Linux Socket Programming

BY EXAMPLE

201 West 103rd Street
Indianapolis, Indiana 46290

Warren W. Gay

Linux Socket Programming by Example

International Standard Book Number: 0-7897-2241-0

Library of Congress Catalog Card Number: 99-66454

Printed in the United States of America

First Printing: April 2000

02   01   00   4   3   2   1

Trademarks

All terms mentioned in this book that are known to be trademarks or service marks have been appropriately capitalized. Que cannot attest to the accuracy of this information. Use of a term in this book should not be regarded as affecting the validity of any trademark or service mark.

Linux® is a registered trademark of Linus Torvalds. Red Hat® Linux™ is a registered trademark of Red Hat Software.

Warning and Disclaimer

Every effort has been made to make this book as complete and as accurate as possible, but no warranty or fitness is implied. The information provided is on an "as is" basis. The author and the publisher shall have neither liability nor responsibility to any person or entity with respect to any loss or damages arising from the information contained in this book.

Associate Publisher
Tracy Dunkelberger

Acquisitions Editor
Todd Green

Development Editor
Laura Bulcher

Managing Editor
Thomas F. Hayes

Project Editor
Karen S. Shields

Copy Editor
Victoria Elzey

Indexer
Aamir Burki

Proofreader
Jeanne Clark

Technical Editor
William Ray

Team Coordinator
Cindy Teeters

Media Developer
Jay Payne

Interior Designer
Karen Ruggles

Cover Designer
Rader Design

Copywriter
Eric Borgert

Production
Lisa England
Steve Geiselman
Liz Johnston

Contents at a Glance

Table of Contents

About the Author

Warren W. Gay is a supervisor at Mackenzie Financial Corporation in Toronto, Canada. There he supervises a small team of programmers that manage the Mackenzie Investment Management System (IMS). Warren is also the author of *Sams Teach Yourself Linux Programming in 24 Hours*.

Warren has been programming professionally since 1980, using many assembler languages, PL/I, C, and C++. He has been programming for UNIX since 1986 and started programming for Linux in 1994. Linux has allowed him to contribute software packages, such as the ftpbackup program and the rewrite of the popular wavplay program. These and his other Linux packages can be found at sunsite.unc.edu and its mirror ftp sites.

Amateur radio is a hobby of Warren's. He holds an advanced amateur radio license and is occasionally active on 75 meters with the radio call sign VE3WWG. Using the 2-meter band on August 3, 1991, he made contact with Musa Manarov, call sign U2MIR, aboard the Soviet MIR space station using a PC and packet radio gear.

Warren lives with his wife, Jacqueline, and his three children, Erin, Laura, and Scott, in St. Catharines, Ontario, Canada.

Dedication

This book is dedicated to my loving wife, Jackie, my daughters, Erin and Laura, and my son, Scott. Only through their collective patience and support was this book made possible.

Acknowledgements

First, thanks go to Brian Gill for his enthusiasm and support, which helped to get this project started. Thanks also to Todd Green who took over for Brian as acquisitions editor and to Laura Bulcher as development editor. I also want to thank William Ray for his enthusiasm and effort as the technical editor.

Thanks also belong to those at Macmillan USA who expended countless hours doing all of the various jobs that take place in the production of a book. As is so often the case in life, accomplishment is achieved with the effort of many.

I would also like to thank the people at Mackenzie Financial Corporation for their support as I juggled my job responsibilities with my writing at home. Particularly, I want to thank Carol Penhale for allowing me to arrange vacation time when I really needed it. I also want to thank Alex Lowitt for his efforts in leasing laptops for Mackenzie employees. The laptop that I used was a great boost to this writing effort.

A warm thank-you goes to Darie Urbanky for his assistance in testing a few program examples for me, under Sun's Solaris. To my various other friends, please accept my general thanks for your encouragement and continued support.

Tell Us What You Think!

As the reader of this book, *you* are our most important critic and commentator. We value your opinion and want to know what we're doing right, what we could do better, what areas you'd like to see us publish in, and any other words of wisdom you're willing to pass our way.

As an Associate Publisher for Que, I welcome your comments. You can fax, email, or write to let me know what you did or didn't like about this book—as well as what we can do to make our books stronger.

Please note that I cannot help you with technical problems related to the topic of this book, and that due to the high volume of mail I receive, I might not be able to reply to every message.

When you write, please be sure to include this book's title and author as well as your name and phone or fax number. I will carefully review your comments and share them with the author and editors who worked on the book.

Fax: 317-581-4666

Email: quetechnical@macmillanusa.com

Mail: Associate Publisher, Programming
            Que
            201 West 103rd Street
            Indianapolis, IN 46290 USA

Introduction

There have been many books written on the topic of computer networking. While many of these are excellent resources for advanced programmers, they tend to be too deep for the beginner who just wants to know how to use it. Why require a potential driver to understand the theory behind his automobile?

This book teaches the reader how to use socket programming, as if networking was an appliance that you can turn on and use. Consequently, a "by example" approach to socket programming is used here. Each chapter builds upon the previous, until all of the basic concepts are mastered in Part 1, "Basic Socket Concepts." Part 2, "Advanced Socket Programming," contains some more advanced topics that might present a challenge for some readers. The last chapter presents a practical application tying together many of the concepts you've learned.

The *by Example* Series

How does the *by Example* series make you a better programmer? The *by Example* series teaches programming using the best method possible—examples. The text acts as a mentor, looking over your shoulder, providing example programs, and showing you new ways to use the concepts covered in each chapter. While the material is still fresh, you will see example after example, demonstrating ways to use what you just learned.

The philosophy of the *by Example* series is simple: The best way to teach computer programming is with multiple examples. Command descriptions, format syntax, and language references are not enough to teach a newcomer a programming language. Only by taking the components, immediately putting them into use, and running example programs can programming students get more than just a feel for the language. Newcomers who learn only a few basics using examples at every step of the way will automatically know how to write programs using those skills.

Who Should Use This Book

This book should be read by anyone wanting to know how to perform network programming on Linux or UNIX platforms. The example programs have been tailored specifically for Linux, in order to provide for the best educational experience to the reader.

The best success with the example programs will occur with Red Hat 6.0 or comparable Linux distribution releases. Older releases of Linux might present some special challenges because the netstat(1) command has been through a lot of change in recent times. Older Linux distributions should also have the /proc file system enabled in order to take full advantage of some of the example programs.

Conventions Used in This Book

This book uses several common conventions to help teach Linux socket programming. Here is a summary of those typographical conventions.

Examples are indicated by the icon shown at the left of this sentence. Code associated with this book will be available at the Que Web site for download (`http://www.quecorp.com/series/by_example/`).

EXAMPLE

You'll find the icon shown to the left of this sentence to indicate output associated with the code listings.

OUTPUT

Some of the typographical conventions used include the following:

- Commands and computer output appear in a special monospaced computer font.

- Words you type appear in a **boldfaced** computer font.

- Any lines of code that are too long to fit on a single line will be broken into two lines, and a code continuation character, ➥, will appear on the second line.

In addition to typographical conventions, the following special elements are included to set off different types of information to make them easily recognizable:

NOTE
Special notes augment the material you read in each chapter. These notes clarify concepts and procedures.

TIP
You'll find numerous tips offering shortcuts and solutions to common problems.

CAUTION
The cautions warn you about roadblocks that sometimes appear when programming for Linux. Reading the caution sections should save you time and trouble, not to mention a few headaches.

Where to Find the Code

Please visit the following *by Example* Web site for example code or additional material associated with this book:

```
http://www.quecorp.com/series/by_example/
```

What's Next

The socket API is not the only way that networking programs can be written. It is, however, the most popular interface due to its elegant simplicity. If you know a little about the C language and Linux programming—and you have an appetite for writing networked programs—then it's time to get started with the first chapter!

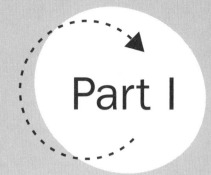

Part I

Basic Socket Concepts

Introducing Sockets

Domains and Address Families

Address Conversion Functions

Socket Types and Protocols

Binding Addresses to a Socket

Connectionless-Oriented Protocols

Connection-Oriented Protocols for Clients

Connection-Oriented Protocols for Servers

Hostname and Network Name Lookups

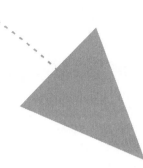

Introducing Sockets

Friday, October 4, 1957, marked the beginning of a startling new era. The Soviet Union had launched the world's first artificial satellite into the Earth's orbit, known as Sputnik. Approximately the size of a basketball, this satellite took 98 minutes to orbit the Earth. Anyone with a shortwave radio was able to hear it during overhead passes, at a frequency of approximately 40.002Mhz. Who would have imagined at that time, that this would later spawn the beginnings of TCP/IP and the Internet?

In this chapter you will be introduced to

- A brief history of how sockets were developed

- The essence of sockets

- How sockets are referenced by the Linux kernel and application programs

- An introductory example of a socket C program

A Brief Historical Introduction

Eisenhower's response to the Sputnik threat was to approach Congress on January 7, 1958, for the startup funds necessary for the Advanced Research Projects Agency (ARPA). At that time, government agencies were required to buy computers from different manufacturers each time they made a purchase, to maintain fairness. The new ARPA organization soon found that they had a collection of machines that spoke completely different languages. Sometime after 1962, J. C. R. Licklider conceived of the idea that computers should be able to communicate with one another, even if they were "highly individualistic."

During the 1960s, the ARPAnet was being conceived and developed by a number of talented people. The humble beginning of the ARPAnet was to become the Internet that we know of today. Eventually ARPA was folded into the Defense Advanced Research Projects Agency (DARPA).

Overlapping with the development of ARPAnet, UNIX development was beginning in 1969. The University of California, Berkeley (UCB) later developed their own flavor of UNIX, which was known as BSD. DARPA wanted to divest itself of the business of networking, and so DARPA provided funding to UCB in 1979, to further develop the ARPAnet. In 1982, 4.1BSD and 4.2BSD versions of UNIX were released by UCB that included a TCP/IP network implementation. The network socket concepts and interfaces that you will learn about in this book are based upon the work done by UCB.

Linux draws upon this rich heritage, and so you'll learn about the Linux specific implementation of the BSD socket interface in this book. Figure 1.1 is provided as a time line overview of the history behind the socket interface.

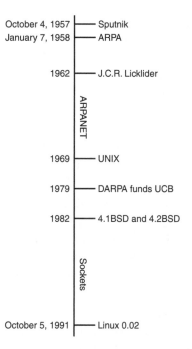

Figure 1.1: *According to the time line, BSD sockets were developed 24 years after the formation of ARPA.*

Understanding Sockets

It is important that you have an understanding of some of the concepts behind the socket interface before you try to apply them. This section outlines some of the high level concepts surrounding the sockets themselves.

Defining a Socket

To communicate with someone using a telephone, you must pick up the handset, dial the other party's telephone number, and wait for them to answer. While you speak to that other party, there are two endpoints of communication established:

- Your telephone, at your location
- The remote party's telephone, at his location

As long as both of you communicate, there are two endpoints involved, with a line of communication in between them. Figure 1.2 shows an illustration of two telephones as endpoints, each connected to the other, through the telephone network.

Figure 1.2: *Without the telephone network, each endpoint of a telephone line is nothing more than a plastic box.*

A socket under Linux, is quite similar to a telephone. Sockets represent endpoints in a line of communication. In between the endpoints exists the data communications network.

Sockets are like telephones in another way. For you to telephone someone, you dial the telephone number of the party you want to contact. Sockets have network addresses instead of telephone numbers. By indicating the address of the remote socket, your program can establish a line of communication between your local socket and that remote endpoint. Socket addresses are discussed in Chapter 2, "Domains and Address Families."

You can conclude then, that a socket is merely an endpoint in communication. There are a number of Linux function calls that operate on sockets, and you learn about all of them in this book.

Using Sockets

You might think that Linux sockets are treated specially, because you've already learned that sockets have a collection of specific functions that operate on them. Although it is true that sockets have some special qualities, they are very similar to file descriptors that you should already be familiar with.

NOTE

Any reference to a function name like pipe(2) means that you should have online documentation (man pages) on your Linux system for that function. For information about pipe(2) for example, you can enter the command:

$ man 2 pipe

where the 2 represents the manual section number, and the function name can be used as the name of the manual page. Although the section number is often optional, there are many cases where you must specify it in order to obtain the correct information.

For example, when you open a file using the Linux open(2) call, you are returned a file descriptor if the open(2) function is successful. After you have this file descriptor, your program uses it to read(2), write(2), lseek(2), and close(2) the specific file that was opened. Similarly, a socket, when it is created, is just like a file descriptor. You can use the same file I/O functions to read, write, and close that socket. You learn in Chapter 15, "Using the inetd Daemon," that sockets can be used for standard input (file unit 0), standard output (file unit 1), or standard error (file unit 2).

> **NOTE**
>
> Sockets are referenced by file unit numbers in the same way that opened files are. These unit numbers share the same "number space"—for example, you cannot have both a socket with unit number 4 and an open file on unit number 4 at the same time.

There are some differences, however, between sockets and opened files. The following list highlights some of these differences:

- You cannot lseek(2) on a socket (this restriction also applies to pipes).

- Sockets can have addresses associated with them. Files and pipes do not have network addresses.

- Sockets have different option capabilities that can be queried and set using ioctl(2).

- Sockets must be in the correct state to perform input or output. Conversely, opened disk files can be read from or written to at any time.

Referencing Sockets

When you open a new file using the open(2) function call, the next available and lowest file descriptor is returned by the Linux kernel. This file descriptor, or *file unit* number as it is often called, is a zero or positive integer value that is used to refer to the file that was opened. This "handle" is used in all other functions that operate upon opened files. Now you know that file unit numbers can also refer to specific sockets.

> **NOTE**
>
> When a new file unit (or file descriptor) is needed by the kernel, the lowest available unit number is returned. For example, if you were to close standard input (file unit number 0), and then open a file successfully, the file unit number returned by the open(2) call will be zero.

Assume for a moment that your program already has file units 0, 1, and 2 open (standard input, output, and error) and the following sequence of program operations is carried out. Notice how the file descriptors are allocated by the kernel:

1. The open(2) function is called to open a file.

2. File unit 3 is returned to reference the opened file. Because this unit is not currently in use, and is the lowest file unit presently available, the value 3 is chosen to be the file unit number for the file.

3. A new socket is created using an appropriate function call.

4. File unit 4 is returned to reference that new socket.

5. Yet, another file is opened by calling open(2).

6. File unit 5 is returned to reference the newly opened file.

Notice how the Linux kernel makes no distinction between files and sockets when allocating unit numbers. A file descriptor is used to refer to an opened file or a network socket.

This means that you, as a programmer, will use sockets as if they were open files. Being able to reference files and sockets interchangeably by file unit number provides you with a great deal of flexibility. This also means that functions like read(2) and write(2) can operate upon both open files and sockets.

Comparing Sockets to Pipes

Before you are introduced to any socket functions, review the pipe(2) function call that you might already be familiar with. Let's see how the file descriptors it returns differ from a socket. The following is a function synopsis taken from the pipe(2) man page:

```
#include <unistd.h>

int pipe(int filedes[2]);
```

The pipe(2) function call returns two file descriptors when the call is successful. Array element filedes[0] contains the file descriptor number for the read end of the pipe. Element filedes[1] receives the file unit number of the write end of the pipe.

This arrangement of two file descriptors is suggestive of a communications link with file descriptors at each end, acting as sockets. How then does this differ from using sockets instead? The difference lies in that the pipe(2) function creates a line of communications in one direction only. Information can only be written to the file unit in filedes[1] and only read by unit filedes[0]. Any attempt to write data in the opposite direction results in the Linux kernel returning an error to your program.

Sockets, on the other hand, allow processes to communicate in both directions. A process is able to use a socket open on file unit 3, for example, to send data to a remote process. Unlike when using a pipe, the same local process can also receive information from file unit 3 that was sent by the remote process it is communicating with.

Creating Sockets

In this section, you see that creating sockets can be almost as easy as creating a pipe. There are a few more function arguments however, which you will learn about. These arguments must be supplied with suitable values to be successful.

The function socketpair(2) synopsis is as follows:

```
#include <sys/types.h>
#include <sys/socket.h>

int socketpair(int domain, int type, int protocol, int sv[2]);
```

The include file sys/types.h is required to define some C macro constants. The include file sys/socket.h is necessary to define the socketpair(2) function prototype.

The socketpair(2) function takes four arguments. They are

- The domain of the socket.

- The type of the socket.

- The protocol to be used.

- The pointer to the array that will receive file descriptors that reference the created sockets.

The domain argument's explanation will be deferred until Chapter 2. For the purpose of the socketpair(2) function, however, always supply the C macro value AF_LOCAL.

The type argument declares what type of socket you want to create. The choices for the socketpair(2) function are

- SOCK_STREAM

- SOCK_DGRAM

The implication of the socket choice will be explored in Chapter 4, "Socket Types and Protocols." For this chapter, we'll simply use SOCK_STREAM for the type of the socket.

For the socketpair(2) function, the protocol argument must be supplied as zero.

The argument sv[2] is a receiving array of two integer values that represent two sockets. Each file descriptor represents one socket (endpoint) and is otherwise indistinguishable from the other.

If the function is successful, the value zero is returned. Otherwise, a return value of –1 indicates that a failure has occurred, and that `errno` should be consulted for the specific reason.

CAUTION

Always test the function return value for success or failure. The value `errno` should only be consulted when it has been determined that the function call has indicated that it failed. Only errors are posted to `errno`; it is never cleared to zero upon success.

Using `socketpair(2)` in an Example

To demonstrate how the `socketpair(2)` function is used, the program in Listing 1.1 is presented for your experimentation.

CAUTION

If you type example programs manually from the listings shown in this book, do not include the line number shown at the extreme left. The line number is shown for ease of reference only.

Listing 1.1: `01LST01.c`—Example Use of `socketpair(2)` Function

```
1:    /* Listing 1.1:
2:     *
3:     * Example of socketpair(2) function:
4:     */
5:    #include <stdio.h>
6:    #include <stdlib.h>
7:    #include <unistd.h>
8:    #include <errno.h>
9:    #include <string.h>
10:   #include <sys/types.h>
11:   #include <sys/socket.h>
12:
13:   int
14:   main(int argc,char **argv) {
15:       int z;                      /* Status return code */
16:       int s[2];                   /* Pair of sockets */
17:
18:       /*
19:        * Create a pair of local sockets:
20:        */
21:       z = socketpair(AF_LOCAL,SOCK_STREAM,0,s);
22:
23:       if ( z == -1 ) {
24:           fprintf(stderr,
25:               "%s: socketpair(AF_LOCAL,SOCK_STREAM,0)\n",
26:               strerror(errno));
```

```
27:          return 1;                /* Failed */
28:      }
29:
30:      /*
31:       * Report the socket file descriptors returned:
32:       */
33:      printf("s[0] = %d;\n",s[0]);
34:      printf("s[1] = %d;\n",s[1]);
35:
36:      system("netstat --unix -p");
37:
38:      return 0;
39:  }
```

NOTE

If you have an older version of Linux (pre Red Hat 6.0) the netstat command used in line 36 of Listing 1.1 may not understand the options used.

If this is the case, you may want to try changing line 36 to read:

```
system("lsof -i tcp");
```

This requires that lsof is installed on your system. lsof command may be obtained from a variety of sources. A good place to start is

```
ftp://vic.cc.purdue.edu/pub/tools/unix/lsof/
```

Various mirror sites are listed there, in addition to the source code. Note also that when using lsof, you may need to execute the program in Listing 1.1 as root.

lsof may also be found in binary (including RPM) and source formats under the various distribution directories under

```
ftp://sunsite.unc.edu/pub/Linux/distributions
```

As a last resort, you may substitute the following statement for line 36:

```
system("netstat | grep tcp");
```

The demonstration program can be described in the following steps:

1. A receiving array s[2] is declared in line 16 to receive the two new file descriptors that will reference the two new sockets being created.

2. The socketpair(2) function is invoked in line 21. The domain argument is specified as AF_LOCAL, the socket type argument is SOCK_STREAM and the protocol is specified as zero.

3. The if statement in line 23 tests to see if the socketpair(2) function was successful. If z contains a value of –1, the failure is reported to standard error (lines 24 to 26) and the program exits in line 27.

4. If the function call is successful, control passes to lines 33 and 34 where the file unit numbers that were returned are reported to standard output.

5. Line 36 invokes the netstat(1) command using the system(3) function. The command option --unix indicates that only UNIX sockets (AF_LOCAL domain) are to be reported, and the -p option tells it to report process information.

Using the supplied Makefile, you can use the make command to compile the program in Listing 1.1 as follows:

```
$ make 01lst01
gcc -c  -D_GNU_SOURCE -Wall 01LST01.c
gcc 01LST01.o -o 01lst01
```

Now you are ready to try out the demonstration program.

Running the Demonstration Program

To invoke the demonstration, use the following method:

```
$ ./01lst01
```

NOTE

Be certain to watch the case of the filename when entering the executable filename at the command prompt. The executable filenames chosen use lowercase letters.

The results of running the program are as follows (with line numbers added for reference purposes):

OUTPUT

```
 1:  $ ./01lst01
 2:  s[0] = 3;
 3:  s[1] = 4;
 4:  (Not all processes could be identified, non-owned process info
 5:   will not be shown, you would have to be root to see it all.)
 6:  Active UNIX domain sockets (w/o servers)
 7:  Proto RefCnt Flags     Type    ... I-Node PID/Program name   Path
 8:  unix  1      [ ]       STREAM  ... 406    -                  @00000019
 9:  unix  1      [ ]       STREAM  ... 490    -                  @0000001f
10:  unix  1      [ ]       STREAM  ... 518    -                  @00000020
11:  unix  0      [ ]       STREAM  ... 117    -                  @00000011
12:  unix  1      [ ]       STREAM  ... 789    -                  @00000030
13:  unix  1      [ ]       STREAM  ... 549    -                  @00000023
14:  unix  1      [ ]       STREAM  ...1032    662/01lst01
15:  unix  1      [ ]       STREAM  ...1031    662/01lst01
16:  unix  1      [ ]       STREAM  ... 793    -                  /dev/log
17:  unix  1      [ ]       STREAM  ... 582    -                  /dev/log
18:  unix  1      [ ]       STREAM  ... 574    -                  /dev/log
19:  unix  1      [ ]       STREAM  ... 572    -                  /dev/log
20:  unix  1      [ ]       STREAM  ... 408    -                  /dev/log
21:  $
```

The executable program 011st01 is invoked in line 1 in the output shown. Lines 2 and 3 show that the socket pair was opened on file descriptors 3 and 4. What follows in lines 4 to 20 are the output lines from the netstat(1) command that was invoked from the system(3) function call, within the program.

Notice lines 14 and 15 in the netstat(1) output of Listing 1.2. Looking under the column for "PID/Program name" we can see that our program named 011st01 had a process ID of 662 and had two "unix" sockets open. Although not shown in the output, you will see under the column "State" that the sockets are shown as connected.

Although the program didn't do anything with the socket pair that it created, it did demonstrate the creation of a socket pair. It also demonstrated that the sockets are allocated to file unit numbers in the same manner that opened files are.

The astute reader also might have noticed that this pair of AF_LOCAL sockets are also referred to as "unix" sockets (we saw this in the netstat(1) output). In fact, the C macro constant AF_UNIX could have been used in place of the macro AF_LOCAL for the domain value in the socketpair(2) function call. These values are equivalent, although standards efforts are now encouraging the use of AF_LOCAL over AF_UNIX.

Performing I/O on Sockets

You learned earlier that sockets can be written to and read from just like any opened file. In this section, you are going to demonstrate this firsthand for yourself. For the sake of completeness however, let's review the function synopsis for the calls read(2), write(2), and close(2) before we put them to work:

```
#include <unistd.h>

ssize_t read(int fd, void *buf, size_t count);
ssize_t write(int fd, const void *buf, size_t count);
int close(int fd);
```

These are Linux input/output functions you should be already familiar with. By way of review, the function read(2) returns input that is available from the file descriptor fd, into your supplied buffer buf of a maximum size of count bytes. The return value represents the number of bytes read. A return count of zero represents *end-of-file*.

The write(2) function writes data to your file descriptor fd, from your supplied buffer buf for a total of count bytes. The returned value represents the actual number of bytes written. Normally, this should match the supplied count argument. However, there are some valid circumstances where this will be less than count, but you won't have to worry about it here.

Finally, close(2) returns zero if the unit was closed successfully.

A return value of -1 for any of these functions indicates that an error occurred, and that the reason for the error is posted to the external variable errno. To make this value accessible, include the file errno.h within the source module that needs it.

Listing 1.2 shows an example that performs some reads and writes upon sockets in both directions.

EXAMPLE

Listing 1.2: 01LST02.c—Example Performing I/O on a Socket Pair

```
1:   /* Listing 1.2:
2:    *
3:    * Example performing I/O on a Socket Pair:
4:    */
5:   #include <stdio.h>
6:   #include <unistd.h>
7:   #include <stdlib.h>
8:   #include <errno.h>
9:   #include <string.h>
10:  #include <sys/types.h>
11:  #include <sys/socket.h>
12:
13:  int
14:  main(int argc,char **argv) {
15:      int z;                  /* Status return code */
16:      int s[2];               /* Pair of sockets */
17:      char *cp;               /* A work pointer */
18:      char buf[80];           /* Work buffer */
19:
20:      /*
21:       * Create a pair of local sockets:
22:       */
23:      z = socketpair(AF_LOCAL,SOCK_STREAM,0,s);
24:
25:      if ( z == -1 ) {
26:          fprintf(stderr,
27:              "%s: socketpair(AF_LOCAL,SOCK_STREAM,"
28:              "0)\n",
29:              strerror(errno));
30:          return 1;           /* Failed */
31:      }
32:
33:      /*
```

```
34:          * Write a message to socket s[1]:
35:          */
36:         z = write(s[1],cp="Hello?",6);
37:         if ( z < 0 ) {
38:             fprintf(stderr,
39:                 "%s: write(%d,\"%s\",%d)\n",
40:                 strerror(errno),s[1],cp,strlen(cp));
41:             return 2;    /* Failed write */
42:         }
43:
44:         printf("Wrote message '%s' on s[1]\n",cp);
45:
46:         /*
47:          * Read from socket s[0]:
48:          */
49:         z = read(s[0],buf,sizeof buf);
50:         if ( z < 0 ) {
51:             fprintf(stderr,
52:                 "%s: read(%d,buf,%d)\n",
53:                 strerror(errno),s[0],sizeof buf);
54:             return 3;    /* Failed read */
55:         }
56:
57:         /*
58:          * Report received message:
59:          */
60:         buf[z] = 0;     /* NUL terminate */
61:         printf("Received message '%s' from socket s[0]\n",
62:             buf);
63:
64:         /*
65:          * Send a reply back to s[1] from s[0]:
66:          */
67:         z = write(s[0],cp="Go away!",8);
68:         if ( z < 0 ) {
69:             fprintf(stderr,
70:                 "%s: write(%d,\"%s\",%d)\n",
71:                 strerror(errno),s[0],cp,strlen(cp));
72:             return 4;    /* Failed write */
73:         }
74:
75:         printf("Wrote message '%s' on s[0]\n",cp);
76:
77:         /*
78:          * Read from socket s[1]:
79:          */
80:         z = read(s[1],buf,sizeof buf);
```

continues

Listing 1.2: continued

```
 81:        if ( z < 0 ) {
 82:            fprintf(stderr,
 83:                "%s: read(%d,buf,%d)\n",
 84:                strerror(errno),s[1],sizeof buf);
 85:            return 3;    /* Failed read */
 86:        }
 87:
 88:        /*
 89:         * Report message received by s[0]:
 90:         */
 91:        buf[z] = 0;      /* NUL terminate */
 92:        printf("Received message '%s' from socket s[1]\n",
 93:            buf);
 94:
 95:        /*
 96:         * Close the sockets:
 97:         */
 98:        close(s[0]);
 99:        close(s[1]);
100:
101:        puts("Done.");
102:        return 0;
103: }
```

The steps invoked by the program can be summarized as follows:

1. The socketpair(2) function is invoked in line 23, returning, if success-ful, a pair of sockets into array elements s[0] and s[1] (line 16).

2. The success of the function is tested in line 25, and the error is reported, if it occurs, in lines 26 to 31.

3. A message consisting of the 6 characters "Hello?" is written to the socket s[1] in line 36. Note that no null byte is written, because only 6 bytes are specified in the count argument of the write(2) function.

4. Lines 37 to 42 check and report any error that might occur.

5. Line 44 announces a successful write operation.

6. The read(2) call in line 49 now attempts to read a message from the other socket s[0]. Any message up to the maximum size of array buf[] can be read in this statement.

7. Lines 50 to 55 check and report any error that might occur in the read statement.

8. Lines 60 to 62 report a successful reception of a message, and report what it was.

9. Lines 67 to 73 write a reply message "Go away!" to socket s[0]. This will demonstrate that information can travel both ways with sockets as endpoints, unlike a pipe.

10. Line 75 announces a successful write in line 67.

11. Lines 80 to 86 should read the "Go away!" message from socket s[1], which is the other endpoint of the communications line.

12. Lines 91 to 93 report this successful reception and its message.

13. The two socket endpoints are closed in lines 98 and 99.

14. The program exits in line 102.

OUTPUT

When the program is invoked, this is what you should see:

```
$ ./011st02
Wrote message 'Hello?' on s[1]
Received message 'Hello?' from socket s[0]
Wrote message 'Go away!' on s[0]
Received message 'Go away!' from socket s[1]
Done.
$
```

If you trace the steps that were previously outlined, you will see that information was sent both ways on that pair of sockets. Furthermore, it was demonstrated that sockets are closed in the same manner that files are.

Closing Sockets

Previously, you saw how a pair of sockets could be easily created and how some elementary input and output can be performed using those sockets. You also saw that these sockets could be closed in the same manner that files are with the use of the close(2) function call. It's now time that you learn what is implied by the closing of a socket.

When reading from a pipe created by the pipe(2) function, the receiving end recognizes that there will be no more data when an end-of-file is received. The end-of-file condition is sent by the writing process, when it closes the write end of the pipe.

This same procedure can be used with a pair of sockets. The receiving end will receive an end-of-file indication when the other endpoint (socket) has been closed.

The problem develops when the local process wants to signal to the remote endpoint that there is no more data to be received. If the local process closes its socket, this much will be accomplished. However, if it needs to receive a confirmation from the remote end, it cannot, because its socket is now closed. Situations like these require a means to half close a socket.

The `shutdown(2)` Function

The following shows the function synopsis of the `shutdown(2)` function:

```
#include <sys/socket.h>
```

```
int shutdown(int s, int how);
```

The function `shutdown(2)` requires two arguments. They are

- Socket descriptor s specifies the socket to be partially shut down.

- Argument how indicates how this socket should be shut down.

The returned value is zero if the function call succeeded. A failure is indicated by returning a value of –1, and the reason for the failure is posted to errno.

The permissible values for how are shown in Table 1.1.

*Table 1.1: Permissible Values of the **shutdown(2) how** Argument*

Value	Macro	Description
0	SHUT_RD	No further reads will be allowed on the specified socket.
1	SHUT_WR	No further writes will be allowed on the specified socket.
2	SHUT_RDWR	No further reads or writes will be allowed on the specified socket.

Notice that when the how value is supplied as 2, this function call becomes almost equivalent to a `close(2)` call.

Shutting Down Writing to a Socket

The following code shows how to indicate that no further writes will be performed upon the local socket:

EXAMPLE

```
int z;
int s;   /* Socket */

z = shutdown(s,SHUT_WR);
if ( z == -1 )
    perror("shutdown()");
```

Shutting down the writing end of a socket solves a number of thorny problems. They are

- Flushes out the kernel buffers that contain any pending data to be sent. Data is buffered by the kernel networking software to improve performance.

- Sends an end-of-file indication to the remote socket. This tells the remote reading process that no more data will be sent to it on this socket.

- Leaves the partially shutdown socket open for reading. This makes it possible to receive confirmation messages after the end-of-file indication has been sent on the socket.

- Disregards the number of open references on the socket. Only the last close(2) on a socket will cause an end-of-file indication to be sent.

The last point requires a bit of explanation, which is provided in the next section.

Dealing with Duplicated Sockets

If a socket's file descriptor is duplicated with the help of a dup(2) or a dup2(2) function call, then only the last outstanding close(2) call actually closes down the socket. This happens because the other duplicated file descriptors are still considered to be in use. This is demonstrated in the following code:

EXAMPLE

```
int s;      /* Existing socket */
int d;      /* Duplicated socket */

d = dup(s); /* duplicate this socket */
close(s);   /* nothing happens yet */
close(d);   /* last close, so shutdown socket */
```

In the example, the first close(2) call would have no effect. It would make no difference which socket was closed first. Closing either s or d first would still leave one outstanding file descriptor for the same socket. Only when closing the last surviving file descriptor for that socket would a close(2) call have any effect. In the example, the close of the d file descriptor closes down the socket.

The shutdown(2) function avoids this difficulty. Repeating the example code, the problem is solved using the shutdown(2) function:

EXAMPLE

```
int s;      /* Existing socket */
int d;      /* Duplicated socket */

d = dup(s);  /* duplicate this socket */
shutdown(s,SHUT_RDWR); /* immediate shutdown */
```

Even though the socket s is also open on file unit d, the shutdown(2) function immediately causes the socket to perform its shutdown duties as requested. This naturally affects both the open file descriptors s and d because they both refer to the same socket.

Another way this problem is manifested is after a fork(2) function has been called upon. Any sockets that existed prior to a fork operation would be duplicated in the child process.

TIP

Use the shutdown(2) function instead of the close(2) function whenever immediate or partial shutdown action is required. Duplicated file descriptors from dup(2), dup2(2), or fork(2) operations can prevent a close(2) function from initiating any shutdown action until the last outstanding descriptor is closed.

Shutting Down Reading from a Socket

Shutting down the read side of the socket causes any pending read data to be silently ignored. If more data is sent from the remote socket, it too is silently ignored. Any attempt by the process to read from that socket, however, will have an error returned to it. This is often done to enforce protocol or to help debug code.

Knowing When Not to Use shutdown(2)

The shutdown(2) function is documented to return the errors shown in Table 1.2.

Table 1.2: Possible errors returned by **shutdown(2)**

Error	Description
EBADF	Given socket is not a valid file descriptor.
ENOTSOCK	Given file descriptor is not a socket.
ENOTCONN	The specified socket is not connected.

From Table 1.2, you can see that you should only call shutdown(2) for connected sockets. Otherwise, the error code ENOTCONN is returned.

NOTE

The shutdown(2) function does not release the socket's file unit number, even when SHUT_RDWR is used. The socket's file descriptor remains valid and in use until the function close(2) is called to release it.

Note also that shutdown(2) can be called more than once for the same file unit, provided that the socket is still connected.

Writing a Client/Server Example

You have now looked at enough of the socket API set to start having some fun with it. In this section, you examine, compile, and test a simple client and server process that communicates with a pair of sockets.

To keep the programming code to a bare minimum, one program will start and then fork into a client process and a server process. The child process will assume the role of the client program, whereas the original parent process will perform the role of the server. Figure 1.3 illustrates the relationship of the parent and child processes and the sockets that will be used.

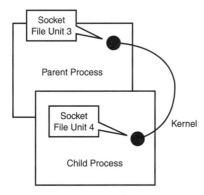

Figure 1.3: A Client/Server example using fork(2) *and* socketpair(2)*.*

The parent process is the original starting process. It will immediately ask for a pair of sockets by calling socketpair(2) and then fork itself into two processes by calling fork(2).

The server will accept one request, act on that request, and then exit. The client likewise in this example will issue one request, report the server response, and then exit.

The request will take the form of the third argument to the strftime(3) function. This is a format string, which will be used to format a date and time string. The server will obtain the current date and time at the time that the request is received. The server will use the client's request string to format it into a final string, which is returned to the client. By way of review, the strftime(3) function's synopsis is as follows:

```
#include <time.h>

size_t strftime(char *buf,
    size_t max,
    const char *format,
    const struct tm *tm);
```

EXAMPLE

The arguments buf and max indicate the output buffer and its maximum length respectively. The argument format is an input string that allows you to format a date and time string (Listing 1.3 line 75 shows an example of such a string). Finally, argument tm is used to supply all the date and time components necessary to create the output date and time string. Review the man page for strftime(3) if you need to.

Listing 1.3 shows the source listing for the demonstration client/server program.

Listing 1.3: 01LST03.c—Client/Server Example Using socketpair(2) and fork(2)

```
1:   /* Listing 1.3
2:    *
3:    * Client/Server Example Using socketpair(2)
4:    * and fork(2):
5:    */
6:   #include <stdio.h>
7:   #include <stdlib.h>
8:   #include <unistd.h>
9:   #include <errno.h>
10:  #include <string.h>
11:  #include <time.h>
12:  #include <sys/types.h>
13:  #include <sys/socket.h>
14:  #include <sys/wait.h>
15:
16:  /*
17:   * As of RedHat-6.0, these are still not defined:
18:   */
19:  #ifndef SHUT_WR
20:  #define SHUT_RD     0
21:  #define SHUT_WR     1
22:  #define SHUT_RDWR   2
23:  #endif
24:
25:  /*
26:   * Main program:
27:   */
28:  int
29:  main(int argc,char **argv) {
30:      int z;          /* Status return code */
31:      int s[2];       /* Pair of sockets */
32:      char *msgp;     /* A message pointer */
33:      int mlen;       /* Message length */
34:      char buf[80];   /* Work buffer */
35:      pid_t chpid;    /* Child PID */
36:
37:      /*
38:       * Create a pair of local sockets:
39:       */
40:      z = socketpair(AF_LOCAL,SOCK_STREAM,0,s);
```

```
41:
42:      if ( z == -1 ) {
43:          fprintf(stderr,"%s: socketpair(2)\n",
44:              strerror(errno));
45:          exit(1);
46:      }
47:
48:      /*
49:       * Now fork() into two processes:
50:       */
51:      if ( (chpid = fork()) == (pid_t)-1 ) {
52:
53:          /*
54:           * Failed to fork into two processes:
55:           */
56:          fprintf(stderr,"%s: fork(2)\n",
57:              strerror(errno));
58:          exit(1);
59:
60:      } else if ( chpid == 0 ) {
61:
62:          /*
63:           * This is the child process (client):
64:           */
65:          char rxbuf[80]; /* Receive buffer */
66:
67:          printf("Parent PID is %ld\n",(long)getppid());
68:
69:          close(s[0]);     /* Server uses s[1] */
70:          s[0] = -1;       /* Forget this unit */
71:
72:          /*
73:           * Form the message and its length:
74:           */
75:          msgp = "%A %d-%b-%Y %l:%M %p";
76:          mlen = strlen(msgp);
77:
78:          printf("Child sending request '%s'\n",msgp);
79:          fflush(stdout);
80:
81:          /*
82:           * Write a request to the server:
83:           */
84:          z = write(s[1],msgp,mlen);
85:
86:          if ( z < 0 ) {
87:              fprintf(stderr,"%s: write(2)\n",
```

continues

Listing 1.3: continued

```
88:                        strerror(errno));
89:                    exit(1);
90:            }
91:
92:            /*
93:             * Now indicate that we will not be writing
94:             * anything further to our socket, by shutting
95:             * down the write side of the socket:
96:             */
97:            if ( shutdown(s[1],SHUT_WR) == -1 ) {
98:                fprintf(stderr,"%s: shutdown(2)\n",
99:                    strerror(errno));
100:                exit(1);
101:            }
102:
103:            /*
104:             * Receive the reply from the server:
105:             */
106:            z = read(s[1],rxbuf,sizeof rxbuf);
107:            if ( z < 0 ) {
108:                fprintf(stderr,"%s: read(2)\n",
109:                    strerror(errno));
110:                exit(1);
111:            }
112:
113:            /*
114:             * Put a null byte at the end of what we
115:             * received from the server:
116:             */
117:            rxbuf[z] = 0;
118:
119:            /*
120:             * Report the results:
121:             */
122:            printf("Server returned '%s'\n",rxbuf);
123:            fflush(stdout);
124:
125:            close(s[1]);    /* Close our end now */
126:
127:        } else {
128:
129:            /*
130:             * This is the parent process (server):
131:             */
132:            int status; /* Child termination status */
133:            char txbuf[80];         /* Reply buffer */
```

```
134:          time_t td;        /* Current date & time */
135:
136:          printf("Child PID is %ld\n",(long)chpid);
137:          fflush(stdout);
138:
139:          close(s[1]);    /* Client uses s[1] */
140:          s[1] = -1;      /* Forget this descriptor */
141:
142:          /*
143:           * Wait for a request from the client:
144:           */
145:          z = read(s[0],buf,sizeof buf);
146:
147:          if ( z < 0 ) {
148:              fprintf(stderr,"%s: read(2)\n",
149:                  strerror(errno));
150:              exit(1);
151:          }
152:
153:          /*
154:           * Put a null byte at the end of the
155:           * message we received from the client:
156:           */
157:          buf[z] = 0;
158:
159:          /*
160:           * Now perform the server function on the
161:           * received message:
162:           */
163:          time(&td);             /* Get current time */
164:
165:          strftime(txbuf,sizeof txbuf,  /* Buffer */
166:              buf,                    /* Input format */
167:              localtime(&td));        /* Input time */
168:
169:          /*
170:           * Send back the response to client:
171:           */
172:          z = write(s[0],txbuf,strlen(txbuf));
173:
174:          if ( z < 0 ) {
175:              fprintf(stderr,"%s: write(2)\n",
176:                  strerror(errno));
177:              exit(1);
178:          }
179:
180:          /*
```

continues

Listing 1.3: continued

```
181:              * Close our end of the socket:
182:              */
183:             close(s[0]);
184:
185:             /*
186:              * Wait for the child process to exit.
187:              * See text.
188:              */
189:             waitpid(chpid,&status,0);
190:     }
191:
192:     return 0;
193: }
```

The program shown in Listing 1.3 can be broken into the following basic steps:

1. Lines 19 to 23 were required to define the SHUT_WR, SHUT_RD, and SHUT_RDWR macro constants (as of Red Hat Linux 6.0 at least). Eventually these constants will be defined for you. The #ifndef statement in line 19 makes certain that lines 20 to 22 are compiled only if SHUT_WR is not already defined.

2. The single process starts at the main function entry point in line 29.

3. A pair of sockets is created in line 40 by calling the function socketpair(2).

4. If an error occurs, lines 42 to 46 report the error and halt the program.

5. The single process forks into a parent and child process by calling fork(2) in line 51. If an error occurs, the error is reported and the program is halted in lines 52 to 58.

6. The new child process executes in lines 61 to 125. The child process will act as the client program, sending a request to the server, and receiving a response back from the server.

7. The original (parent) process, executes lines 129 to 189. This process acts as a server by waiting for one input request and returns a response to that request.

Now you'll examine the server steps in more detail:

1. Lines 136 and 137 announce that the parent process is beginning as a server process and reports the child process ID.

2. Line 139 closes the extra socket that will not be used by the server. Socket s[1] is the file unit that will be used only by the child process.

Refer to Figure 1.3 to visualize the processes and the sockets used (s[1] will contain file descriptor 4).

3. Line 140 is just a precaution that helps debugging. By setting s[1] to -1 it is abundantly clear that the file unit is no longer available to that process.

4. The server calls upon read(2) at line 145. The server process will block there until a message arrives on the socket to be read. Lines 147 to 151 check and report any error that might occur from the read(2) call.

5. Line 157 places a null byte at the end of the received message. This is done to turn the message into a C string that can be used in line 166.

6. The function strftime(3) is called to format a new time string according to the message that was received from the client program. The current date and time was determined by the server in line 163.

7. Line 172 writes a message back to the client process using the write(2) function. Errors are checked and reported in lines 174 to 178.

8. Because our demonstration program only serves one request, it simply closes the socket in line 183.

9. The waitpid(2) function is called in this demonstration so that the parent process will not exit back to the shell until the child process has completed.

10. When the child process has terminated, the parent process exits in line 192.

Now let's examine the child process that is acting as the client program:

1. The child process announces its beginning in line 67 by reporting its parent process ID.

2. The client program does not use the duplicated socket in s[0] (which holds file unit 3 according to Figure 1.3). Consequently, it is closed in line 69. Line 70 again just represents a good programming practice.

3. The client program is about to send a format string to the server. This is established in line 75 by the use of variable msgp. The length of the message is established in line 76 in the variable mlen.

4. The message being sent is announced in lines 78 and 79.

5. The write(2) function is used to send the message from the client's socket to the server's socket in line 84. Errors are reported in lines 86 to 90.

6. The client at this point has no intention to send any more data to the server. The shutdown(2) function is called in line 97 to indicate this. Errors are reported in lines 98 to 101.

7. The client now calls read(2) to wait for a response message (line 106). The client process will wait indefinitely here until a response arrives. Errors are reported in lines 107 to 111.

8. A null byte is placed at the end of the received response in line 117.

9. The received response is reported in lines 122 to 123.

10. The client socket is now closed in line 125.

11. The client process exits at line 192.

C A U T I O N

It has been reported that on Red Hat 5.1 (and perhaps older releases of Linux kernels in general) that the shutdown(2) function is not correctly implemented. It would appear that these kernels have SHUT_WR blocking reads, while SHUT_RDWR doesn't block reads at all.

If the server example fails to work correctly, then your Linux kernel may have this problem.

You can work around this problem by deleting lines 97 to 101. The program works without this code because the kernel will eventually deliver what has been placed into the socket buffers. The shutdown(2) function, however, can make this happen sooner.

OUTPUT

Running the program should yield results similar to what appears in output shown next. Note that your date and time will differ, of course.

```
$ ./011st03
Child PID is 879
Parent PID is 878
Child sending request '%A %d-%b-%Y %l:%M %p'
Server returned 'Thursday 15-Jul-1999  6:39 PM'
$
```

In the output, you can see that the child process (client) requested that the date and time be formatted according to the string shown. The server process obtained the current date and sent the response back to the client, which it was able to report.

As an experiment, try modifying the program in Listing 1.3 at line 75 to use a different format. Recompile it and run it again. For example, change line 75 to read:

```
msgp = "%d-%b-%y";
```

You should be able to obtain a result looking similar to

```
15-Jul-99
```

when the program is run.

What's Next

In this chapter, you have briefly seen how sockets can be used to communicate between two different processes. When the socketpair(2) function was introduced, it was noted that a socket domain, socket type, and a socket protocol had to be specified. The next chapter teaches you how to choose the socket domain and how to adorn a socket with an address. You will cover anonymous and addressed sockets and how to initialize address structures for each domain.

Domains and Address Families

In the last chapter, you read about the telephone analogy where the caller gets in touch with the other person by dialing that person's telephone number. In the telephone network, each person's telephone number is like a socket address. Sockets have addresses of their own to allow them to be specifically identified. The socket address will be the primary focus of this chapter.

In this chapter you will

- Understand address families
- Learn how to form socket addresses
- Understand the difference between big-endian and little-endian byte ordering
- Learn what an abstract local address is and how to form one
- Learn when socket addresses are not required

This chapter is very important to you because many programmers struggle with this very aspect of socket programming. A little extra effort spent here will reward you later.

Nameless Sockets

Sockets do not always need to have an address. The socketpair(2) function, for example, creates two sockets that are connected to each other, but without addresses. They are, in essence, "nameless" sockets. Imagine a red telephone between the U.S. president's office and the Soviet Union, during the Cold War. There is no need for a telephone number at either end, because they are directly connected. In the same way, the sockets created by socketpair(2) are directly connected and have no need for addresses.

Anonymous Calls

Sometimes in practice, one of the two sockets in a connection will have no address. For a remote socket to be contacted, it must have an address to identify it. However, the local socket that is "placing the call" can be anonymous. The connection that becomes established has one remote socket with an address and another socket without an address.

Generating Addresses

Sometimes you don't care what your local address is, but you need one to communicate. This is particularly true of programs that need to connect to a service, like a RDBMS database server. Their local address is only required for the duration of the communication. Allocating fixed addresses could be done, but this increases network administration work. Consequently, address generation is often used when it is available.

Understanding Domains

When the BSD socket interface was being conceived by the Berkeley team, the TCP/IP protocol was still undergoing development. At the same time, there were a number of other competing protocols being used by different organizations like the X.25 protocol. Still other protocols were being researched.

The socketpair(2) function that you have seen in the last chapter, and the socket(2) function, which has yet to be introduced, wisely allowed for the possibility that other protocols might be used instead of TCP/IP. The domain argument of the socketpair(2) function allows for this contingency. For ease of discussion, let's restate the function synopsis for the following socketpair(2) function:

```
#include <sys/types.h>
#include <sys/socket.h>

int socketpair(int domain, int type, int protocol, int sv[2]);
```

NOTE

Here you will simply learn about the domain and the protocol arguments. The discussion for the type argument will be deferred until later in the chapter.

Normally, the protocol argument is specified as zero. A zero allows the operating system to choose the correct default protocol to be used for the domain that has been selected. There are exceptions to this rule, but this is beyond the scope of the present discussion.

This leaves the domain argument to be explained. For the socketpair(2) function, this value must always be AF_LOCAL or AF_UNIX. In the last chapter, it was pointed out that the macro AF_UNIX is the equivalent of and the older macro name for AF_LOCAL. What does AF_LOCAL mean however? What does it select?

The AF_ prefix of the constant indicates the *address family*. The domain argument selects the address family to be used.

Chapter 4, "Socket Types and Protocols," will expand upon the domain· argument further. In that chapter you will learn about C macros with a prefix of PF_, like PF_LOCAL. For the purposes of this chapter, however, you may consider AF_ prefixed macros equivalent to the PF_ prefixed macros.

Forming Socket Addresses

Each communication protocol specifies its own format for its networking address. Consequently, the address family is used to indicate which type of addressing is being used. The constant AF_LOCAL (AF_UNIX) specifies that the address will be formed according to local (UNIX) address rules. The constant AF_INET indicates that the address will conform to IP address rules, and so on. These are examples of address families.

Within one address family, there can be variations. You will see an example of this when you learn how to form AF_LOCAL addresses.

In the sections that follow, you will examine the format and the physical layout of various address families. This is an important section to master. Much of the difficulty that people experience with the BSD socket interface is related to address initialization.

Examining the Generic Socket Address

Because the BSD socket interface was developed before the ANSI C standard was adopted, there was no (void *) data pointer type to accept any structure address. Consequently, the BSD solution chosen was to define a generic address structure. The generic structure is defined by the C language statement

```
#include <sys/socket.h>
```

EXAMPLE

Listing 2.1 illustrates how the structure is defined in C language terms.

Listing 2.1: The Generic Socket Address

```
struct sockaddr {
    sa_family_t  sa_family;   /* Address Family */
    char         sa_data[14]; /* Address data.  */
};
```

Presently the data type sa_family_t is an unsigned short integer, which is two bytes in length under Linux. The total structure size is 16 bytes. The structure element sa_data[14] represents 14 remaining bytes of address information.

Figure 2.1 provides a physical view of the generic socket address structure.

```
┌──────────────┬──────────┬──────────┐
│              │          │          │
│   sa_family  │          │          │
│              │          │          │
├──────────────┼──────────┼──────────┤
│              │          │          │
│              │          │          │
├──────────────┼──────────┼──────────┤
│         ─ sa_data[14] ─            │
│              │          │          │
├──────────────┼──────────┼──────────┤
│              │          │          │
│              │          │          │
└──────────────┴──────────┴──────────┘
```

Figure 2.1: *Here is a representation of the generic socket address layout.*

The generic socket address structure itself is not that useful to the programmer. It does, however, provide a reference model from which all other address structures must fit. For example, you will learn that all addresses must define the sa_family member in exactly the same location in the structure, because this element determines how the remaining bytes of the address are interpreted.

Forming Local Addresses

This address format is used by sockets that are local to your host (your PC running Linux). For example, when you queue a file to be printed using the lpr(1) command, it uses a local socket to communicate with the spooling service on your PC. While it is also possible to use TCP/IP for local communication, it turns out that this is less efficient.

Traditionally, the local address family has been referred to as the AF_UNIX domain (for example, a UNIX socket address). This is because these addresses use local UNIX filenames to act as the socket name. Linux kernels 2.2.0 and later support abstract socket names, which you'll learn about shortly.

The structure name for `AF_LOCAL` or `AF_UNIX` addresses is `sockaddr_un`. This structure is defined by including the following statement in your C program:

```
#include <sys/un.h>
```

EXAMPLE

An example of the `sockaddr_un` structure is shown in Listing 2.2.

Listing 2.2: The `sockaddr_un` Address Structure

```
struct sockaddr_un {
    sa_family_t  sun_family;/* Address Family */
    char         sun_path[108];  /* Pathname */
};
```

The structure member sun_family must have the value `AF_LOCAL` or `AF_UNIX` assigned to it (these macros represent the same value, though usage of `AF_LOCAL` is now being encouraged). This value indicates the structure is formatted according to the structure `sockaddr_un` rules.

The structure member sun_path[108] contains a valid UNIX pathname. There is no `null` byte required at the end of the character array, as you will find out.

CAUTION

Note that the total size for the sockaddr_un address is much larger than the 16 bytes of the generic address structure. Make sure you allocate sufficient storage to accommodate the AF_LOCAL/AF_UNIX address if you are working with multiple address families within your code.

In the next sections, you will learn how to initialize an `AF_LOCAL` address and define its length.

TIP

Information about local socket addresses can be found in the unix(4) man page.

Forming Traditional Local Addresses

The address name space for traditional local addresses are file system pathnames. A process might name its local socket by any valid pathname. To be valid, however, the process naming the socket must have access to all directory components of the pathname and permissions to create the final socket object in the directory named. Figure 2.2 shows the physical layout of a socket /dev/printer, which you may have active on your system. The lpd printer daemon listens on this local socket address.

sun_family=AF_LOCAL		/	d
e	v	/	p
r	i	n	t
e	r		
	sun_path[108]		

Figure 2.2: *Here is the* AF_LOCAL / AF_UNIX *Socket Address for* /dev/printer.

Notice that the first two bytes indicate the address type of AF_LOCAL. The remaining bytes are the characters /dev/printer with no null byte present. Now you'll turn your attention to the C code to initialize such an address.

Some programmers like to initialize the address structure completely to zero before filling it in. This is often done using the memset(3) function and is probably a good idea:

```
struct sockaddr_un uaddr;

memset(&uaddr,0,sizeof uaddr);
```

This function call will zero out all bytes of the address structure for you.

NOTE

Zeroing out the address structure is not required if you properly initialize the mandatory address elements. However, it does make debugging easier because it eliminates any leftover data that might otherwise remain.

In this chapter, memset(3) is used to zero the address structures, as a demonstration of how it would be done.

EXAMPLE

Listing 2.3 illustrates a small C program that initializes the sockaddr_un structure and then invokes the netstat(1) command to prove that it worked. Keep in mind that the program calls upon the functions socket(2) and bind(2), which have not been covered yet. The socket(2) function is covered in detail in Chapter 4. The bind(2) function is covered in Chapter 5, "Binding Addresses to a Socket."

Listing 2.3: af_unix.c—Initializing an AF_LOCAL/AF_UNIX Socket Address to /dev/printer

```
 1:   /* af_unix.c:
 2:    *
 3:    * AF_UNIX Socket Example:
 4:    */
 5:   #include <stdio.h>
 6:   #include <unistd.h>
 7:   #include <stdlib.h>
 8:   #include <errno.h>
 9:   #include <string.h>
10:   #include <sys/types.h>
11:   #include <sys/stat.h>
12:   #include <sys/socket.h>
13:   #include <sys/un.h>
14:
15:   /*
16:    * This function reports the error and
17:    * exits back to the shell:
18:    */
19:   static void
20:   bail(const char *on_what) {
21:       perror(on_what);
22:       exit(1);
23:   }
24:
25:   int
26:   main(int argc,char **argv,char **envp) {
27:       int z;                /* Status return code */
28:       int sck_unix;                /* Socket */
29:       struct sockaddr_un adr_unix;/* AF_UNIX */
30:       int len_unix;                /* length */
31:       const char pth_unix[]        /* pathname */
32:           = "/tmp/my_sock";
33:
34:       /*
35:        * Create a AF_UNIX (aka AF_LOCAL) socket:
36:        */
37:       sck_unix = socket(AF_UNIX,SOCK_STREAM,0);
38:
39:       if ( sck_unix == -1 )
40:           bail("socket()");
41:
42:       /*
43:        * Here we remove the pathname for the
44:        * socket, in case it existed from a
45:        * prior run. Ignore errors (it might
46:        * not exist).
```

continues

Listing 2.3: continued

```
47:        */
48:        unlink(pth_unix);
49:
50:        /*
51:         * Form an AF_UNIX Address:
52:         */
53:        memset(&adr_unix,0,sizeof adr_unix);
54:
55:        adr_unix.sun_family = AF_UNIX;
56:
57:        strncpy(adr_unix.sun_path,pth_unix,
58:            sizeof adr_unix.sun_path-1)
59:            [sizeof adr_unix.sun_path-1] = 0;
60:
61:        len_unix = SUN_LEN(&adr_unix);
62:
63:        /*
64:         * Now bind the address to the socket:
65:         */
66:        z = bind(sck_unix,
67:            (struct sockaddr *)&adr_unix,
68:            len_unix);
69:
70:        if ( z == -1 )
71:            bail("bind()");
72:
73:        /*
74:         * Display all of our bound sockets:
75:         */
76:        system("netstat -pa --unix 2>/dev/null| "
77:            "sed -n '/^Active UNIX/,/^Proto/p;"
78:            "/af_unix/p'");
79:
80:        /*
81:         * Close and unlink our socket path:
82:         */
83:        close(sck_unix);
84:        unlink(pth_unix);
85:
86:        return 0;
87:    }
```

The steps used in Listing 2.3 are as follows:

1. Variable sck_unix is defined in line 28 to hold the file descriptor for the created socket.

2. The local address structure is defined in line 29 and named `adr_unix`. The program will populate this structure with an `AF_LOCAL` socket address.

3. A socket is created in line 37 by calling upon the function `socket(2)`. Errors are tested in line 39 and reported if necessary.

4. The `unlink(2)` function is called in line 48. Because the `AF_UNIX` address results in a file system object being created, it must be removed when it is no longer required. This statement attempts to remove it, in case it was not removed the last time this program was run.

5. The address structure `adr_unix` is cleared to zero bytes in line 53.

6. The address family is initialized as `AF_UNIX` in line 55.

7. Lines 57 to 59 copies the pathname "/tmp/my_sock" into the address structure. The code used here, also places a null byte into the structure, because the Linux-provided macro `SUN_LEN()` in line 61 needs it.

8. The length of the address is computed in line 61. The program presented uses the Linux-provided macro for this. The macro depends upon a null-terminated string being present in the `adr_unix.sun_path[]` structure member, however.

9. The function `bind(2)` is called (lines 66 to 68) to assign the address that was formed to the socket that was created in line 37.

10. The `netstat(1)` command is invoked in line 76 to prove that our address was bound to our socket.

11. The socket is closed in line 83.

12. The UNIX pathname created for the socket when `bind(2)` was called in line 66 is removed (unlinked).

The length that is assigned to `len_unix` in line 61, using the `SUN_LEN()` macro, does not count the null byte that was copied into the `adr_unix.sun_path[]` character array. However, it was necessary to place the `null` byte there, because the `SUN_LEN()` macro calls upon `strlen(3)` to compute the string length of the UNIX pathname.

To compile and run the program, you can take advantage of the supplied `Makefile`. Perform the following:

```
$ make af_unix
gcc -c  -D_GNU_SOURCE -Wall af_unix.c
gcc af_unix.o -o af_unix
$
```

After the program has been compiled, you can simply invoke it as follows without any arguments:

```
$ ./af_unix
```

Listing 2.4 shows a modified view of the output you would receive from running the command.

Listing 2.4: The Output from the `af_unix` Demonstration Program

```
$ ./af_unix
Active UNIX domain sockets (servers and established)
Proto RefCnt Flags    Type      State  I-Node PID/Program name    Path
unix  0      [ ]       STREAM            104129 800/af_unix         /tmp/my_sock
$
```

Listing 2.4 shows that there was a `unix` socket created, of type `STREAM` (`SOCK_STREAM`), and that `af_unix` was the name of the program that created it. At the right end of the line, you will see that indeed the socket name was `/tmp/my_sock` as it was expected to be.

Forming Abstract Local Addresses

One of the annoyances of the traditional `AF_UNIX` socket name was that a file system object was always involved. This was often unnecessary and inconvenient. If the original file system object was not removed and the same name was used in a call to `bind(2)`, the name assignment would fail.

Linux kernel version 2.2 has made it possible to create an abstract name for a local socket. The trick to this is to make the first byte of the pathname a null byte. Only the bytes that follow that first null byte in the pathname then become part of the abstract name.

The example in Listing 2.5 shows a modified version of the last program. This program takes some different steps to create the abstract name.

Listing 2.5: `af_unix2.c`—Program Creating an Abstract Named `AF_LOCAL`/`AF_UNIX` Socket

```
1:   /* af_unix2.c:
2:    *
3:    * AF_UNIX Socket Example:
4:    */
5:   #include <stdio.h>
6:   #include <unistd.h>
7:   #include <stdlib.h>
8:   #include <errno.h>
9:   #include <string.h>
10:  #include <sys/types.h>
11:  #include <sys/stat.h>
12:  #include <sys/socket.h>
13:  #include <sys/un.h>
```

```
14:
15:   /*
16:    * This function reports the error and
17:    * exits back to the shell:
18:    */
19:   static void
20:   bail(const char *on_what) {
21:       perror(on_what);
22:       exit(1);
23:   }
24:
25:   int
26:   main(int argc,char **argv,char **envp) {
27:       int z;              /* Status return code */
28:       int sck_unix;                /* Socket */
29:       struct sockaddr_un adr_unix;/* AF_UNIX */
30:       int len_unix;                /* length */
31:       const char pth_unix[]      /* Abs. Name */
32:           = "Z*MY-SOCKET*";
33:
34:       /*
35:        * Create an AF_UNIX (aka AF_LOCAL) socket:
36:        */
37:       sck_unix = socket(AF_UNIX,SOCK_STREAM,0);
38:
39:       if ( sck_unix == -1 )
40:           bail("socket()");
41:
42:       /*
43:        * Form an AF_UNIX Address:
44:        */
45:       memset(&adr_unix,0,sizeof adr_unix);
46:
47:       adr_unix.sun_family = AF_UNIX;
48:
49:       strncpy(adr_unix.sun_path,pth_unix,
50:           sizeof adr_unix.sun_path-1)
51:           [sizeof adr_unix.sun_path-1] = 0;
52:
53:       len_unix = SUN_LEN(&adr_unix);
54:
55:       /* Now make first byte null */
56:       adr_unix.sun_path[0] = 0;
57:
58:       /*
59:        * Now bind the address to the socket:
60:        */
```

continues

Listing 2.5: continued

```
61:     z = bind(sck_unix,
62:         (struct sockaddr *)&adr_unix,
63:         len_unix);
64:
65:     if ( z == -1 )
66:         bail("bind()");
67:
68:     /*
69:      * Display all of our bound sockets:
70:      */
71:     system("netstat -pa --unix 2>/dev/null| "
72:         "sed -n '/^Active UNIX/,/^Proto/p;"
73:         "/af_unix/p'");
74:
75:     /*
76:      * Close and unlink our socket path:
77:      */
78:     close(sck_unix);
79:     return 0;
80: }
```

To make and run the program in Listing 2.5, perform the following commands:

```
$ make af_unix2
gcc -c  -D_GNU_SOURCE -Wall af_unix2.c
gcc af_unix2.o -o af_unix2
$ ./af_unix2
```

The output from the running the program is shown in Listing 2.6.

Listing 2.6: Output of the af_unix2 Example Program

```
$ ./af_unix2
Active UNIX domain sockets (servers and established)
Proto RefCnt Flags    Type     State  I-Node PID/Program name   Path
unix  0      [ ]      STREAM          104143 5186/af_unix2      @*MY-SOCKET*
$
```

From Listing 2.6, you can see the socket address appears as the name @*MY-SOCKET*. The leading @ sign is used by netstat(1) to indicate abstract UNIX socket names. The remaining characters are the ones that were copied into the rest of the character array. Notice that the @ character appears where our placeholder 'Z' character was (see line 32 in Listing 2.5).

The overall program steps were the same as the earlier program in Listing 2.3. However, the address initialization steps were a bit different in Listing 2.5. Those steps will be described here:

1. The abstract name of the socket is defined as a string constant in lines 31 and 32. Notice the first character of the string is Z. This extra character is just a placeholder in this string, because it will be eventually replaced by a null byte in step 6.

2. The optional zeroing of the structure was done in line 45 by calling upon memset(3).

3. The address family was set to AF_UNIX in line 47.

4. The abstract pathname is copied to adr_unix.sun_path in line 49 using the strncpy(3) function as before. Notice again, that the terminating null byte is placed into the destination character array for the benefit of the Linux SUN_LEN() macro. Otherwise, the terminating null byte is not required.

5. The length of the address is computed with the help of the Linux provided SUN_LEN() C macro in line 53. This macro invokes strlen(3) on sun_path[], so it is necessary that a terminating null byte is present.

6. This is new: The first byte of the sun_path[] array is set to a null byte. This step must be performed last, if the SUN_LEN() macro is used (step 5).

CAUTION

If you use the Linux-provided SUN_LEN() macro to compute the length of an abstract AF_LOCAL or AF_UNIX socket address, be sure to check that the first byte is not yet null. Make the sun_path[0] byte null after the address length has been computed; otherwise, the computed length will be incorrect.

In this section, you have learned what you need to know about creating AF_LOCAL and AF_UNIX socket addresses. To compute the length of the socket address, you use the SUN_LEN() macro that is provided. Special attention must be paid, however, when computing the length of abstract socket names.

Forming Internet (IPv4) Socket Addresses

The most commonly used address family under Linux is the AF_INET family. This gives a socket an IPv4 socket address to allow it to communicate with other hosts over a TCP/IP network. The include file that defines the structure sockaddr_in is defined by the C language statement:

```
#include <netinet/in.h>
```

EXAMPLE

Listing 2.7 shows an example of the structure sockaddr_in which is used for Internet addresses. An additional structure in_addr is also shown, because the sockaddr_in structure uses it in its definition.

Listing 2.7: The sockaddr_in Structure

```
struct sockaddr_in {
    sa_family_t    sin_family;   /* Address Family */
    uint16_t       sin_port;     /* Port number */
    struct in_addr sin_addr;     /* Internet address */
    unsigned char  sin_zero[8];  /* Pad bytes */
};

struct in_addr {
    uint32_t       s_addr;       /* Internet address */
};
```

Listing 2.7 can be described as follows:

- The sin_family member occupies the same storage area that sa_family does in the generic socket definition. The value of sin_family is initialized to the value of AF_INET.

- The sin_port member defines the TCP/IP port number for the socket address. This value must be in network byte order (this will be elaborated upon later).

- The sin_addr member is defined as the structure in_addr, which holds the IP number in network byte order. If you examine the structure in_addr, you will see that it consists of one 32-bit unsigned integer.

- Finally, the remainder of the structure is padded to 16 bytes by the member sin_zero[8] for 8 bytes. This member does not require any initialization and is not used.

Now turn your attention to Figure 2.3 to visualize the physical layout of the address.

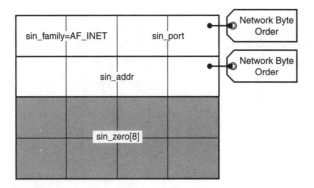

Figure 2.3: *Here is the structure sockaddr_in physical layout.*

In Figure 2.3, you see that the sin_port member uses two bytes, whereas the sin_addr member uses four bytes. Both of these members show a tag on them indicating that these values must be in network byte order.

TIP

Information about IPv4 Internet addresses can be obtained by examining the ip(4) man page.

Understanding Network Byte Order

Different CPU architectures have different arrangements for grouping multiple bytes of data together to form integers of 16, 32, or more bits. The two most basic byte orderings are

- big-endian

- little-endian

Other combinations are possible, but they need not be considered here. Figure 2.4 shows a simple example of these two different byte orderings.

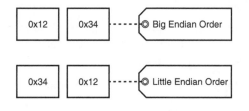

Hexadecimal value 0x1234 (4660 decimal) in
a 16 bit integer (2 bytes)

Figure 2.4: *Here is an example of the basic big- and little-endian byte ordering.*

The value illustrated in Figure 2.4 is decimal value 4660, which, in hexadecimal, is the value 0x1234. The value requires that 2 bytes be used to represent it. It can be seen that you can either place the most significant byte first (big-endian) or you can place the least significant byte value first (little-endian.) The choice is rather arbitrary and it boils down to the design of the CPU.

You might already know that the Intel CPU uses the little-endian byte order. Other CPUs like the Motorola 68000 series use the big-endian byte order. The important thing to realize here is that CPUs of both persuasions exist in the world and are connected to a common Internet.

What happens if a Motorola CPU were to write a 16-bit number to the network and is received by an Intel CPU? "Houston, we have a problem!" The bytes will be interpreted in the reverse order for the Intel CPU, causing it to see the value as 0x3412 in hexadecimal. This is the value 13330 in decimal, instead of 4660!

For agreement to exist over the network, it was decided that big-endian byte order would be the order used on a network. As long as every message communicated over the network obeys this sequence, all software will be able to communicate in harmony.

This brings you back to AF_INET addresses. The TCP/IP port number (sin_port) and the IP number (sin_addr) must be in network byte order. The BSD socket interface requires that you as the programmer consider this when forming the address.

Performing Endian Conversions

A few functions have been provided to help simplify this business of endian conversions. There are two directions of conversion to be considered:

- Host ordering to network ordering
- Network ordering to host ordering

By "host order" what is meant is the byte ordering that your CPU uses. For Intel CPUs, this will mean little-endian byte order. Network order, as you learned earlier, is big-endian byte order.

There are also two categories of conversion functions:

- Short (16-bit) integer conversion
- Long (32-bit) integer conversion

The following provides a synopsis of the conversion functions that you have at your disposal:

```
#include <netinet/in.h>

unsigned long htonl(unsigned long hostlong);

unsigned short htons(unsigned short hostshort);

unsigned long ntohl(unsigned long netlong);

unsigned short ntohs(unsigned short netshort);
```

TIP

These functions are all described in the byteorder(3) man page.

EXAMPLE

Use of these functions is quite simple. For example, to convert a short integer to network order, the following code can be used:

```
short host_short = 0x1234;
short netw_short;

netw_short = htons(host_short);
```

The value netw_short will receive the appropriate value from the conversion to network order. To convert a value from network order back into host order is equally simple:

```
host_short = ntohs(netw_short);
```

Initializing a Wild Internet Address

Now you are ready to create an Internet address. The example shown here will request that the address be wild. This is often done when you are connecting to a remote service. The reason for doing this is that your host might have two or more network interface cards, each with a different IP number. Furthermore, Linux also permits the assignment of more than one IP number to each interface. When you specify a wild IP number, you allow the system to pick the route to the remote service. The kernel will then determine what your final local socket address will be at the time the connection is established.

There are also times when you want the kernel to assign a local port number for you. This is done by specifying sin_port as the value zero. The example code shown in Listing 2.8 demonstrates how to initialize an AF_INET address with both a wild port number and a wild IP number.

EXAMPLE

Listing 2.8: Initializing an IN_ADDRANY AF_INET Address

```
1:        struct sockaddr_in adr_inet;
2:        int adr_len;
3:
4:        memset(&adr_inet,0,sizeof adr_inet);
5:
6:        adr_inet.sin_family = AF_INET;
7:        adr_inet.sin_port = ntohs(0);
8:        adr_inet.sin_addr.s_addr = ntohl(INADDR_ANY);
9:        adr_len = sizeof adr_inet;
```

The steps used in Listing 2.8 are as follows:

1. The value adr_inet is defined using the structure sockaddr_in (line 1).

2. The address adr_inet is zeroed by calling memset(3) in line 4. (This is optional.)

3. The address family is established by assigning the value AF_INET to adr_inet.sin_family (line 6).

4. A wild port number is specified in line 7. Notice the use of the function ntohs(3). The value zero indicates a wild port number.

5. A wild IP number is assigned in line 8. Again, note the use of the ntohl(3) function to perform the endian conversion.

6. The size of the address is simply computed as the size of the structure adr_inet (line 9).

Another commonly used IP number is 127.0.0.1. This refers to the *loopback* device. The loopback device lets you communicate with another process on the same host as your process. You'll see more of this IP number later. For now, just note how the address can be assigned below. Line 8 of Listing 2.8 could be changed to the following statement:

```
adr_inet.sin_addr.s_addr = ntohl(INADDR_LOOPBACK);
```

This will address your current host through the loopback device. In the next section, you will learn how to set up any IP number and port number.

Initializing a Specific Internet Address

The previous section dealt with a simple case for AF_INET addresses. Things get more complicated when you want to establish a specific IP number in the address. Listing 2.9 shows a complete program listing that you can compile by simply performing the following command:

```
$ make af_inet
```

Then, just invoke the compiled program by the name af_inet.

Listing 2.9: af_inet.c—Establishing a Specific AF_INET Address

```
1:   /* af_inet.c:
2:    *
3:    * Establishing a Specific AF_INET
4:    * Socket Address:
5:    */
6:   #include <stdio.h>
7:   #include <unistd.h>
8:   #include <stdlib.h>
9:   #include <errno.h>
10:  #include <string.h>
11:  #include <sys/types.h>
12:  #include <sys/stat.h>
13:  #include <sys/socket.h>
14:  #include <netinet/in.h>
15:
16:  /*
17:   * This function reports the error and
18:   * exits back to the shell:
19:   */
20:  static void
21:  bail(const char *on_what) {
22:      perror(on_what);
23:      exit(1);
24:  }
25:
26:  int
27:  main(int argc,char **argv,char **envp) {
28:      int z;                /* Status return code */
29:      int sck_inet;                  /* Socket  */
30:      struct sockaddr_in adr_inet;/* AF_INET */
31:      int len_inet;                  /* length   */
32:      const unsigned char IPno[] = {
33:          127, 0, 0, 23    /* Local loopback */
34:      };
35:
36:      /* Create an IPv4 Internet Socket */
37:      sck_inet = socket(AF_INET,SOCK_STREAM,0);
38:
39:      if ( sck_inet == -1 )
40:          bail("socket()");
41:
42:      /* Create an AF_INET address */
43:      memset(&adr_inet,0,sizeof adr_inet);
44:
```

continues

Listing 2.9: continued

```
45:        adr_inet.sin_family = AF_INET;
46:        adr_inet.sin_port = htons(9000);
47:        memcpy(&adr_inet.sin_addr.s_addr,IPno,4);
48:        len_inet = sizeof adr_inet;
49:
50:        /* Now bind the address to the socket */
51:        z = bind(sck_inet,
52:            (struct sockaddr *)&adr_inet,
53:            len_inet);
54:
55:        if ( z == -1 )
56:            bail("bind()");
57:
58:        /* Display all of our bound sockets */
59:        system("netstat -pa --tcp 2>/dev/null | "
60:            "sed -n '1,/^Proto/p;/af_inet/p'");
61:
62:        close(sck_inet);
63:        return 0;
64:  }
```

The steps used in this program are almost identical to the others shown in
Listings 2.3 and 2.5. Lines 43 to 48, however, require some explanation:

1. Line 30 defines the sockaddr_in structure with the name adr_inet.
   Additionally, the socket address length is defined as an integer in line
   31 as len_inet.

2. An unsigned character array is defined as IPno[4] in lines 32 and 33.
   Here the individual bytes spell out a specific IP address 127.0.0.23.

3. Line 43 zeros out adr_inet as usual. Note that, again, this is optional.

4. Line 45 establishes the address family as AF_INET.

5. This example chose to establish a TCP/IP port number 9000 in line 46.
   Note the use of the conversion function htons(3) in line 46.

6. The character array IPno[4] is copied to the location
   adr_inet.sin_addr.s_addr in line 47. Because the bytes are defined in
   network order back in step 2, there is no endian conversion required
   here. You will recall that network byte ordering has the most significant byte presented first.

7. The size of the address structure is computed as before (line 48).

You might have noticed that Internet addresses have a fixed length. If you
review Figure 2.3, this is readily apparent. However, you will remember
that the AF_LOCAL address was variable in length (refer to Figure 2.2). For

AF_INET addresses, you merely need to supply the size of the socket structure sockaddr_in. In C language terms, this is

```
sizeof(struct sockaddr_in)
```

You should be well equipped now for forming Internet IPv4 addresses. To broaden your knowledge on socket addressing, the next sections will show you how some other address families can be specified.

Specifying an X.25 Address

The socket interface allows the programmer to use other protocols that are available under Linux with very little effort. The only major part of the code that is different has to do with how the sockets are addressed. You have already seen the initialization required for AF_LOCAL and AF_INET addresses. The creation of an X.25 address is very similar.

The structure used to define an X.25 protocol address is the sockaddr_x25 structure. The include statement that defines this structure is as follows:

```
#include <linux/x25.h>
```

Listing 2.10 shows the socket address structure for the AF_X25 address family.

EXAMPLE

Listing 2.10: The X.25 Socket Address Structure

```
struct sockaddr_x25 {
    sa_family_t  sx25_family; /* Must be AF_X25 */
    x25_address  sx25_addr;   /* X.121 Address */
};

typedef struct {
    char          x25_addr[16];
} x25_address;
```

You will notice that, again, a member sx25_family occupies the first two bytes of the generic socket structure. For this address, it must have the value AF_X25.

TIP

Information about X.25 socket addresses can be found in the x25(4) man page.

An X.25 network address (the X.121 standard defines this address) consists of a series of decimal digits. The program af_x25.c has been provided to show you how you can establish an X.25 address and have netstat(1) display it. Listing 2.11 shows the program listing.

Listing 2.11: `af_x25.c`—Establishing an X.25 Protocol Address

```
1:    /* af_x25.c:
2:     *
3:     * X.25 Socket Address Example:
4:     *
5:     */
6:    #include <stdio.h>
7:    #include <unistd.h>
8:    #include <stdlib.h>
9:    #include <errno.h>
10:   #include <string.h>
11:   #include <sys/types.h>
12:   #include <sys/socket.h>
13:   #include <linux/x25.h>
14:
15:   /*
16:    * This function reports the error and
17:    * exits back to the shell:
18:    */
19:   static void
20:   bail(const char *on_what) {
21:       perror(on_what);
22:       exit(1);
23:   }
24:
25:   int
26:   main(int argc,char **argv,char **envp) {
27:       int z;              /* Status return code */
28:       int sck_x25;                /* Socket */
29:       struct sockaddr_x25 adr_x25;/* AF_X25 */
30:       int len_x25;                /* length */
31:       const char x25_host[]   /* X.121 addr */
32:           = "79400900";
33:
34:       /* Create an AF_X25 socket */
35:       sck_x25 = socket(AF_X25,SOCK_SEQPACKET,0);
36:
37:       if ( sck_x25 == -1 )
38:           bail("socket()");
39:
40:       /* Form an AF_X25 Address */
41:       adr_x25.sx25_family = AF_X25;
42:       strcpy(adr_x25.sx25_addr.x25_addr,x25_host);
43:       len_x25 = sizeof adr_x25;
44:
45:       /* Bind the address to the socket */
46:       z = bind(sck_x25,
```

```
47:              (struct sockaddr *)&adr_x25,
48:              len_x25);
49:
50:      if ( z == -1 )
51:          bail("bind()");
52:
53:      puts("X.25 SOCKETS :");
54:      system("cat /proc/net/x25");
55:      return 0;
56:  }
```

To compile the program in Listing 2.11, perform the following:

```
$ make af_x25
```

NOTE

You will not be successful running the program in Listing 2.11 if you do not have X.25 support compiled into your kernel. Be sure to enable X.25 support if you want to experiment with that protocol. To enable X.25 support you must configure and recompile your Linux kernel.

The address establishing code consists of the following basic steps:

1. The sockaddr_x25 structure is used in line 29 to define adr_x25. The length variable len_x25 is defined as an int on line 30.

2. A character array constant x25_host[] is defined on lines 31 and 32 as the X.25 address is to be establish.

3. The address family is specified as AF_X25 in line 41.

4. The host address number is copied into the address structure with a terminating null byte in line 42.

5. The length of the sockaddr_x25 structure is the correct length to use with the current Linux implementation (line 43).

Note that the program does not call upon netstat(1) this time. This is because netstat(1) does not report AF_X25 sockets at this time. Instead, the example program uses cat(1) to copy the contents of /proc/net/x25 to standard output. For this to be successful, however, you must have the proc file system support compiled into your kernel (this is now standard practice).

NOTE

Normally socket addresses with variable elements like the AF_UNIX address family require a computed length of the address. The Linux implementation of the AF_X25 socket address, however, simply requires the fixed length of sizeof(sockaddr_x25). The host number must be null terminated within the sockaddr_x25 structure.

Running the program af_x25 provides the results shown in Listing 2.12.

OUTPUT

Listing 2.12: The Output of the af_x25 Program

```
$ ./af_x25
X.25 SOCKETS :
dest_addr  src_addr  dev  lci st vs vr va  t t2 t21 t22 t23 Snd-Q Rcv-Q inode
*          79400900  ???  000  0  0  0  0  0 3 200 180 180     0     0 104172
$
```

In the program output in Listing 2.12, you can see the host number listed under the src_addr column heading as 79400900.

Specifying Other Address Families

The scope of this book does not permit a full coverage of all address families supported by Linux. The list of supported protocols is growing longer with each new year. If you are looking for a fast track to TCP/IP programming, you can skip this section and advance to the next section.

In this section, you will read briefly about a few other protocols that might be of interest to you. This section is intended as a roadmap to other places of interest, should you feel like some adventure.

There are at least three more address families that Linux can support. They are

- AF_INET6—IPv6, which is under development
- AF_AX25—Amateur Radio X.25 protocol
- AF_APPLETALK—Linux AppleTalk protocol implementation

Each of these protocols requires that you have the corresponding support compiled into your kernel. Some of these protocols may not be complete implementations—programmer beware! Incomplete or experimental protocols will be buggy or sometimes even crash your system.

TIP

The AF_APPLETALK address family is documented in the ddp(4) man page.

Listing 2.13 shows some of the C structures that are important to these other socket address families. These structures will help you visualize the address components that must be initialized when creating an address for the protocol chosen.

Listing 2.13: Other Address Family Structures

EXAMPLE

```
/*
 * IPv6 Address (AF_INET6):
 */
```

```
struct sockaddr_in6 {
    sa_family_t     sin6_family;
    uint16_t        sin6_port;          /* port # */
    uint32_t        sin6_flowinfo; /* flow info */
    struct in6_addr sin6_addr;   /* IPv6 address */
};

struct in6_addr {
    union {
        uint8_t     u6_addr8[16];
        uint16_t    u6_addr16[8];
        uint32_t    u6_addr32[4];
    } in6_u;
};

/*
 * Amateur Radio AX.25 Address (AF_AX25):
 */
struct full_sockaddr_ax25 {
    struct sockaddr_ax25 fsa_ax25;
    ax25_address  fsa_digipeater[AX25_MAX_DIGIS];
};

struct sockaddr_ax25 {
    sa_family_t     sax25_family;
    ax25_address    sax25_call;
    int             sax25_ndigis;
};

typedef struct {
    /* 6 call + SSID (shifted ascii!) */
    char            ax25_call[7];
} ax25_address;

#define sax25_uid       sax25_ndigis

/*
 * AppleTalk Address (AF_APPLETALK):
 */
struct sockaddr_atalk {
    sa_family_t     sat_family; /* addr family */
    u_char          sat_port;   /* port */
    struct at_addr  sat_addr;   /* net/node */
};

struct at_addr {
    u_short         s_net;
    u_char          s_node;
};
```

Fully addressing the steps to initialize each of these different protocols would require some knowledge about the underlying protocols themselves. This is outside of the scope of what you want to accomplish at this point in this book.

However, if you would like to experiment further with the AF_AX25 family, there is one other program available for the purpose in source file af_ax25.c. Using the Makefile provided at the Web site associated with this book, you can compile it as follows:

```
$ make af_ax25
gcc -c  -D_GNU_SOURCE -Wall af_ax25.c
gcc af_ax25.o -o af_ax25
$
```

NOTE

All source code and make files for this book are provided at the following URL:

```
http://www.quecorp.com/series/by_example
```

To run this program, the following conditions must be met:

1. You have Amateur Radio AX.25 support compiled into your kernel.

2. You might require an AX.25 compatible interface to establish a socket name. See the note that follows.

3. If condition two is required, and you have no AX.25 interfaces, you can satisfy this requirement by using a BPQ device on top of an ethernet device. See instructions that follow the note.

NOTE

The author found that the program af_ax25 could call bind(3) and establish an AF_AX25 address with no AX.25 interfaces present in the system (using Red Hat Linux 6.0, kernel 2.2.10). However, this may depend upon the kernel release that you have and could be subject to change.

If you require an AX.25 device, either to run the af_ax25 program or to perform further network programming experiments, you can establish a BPQ interface if you already have an ethernet interface. To check, perform the following:

```
$ netstat -i
Kernel Interface table
Iface  MTU Met   RX-OK RX-ERR RX-DRP RX-OVR   TX-OK TX-ERR TX-DRP TX-OVR Flg
eth0   1500  0   81764      0      0      0   51634      0      0      0 BRU
lo     3924  0   16969      0      0      0   16969      0      0      0 LRU
$
```

In the display shown, eth0 represents one ethernet interface. If you have BPQ support compiled into your kernel, you can create a BPQ device as follows:

```
$ su -
Password:
# ifconfig bpq0 hw ax25 VE3WWG-5 up
```

Then, you can check the status of the interface, as shown in Listing 2.14.

Listing 2.14: Checking the Interface Status of bpq0

OUTPUT

```
# /sbin/ifconfig
bpq0      Link encap:AMPR AX.25   HWaddr VE3WWG-5
          UP RUNNING  MTU:256  Metric:1
          RX packets:0 errors:0 dropped:0 overruns:0 frame:0
          TX packets:0 errors:0 dropped:0 overruns:0 carrier:0
          collisions:0 txqueuelen:0

eth0      Link encap:Ethernet   HWaddr 00:A0:4B:06:F4:8D
          inet addr:192.168.0.1  Bcast:192.168.0.255  Mask:255.255.255.0
          UP BROADCAST RUNNING PROMISC MULTICAST  MTU:1500  Metric:1
          RX packets:10945 errors:0 dropped:0 overruns:0 frame:100
          TX packets:4959 errors:0 dropped:0 overruns:0 carrier:0
          collisions:0 txqueuelen:100
          Interrupt:9 Base address:0xe400
```

The bpq0 interface is a pseudo device, because it interfaces with the real device eth0. However, this trick allows you to experiment with the AX.25 radio protocol without using any packet radio hardware. In the output Listing 2.14, you can see that the bpq0 interface is up, with the hardware AX.25 address of VE3WWG-5.

The AF_UNSPEC Address Family

The C macro AF_UNSPEC represents the unspecified address family. This might seem like a rather useless macro, but it does have its uses. If you write a program that must work with many different protocols and address families, then you need a way to indicate an unspecified address family. Consider the union of different address families in Listing 2.15.

Listing 2.15: A Union of Address Families

EXAMPLE

```
union {
    sockaddr        sa;
    sockaddr_un     un;
    sockaddr_in     in;
    sockaddr_in6    in6;
    sockaddr_x25    x25;
    full_sockaddr_ax25 ax25;
    sockaddr_atalk  at;
} u;
```

Before any value is placed into this union, your C program might initialize the union as follows:

```
u.sa.sa_family = AF_UNSPEC;
```

Later in the program, when you go to place an AF_INET address into this union, you would use:

```
u.in.sin_family = AF_INET;
```

The AF_UNSPEC acts as a safe placeholder for you when you don't know what the address family is yet.

What's Next

Socket addressing is the messiest part of socket programming, but that is all behind you now. With the examples that you have worked through, you now know how to apply local addresses, Internet addresses, and a few others. You learned that each address structure must have its corresponding address family constant stored in it (AF_INET, for example).

In this chapter, you learned that the AF_INET address was sensitive about network ordered bytes in the sin_port and sin_addr members. The byteorder(3) conversion functions were mastered to deal with this problem.

You also saw that each address family has its own quirks for establishing both the address itself and the length of the address. Consequently, this chapter will continue to serve as a reference for you.

In the next chapter, you'll build upon the concept of network addresses that you've learned and you'll be introduced to new library functions that manipulate addresses for you.

Address Conversion Functions

In the last chapter, you learned how various types of socket addresses could be allocated and initialized. These were all simple cases of initializing from a constant. Setting up an address from a C string with varying addresses requires more programming effort. In this chapter, you will focus on the additional issues pertaining to establishing Internet addresses, and learning about the functions that can assist you in this area.

In this chapter, you will learn about

- Classes of internet addresses
- IP netmasks
- Private and reserved IP numbers
- Functions that convert IP numbers

Before you get started however, it's a good time to review the design of an IP address. Then, you'll have a greater insight into the job that is ahead of you.

Internet IP Numbers

The IP number consists of four decimal values separated by decimal points, often referred to as "dots." This convention is frequently called *dotted-quad* notation, or sometimes *dotted-decimal* notation. Each decimal value represents the unsigned value of one byte, in network byte sequence. Remember that network order requires that the most significant bytes appear first.

Each byte is considered as an unsigned 8-bit value. This restricts each byte to a decimal value range of zero to 255. Because the value is unsigned, the value cannot be negative, and a plus sign is not permitted. Consider the address 192.168.0.1, for example; you know that the first byte in network order must have the value of 192 decimal.

When you see a movie showing an IP number on the screen with a value such as 192.168.300.5, you know that the producer knew very little about TCP/IP networking! Although this IP number is syntactically correct, the decimal value 300 obviously exceeds the maximum unsigned value of 255.

Later, starting with the section "Manipulating IP Numbers," you will look at functions that can parse a C string into network address bytes, and range check the decimal values for you.

Internet Address Classes

Internet addresses are made up of two components:

- Network number (most significant bits)
- Host number (least significant bits)

The network number identifies the network where the host can be contacted. The host number identifies one host (your PC, for example) out of several on that particular network.

As you already know, the IP number is a 32-bit value (or four 8-bit bytes). However, the division between the network number and host number components is not at a fixed location. The dividing line depends upon the classification of the address, which is determined by examining the most significant byte of the address. Table 3.1 summarizes how IP numbers are classified.

Table 3.1: Internet Address Classes

Class	Lowest	Highest	Network Bits	Host Bits
A	0.0.0.0	127.255.255.255	7	24
B	128.0.0.0	191.255.255.255	14	16
C	192.0.0.0	223.255.255.255	21	8
D	224.0.0.0	239.255.255.255	28	N/A
E	240.0.0.0	247.255.255.255	27	N/A

Class A, B, and C define specific IP addresses of hosts. For class D and E addresses, there are zero host bits available in the address. Class D addresses are used for multicasting where the 28 bits are used to describe a multicast group. The 27 bits of the class E address are reserved.

Figure 3.1 helps you visualize the breakdown of the 32-bit IP address. The frequently used classes A, B, and C are shown.

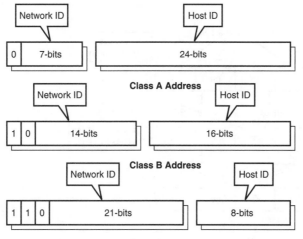

Figure 3.1: *This figure illustrates the Internet address classes A, B, and C.*

Understanding Netmask Values

There are situations in which you must determine the *netmask* value of an address. This is particularly true if you are setting up your own network. So, just what is a netmask value anyway?

If you take the Internet IP Address as a 32-bit number, then you know that the network ID is specified in the most significant bits of the address. Additionally, the host ID is specified by the least significant bits of the same address (review Figure 3.1 if necessary). The netmask is simply the value that you would "bit-wise and" with the address to leave only the network ID. Figure 3.2 illustrates how the IP address 192.168.9.1 is masked to extract only the network ID bits.

TIP

You will often hear people use the terms net and subnet interchangeably. Technically speaking, these terms represent two distinctly different network ID values. The network ID identifies the network ID number proper.

continues

continued

However, within an IPv4 number, it is possible to further subdivide the host ID leaving a subnetwork ID in the most significant bits of the host ID and the final host ID in the least significant bits. When subnetting is used, the netmask value will take into account these additional subnetwork ID bits.

Consequently, when subnetting is in use, the network mask will differ from the ones presented in this chapter.

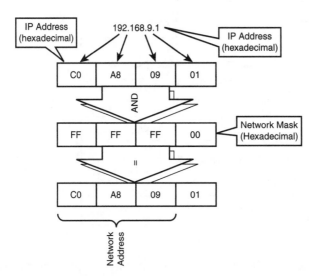

Figure 3.2: *Applying a netmask to* 192.168.9.1 *yields a network address.*

The resulting most significant bits represent the network portion of the IP address without the host ID. Figure 3.3 illustrates how the network mask is converted from hexadecimal back into dotted-quad notation.

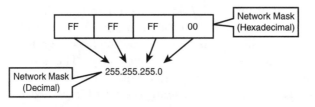

Figure 3.3: *Here is the netmask expressed in dotted-quad notation.*

If you must set up your own IP network, then you will need to determine what the netmask values should be. Table 3.2 lists the netmask values for class A, B, and C addresses.

Table 3.2: Netmask Values by IP Class

Class	Lowest	Highest	Netmask
A	0.0.0.0	127.255.255.255	255.0.0.0
B	128.0.0.0	191.255.255.255	255.255.0.0
C	192.0.0.0	223.255.255.255	255.255.255.0

Sometimes, in networking software, your software must be able to classify a network address. Sometimes this is simply done in order to determine a default netmask value.

Listing 3.1 provides a short program that illustrates how to classify an IP address, starting from a socket address. To compile and run the provided source code, perform the following:

```
$ make netmask
gcc -c  -D_GNU_SOURCE -Wall netmask.c
gcc netmask.o -o netmask
$ ./netmask
```

The program in Listing 3.1 sets up four different IP addresses in an Internet socket address structure. Then, the address is examined and classified. This is done to demonstrate how you would classify an IP address of a remote client that has connected to your server.

EXAMPLE

Listing 3.1: netmask.c—Classifying and Determining a Netmask

```
1:    /* netmask.c:
2:     *
3:     * Classify an IP address:
4:     */
5:    #include <stdio.h>
6:    #include <unistd.h>
7:    #include <stdlib.h>
8:    #include <sys/types.h>
9:    #include <sys/socket.h>
10:   #include <netinet/in.h>
11:
12:   int
13:   main(int argc,char **argv) {
14:       int x;                  /* Index variable */
15:       struct sockaddr_in adr_inet;/* AF_INET */
16:       int len_inet;              /* length  */
17:       unsigned msb; /* Most significant byte */
18:       char class;
19:       char *netmask;
20:       static struct {
21:           unsigned char   ip[4];
22:       } addresses[] = {
```

continues

Listing 3.1: continued

```
23:              { { 44,135,86,12 } },
24:              { { 127,0,0,1 } },
25:              { { 172,16,23,95 } },
26:              { { 192,168,9,1 } }
27:          };
28:
29:      for ( x=0; x<4; ++x ) {
30:          /*
31:           * Set up the socket address, to
32:           * demonstrate how to classify it:
33:           */
34:          memset(&adr_inet,0,sizeof adr_inet);
35:          adr_inet.sin_family = AF_INET;
36:          adr_inet.sin_port = htons(9000);
37:          memcpy(&adr_inet.sin_addr.s_addr,
38:              addresses[x].ip,4);
39:          len_inet = sizeof adr_inet;
40:
41:          /*
42:           * Classify this address:
43:           *
44:           * 1. Get the Most Significant Byte
45:           * 2. Classify by that byte
46:           */
47:          msb = *(unsigned char *)
48:              &adr_inet.sin_addr.s_addr;
49:
50:          if ( (msb & 0x80) == 0x00 ) {
51:              class = 'A';
52:              netmask = "255.0.0.0";
53:          } else if ( (msb & 0xC0) == 0x80 ) {
54:              class = 'B';
55:              netmask = "255.255.0.0";
56:          } else if ( (msb & 0xE0) == 0xC0 ) {
57:              class = 'C';
58:              netmask = "255.255.255.0";
59:          } else if ( (msb & 0xF0) == 0xE0 ) {
60:              class = 'D';
61:              netmask = "255.255.255.255";
62:          } else {
63:              class = 'E';
64:              netmask = "255.255.255.255";
65:          }
66:
67:          printf("Address %u.%u.%u.%u is class %c "
68:              "netmask %s\n",
69:              addresses[x].ip[0],
```

```
70:                 addresses[x].ip[1],
71:                 addresses[x].ip[2],
72:                 addresses[x].ip[3],
73:                 class,
74:                 netmask);
75:         }
76:
77:         return 0;
78:     }
```

The operation of this demonstration program can be summarized in the following steps:

1. The socket address structure adr_inet is defined in line 15. This will be the address that will be examined for classification.

2. The addresses to be tested are defined in a static array of structures, defined in lines 20 to 27. You might want to experiment by trying other address numbers in lines 23 to 26.

3. Line 29 starts a loop that will iterate through four entries in the addresses[] array. The subscript value will be the variable x.

4. A socket address is initialized in lines 34 to 39, from addresses[x]. This is done in the same manner it was presented in the last chapter, and should look familiar to you now.

5. The most significant byte is extracted out of the socket address adr_inet in line 47. You will remember that the most significant byte is the first byte of the address, in network byte order (big-endian). With this byte lifted from the socket address, it will be possible to classify the address based upon the high-order bits in this byte.

6. The if statement in line 50 tests to see whether the high-order bit is zero (review Figure 3.1, looking at the class A address). If the high-order bit is zero, you know you have a class A address (lines 51 and 52 execute).

7. The if statement in line 53 tests to see whether the high-order bit is 1, and the 2nd highest bit is a 0 (review the class B address in Figure 3.1). If this is true, then the statements in lines 54 and 55 classify this address as class B.

8. The if statement in line 56 tests to see whether the highest two bits are 11 (binary), followed by a 0 bit. If this is true, then lines 57 and 58 classify the address as a class C address (review Figure 3.1 for class C addresses).

9. The if statement in line 59 tests for the high-order bit pattern of 1110. This causes the address to be classified as a class D address. Note for class D and class E, the netmask is set to 255.255.255.255 because the entire address is a network address.

10. The else statement in line 62 evaluates everything remaining as a class E address, and sets the netmask also to 255.255.255.255 (see step 9).

11. The results of the classification are reported in lines 67 to 74.

Listing 3.2 shows the output that results from running this demonstration program.

OUTPUT

Listing 3.2: The Output of the netmask.c Demonstration Program

```
$ ./netmask
Address 44.135.86.12 is class A netmask 255.0.0.0
Address 127.0.0.1 is class A netmask 255.0.0.0
Address 172.16.23.95 is class B netmask 255.255.0.0
Address 192.168.9.1 is class C netmask 255.255.255.0
$
```

With the example code demonstrated in Listing 3.1, you will be ready to classify any IP number that you must process.

While your attention is still focused upon IP numbers, now is a good time to cover private IP number allocations. These are addresses that you will use if you decide to establish your own private network.

Allocating IP Addresses

You learned how Internet addresses are classified in the previous section. IP addresses are allocated to various individuals and groups by an organization known as the InterNIC. However, some ranges of IP addresses have been set aside for private use, and still others are reserved for special uses.

Private IP Numbers

Normally, IP numbers must be registered by the InterNIC at rs.internic.net. (Prior to April 1, 1993, this was handled by the NIC at nic.ddn.mil.) However, if your system is not directly connected to the Internet, you do not need to have a globally unique address. You can use "private" IP numbers instead.

The first question that immediately follows, then, is "What IP numbers should I use?" This section is provided to help you make that decision, and to act as a future reference guide.

RFC 1597 is an Internet standards document that describes how private IP numbers are allocated. Table 3.3 provides a quick summary for you, complete with netmask values.

Table 3.3: Private IP Number Allocations

Class	Lowest	Highest	Netmask
A	10.0.0.0	10.255.255.255	255.0.0.0
B	172.16.0.0	172.31.255.255	255.255.0.0
C	192.168.0.0	192.168.255.255	255.255.255.0

Your choice of a class A, B, or C IP number series will depend largely upon the number of separate networks and hosts that you plan to establish. If the total number of networks and hosts is small, then a class C address might be sufficient. Alternatively, a class A address allows for one network (without subnetting), but a very large total number of hosts. Class B provides a large number of both networks and hosts.

Reserved IP Numbers

There are a large number of reserved IP numbers and these blocks are listed in RFC 1166. As one example of a reserved series of numbers, the Amateur Radio IP number series are shown in Table 3.4 as an example. These are used by amateur radio operators using the Internet protocol on packet radio equipment. Now that the AX.25 protocol is built into the Linux kernel (as of 2.2.0), it is certain that more radio amateurs will be exercising these IP numbers!

Table 3.4: Amateur Radio Reserved IP Numbers

Class	Lowest	Highest	Netmask
A	44.0.0.0	44.255.255.255	255.0.0.0

This brings you to the end of the IP number tour. Now, it's time to apply your knowledge of socket addresses and IP numbers to functions that Linux provides to make IP address conversion easier.

Manipulating IP Numbers

To ease the programming burden of turning IP numbers in string form into usable socket addresses, a number of conversion functions have been provided. These and other useful functions will be presented in the following sections.

Using the `inet_addr(3)` Function

The first function that you will learn about is an older function, which should probably no longer be used in new code. However, you will find it in a lot of existing network code, and so you should become familiar with it and know its limitations.

The synopsis for inet_addr(3) is as follows:

```
#include <sys/socket.h>
#include <netinet/in.h>
#include <arpa/inet.h>

unsigned long inet_addr(const char *string);
```

This function accepts an input C string argument string and parses the dotted-quad notation into a 32-bit Internet address value. The 32-bit value returned is in network byte order.

If the input argument string does not represent a valid dotted-quad address, the value INADDR_NONE is returned. Any other returned value represents the converted value.

NOTE

The 32-bit value returned by inet_addr(3) is in network byte order. Do not use htonl(3) on the returned value, because it is already in network byte order.

CAUTION

The inet_addr(3) does not establish a reason code in errno when INADDR_NONE is returned. So, do not test errno or report it when an error indication is returned by this function.

The program shown in Listing 3.3 is an example of how you would use this function. To compile and run the program, perform the following:

```
$ make inetaddr
gcc -c -D_GNU_SOURCE -Wall inetaddr.c
gcc inetaddr.o -o inetaddr
$ ./inetaddr
```

The program in Listing 3.3, when it is run, converts a C string constant containing an IP number into a network sequenced 32-bit IP address. This value is then placed into an AF_INET socket address and bound to the socket.

EXAMPLE

Listing 3.3: inetaddr.c—Example Program Using inet_addr(3)

```
1:   /* inetaddr.c:
2:    *
3:    * Example using inet_addr(3):
4:    */
5:   #include <stdio.h>
6:   #include <unistd.h>
7:   #include <stdlib.h>
8:   #include <errno.h>
```

```
9:   #include <string.h>
10:  #include <sys/types.h>
11:  #include <sys/socket.h>
12:  #include <netinet/in.h>
13:  #include <arpa/inet.h>
14:
15:  /*
16:   * This function reports the error and
17:   * exits back to the shell:
18:   */
19:  static void
20:  bail(const char *on_what) {
21:      fputs(on_what,stderr);
22:      fputc('\n',stderr);
23:      exit(1);
24:  }
25:
26:  int
27:  main(int argc,char **argv) {
28:      int z;
29:      struct sockaddr_in adr_inet;/* AF_INET */
30:      int len_inet;                    /* length  */
31:      int sck_inet;                    /* Socket */
32:
33:      /* Create a Socket */
34:      sck_inet = socket(AF_INET,SOCK_STREAM,0);
35:
36:      if ( sck_inet == -1 )
37:          bail("socket()");
38:
39:      /* Establish address */
40:      memset(&adr_inet,0,sizeof adr_inet);
41:
42:      adr_inet.sin_family = AF_INET;
43:      adr_inet.sin_port = htons(9000);
44:
45:      adr_inet.sin_addr.s_addr =
46:          inet_addr("127.0.0.95");
47:
48:      if ( adr_inet.sin_addr.s_addr == INADDR_NONE )
49:          bail("bad address.");
50:
51:      len_inet = sizeof adr_inet;
52:
53:      /* Bind it to the socket */
54:      z = bind(sck_inet,
```

continues

Listing 3.3: continued

```
55:             (struct sockaddr *)&adr_inet,
56:             len_inet);
57:
58:     if ( z == -1 )
59:         bail("bind()");
60:
61:     /* Display our socket address */
62:     system("netstat -pa --tcp 2>/dev/null"
63:         "| grep inetaddr");
64:
65:     return 0;
66:  }
```

NOTE

If netstat(1) command on your system does not support the options used in lines 62 and 63 of Listing 3.3, substitute the following call if you have lsof installed:

```
system("lsof -i tcp | grep inetaddr");
```

The general program structure is very similar to the ones used in the previous chapter. However, the steps used to set up the socket address are a bit different. They are

1. The socket address structure is zeroed out in line 40. This is an optional step, but many find that this helps debugging should it become necessary.

2. The address family is established as AF_INET in line 42.

3. The port number has been established as port 9000 in this example (line 43).

4. The function inet_addr(3) is called in line 46 to convert the string constant "127.0.0.95" into a network 32-bit address. This value is stored into the socket address member adr_inet.sin_addr.s_addr.

5. The value returned from the conversion in step 4 is tested to see whether it matches the value INADDR_NONE in line 48. If it does, this indicates that the value provided in the C string was not a good Internet IP number (the program bails out in line 49 if this happens).

6. Finally, the length of the socket address is established in line 51 as before.

The above procedure has established the socket address in the variable adr_inet. This is later passed to bind(2) in line 54, which has not been covered yet. The bind(3) call just applies the address to the socket (the full discussion will otherwise be deferred for now).

The important thing that you accomplish with the use of the inet_addr(3) function is that you are spared from performing all parsing and testing of the input IP number.

TIP

Avoid using inet_addr(3) in new programs. Use the function inet_aton(3) instead.

The inet_addr(3) function has the limitation that it returns the value INADDR_NONE if the input argument is an invalid IP number. The limitation is that it also returns the value INADDR_NONE if you pass it the valid IP address of 255.255.255.255.

This creates a problem for programs like the ping(8) command where this is a valid broadcast address to use.

OUTPUT

Running the program yields the following output:

```
$ ./inetaddr
tcp 0 0 127.0.0.95:9000  *:*  CLOSE  992/inetaddr
$
```

The program invokes netstat(1) using grep to look for the program name inetaddr. Consequently, you see one output line showing the address established for the socket as 127.0.0.95:9000. You'll remember that the program arbitrarily chose the port number 9000 for this experiment.

The inet_aton(3) Function

The inet_aton(3) is an improved way to convert a string IP number into a 32-bit networked sequenced IP number. The synopsis of the function is given as follows:

```
#include <sys/socket.h>
#include <netinet/in.h>
#include <arpa/inet.h>

int inet_aton(const char *string, struct in_addr *addr);
```

The inet_aton(3) function accepts two arguments. They are

1. The input argument string, which contains the ASCII representation of the dotted-quad IP number.

2. The output argument addr is the structure that will be updated with the new IP address.

The return value of the function is nonzero (true) if the conversion succeeds. The value zero (false) is returned if the input address is incorrect. There is no error code established in errno, so its value should be ignored.

What is a little bit confusing about this function is the pointer required for argument two of this function call. If you define an AF_INET socket address as

```
struct sockaddr_in adr_inet; /* AF_INET */
```

the pointer that should be supplied as argument two of the inet_aton(3) function is the following:

```
&adr_inet.sin_addr
```

✔ Review Listing 2.7 in Chapter 2, "Domains and Address Families," page 48, if this does not seem clear to you. It will make more sense when you review the definition of the sockaddr_in structure.

Listing 3.4 shows a program that calls upon inet_aton(3) instead of the older inet_addr(3) function that you learned about in the previous section. This program operates the same way, except that it is compiled and executed as follows:

```
$ make inetaton
gcc -c  -D_GNU_SOURCE -Wall inetaton.c
gcc inetaton.o -o inetaton
$ ./inetaton
```

Now, spend a few moments examining Listing 3.4. You'll find that the new function is invoked in lines 45 to 47.

EXAMPLE

Listing 3.4: inetaton.c—Using inet_aton(3)

```
1:    /* inetaton.c:
2:      *
3:      * Example using inet_aton(3) :
4:      */
5:    #include <stdio.h>
6:    #include <unistd.h>
7:    #include <stdlib.h>
8:    #include <errno.h>
9:    #include <string.h>
10:   #include <sys/types.h>
11:   #include <sys/socket.h>
12:   #include <netinet/in.h>
13:   #include <arpa/inet.h>
14:
15:   /*
16:     * This function reports the error and
17:     * exits back to the shell:
18:     */
19:   static void
20:   bail(const char *on_what) {
21:       fputs(on_what,stderr);
```

```
22:        fputc('\n',stderr);
23:        exit(1);
24:  }
25:
26:  int
27:  main(int argc,char **argv) {
28:        int z;
29:        struct sockaddr_in adr_inet;/* AF_INET */
30:        int len_inet;              /* length  */
31:        int sck_inet;               /* Socket */
32:
33:        /* Create a Socket */
34:        sck_inet = socket(AF_INET,SOCK_STREAM,0);
35:
36:        if ( sck_inet == -1 )
37:            bail("socket()");
38:
39:        /* Establish address */
40:        memset(&adr_inet,0,sizeof adr_inet);
41:
42:        adr_inet.sin_family = AF_INET;
43:        adr_inet.sin_port = htons(9000);
44:
45:        if ( !inet_aton("127.0.0.23",
46:                  &adr_inet.sin_addr) )
47:            bail("bad address.");
48:
49:        len_inet = sizeof adr_inet;
50:
51:        /* Bind it to the socket */
52:        z = bind(sck_inet,
53:            (struct sockaddr *)&adr_inet,
54:            len_inet);
55:
56:        if ( z == -1 )
57:            bail("bind()");
58:
59:        /* Display our socket address */
60:        system("netstat -pa --tcp 2>/dev/null"
61:            "| grep inetaton");
62:
63:        return 0;
64:  }
```

Running this program yields the following results:

```
$ ./inetaton
tcp 0 0 127.0.0.23:9000  *:*  CLOSE  1007/inetaton
$
```

OUTPUT

NOTE

If netstat(1) command on your system does not support the options used in lines 60 and 61 of Listing 3.4, substitute the following call if you have lsof installed:

```
system("lsof -i tcp | grep inetaton");
```

While the bulk of the program was the same as the previous one in Listing 3.3, the following steps are of particular importance:

1. The new function inet_aton(3) is invoked from within the if statement in line 45.

2. Note the second argument in line 46, given as the value &adr_inet.sin_addr. This is the required pointer for argument two.

3. If the return value of the function in line 45 is zero, this indicates the conversion failed, and line 47 is executed.

The program in Listing 3.4 shows you how easily the newer function inet_aton(3) can be put to work in place of the older function inet_addr(3). There are perhaps three things that you need to remember about this function:

- The pointer in argument two always refers to the sockaddr_in member sin_addr (&adr_inet.sin_addr in the example program).

- The return value indicates a Boolean success value. A return value of true (nonzero) means that the call succeeded, whereas false (zero) means that it failed.

- Do not consult the value in errno. No meaningful code is established by inet_aton(3) for errno.

In the next section, you'll see how you can take a socket IP address and convert it back to a string for reporting purposes.

Using the inet_ntoa(3) Function

There are times when a socket address represents the address of a user that has connected to your server, or represents the sender of a UDP packet. The job of converting a network sequenced 32-bit value into dotted-quad notation is inconvenient. Hence, the inet_ntoa(3) function has been provided. The synopsis of the function is as follows:

```
#include <sys/socket.h>
#include <netinet/in.h>
#include <arpa/inet.h>

char *inet_ntoa(struct in_addr addr);
```

The function requires only one input argument addr. Note that the struct in_addr is an internal part of the Internet socket address. The address is converted into a static buffer, which is internal to the function. This character array pointer is returned as the return value. The results will be valid only until the next call to this function.

✔ Review the sockaddr_in structure in Figure 2.3 of Chapter 2, "Domains and Address Families," page 48. This will help you visualize the physical address structure that you are working with.

If a socket address addr exists in your program as a sockaddr_in structure, then the following code shows how to use inet_ntoa(3) to perform the conversion. The IP number is converted to a string and reported, using the printf(3) function:

```
struct sockaddr_in addr;    /* Socket Address */

printf("IP ADDR: %s\n",
    inet_ntoa(addr.sin_addr));
```

A complete example program is provided in Listing 3.5. To compile and run this program, the following steps are required:

```
$ make inetntoa
gcc -c  -D_GNU_SOURCE -Wall inetntoa.c
gcc inetntoa.o -o inetntoa
$ ./inetntoa
```

The program in Listing 3.5 uses the same steps to set up the address as did the previous example program. The function inet_ntoa(3) is called upon to allow the IP number to be displayed.

EXAMPLE

Listing 3.5: inetntoa.c—Demonstration of inet_ntoa(3) Function

```
1:   /* inetntoa.c:
2:    *
3:    * Example using inet_ntoa(3):
4:    */
5:   #include <stdio.h>
6:   #include <unistd.h>
7:   #include <stdlib.h>
8:   #include <sys/types.h>
9:   #include <sys/socket.h>
10:  #include <netinet/in.h>
11:  #include <arpa/inet.h>
12:
13:  int
14:  main(int argc,char **argv) {
15:      struct sockaddr_in adr_inet;/* AF_INET */
```

continues

Listing 3.5: continued

```
16:        int len_inet;                    /* length  */
17:
18:        /*
19:         * Establish address (pretend we got
20:         * this address from a connecting
21:         * client):
22:         */
23:        memset(&adr_inet,0,sizeof adr_inet);
24:
25:        adr_inet.sin_family = AF_INET;
26:        adr_inet.sin_port = htons(9000);
27:
28:        if ( !inet_aton("127.0.0.23",
29:                    &adr_inet.sin_addr) )
30:            puts("bad address.");
31:
32:        len_inet = sizeof adr_inet;
33:
34:        /*
35:         * Demonstrate use of inet_ntoa(3):
36:         */
37:        printf("The IP Address is %s\n",
38:            inet_ntoa(adr_inet.sin_addr));
39:
40:        return 0;
41:    }
```

Now, review the steps that were taken in the program:

1. The structure adr_inet is declared as a sockaddr_in type in line 15. This is the form of the address that you'll work with most of the time.

2. Lines 23 to 32 set up the address, just as before. In this example, the socket(2) and bind(2) calls were omitted because they don't help in this illustration.

3. Line 37 shows a call to printf(3). Here, the statement calls upon inet_ntoa(3) in line 38 to convert the IP address in adr_inet to string form so that it can be printed.

NOTE

The results returned from inet_ntoa(3) are valid only until the next call to this function.

CAUTION

Due to the limitation given in the previous note, if you use this function in threaded code, you must make certain that only one thread at a time calls this function. Failure to heed this advice will result in returned results being overwritten by other threads.

The program's output is shown as follows:

```
$ ./inetntoa
The IP Address is 127.0.0.23
$
```

You know, because of the initialization in line 28, that this is the correct result. Line 38 converts this value back into a string.

Using `inet_network(3)`

There might be occasions in which it is more convenient to have the dotted-quad IP number converted into a 32-bit host-ordered value. This is more convenient when you are applying mask values to extract host or network bits from the addresses.

The function synopsis for `inet_network(3)` is as follows:

```
#include <sys/socket.h>
#include <netinet/in.h>
#include <arpa/inet.h>

unsigned long inet_network(const char *addr);
```

This function takes one input string containing a dotted quad address in argument `addr`. The return value is the 32-bit value of the IP address, but in host-order format. However, if the input value is malformed, the returned result will be `0xFFFFFFFF` (all 1 bits).

Having the returned value in host-endian order means that you can safely assume constants for mask values and bit positions. If the returned value were in network-endian order, the constants and code would then be different for different CPU platforms.

An example of how `inet_network(3)` might be used is shown next. The following shows how to extract the network address from a class C address:

```
unsigned long net_addr;

net_addr =
    inet_network("192.168.9.1") & 0xFFFFFF00;
```

The value assigned to `net_addr` would be the value `0xC0A80900` (or `192.168.9.0` in dotted-quad notation). The logical and operation masked out the low-order eight bits to arrive at the network ID without the host ID.

The example shown in Listing 3.6 illustrates how the `inet_network(3)` function can be used. The program also calls upon the `htonl(3)` function to display how the value looks in network-endian order.

Listing 3.6: `network.c`—Demonstration of the `inet_network(3)` Function

```
1:    /* network.c:
2:     *
3:     * Example using inet_network(3):
4:     */
5:    #include <stdio.h>
6:    #include <unistd.h>
7:    #include <stdlib.h>
8:    #include <sys/types.h>
9:    #include <sys/socket.h>
10:   #include <netinet/in.h>
11:   #include <arpa/inet.h>
12:
13:   int
14:   main(int argc,char **argv) {
15:       int x;
16:       const char *addr[] = {
17:           "44.135.86.12",
18:           "127.0.0.1",
19:           "172.16.23.95",
20:           "192.168.9.1"
21:       };
22:       unsigned long net_addr;
23:
24:       for ( x=0; x<4; ++x ) {
25:           net_addr = inet_network(addr[x]);
26:           printf("%14s = 0x%08lX net 0x%08lX\n",
27:               addr[x],net_addr,
28:               (unsigned long)htonl(net_addr));
29:       }
30:
31:       return 0;
32:   }
```

This program is compiled and run as follows:

```
$ make network
gcc -c  -D_GNU_SOURCE -Wall network.c
gcc network.o -o network
$
```

The steps used in the program shown in Listing 3.6 are as follows:

1. Four arbitrarily picked IP numbers are declared in lines 17 to 20 to initialize the array addr[].

2. Lines 24 to 29 loop through each of the four strings in the addr[] array, starting with the first.

3. The `inet_network(3)` function is called in line 25 to convert the string into a host-endian ordered 32-bit value representing the IP number given.

4. The `printf(3)` function is called in line 26 to illustrate the output values. The first is the original string that was given to `inet_network(3)` in line 25. The second value printed is the value returned by `inet_network(3)`, which is in host-endian form. The last value displayed on the line is the network-endian ordered value. For Intel CPU platforms, the last two columns will display differently.

OUTPUT

The program is run as follows:

```
$ ./network
 44.135.86.12 = 0x2C87560C net 0x0C56872C
    127.0.0.1 = 0x7F000001 net 0x0100007F
 172.16.23.95 = 0xAC10175F net 0x5F1710AC
  192.168.9.1 = 0xC0A80901 net 0x0109A8C0
$
```

This program was run on an Intel CPU running Linux. Consequently, because an Intel CPU is little-endian by design, its host-ordered value (second column) and the networked-ordered value (last column) appear different. If you run this same program on a big-endian machine, the last two columns will be identical.

Using the `inet_lnaof(3)` Function

The `inet_lnaof(3)` function converts the IP number contained in a socket address, which is in network byte order, to a host ID number with the network ID removed. The return value is in host-endian order.

This function saves you from having to determine the class of the IP number and then extracting the host ID portion. The function synopsis for `inet_lnaof(3)` is given as follows:

```
#include <sys/socket.h>
#include <netinet/in.h>
#include <arpa/inet.h>

unsigned long inet_lnaof(struct in_addr addr);
```

The input argument addr must be the `struct in_addr` member of the socket address that you will normally be working with. This value will be in network byte sequence, which is what the function expects. An example of how to invoke the function using a `sockaddr_in` address is given as follows:

```
struct sockaddr_in addr;   /* Socket Address */
unsigned long host_id;     /* Host ID number */

host_id = inet_lnaof(addr.sin_addr);
```

Table 3.5 shows some example values that can be supplied to the input of
inet_lnaof(3) and the values that result. To make the reasons for the
results clearer, the class of each example address is included in the table.

Table 3.5: Example Values Returned from **inet_lnaof(3)** *(the Hexadecimal
Values Are Host-Endian Ordered)*

IP Number	Class	Hexadecimal	Dotted-Quad
44.135.86.12	A	0087560C	0.135.86.12
127.0.0.1	A	00000001	0.0.0.1
172.16.23.95	B	0000175F	0.0.23.95
192.168.9.1	C	00000001	0.0.0.1

You should notice in the table's class A examples only the first byte is
zeroed in the returned result (review Figure 3.1 to visualize the class
boundaries again if you need to). In the class B example, the upper 16 bits
are zeroed in the returned result. Finally, the class C example in Table 3.5
zeroes out the upper 3 bytes of the address, leaving the host ID behind in
the last byte.

NOTE

The input is in network-endian sequence. The returned value is in host-endian sequence.

Using the inet_netof(3) Function

The inet_netof(3) function is the companion to the inet_lnaof(3) function.
The inet_netof(3) function returns the network ID instead of the host ID
value. In all other respects, these functions are the same. The following
lists the function synopsis:

```
#include <sys/socket.h>
#include <netinet/in.h>
#include <arpa/inet.h>

unsigned long inet_netof(struct in_addr addr);
```

Again, the input is the struct in_addr member of the socket address
sockaddr_in structure that you'll normally be working with. An example
of its use is given as follows:

```
struct sockaddr_in addr;    /* Socket Address */
unsigned long net_id;       /* Network ID number */

net_id = inet_netof(addr.sin_addr);
```

Table 3.6 shows the same example IP numbers used in Table 3.5. Table 3.6
shows the values returned for the function inet_netof(3) function, however.

Table 3.6: Example Values Returned from `inet_netof(3)` *(the Hexadecimal Values Are Host-Endian Ordered)*

IP Number	Class	Hexadecimal	Dotted-Quad
44.135.86.12	A	0000002C	0.0.0.44
127.0.0.1	A	0000007F	0.0.0.127
172.16.23.95	B	0000AC10	0.0.172.16
192.168.9.1	C	00C0A809	0.192.168.9

You might find the values in Table 3.6 to be a bit of a surprise. These return values are the network bits shifted right, in order to eliminate the host ID bits. What you are left with is the right-justified network ID number.

NOTE

The return values from `inet_netof(3)` are right-justified. The host ID bits are shifted out.

Using the `inet_makeaddr(3)` Function

With the functions `inet_lnaof(3)` and `inet_netof(3)`, you have the ability to extract host and network ID values. To re-create a consolidated IP address with the network and host ID values combined, you need to use the `inet_makeaddr(3)` function. Its function synopsis is as follows:

```
#include <sys/socket.h>
#include <netinet/in.h>
#include <arpa/inet.h>

struct in_addr inet_makeaddr(int net,int host);
```

The arguments to the `inet_makeaddr(3)` function are described as follows:

1. The `net` argument is the network ID, right-justified and in host-endian order. This same value is returned from the function `inet_netof(3)`.

2. The `host` argument is the host ID, which is in host-endian order. This same value is returned from the function `inet_lnaof(3)`.

The value returned in the `struct in_addr` member of the `sockaddr_in` socket address. This value is in network-endian sequence, which is correct for the socket address.

A program has been provided in Listing 3.7 that uses the three functions `inet_lnaof(3)`, `inet_netof(3)`, and `inet_makeaddr(3)`. The IP address is split apart from a `sockaddr_in` structure into its network and host ID parts. Then, the socket address is zeroed out and reconstructed from just the network and host ID parts.

EXAMPLE

Listing 3.7: makeaddr.c—Demonstration of inet_netof(3), inet_lnaof(3), and inet_makeaddr(3)

```
1:   /* makeaddr.c:
2:    *
3:    * Demonstrate inet_lnaof, inet_netof
4:    * and inet_makeaddr(3) functions;
5:    */
6:   #include <stdio.h>
7:   #include <unistd.h>
8:   #include <stdlib.h>
9:   #include <sys/types.h>
10:  #include <sys/socket.h>
11:  #include <netinet/in.h>
12:  #include <arpa/inet.h>
13:
14:  int
15:  main(int argc,char **argv) {
16:      int x;
17:      struct sockaddr_in adr_inet;/* AF_INET */
18:      const char *addr[] = {
19:          "44.135.86.12",
20:          "127.0.0.1",
21:          "172.16.23.95",
22:          "192.168.9.1"
23:      };
24:      unsigned long net, hst;
25:
26:      for ( x=0; x<4; ++x ) {
27:          /*
28:           * Create a socket address:
29:           */
30:          memset(&adr_inet,0,sizeof adr_inet);
31:          adr_inet.sin_family = AF_INET;
32:          adr_inet.sin_port = htons(9000);
33:          if ( !inet_aton(addr[x],
34:                  &adr_inet.sin_addr) )
35:              puts("bad address.");
36:
37:          /*
38:           * Split address into Host & Net ID
39:           */
40:          hst = inet_lnaof(adr_inet.sin_addr);
41:          net = inet_netof(adr_inet.sin_addr);
42:
43:          printf("%14s : net=0x%08lX host=0x%08lX\n",
44:              inet_ntoa(adr_inet.sin_addr),net,hst);
45:
46:          /*
```

```
47:              * Zero the address to prove later that
48:              * we can reconstruct this value:
49:              */
50:             memset(&adr_inet,0,sizeof adr_inet);
51:             adr_inet.sin_family = AF_INET;
52:             adr_inet.sin_port = htons(9000);
53:
54:             adr_inet.sin_addr =
55:                 inet_makeaddr(net,hst);
56:
57:             /*
58:              * Now display the reconstructed
59:              * address:
60:              */
61:             printf("%14s : %s\n\n",
62:                 "inet_makeaddr",
63:                 inet_ntoa(adr_inet.sin_addr));
64:         }
65:
66:     return 0;
67: }
```

To compile the program in Listing 3.7, perform the following:

```
$ make makeaddr
gcc -c  -D_GNU_SOURCE -Wall makeaddr.c
gcc makeaddr.o -o makeaddr
$
```

The procedure used in Listing 3.7 is as follows:

1. The socket address is declared in line 17 as a sockaddr_in structure. This is the form of the socket address that you'll normally work with.

2. Four example addresses are declared in lines 18 to 23.

3. The loop starts in line 26, and iterates through each of the four example IP numbers declared in step 2.

4. Lines 30 to 35 set up a sockaddr_in socket address. Port 9000 was just an arbitrary port number used as an example.

5. The host ID is extracted from the socket address adr_inet in line 40.

6. The network ID is extracted from the socket address adr_inet in line 41.

7. The example IP number, network ID, and host ID numbers are reported in lines 43 and 44.

8. The entire socket address adr_inet is zeroed out in line 50. This was done to eliminate any doubt that the socket address is re-created later.

9. The address family and example port number are re-established in lines 51 and 52.

10. The IP number is reconstructed by calling inet_makeaddr(3) in lines 54 and 55. The input values are the extracted values net and hst from steps 5 and 6.

11. The reconstructed address is reported in lines 61 to 63.

Running the program yields the following results:

```
$ ./makeaddr
  44.135.86.12 : net=0x0000002C host=0x0087560C
inet_makeaddr : 44.135.86.12

     127.0.0.1 : net=0x0000007F host=0x00000001
inet_makeaddr : 127.0.0.1

  172.16.23.95 : net=0x0000AC10 host=0x0000175F
inet_makeaddr : 172.16.23.95

   192.168.9.1 : net=0x00C0A809 host=0x00000001
inet_makeaddr : 192.168.9.1

$
```

OUTPUT

In each case, you can see for yourself that the program did indeed re-create the final IP numbers from the extracted host and network ID numbers.

What's Next

The beginning of this chapter might have been review to some, but perhaps new to you. However, you can see now that this topic was important to cover, because the makeup of IP numbers and their classification plays quite a large role when working with IP addresses. You also learned about private IP number ranges, which might help you set up your own network.

One example program was described early in this chapter, which classified IP numbers. From this example, you learned how this can be done. However, toward the end of this chapter, you also learned that you do not always have to do this yourself. The functions inet_lnaof(3) and inet_netof(3) were able to do this for you and extract the parts that you were interested in.

The remainder of this chapter dealt with conversion from strings to addresses, and addresses back to strings. These are important functions for the network application designer to know. These functions ease your workload and provide reliability and consistency. This is accomplished by having these operations done in the same manner in each program that they are used in.

The next chapter will introduce you to socket types and protocols. With this knowledge, you will learn how to create sockets to match your networking needs using the socket(2) function call.

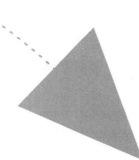

4

Socket Types and Protocols

In Chapter 1, "Introducing Sockets," you saw how the socketpair(2) function was used to create a pair of local sockets. In this chapter, you will also learn about the socket(2) function to create a socket. These two functions have the domain, the socket type, and the protocol ingredients in common.

This chapter will build on the previous chapters by primarily focusing on the socket(2) function call. This includes expanding upon the following:

- The domain argument
- The socket type argument
- The protocol argument

Specifying the Domain of a Socket

In Chapter 1, you read that for the socketpair(2) function, the domain argument must be the value AF_LOCAL or AF_UNIX (remember, these were equivalent). Then in Chapter 2, you might have noticed that there was a socket(2) function called in Listing 2.9 that gave an AF_INET value in the domain argument there (although we haven't properly covered socket(2) just yet). In these and other cases, you've probably concluded that the domain argument in some way specifies the protocol to be used.

Technically, the domain argument actually specifies the protocol family to be used rather than a specific protocol. A bit of history is required, by way of explanation.

The BSD socket interface went through a series of evolutionary changes. In early socket implementations, it was imagined that there might be the following breakdowns possible when specifying a socket:

- One or more protocols of a protocol family

- One or more address formats for one or more protocols

Given this perceived possibility, the original socket interface provided ways to define the following before a socket was created:

1. The protocol family to use. For example, the C macro constant PF_INET would indicate that the Internet IP family of protocols should be used.

2. The specific protocol within the family to use. For example, the macro IPPROTO_UDP would specify that the UDP protocol should be used.

3. The address family to use. For example, the macro constant AF_INET would indicate that an Internet IP address is to be used with the specified protocol.

Experience later showed that there is never more than one address format defined for a given family of protocols. The result of this is the inherited modern socket interface Linux uses today. What does this mean to you? It means simply that the socket interface accepts either the PF_INET macro or the AF_INET macro to specify the domain to be used.

Choosing PF_INET or AF_INET

Standards are encouraging that the PF_INET macro be used in preference over the AF_INET macro to specify the domain (that is, the protocol family to use). However, such a large amount of existing C program code has conformed to the older convention, and many programmers have resisted making the change.

In the previous chapters, the AF_UNIX, AF_LOCAL, and AF_INET macros were used in the domain argument of the socketpair(2) and the socket(2) function calls. This works because of AF_UNIX=PF_UNIX and AF_INET=PF_INET and so on. However, this might not always be the case in the future.

To foster new standards and practices, the examples and illustrations in the remainder of this book will follow the new standard. What this means is that socketpair(2) when called will be given PF_LOCAL instead of AF_LOCAL for the domain argument value. Likewise, calls to socket(2) will make a similar shift in practice.

NOTE

Note that the AF_UNIX constant is defined to be the same value as the PF_UNIX constant under Linux. The same applies to all other constants of this series (AF_INET is the same as PF_INET, for example). You will see valid program code that uses the AF_INET value for the domain argument of the socketpair(2) and socket(2) functions. Still other programs will use the PF_INET value instead. This is confusing, but presently, both are valid.

The best advice seems to be that the PF_LOCAL series of macros should be used in the socketpair(2) and socket(2) domain argument. The AF_LOCAL series of macros should be used when initializing the socket address structures.

Using the PF_LOCAL and AF_LOCAL Macros

You should note that socket addresses themselves should still be initialized with the correct address family constants such as AF_INET. The PF_INET chooses the protocol family in the socket creation function, whereas the AF_INET macro chooses an address family in the socket address structure. The following code shows how the C macro constants PF_LOCAL and AF_LOCAL are applied:

EXAMPLE

```
int z;                     /* Status Code */
int sp[2];                 /* Socket Pair */
struct sockaddr_un adr_unix; /* AF_LOCAL */

z = socketpair(PF_LOCAL,SOCK_STREAM,0,sp);
…
adr_unix.sun_family = AF_LOCAL;
```

The PF_LOCAL macro is used in the socketpair(2) function to specify the protocol family to use in the domain argument. Note that when the socket address is established in structure adr_unix, the AF_LOCAL address family macro is used instead.

Using the `socket(2)` Function

Before you learn more about the socket type argument and the protocol argument, the `socket(2)` function itself will be presented. Unlike the `socketpair(2)` function, which can have its domain specified only as `PF_LOCAL` (or its older equivalent `PF_UNIX`), the `socket(2)` function can be used to create one socket of any supported protocol family. The function synopsis for `socket(2)` is provided as follows:

```
#include <sys/types.h>
#include <sys/socket.h>

int socket(int domain, int type, int protocol);
```

This function accepts three input arguments:

1. The `domain` of the socket (the protocol family to use)

2. The `type` of the socket required

3. The specific `protocol` to use within the protocol family

The socket is returned as the function return value if the call is successful. Like file descriptors, a socket is returned if the value is zero or positive in value. A value of -1 is returned if there was an error. The external variable `errno` will have the reason code posted to it when an error has been returned.

One difficult aspect of the `socket(2)` function for new programmers is the bewildering array of choices that must be made for the three input arguments. The purpose of this entire chapter is to teach you what those choices are and how to choose between them.

Choosing a Socket Type

You already know that choosing a domain value for the `socket(2)` or `socketpair(2)` function chooses a protocol family to be used. For example, you know that

- `PF_LOCAL` (which is the same as `PF_UNIX`) indicates that a local UNIX socket protocol family is being specified.

- `PF_INET` indicates that the Internet family of protocols is used.

Consequently, you now have to learn about only two more input arguments.

The socket type argument in the `socket(2)` and `socketpair(2)` function calls indicates how a socket will interface with your program. But this is not the whole story, as this parameter also has implications for the protocol that is selected. (You'll understand this better as you progress through this chapter.)

The programmer typically chooses one of the following values for the socket type argument:

- SOCK_STREAM *

- SOCK_DGRAM *

- SOCK_SEQPACKET

- SOCK_RAW

The entries marked with an asterisk (*) are the two you'll normally use. The SOCK_SEQPACKET type is commonly used on non-Internet protocols such as X.25, or the amateur radio protocol AX.25. There are a few additional types that could be listed here. However, they are outside of the scope of this text.

NOTE

The SOCK_RAW macro specifies that the programmer wants a "raw" interface to the socket. This allows the programmer more direct control over the communications and its packets. However, it also requires an intimate knowledge of the protocol and its underlying packet structure. For this reason, the SOCK_RAW socket will not be studied in this book.

Understanding the SOCK_STREAM Socket Type

The SOCK_STREAM socket type is used when you want to perform stream I/O with a remote socket. A stream in the socket sense is the same concept that applies to a UNIX pipe. Bytes written to one end of the pipe (or socket) are received at the other end as one continuous stream of bytes. There are no dividing lines or boundaries. There is no record length, block size, or concept of a packet at the receiving end. Whatever data is currently available at the receiving end is returned in the caller's buffer.

EXAMPLE

An example to review might help illustrate the stream I/O concept. In this example, there is a local process on your host that has connected to a remote process on a remote host. The local host is going to send data to the remote host in two separate write(2) calls as follows:

1. The local process writes 25 bytes of data to be sent to the remote process, by socket. The Linux kernel might or might not choose to buffer this data. Buffering helps improve the performance of the kernel and the network facilities.

2. Another 30 bytes are written by the local process to be sent to the remote process.

3. The remote process executes a function designed to receive data from the socket. The receiving buffer in this example allows up to 256 bytes to be read. The remote process receives the 55 bytes that were written in steps 1 and 2.

Note what has happened. The local process has performed two separate writes to the socket. These could be two different messages or two different data structures. Yet, the remote process received all of the written data as one combined unit of 55 bytes.

Another way to look at this example is that the local process might have had to create one message in two partial writes. The receiving end received the message as one combined unit.

At other times, depending on timing and buffer availability, the remote process might first get the original piece of 25 bytes (or perhaps even less). Then, on a successive receive function call, obtain the remaining 30 bytes. In short, a stream socket does not preserve any message boundary. It simply returns the data it has to the receiving application.

The receiving end cannot tell what the original message boundaries were. In our example, it cannot tell that the first write(2) was for 25 bytes and the second was for 30. All it can know is the data bytes that it received and that the total bytes sent was 55.

A stream socket has one other important property. Like a UNIX pipe, the bytes written to a stream socket are guaranteed to arrive at the other end in the exact same order in which they were written. With protocols such as IP, in which packets can take different routes to their destination, it frequently happens that later packets arrive ahead of their earlier cousins. The SOCK_STREAM socket ensures that your receiving application accepts data bytes in precisely the same sequence in which they were originally written.

Let's recap the properties of a SOCK_STREAM socket:

- No message boundaries are preserved. The receiving end cannot determine how many write(2) calls were used to send the received data. Nor can it determine where the write(2) calls began or ended in the stream of bytes received.

- The data bytes received are guaranteed to be in precisely the same order in which they were written.

- All data written is guaranteed to be received by the remote end without error. If a failure occurs, an error is reported after all reasonable attempts at recovery have been made. Any recovery attempts are automatic and are not directed by your application program.

The last point presented is a new one to this discussion. A stream socket implies that every reasonable effort will be made to deliver data written to one socket, to the socket at the other end. If this cannot be done, the error will be made known to the receiving end as well as the writing end. In this respect, SOCK_STREAM socket is a reliable data transport. This feature makes it a very popular socket type.

There is one more property of the SOCK_STREAM type of socket. It is

- The data is transported over a pair of connected sockets.

In order to guarantee delivery of data, and to enforce byte ordering, the underlying protocols use a connected pair of sockets. For the moment, simply know that the SOCK_STREAM type implies that a connection must be established before communications can proceed.

Understanding the SOCK_DGRAM Socket Type

There are some situations in which it is not absolutely required that data must arrive at the remote end in sequence. Additionally, it might not even be required that the data delivery be reliable. The following lists the characteristics of a SOCK_DGRAM socket type:

- Packets are delivered, possibly out of order at the receiving end.

- Packets might be lost. No attempt is made at recovering from this type of error. Nor is it necessarily known at the receiving end that a packet was lost.

- Datagram packets have practical size limits. Exceeding these limits will make them undeliverable through certain routers and nodes.

- Packets are sent to remote processes in an unconnected manner. This permits a program to address its message to a different remote process, with each message written to the same socket.

NOTE

Reliability is not a concern when noncritical logging information is transmitted. This information is transmitted on a "best efforts" basis. When a noncritical log packet is lost, it is considered an acceptable loss.

Unlike a streamed connected socket, a datagram socket simply passes data by individual packets. Remember that for protocols such as IP, individual packets can be routed different ways. This frequently causes packets to arrive at the destination in a different sequence from which they were sent. The socket type SOCK_DGRAM implies that receiving these messages out of order is acceptable to the application.

Sending a datagram packet is unreliable. If a packet is transmitted and not received correctly by an intervening router or the receiving host, then the packet is simply lost. No record of its existence is kept, and no attempt to recover from the transmission error is made.

Packets can also be lost if they are unsuitably large. Routers in the path between the sending host and the receiving host will drop a packet if it is too large or lacks the buffer space to pass it. Again, there is no error recovery implied in a SOCK_DGRAM socket when this happens.

The last characteristic that is of interest to you is the fact that the SOCK_DGRAM type does not imply a connection. Each time you send a message with your socket, it can be destined for another recipient. This property of the SOCK_DGRAM type makes it attractive and efficient.

A connection-oriented protocol, on one hand, requires that a connection establishment procedure be carried out. This requires a certain number of packets to be sent and received in order to establish the connection. The SOCK_DGRAM type, on the other hand, is efficient because no connection is established.

Before choosing to use SOCK_DGRAM, however, you must carefully weigh the following:

- Need for reliability
- Need for sequenced data
- Data size requirements

Understanding the SOCK_SEQPACKET Socket Type

Although the SOCK_SEQPACKET type will not be used in this book, you should at least become familiar with it. This socket type is important for protocols such as X.25 and AX.25 that use it. It is very similar to SOCK_STREAM but has one subtle distinction. The difference is that although the SOCK_STREAM socket does not preserve message boundaries, the SOCK_SEQPACKET does. When X.25 is used, for example, and SOCK_SEQPACKET is chosen, each packet is received in the same unit size in which it was originally written.

For example, imagine the sending end performing the following two writes:

1. Write a message one of 25 bytes.
2. Write a message two of 30 bytes.

Although the receiving process might indicate that it can accept up to 256 bytes in one read(2) call, the following receive events will occur:

1. A message will be received with a length of 25 bytes. This corresponds to the length of the first message that was written by the sending process.
2. A second message will be received with a length of 30 bytes. This corresponds to the length of the second write of the sending process.

Although the receiving buffer was able to receive the total combined message length of 55 bytes, only the first message for 25 bytes is received by the first read(2) call on the socket. This tells the application that this message was precisely 25 bytes in length. The next call to read(2) will fetch the next message of 30 bytes, regardless of whether there is more data that could be returned.

With this behavior, you can see that SOCK_SEQPACKET preserves the original message boundaries. The following provides a summary of characteristics for this socket type:

- Message boundaries are preserved. This feature distinguishes the SOCK_SEQPACKET type from the SOCK_STREAM type.

- The data bytes received are guaranteed to be in precisely in the same order in which they were written.

- All data written is guaranteed delivered to the remote end without error. If it cannot be delivered after reasonable attempts at automatic recovery, an error is reported to the sending and receiving processes.

- The data is transported over a pair of connected sockets.

NOTE

Not all socket types can be used with all protocols. For example, SOCK_STREAM is supported for the PF_INET protocol family, but SOCK_SEQPACKET is not. Conversely for PF_X25, the socket type SOCK_SEQPACKET is supported, but SOCK_STREAM is not.

Choosing a Protocol

You might think that with the protocol family specified, and the socket type specified for a new socket, there would be little need for anything else. Although normally there is only one protocol used for a given protocol family and socket type, there are some situations where this isn't true. The protocol parameter of the socket(2) or socketpair(2) function allows you to be more specific when this need arises.

The good news is that it is rare that you need to choose a value for this parameter. Normally, you simply specify zero for the protocol. This allows the Linux kernel to choose the correct protocol for the other parameters that you have specified.

NOTE

The protocol argument of the socket(2) or socketpair(2) function is normally supplied as the value zero. This tells the kernel to choose the correct protocol according to the domain and socket type parameter values chosen.

See protocols(5) or the include file <netinet/in.h> for macro entries such as IPPROTO_TCP.

Some programmers prefer, however, to explicitly describe the protocol argument value. This might be important for certain applications in which a specific protocol is required, and no substitution is permitted. This allows you to choose the final protocol used rather than rely on today's "kernel of the month." The downside of this is that when networks and protocols evolve, someone might have to go back and revisit your source code to make it work.

In this book, you'll learn about the only four combinations you'll need to use.

Using PF_LOCAL and SOCK_STREAM

You will use a zero for the protocol argument in the socket(2) or socketpair(2) functions for PF_LOCAL sockets. This is the only supported value for that argument. A valid socket(2) call using PF_LOCAL and SOCK_STREAM is shown as follows:

EXAMPLE

```
int s;

s = socket(PF_LOCAL,SOCK_STREAM,0);

if ( s == -1 )
    perror("socket()");
```

This creates a stream socket to allow one process to communicate with another process within the same host. The steps are

1. Integer s is declared to receive the socket number (it is treated the same as a file descriptor).

2. The socket(2) function is called. The domain argument is set to PF_LOCAL, and the socket type argument is set to SOCK_STREAM to request a stream socket. The protocol argument is set to zero, which is the only valid value for PF_LOCAL sockets.

3. The value s is tested to see whether it is the value -1. If it is, then an error has occurred, and errno has the reason for it. Function perror(3) is used in this example to report what the errno code indicates.

4. If s is not -1, then it represents a valid socket. It can be used in most places in which a file descriptor is valid (in read(2) and write(2) function calls, for example).

NOTE

At the present time, zero is the only valid value for the protocol argument of the socket(2) or socketpair(2) function calls, when the domain argument is PF_LOCAL (or PF_UNIX).

Using PF_LOCAL and SOCK_DGRAM

You will use SOCK_DGRAM on a local socket when you want to preserve message boundaries. Again, no specific protocol type is permitted for PF_LOCAL domain sockets at this time. Take a look at the following example:

EXAMPLE

```
int s;

s = socket(PF_LOCAL,SOCK_DGRAM,0);

if ( s == -1 )
    perror("socket()");
```

The steps used to create this local datagram socket are

1. Integer s is declared to receive the socket number (it is treated the same as a file descriptor).

2. The socket(2) function is called. The domain argument is set to PF_LOCAL, and the socket type argument is set to SOCK_DGRAM to request a datagram socket. The protocol argument is set to zero, which is the only valid value for PF_LOCAL sockets.

3. The value s is tested to see whether it is the value -1. If it is, then an error has occurred, and errno has the reason for it. Function perror(3) is used in this example to report what the errno code indicates.

4. If s is not -1, then it represents a valid socket.

Datagram sockets are attractive to use for PF_LOCAL sockets because they are mostly reliable and they preserve message boundaries. They don't get lost in network transmission errors as PF_INET datagrams can, because they remain internal to the local host. However, you should assume that kernel buffer shortages might cause PF_LOCAL packets to be lost, even if this rarely occurs.

NOTE

When a socket is created, it is nameless (without an address). A valid socket address must be set up and the function bind(2) called to give the socket an address.

Using PF_INET and SOCK_STREAM

At the present time, a zero in the protocol argument of the socket(2) function for the domain PF_INET will cause the kernel to choose IPPROTO_TCP. This causes the socket to use the TCP/IP protocol. The TCP part of the TCP/IP designation is the transport level protocol that is built on top of the IP layer. This provides the data packet sequencing, error control, and recovery. In short, TCP makes it possible to provide a stream socket using the Internet protocol.

As you see in the following example, most application programmers will choose to simply specify the protocol argument as zero, allowing the kernel to correctly choose the protocol:

EXAMPLE

```
int s;

s = socket(PF_INET,SOCK_STREAM,0);

if ( s == -1 )
    perror("socket()");
```

The steps used to create Internet stream sockets are

1. Integer s is declared to receive the socket number.

2. The socket(2) function is called. The domain argument is set to PF_INET to choose the Internet family of protocols. The socket type argument is set to SOCK_STREAM to request a stream socket. The protocol argument is set to zero, which allows the kernel to choose the correct protocol for the combination of PF_INET and SOCK_STREAM.

3. The value s is tested to see whether it is the value -1. If it is, then an error has occurred, and errno has the reason for it. Function perror(3) is used in this example to report what the errno code indicates.

4. If s is not -1, then it represents a valid socket. It can be used in most places where a file descriptor is valid (in read(2) and write(2) function calls, for example).

EXAMPLE

Specifying zero for the protocol argument of socket(2) will imply the use of TCP/IP. However, if you like having full control, or worry that future kernel defaults might be unsuitable, you can explicitly choose the protocol as follows:

```
int s;

s = socket(PF_INET,SOCK_STREAM,IPPROTO_TCP);

if ( s == -1 )
    perror("socket()");
```

Looking only at the socket(2) function call, the arguments can be explained as follows:

1. The domain argument is specified as PF_INET as before, to indicate that the Internet family of protocols is required.

2. The socket type argument is specified as SOCK_STREAM to request a stream I/O socket, as before.

3. The protocol argument, however, has been explicitly specified as
IPPROTO_TCP in this case. This chooses the use of the TCP/IP protocol
for this socket.

The IPPROTO_TCP macro is defined by the include file:

```
#include <netinet/in.h>
```

Using PF_INET and SOCK_DGRAM

This section describes the last socket combination that you will use in the
applications within this book. The combination of PF_INET and SOCK_DGRAM
causes the kernel to choose the UDP protocol. UDP is short for User
Datagram Protocol. A datagram is a standalone packet of information.

This protocol allows the application to send datagrams from your socket to
the remote socket, to which you have addressed it. Note again that this service is not reliable, but it is suitable for many types of services in which
efficiency is highly desirable. For example, the Network Time Protocol
(NTP) uses UDP because it is efficient and message-oriented, and lost messages can be tolerated. The impact of a lost message is that the time syn-
chronization might take longer to achieve or that some accuracy is lost
when expecting replies from multiple NTP servers.

To create a UDP socket, you can use zero for the protocol argument. The
following shows an example:

EXAMPLE

```
int s;

s = socket(PF_INET,SOCK_DGRAM,0);
if ( s == -1 )
    perror("socket()");
```

The procedure used is the same general procedure that has been used in
the preceding sections. However, the arguments used in the socket(2) function require explanation:

1. The domain argument is specified as PF_INET, as before, to indicate
that the Internet family of protocols is required.

2. The socket type argument is specified as SOCK_DGRAM to request a datagram socket.

3. The protocol argument is specified as zero to allow the kernel to choose
the correct protocol for the PF_INET and SOCK_DGRAM combination.

EXAMPLE

However, if you prefer to specify UDP explicitly, you might do it like this
instead:

```
int s;
```

```
s = socket(PF_INET,SOCK_DGRAM,IPPROTO_UDP);

if ( s == -1 )
    perror("socket()");
```

The arguments for this socket(2) call are described as follows:

1. The domain argument is specified as PF_INET, as before, to indicate that the Internet family of protocols is required.

2. The socket type argument is specified as SOCK_DGRAM to request a datagram socket.

3. The protocol argument is specified as IPPROTO_UDP to explicitly indicate that only the UDP protocol is permitted for this socket.

There is a number of other socket combinations that can be created, but these are too advanced to be considered here. You will be happy to know that most of the time you will use only the four socket(2) parameter combinations that have just been described and are summarized in Table 4.1.

Table 4.1: Table of Commonly Used Socket Argument Values

Domain	Socket Type	Protocol	Description
PF_LOCAL	SOCK_STREAM	0	Local stream socket
PF_LOCAL	SOCK_DGRAM	0	Local datagram socket
PF_INET	SOCK_STREAM	IPPROTO_TCP	TCP/IP stream socket
PF_INET	SOCK_DGRAM	IPPROTO_UDP	UDP datagram socket

Note that the last two entries (domain PF_INET) shown in Table 4.1 may have zero specified instead for the protocol argument. This decision is left to the discretion of the programmer.

Socket Domain and Type Summary

This section has been provided to allow you to review in summary form what you have learned in this chapter. Figure 4.1 illustrates the relationship that exists between the three socket(2) function arguments.

You'll notice that the domain argument appears on the left of Figure 4.1. The domain argument is the first argument of the socket(2) and socketpair(2) functions. It is also the least specific of the three values. The domain argument chooses a family of protocols that you want to work with.

The second argument defines the socket type. Choosing the socket type eliminates a number of variations within the specified protocol family. Looking at Figure 4.1, you can see that choosing SOCK_DGRAM excludes protocols that stem from SOCK_STREAM above it.

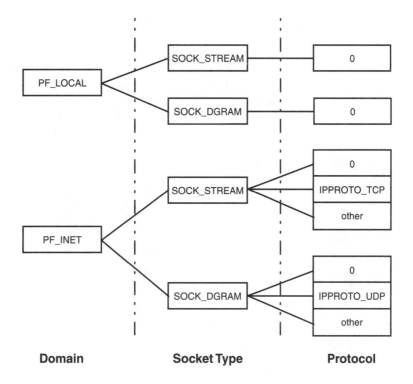

Figure 4.1: *This diagram summarizes* socket(2) *parameter relationships.*

Finally, on the very right, Figure 4.1 provides a sampling of the protocol choices that are available in the socket(2) function call. This parameter finalizes the protocol to be used.

NOTE

The remainder of this book will focus on the use of the PF_LOCAL and PF_INET protocol families from the socket interface. This is done in part to keep you focused on the important socket concepts that you need to master. Additionally, these will be the protocol families that you will use most of the time.

Other Linux-Supported Protocols

Linux is collecting new protocols within the kernel, almost with each new release. Each protocol has its use. For example, the PF_APPLETALK protocol family might be just what you need to make that dusty old Mac more useful to you. With the knowledge of sockets that you will gain in this book, you'll be able to write programs using these and other exotic protocols.

Table 4.2 summarizes some of this chapter's information about the local and Internet protocols.

Table 4.2: Table of Local and Internet **socket(2)** *Parameters*

Domain	Socket Type	Description/Notes
PF_LOCAL	SOCK_STREAM	Provides a stream-oriented socket within the local host. This is a connection-oriented service—reliable and sequenced. Note that PF_UNIX is equivalent to PF_LOCAL.
PF_LOCAL	SOCK_DGRAM	Provides datagram services within the local host. Note that this service is connectionless, but reliable, with the possible exception that packets might be lost if kernel buffers should become exhausted.
PF_INET	SOCK_STREAM	Stream I/O services for Internet connected sockets. Implies the TCP/IP protocol—reliable and sequenced.
PF_INET	SOCK_DGRAM	Datagram I/O services for Internet connectionless sockets. This combination implies UDP (User Datagram Protocol). This service is unreliable.
PF_INET6	SOCK_STREAM	Stream I/O services for Internet IPv6 connected sockets. Implies the TCP/IP protocol, reliable, and sequenced.
PF_INET6	SOCK_SEQPACKET	Stream I/O services for Internet IPv6 connected sockets. Implies the use of the TCP/IP protocol. This service is reliable, message boundaries are preserved, and sequence of data is preserved.
PF_INET6	SOCK_DGRAM	Datagram I/O services for Internet IPv6 connectionless sockets. This combination implies UDP (User Datagram Protocol). This service is unreliable.

Table 4.3 includes references to a few exotic protocol families that will not be explored in this book. However, look at this summary as a reference for you to use someday when you go to create that exotic socket.

Table 4.3: Table of Exotic **socket(2)** *Parameters*

Domain	Socket Type	Description/Notes
PF_X25	SOCK_SEQPACKET	Stream I/O services for the X.25 protocol. This service is connection-oriented and reliable, message boundaries are preserved, and data sequence is preserved.
PF_AX25	SOCK_SEQPACKET	Stream I/O services for the amateur radio protocol AX.25. This service is connection-oriented and reliable, message boundaries are preserved, and data sequence is preserved.

Domain	Socket Type	Description/Notes
PF_AX25	SOCK_DGRAM	Datagram service for the amateur radio protocol AX.25. This provides for unreliable connectionless communications.
PF_APPLETALK	SOCK_STREAM	Stream I/O services for the AppleTalk-connected sockets. This connection-oriented service is reliable and data sequence is preserved.
PF_APPLETALK	SOCK_DGRAM	This has been provided in Linux as an extension. See kernel documentation or sources for more details.
PF_ECONET	SOCK_DGRAM	An implementation of the Acorn Econet and AUN protocols.
PF_IPX	SOCK_STREAM	IPX protocol, stream socket.
PF_IPX	SOCK_DGRAM	IPX protocol, datagram socket.
PF_IPX	SOCK_SEQPACKET	IPX protocol, sequential packet socket.
PF_IRDA	SOCK_STREAM	IrDA subsystem support, using a stream socket (infrared communications).
PF_IRDA	SOCK_SEQPACKET	IrDA subsystem support, using a stream socket that preserves message boundaries (infrared communications).
PF_NETROM	SOCK_SEQPACKET	Amateur radio NetROM protocol.
PF_ROSE	SOCK_SEQPACKET	Amateur radio X.25 PLP 1protocol.

Researching Other Protocols

Many of the protocols listed in Table 4.3 are still undergoing development. Consequently, documentation is sparse in some areas. Nevertheless, here are some ideas regarding where you can scare up more information:

- Linux HOWTO and MINI-HOWTO documents.

- Linux FAQ documents.

- The /usr/src/linux/Documentation/networking Linux source directory. If you use a different source directory, then substitute that for the directory /usr/src/linux.

- The Linux source directory /usr/src/linux/net. There, you will find other subdirectories of source code, many of which have to do with specific protocols.

There are many HOWTO and MINI-HOWTO documents on the Internet that you can search out. FAQ is short for Frequently Asked Questions. Sometimes these files can be very helpful.

DISCOVERING PROTOCOL FAMILIES

Most of the time, the undocumented features will require that you look at some kernel source code and include files. Do not be daunted by this prospect. Many useful bits of information can be determined by looking at this code, without getting too intimate with the details.

The protocol family macros are defined by including the file:

```
#include <sys/socket.h>
```

However, this include file actually includes another file, which then defines the protocol macro constants. The file of interest is the pathname:

```
/usr/include/bits/socket.h
```

A simple way to list all of the protocols that might have support in the kernel is to perform a simple grep command. Listing 4.1 shows how to perform this, and what the results might look like.

OUTPUT

Listing 4.1: Grepping for Protocol Family Support

```
$ grep PF_ /usr/include/bits/socket.h
#define PF_UNSPEC       0           /* Unspecified.  */
#define PF_LOCAL        1           /* Local to host (pipes and file-domain).  */
#define PF_UNIX         PF_LOCAL /* Old BSD name for PF_LOCAL.  */
#define PF_FILE         PF_LOCAL /* Another non-standard name for PF_LOCAL.  */
#define PF_INET         2           /* IP protocol family.  */
#define PF_AX25         3           /* Amateur radio AX.25.  */
#define PF_IPX          4           /* Novell Internet Protocol.  */
#define PF_APPLETALK    5           /* AppleTalk DDP.  */
#define PF_NETROM       6           /* Amateur radio NetROM.  */
#define PF_BRIDGE       7           /* Multiprotocol bridge.  */
#define PF_ATMPVC       8           /* ATM PVCs.  */
#define PF_X25          9           /* Reserved for X.25 project.  */
#define PF_INET6        10          /* IP version 6.  */
#define PF_ROSE         11          /* Amateur radio X.25 PLP.  */
#define PF_DECnet       12          /* Reserved for DECnet project.  */
#define PF_NETBEUI      13          /* Reserved for 802.2LLC project.  */
#define PF_SECURITY     14          /* Security callback pseudo AF.  */
#define PF_KEY          15          /* PF_KEY key management API.  */
#define PF_NETLINK      16
#define PF_ROUTE        PF_NETLINK /* Alias to emulate 4.4BSD.  */
#define PF_PACKET       17          /* Packet family.  */
#define PF_ASH          18          /* Ash.  */
#define PF_ECONET       19          /* Acorn Econet.  */
#define PF_ATMSVC       20          /* ATM SVCs.  */
#define PF_SNA          22          /* Linux SNA project. */
#define PF_IRDA         23          /* IRDA sockets.  */
#define PF_MAX          32          /* For now..  */
#define AF_UNSPEC       PF_UNSPEC
#define AF_LOCAL        PF_LOCAL
```

```
#define AF_UNIX          PF_UNIX
#define AF_FILE          PF_FILE
#define AF_INET          PF_INET
#define AF_AX25          PF_AX25
#define AF_IPX           PF_IPX
#define AF_APPLETALK     PF_APPLETALK
#define AF_NETROM        PF_NETROM
#define AF_BRIDGE        PF_BRIDGE
#define AF_ATMPVC        PF_ATMPVC
#define AF_X25           PF_X25
#define AF_INET6         PF_INET6
#define AF_ROSE          PF_ROSE
#define AF_DECnet        PF_DECnet
#define AF_NETBEUI       PF_NETBEUI
#define AF_SECURITY      PF_SECURITY
#define pseudo_AF_KEY    PF_KEY
#define AF_NETLINK       PF_NETLINK
#define AF_ROUTE         PF_ROUTE
#define AF_PACKET        PF_PACKET
#define AF_ASH           PF_ASH
#define AF_ECONET        PF_ECONET
#define AF_ATMSVC        PF_ATMSVC
#define AF_SNA           PF_SNA
#define AF_IRDA          PF_IRDA
#define AF_MAX           PF_MAX
$
```

Listing 4.1 illustrates one other interesting fact. Note how the PF_ series of macros are defined in terms of AF_ series macro constants in most cases. Earlier, it was mentioned that the AF_ constants are equivalent to the PF_ constants, although this might not always be the case in the future.

In any case, Listing 4.1 shows a plethora of protocol families. All of these are not necessarily supported, however. Some will be defined here for future use. Others are in development. In almost all cases, you'll need to be sure that you have compiled in kernel support for the protocol families that you want to use.

NOTE

You must have the appropriate support compiled into the kernel before you can use certain protocol families. Exotic protocols are often not compiled into standard distribution releases.

CAUTION

Some protocol implementations in Linux are in the development stage, and might cause the kernel to crash with their use. Consequently, you should use backup precautions, or exercise new protocol options on a development host where you can afford to crash it.

DISCOVERING SOCKET TYPES

Knowing about the protocol families is part of the battle when attempting to create an exotic socket. You now need to know about the socket types that are supported by the protocol family that you have selected. This can usually be done using the following simple procedure:

1. Change to the Linux kernel source directory (you might need to install it first). For example, this might require you to do `cd /usr/linux/src`.

2. Change to the Linux network source code subdirectory. For example, you would do `cd ./net` in order to change to that subdirectory.

3. List the directory with the command `ls -F`. This will cause the subdirectories to be shown with a trailing / (slash) after them.

4. Usually, the subdirectory name is indicative of the protocol in which you might be interested. Change to that subdirectory (for example, `cd ipx`).

5. Perform a `grep` command for anything starting with `SOCK_`.

OUTPUT

Usually, this is sufficient to list the socket types that you want to know about. Listing 4.2 shows an example session, following these steps.

Listing 4.2: Listing the Supported Socket Types for a Protocol Family

```
$ cd /usr/src/linux
$ cd ./net
$ ls -F
802/         decnet/     netsyms.c      socket.o
Changes      econet/     netsyms.o      sunrpc/
Config.in    ethernet/   network.a      sysctl_net.c
Makefile     ipv4/       packet/        sysctl_net.o
README       ipv6/       protocols.c    unix/
TUNABLE      ipx/        protocols.o    wanrouter/
appletalk/   irda/       rose/          x25/
ax25/        lapb/       sched/
bridge/      netlink/    sock_n_syms.o
core/        netrom/     socket.c
$ cd ipx
$ ls -F
Config.in  af_ipx.c  sysctl_net_ipx.c
Makefile   af_spx.c
$ grep SOCK_ *.c
af_ipx.c:        s->state, SOCK_INODE(s->socket)->i_uid);
af_ipx.c:    case SOCK_DGRAM:
af_ipx.c:    case SOCK_SEQPACKET:
af_ipx.c:        case SOCK_STREAM: /* Allow higher levels to piggyback */
af_ipx.c:    if(sock->type == SOCK_DGRAM)
af_ipx.c:        SOCK_DEBUG(sk,
```

```
af_ipx.c:       SOCK_DEBUG(sk,
af_ipx.c:       SOCK_DEBUG(sk, "IPX: bind failed because port %X in use.\n",
af_ipx.c:       SOCK_DEBUG(sk, "IPX: bound socket 0x%04X.\n",
af_ipx.c:       if(sock->type == SOCK_DGRAM )
af_spx.c:           case SOCK_SEQPACKET:
af_spx.c:       if(sock->type != SOCK_SEQPACKET)
af_spx.c:       if(sock->type != SOCK_SEQPACKET)
af_spx.c: /* route socket(PF_IPX,SOCK_SEQPACKET) calls through spx_create() */
$
```

From the grep output shown in Listing 4.2, you can immediately see that socket types SOCK_DGRAM and SOCK_STREAM are probably supported (to be certain, you need to examine the logic of the code, however). Toward the end, there also appears to be a reference to SOCK_SEQPACKET, suggesting that it, too, might be supported.

The other item of interest is that you know that you probably want to peruse the file af_ipx.c for notes and comments. Sometimes, the comments can be useful to find out what is supported and what is not.

What's Next

In this chapter, you have taken a careful look at the socket(2) function call. The extra level of theory and detail in this chapter was necessary for you to cover because much hinges upon the choices you make in the socket(2) call. With this working knowledge of the socket(2) function, you are well on your way to putting sockets to work.

The next chapter will turn your attention primarily to the bind(2) function call. This function is important because it enables you to assign addresses to the sockets that you have learned how to create in this chapter.

Binding Addresses to a Socket

The preceding chapters prepared you with the means to create sockets and to form addresses for them. This chapter will expand upon this, enabling you to understand how bind(2) works and how to apply it correctly.

In this chapter, you will learn

- How the bind(2) function call assigns an address to a socket

- How to obtain the local socket address from a socket that already has an existing address

- How to obtain the peer socket address

- How bind(2) can choose the network interface that is used for communication

Chapter 2, "Domains and Address Families," covered addresses in detail. This background will make this chapter easy for you to follow. Having mastered the bind function, you will be able to put sockets to work in the next chapter.

The Purpose of the `bind(2)` Function

When your socket is created by the `socket(2)` function, it is nameless. You saw in Chapter 1, "Introducing Sockets," that sockets could be used without addresses when the `socketpair(2)` function was illustrated. However, this worked only because those sockets were created this way, within one Linux kernel. This cannot be done for sockets that must be joined between two different hosts.

A nameless socket is otherwise difficult to use. No one can send information to your nameless socket, because it is like a telephone without a telephone number. Consequently, programmers must bind a name to the socket to make it reachable by someone else. This is like assigning a telephone number to a new telephone so that it can be called. The `bind(2)` function call permits you to assign an address to a socket in the same manner.

A "name" in the context of this chapter has nothing to do with hostnames such as `sunsite.unc.edu`. The word "name" is often used when discussing the `bind(2)` function, and it refers to the address of the socket. The address, after all, is a name of sorts. To avoid confusion, however, the term *address* will be favored in this chapter.

Using the `bind(2)` Function

The purpose of the `bind(2)` function is to assign a socket address to a nameless socket. The function synopsis is given as follows:

```
#include <sys/types.h>
#include <sys/socket.h>

int bind(int sockfd, struct sockaddr *my_addr, int addrlen);
```

The function accepts the following three input arguments:

1. The socket `sockfd` file descriptor that was returned by a prior `socket(2)` call.

2. The address `my_addr` to assign to the socket.

3. The length of the address `my_addr` in bytes (argument `addrlen`).

The function, if it is successful, returns the value zero. Otherwise, the value –1 is returned and the variable `errno` has the reason for the failure posted to it.

NOTE

The socket provided to `bind(2)` must be presently nameless (without an address). You cannot rebind a socket to a new address.

The address argument must be a pointer to the address structure. You will note that the generic address type used is the sockaddr structure type. This means that you will need to apply a C language cast operator to satisfy the compiler that you have passed the correct pointer type. Listing 5.1 shows a program that calls upon bind(2) to establish an Internet address. Note the use of the inet_aton(3) and bind(2) function calls.

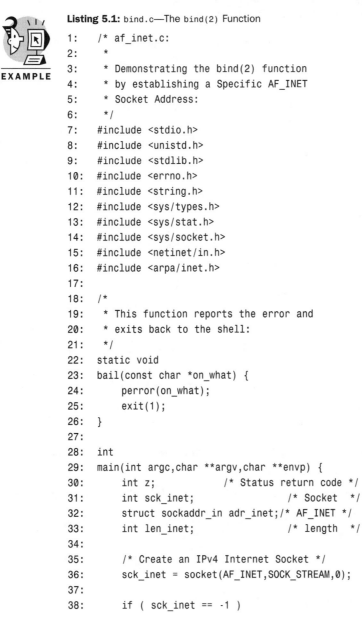

Listing 5.1: bind.c—The bind(2) Function

```
1:   /* af_inet.c:
2:    *
3:    * Demonstrating the bind(2) function
4:    * by establishing a Specific AF_INET
5:    * Socket Address:
6:    */
7:   #include <stdio.h>
8:   #include <unistd.h>
9:   #include <stdlib.h>
10:  #include <errno.h>
11:  #include <string.h>
12:  #include <sys/types.h>
13:  #include <sys/stat.h>
14:  #include <sys/socket.h>
15:  #include <netinet/in.h>
16:  #include <arpa/inet.h>
17:
18:  /*
19:   * This function reports the error and
20:   * exits back to the shell:
21:   */
22:  static void
23:  bail(const char *on_what) {
24:      perror(on_what);
25:      exit(1);
26:  }
27:
28:  int
29:  main(int argc,char **argv,char **envp) {
30:      int z;              /* Status return code */
31:      int sck_inet;              /* Socket  */
32:      struct sockaddr_in adr_inet;/* AF_INET */
33:      int len_inet;              /* length  */
34:
35:      /* Create an IPv4 Internet Socket */
36:      sck_inet = socket(AF_INET,SOCK_STREAM,0);
37:
38:      if ( sck_inet == -1 )
```

continues

Listing 5.1: continued

```
39:          bail("socket()");
40:
41:      /* Create an AF_INET address */
42:      memset(&adr_inet,0,sizeof adr_inet);
43:
44:      adr_inet.sin_family = AF_INET;
45:      adr_inet.sin_port = htons(9000);
46:
47:      inet_aton("127.0.0.24",&adr_inet.sin_addr);
48:
49:      len_inet = sizeof adr_inet;
50:
51:      /* Now bind the address to the socket */
52:      z = bind(sck_inet,
53:          (struct sockaddr *)&adr_inet,
54:          len_inet);
55:
56:      if ( z == -1 )
57:          bail("bind()");
58:
59:      /* Display all of our bound sockets */
60:      system("netstat -pa --tcp 2>/dev/null | "
61:          "sed -n '1,/^Proto/p;/bind/p'");
62:
63:      close(sck_inet);
64:      return 0;
65:  }
```

N O T E

If the netstat(1) command on your system does not support the options used in lines 60 and 61 of Listing 5.1, substitute the following call if you have the lsof command installed:

```
system("lsof -i tcp | sed -n '1p;/bind/p'");
```

The program in Listing 5.1 is much like the ones you saw in Chapter 2. The steps used in the program are

1. Variable sck_inet will receive the socket when it is created (line 31).

2. Variable adr_inet will hold the sockets address that will be bound to it (line 32).

3. Variable len_inet will hold the length of the socket address in bytes (line 33).

4. The socket is created by socket(2) in line 36.

5. Step 4 is checked for errors in lines 38 and 39. If an error is detected, the function bail() is called. bail() reports the error and exits the program.

6. Lines 42 to 47 initialize the new socket address that is to be bound to the socket.

7. Variable len_inet is set to the size of the socket address (line 49).

8. The bind(2) function is called in lines 52 to 54. The value sck_inet represents the socket that is to be bound to the socket address adr_inet. This address is of length len_inet bytes. Note the use of the cast operator (struct sockaddr *) which is used to satisfy the compiler. This prevents a warning from being reported at compile time.

9. Step 8 is checked for errors in line 56. If an error occurs, bind(2) returns the value -1 instead of zero.

10. The system(3) call invokes the netstat(1) command to prove that our socket has an address bound to it (lines 60 and 61).

The following output shows how to compile and run this program:

OUTPUT

```
$ make bind
gcc -c  -D_GNU_SOURCE -Wall bind.c
gcc bind.o -o bind
$ ./bind
Active Internet connections (servers and established)
Proto Recv-Q Send-Q Local Address     Foreign Address  State   PID/Program name
tcp       0      0 127.0.0.24:9000    *:*              CLOSE   934/bind
$
```

The output shows that when it was run, the address 127.0.0.24:9000 was bound to the socket. The 9000 part represents the arbitrary port number that was chosen for this example program.

If you ran the program using the lsof command instead (see prior note), the output will appear slightly different:

```
$ ./bind
COMMAND    PID USER   FD   TYPE DEVICE SIZE NODE NAME
bind     16616 root    4u  inet 142319      TCP 127.0.0.24:9000 (CLOSE)
$
```

From this output, you can verify that the program named bind (under the heading "COMMAND") had a socket open on file unit 4 (column "FD"), and was bound to the TCP address 127.0.0.24, port 9000.

Obtaining the Socket Address

If a C library function that you wrote receives a socket as an input argument, then you will not know what the socket address of that socket is. This is because your function did not create the socket; and, unless the socket address is also passed to your function as input, you will not know what the address is. The function getsockname(2) permits your function to obtain it.

The function synopsis for getsockname(2) is as follows:

```
#include <sys/socket.h>
```

```
int getsockname(int s, struct sockaddr *name, socklen_t *namelen)
```

This function takes the following three input arguments:

1. The socket s to query for the socket address.

2. The pointer to the receiving buffer (argument name).

3. Pointer to the maximum length variable. This variable provides the maximum length in bytes that can be received in the buffer (argument namelen). This value is updated with the actual number of bytes written to the receiving buffer.

Note that like the bind(2) function, getsockname(2) uses the generic address structure sockaddr because it can be used for any type of socket address. This will mean that you will likely need to apply the C language casting operator on the pointer supplied in this argument.

The length argument namelen specifies the maximum number of bytes that can be received into argument two (name). Prior to returning to the caller, however, the value of namelen is overwritten to indicate how many bytes were actually returned in the receiving buffer. This will be less than or equal to the original value supplied.

CAUTION

Never supply the address of a constant for the socket address length in a call to getsockname(2). This should not be done because the length variable is updated with the actual number of bytes placed into the receiving address structure.

If you do supply the address of a constant, the value of the constant will be overwritten. This will cause havoc in your program. On some CPU platforms, you might experience a program fault instead.

The function returns zero if it is successful. If an error occurs, the return value -1 is returned, and the reason for the error is posted to the variable errno.

Writing a sock_addr() Function

To illustrate the use of getsockaddr(2), a small function has been presented in Listing 5.2, which accepts as input a socket descriptor. The function obtains the socket's address by calling getsockaddr(2), and then formats a string to be returned to the caller which can be used in a printf(3) call.

EXAMPLE

Listing 5.2: sckname.c—The getsockaddr(2) Function Call

```
 1:    /* sckname.c:
 2:     *
 3:     * Demonstrate getsockname(2):
 4:     */
 5:    #include <stdio.h>
 6:    #include <unistd.h>
 7:    #include <stdlib.h>
 8:    #include <errno.h>
 9:    #include <string.h>
10:    #include <sys/types.h>
11:    #include <sys/stat.h>
12:    #include <sys/socket.h>
13:    #include <netinet/in.h>
14:    #include <arpa/inet.h>
15:
16:    /*
17:     * This saves lines of code later:
18:     */
19:    static void
20:    bail(const char *on_what) {
21:        perror(on_what);      /* Report error */
22:        exit(1);              /* Exit Program */
23:    }
24:
25:    /*
26:     * This function accepts as input a socket
27:     * for which a socket address must be
28:     * determined for it. Then the address
29:     * is converted into a string and returned.
30:     *
31:     * If an error occurs, NULL is returned.
32:     */
33:    char *
34:    sock_addr(int s,char *buf,size_t bufsiz) {
35:        int z;             /* Status return code */
36:        struct sockaddr_in adr_inet;/* AF_INET */
37:        int len_inet;              /* length  */
38:
```

continues

Listing 5.2: continued

```
39:        /*
40:         * Obtain the address of the socket:
41:         */
42:        len_inet = sizeof adr_inet;
43:
44:        z = getsockname(s,
45:            (struct sockaddr *)&adr_inet,
46:            &len_inet);
47:
48:        if ( z == -1 )
49:            return NULL;      /* Failed */
50:
51:        /*
52:         * Convert address into a string
53:         * form that can be displayed:
54:         */
55:        snprintf(buf,bufsiz,
56:            "%s:%u",
57:            inet_ntoa(adr_inet.sin_addr),
58:            (unsigned)ntohs(adr_inet.sin_port));
59:
60:        return buf;
61:    }
62:
63:    /*
64:     * Main Program:
65:     */
66:    int
67:    main(int argc,char **argv,char **envp) {
68:        int z;              /* Status return code */
69:        int sck_inet;               /* Socket   */
70:        struct sockaddr_in adr_inet;/* AF_INET */
71:        int len_inet;               /* length   */
72:        char buf[64];          /* Work buffer */
73:
74:        /*
75:         * Create an IPv4 Internet Socket:
76:         */
77:        sck_inet = socket(AF_INET,SOCK_STREAM,0);
78:
79:        if ( sck_inet == -1 )
80:            bail("socket()");
81:
82:        /*
83:         * Create an AF_INET address:
84:         */
```

```
85:        memset(&adr_inet,0,sizeof adr_inet);
86:        adr_inet.sin_family = AF_INET;
87:        adr_inet.sin_port = htons(9000);
88:        inet_aton("127.0.0.24",&adr_inet.sin_addr);
89:        len_inet = sizeof adr_inet;
90:
91:        /*
92:         * Now bind the address to the socket:
93:         */
94:        z = bind(sck_inet,
95:            (struct sockaddr *)&adr_inet,
96:            len_inet);
97:        if ( z == -1 )
98:            bail("bind()");
99:
100:       /*
101:        * Now test our sock_addr() function:
102:        */
103:       if ( !sock_addr(sck_inet,buf,sizeof buf) )
104:           bail("sock_addr()");
105:
106:       printf("Address is '%s'\n",buf);
107:
108:       close(sck_inet);
109:       return 0;
110: }
```

Listing 5.2 shows how getsockname(2) could be used by a library C function. Much of the main() program is review for you, because it is very similar to the main() program in Listing 5.1. The general steps used in the main() program are

1. Declarations for the socket sck_inet, the address adr_inet, and the address length len_inet are given in lines 69 to 71.

2. A character array buffer buf[64] is declared in line 72 for use later in the program.

3. The socket is created by socket(2) in line 77.

4. A socket address is established in lines 85 to 95 with the use of the bind(2) function call.

5. The sock_addr() function is called inside the if statement in line 103. If the function returns a null pointer, the statement in line 104 is executed and the program will terminate.

6. If Step 5 succeeds, however, the buffer buf[] will contain a string that represents the socket address for socket sck_inet. The printf(3) call in line 106 reports this result.

In short, the main program does two things:

- Creates a socket and establishes an address for it.

- Calls the function sock_addr() to see whether it can find out what the socket's address is.

Now, examine the steps used by the sock_addr() function that was shown in Listing 5.2:

1. The function declaration for sock_addr() starts in line 33. It accepts as input the socket s for which the function must determine the address. The printable socket address is returned in the supplied buffer buf, which is a maximum size of bufsiz bytes.

2. Declarations for temporary values adr_inet and len_inet are declared in lines 36 and 37.

3. The maximum length is established in variable len_inet before calling getsockname(2). This establishes the maximum number of bytes of address information that can be returned.

4. The getsockname(2) function is called in line 44. If successful, z will be set to zero, and the address will be loaded into the structure adr_inet. The length variable len_inet will be overwritten with the actual size used.

5. Check for errors in line 48. When the return value is -1, an error has occurred. The function returns a null value to indicate that an error has occurred. The caller can test errno for the cause of the error.

6. Lines 55 to 58 format a string into the caller's buffer buf of maximum length bufsiz. The value of bufsiz must include the terminating null byte.

7. The pointer to the caller's buffer is returned in line 60 to indicate that the call was successful.

The function sock_addr() not only determines the socket address for the caller, but formats it nicely into a string that can be used in a printf(3) call.

TIP

Did you notice the use of the snprintf(3) call instead of the more traditional sprintf(3) function? The newer snprintf(3) call is able to limit its formatting to the maximum size of the buffer it is formatting to. This is extremely important for software integrity, and you should use the snprintf(3) instead, whenever possible.

OUTPUT

The following shows how to compile the program in Listing 5.2:

```
$ make sckname
gcc -c  -D_GNU_SOURCE -Wall sckname.c
gcc sckname.o -o sckname
```

After the program is compiled, you can invoke it to produce its output as follows:

```
$ ./sckname
Address is '127.0.0.24:9000'
$
```

Looking at the line of output where the address is reported as '127.0.0.24:9000', you can see that the function sock_addr() was successful at performing its mission. This was the address that was established in the main() program in lines 87 and 88.

Obtaining a Peer Socket Address

In the last section, you saw that the function getsockname(2) is quite useful at obtaining a socket's address. However, there will be times when your code will want to determine the remote address that your socket is connected to. Determining the remote address of a socket is like finding out the caller's telephone number when they have called you—similar to North America's CallerID.

The function to do this is called getpeername(2). This function will be useful to you when you start examining and writing server code. It is introduced here because it is so similar to getsockname(2). The function synopsis for getpeername(2) is as follows:

```
#include <sys/socket.h>

int getpeername(int s, struct sockaddr *name, socklen_t *namelen);
```

You can see that the function arguments are identical to the getsockname(2) function. For completeness, the arguments are described again as follows:

1. The socket s to query for the socket address.

2. The pointer to the receiving buffer (argument name).

3. Pointer to the maximum length variable. This variable provides the maximum length in bytes that can be received in the buffer (argument namelen). This value is updated with the actual number of bytes written to the receiving buffer.

The function returns zero if the operation succeeds. If an error occurs, the value -1 is returned and the value errno will contain the reason for the error.

Listing 5.3 shows some code that defines a function named peer_addr().
This code is very similar in design to the sock_addr() function of Listing
5.2. This is not a complete example, however, because it shows the source
code only for the function itself (it lacks a main program). This code can be
revisited later in this book, when connection-oriented communications are
discussed. For now, simply appreciate it as an example of how the function
getpeername(2) can be used.

EXAMPLE

Listing 5.3: getpeer.c—The getpeername(2) Function

```
1:    /* getpeer.c:
2:     *
3:     * Demonstrate getpeername(2):
4:     */
5:    #include <stdio.h>
6:    #include <unistd.h>
7:    #include <stdlib.h>
8:    #include <errno.h>
9:    #include <string.h>
10:   #include <sys/types.h>
11:   #include <sys/stat.h>
12:   #include <sys/socket.h>
13:   #include <netinet/in.h>
14:   #include <arpa/inet.h>
15:
16:   /*
17:    * This function accepts as input a socket
18:    * for which a peer socket address must be
19:    * determined for it. Then the address
20:    * is converted into a string and returned.
21:    *
22:    * If an error occurs, NULL is returned.
23:    */
24:   char *
25:   peer_addr(int s,char *buf,size_t bufsiz) {
26:       int z;              /* Status return code */
27:       struct sockaddr_in adr_inet;/* AF_INET */
28:       int len_inet;               /* length   */
29:
30:       /*
31:        * Obtain the address of the socket:
32:        */
33:       len_inet = sizeof adr_inet;
34:
35:       z = getpeername(s,
36:           (struct sockaddr *)&adr_inet,
37:           &len_inet);
38:
```

```
39:     if ( z == -1 )
40:         return NULL;     /* Failed */
41:
42:     /*
43:      * Convert address into a string
44:      * form that can be displayed:
45:      */
46:     z = snprintf(buf,bufsiz,
47:         "%s:%u",
48:         inet_ntoa(adr_inet.sin_addr),
49:         (unsigned)ntohs(adr_inet.sin_port));
50:
51:     if ( z == -1 )
52:         return NULL;     /* Buffer too small */
53:
54:     return buf;
55: }
```

The steps used in peer_name() are the same basic steps as sock_addr().
However, one small improvement was made to the program. Let's take a
look at the steps:

1. The function declaration for sock_addr() starts in line 24. It accepts
   as input the socket s for which the function must determine the peer
   address. The printable socket address is returned in the supplied
   buffer buf, which is a maximum size of bufsiz bytes.

2. Declarations for temporary values adr_inet and len_inet are declared
   in lines 27 and 28.

3. The maximum length is established in variable len_inet before calling
   getsockname(2) (line 33). This establishes the maximum number of
   bytes of address information that can be returned.

4. The getpeername(2) function is called in line 35. If successful, z will be
   set to zero, and the address will be loaded into the structure adr_inet.
   The length variable len_inet will be overwritten with the actual size
   used.

5. Check for errors in line 39. When the return value is -1, an error has
   occurred. The function returns a null value to indicate that an error
   has occurred. The caller can test errno for the cause of the error.

6. Lines 46 to 49 format a string into the caller's buffer buf of maximum
   length bufsiz. The value of bufsiz must include the terminating null
   byte.

7. A small improvement to the program was added at lines 51 and 52.
   The snprintf(3) function returns -1 if the formatted result is too
   large to fit into the user's buffer buf of maximum length bufsiz. If this

should happen, the program returns a null pointer in line 52 to indicate that the peer_addr() function was not fully successful.

8. The pointer to the caller's buffer is returned in line 54 to indicate that the call was successful.

If you skimmed over the steps described, the improvement that was made to the program is described in step 7.

Interfaces and Addressing

Before you move onto other aspects of socket programming in the chapters that follow, there is one other concept related to socket addresses that must be understood. This is the concept of interface addresses.

Using the familiar telephone example again, imagine the President's office where there are two (or more) telephones on his desk. Using one of the telephones, he can contact his wife to see how her day is going. On the other hand, using the red telephone gets him in touch with the Russian president. Each of these two telephones is, in a sense, an interface between two different networks. These are

- The normal domestic telephone network.

- A private network to the Russian president's high-ranking office(s) on secure lines.

The important point in this example is that you must use the correct interface (telephone) to reach the correct network. For example, the President would be unable to call his wife on the red telephone. Conversely, the domestic telephone would not be able to reach the Russian president's high-ranking office telephones, which are on secure lines.

In a similar manner, there are times when you want your socket program to specify which interface to use when attempting to contact a remote socket. This is done when you know that one interface is the only way to reach the destination network.

When you are expecting to receive a telephone call, there are times when you want to receive calls only on a particular telephone. For example, the teenage daughter might want to receive calls only on the telephone installed in her bedroom. For others in the household, they expect to receive telephone calls only in a downstairs room where the other telephone is installed. Your socket program will likewise sometimes want to accept connections from only one specific interface and ignore all others.

Specifying an Interface Address Example

A concrete example is shown in Figure 5.1, which specifies an interface address.

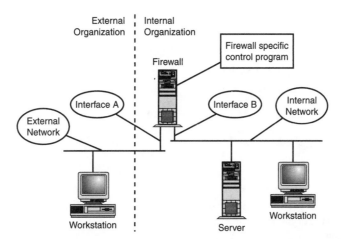

Figure 5.1: *Here is a firewall example using a specific interface.*

In the middle of Figure 5.1, you see a server that is acting as a firewall between an internal organization and an external one that is not trusted. Assume that you have written a socket program that runs on the firewall server, which accepts firewall control commands from your workstation at the extreme right of the figure (from within the internal organization). The server program accepts connections from the internal network by permitting connections to arrive only on the network interface "B."

For security reasons, your control program on the firewall host will not accept connection attempts from the external organization. This is done by ignoring all connection attempts on the firewall network interface "A." This protects your control program from attempted break-ins that might be initiated by the workstation at the extreme left in Figure 5.1.

Binding a Specific Interface Address

In order to specify a particular interface for communications, you must perform the following steps:

1. Create your socket using the socket(2) function as usual.

2. Bind the IP address of the interface that you are willing to accept connections onto the local socket using the function bind(2).

In Figure 5.1, you would use the IP address of interface "B" in your call to bind(2), in order to accept connections from the internal network only.

Listing 5.4 shows how to bind to a specific network interface address, using some lines of code that you have seen before. This must be done before any socket communication begins.

Listing 5.4: Binding a Specific IP Interface

```
int z;
int sck_inet;                    /* Socket */
struct sockaddr_in adr_inet;     /* AF_INET */
int len_inet;                    /* length  */

sck_inet = socket(AF_INET,SOCK_STREAM,0);

if ( sck_inet == -1 )
    abort(); /* Failed */

/* Establish address */
memset(&adr_inet,0,sizeof adr_inet);
adr_inet.sin_family = AF_INET;
adr_inet.sin_port = htons(9000);

adr_inet.sin_addr.s_addr = inet_addr("192.168.0.1");

if ( adr_inet.sin_addr.s_addr == INADDR_NONE )
    abort(); /* Failed */

len_inet = sizeof adr_inet;

z = bind(sck_inet, (struct sockaddr *)&adr_inet, len_inet);
```

The steps shown in Listing 5.4 are as follows:

1. A socket is created by calling socket(2) and assigning the descriptor to variable sck_inet. Errors are also tested for and, in this example, abort(3) is called for simplicity if an error occurs.

2. An IP address of 192.168.0.1 is established prior to calling upon bind(2). TCP port 9000 was arbitrarily used in this example.

3. The function bind(2) is called, which then binds the established address.

Note that the bind(2) function call will fail if there is no interface with that IP number for that host.

Binding for Any Interface

How do you accept connections from any interface? You perform the following steps:

1. Create your socket using the socket(2) function as usual.

2. Bind the IP address INADDR_ANY to the socket using the function bind(2).

Listing 5.5 shows some code that will explicitly indicate that any interface will do.

EXAMPLE

Listing 5.5: Specifying Any Interface Using `bind(2)`

```
int z;
int sck_inet;                    /* Socket */
struct sockaddr_in adr_inet;   /* AF_INET */
int len_inet;                    /* length  */

sck_inet = socket(AF_INET,SOCK_STREAM,0);

if ( sck_inet == -1 )
    abort(); /* Failed */

/* Establish address */
memset(&adr_inet,0,sizeof adr_inet);
adr_inet.sin_family = AF_INET;
adr_inet.sin_port = htons(9000);

adr_inet.sin_addr.s_addr = htonl(INADDR_ANY);

if ( adr_inet.sin_addr.s_addr == INADDR_NONE )
    abort(); /* Failed */

len_inet = sizeof adr_inet;

z = bind(sck_inet, (struct sockaddr *)&adr_inet, len_inet);
```

Listing 5.5 is functionally identical to Listing 5.4, with the exception that the address value assigned was `htonl(INADDR_ANY)` instead of a specific IP address. A socket bound in this way can accept connections from any interface. It can also connect to a remote socket going out from any interface (this is automatically determined by routing tables).

NOTE

The value `INADDR_ANY` is also known as a *wildcard* address.

What's Next

Although you had seen the `bind(2)` function used earlier in this book, this chapter focused on why and how it is used. You then learned the details about its function arguments, and reviewed its use in actual code.

Now that you have completely mastered the socket-addressing techniques involved, you will be fully prepared to use sockets in the chapters that follow. The next chapter will introduce you to two modes of socket operation. Then, it will show you how to use sockets in the connectionless mode of operation.

Connectionless-Oriented Protocols

Up to this point in this book, the nature of socket communications has largely been avoided. Instead, you have been focused on creating sockets, binding addresses to them, shutting them down, or closing them. Now it is time for some real fun in actually using sockets.

There are two basic modes of communication for sockets. They are connectionless- and connection-oriented communications.

In this chapter, you will learn

- The differences between connectionless- and connection-oriented communication

- How to perform connectionless input and output operations

- How to write a datagram server

- How to write a datagram client

Now turn your attention to a comparison between connectionless- and connection-oriented communication.

The Methods of Communication

Connectionless-oriented communication, as you might have surmised, requires no connection to be established before communication begins. This is like a person with a megaphone shouting to a specific person of his choice in a crowd. With each new shout, the person sending the message can address his statement to another person without any prior agreement.

In a similar manner, after you create a connectionless socket, you will be able to send messages to any socket that is willing to receive your messages. There will be no connection establishment, and each message can be directed to a different receiving socket.

Understanding the Advantages

Connectionless-oriented communications offer some advantages over connection-oriented protocols. Some of these include the following:

- **Simpler**—No connection to establish.

- **Flexible**—Can send messages to a different recipient with each message-sending operation.

- **Efficient**—Requires no connection establishment or tear down, which can add a significant number of overhead message packets to the network.

- **Fast**—Since there is no connection establishment or tear-down, only the message itself is sent.

- **Broadcast capability**—The capability to direct one message to many recipients.

Many of the advantages of a connectionless-oriented protocol have to do with efficiency and speed. To establish a connection requires a number of packets to be exchanged between the two endpoints before any data can be exchanged. The tear-down of an established communication channel requires that additional packets be exchanged. Again, this results in additional overhead and elapsed time.

One other advantage of a connectionless protocol is its broadcast capability. It is possible to address one message to several recipients. This makes very efficient use of the network bandwidth.

In this chapter, you will study the UDP protocol (User Datagram Protocol), which is a connectionless-oriented protocol. This protocol enjoys all of the advantages that were just presented.

Understanding the Disadvantages of Connectionless Communications

With all of the advantages that connectionless-oriented protocols offer, you might wonder why they aren't always used. As with most things, even connectionless communication has its disadvantages.

The UDP protocol is a very simple transport-layer protocol, and it is connectionless as noted previously. In the context of the UDP protocol, there exist the following disadvantages:

- The protocol is not reliable.

- There is no sequencing of multiple datagrams.

- There are message size limitations.

The problem of reliability is the most serious limitation for most applications. The UDP datagram can be written out to the network by your application, but there is no assurance that the intended recipient will ever receive it. The message could be garbled and not received by the receiver on the same network. Alternatively, the message could be lost because one of many routers in the network path failed to receive the message without checksum errors. When a packet is received with an error, the UDP packet is quietly discarded and lost forever.

NOTE

A datagram is simply a unit of data that is sent and received over the network. It can be compared to a telegram in the sense that it represents one complete message.

Other problems can cause UDP packets to be lost. If the receiving host or router is unable to allocate enough buffer space to hold the UDP packet, it will be quietly discarded. It follows, then, that if your UDP packet must travel longer distances, there is a greater chance of it being dropped along the way.

Another problem must be considered before you decide to use UDP for your applications. If you send two or more datagrams to your destination in quick succession, there is a possibility that some datagrams will arrive out of sequence. The UDP protocol uses the Internet Protocol (IP) to deliver the final datagram. IP packets can be routed differently with each transmission, and routes vary according to current network conditions. This often results in some packets arriving at the destination before earlier packets. The bottom line is that UDP packets can arrive out of sequence.

Finally, there is the issue of datagram size. The theoretical maximum size of a UDP datagram is slightly less than 64KB. However, many UNIX hosts will only support a maximum near 32KB. Other UNIX kernel built-in restrictions limit the size even further. This is often as low as 8KB. Finally, the receiving socket program will restrict this to the maximum size of its receiving buffer. For this reason, some programs restrict themselves to UDP messages of 512 bytes or less.

If a large UDP packet is sent, it will have to be broken up into several smaller IP fragments and later re-assembled at the receiving end. The re-assembly process requires buffers to be allocated in order to hold the received fragments. This is only done for a given timeout period, until the entire packet can be re-assembled. Competition for buffers may cause the re-assembly to be abandoned, with the effect that your UDP packet will be quietly dropped. The UDP datagram must endure a number of perils before it successfully arrives at its destination.

For some applications, these caveats will steer you toward the more reliable connection-oriented protocols such as TCP/IP. These might not be serious limitations for other applications. Only you can decide whether UDP is appropriate for use in your application.

Performing Input/Output of Datagrams

In the example program shown in Listing 1.3 of Chapter 1, "Introducing Sockets," you saw the functions read(2) and write(2) being used when reading from and writing to sockets. While it was not pointed out at the time, the socketpair(2) function call shown created a pair of sockets using a connection-oriented protocol. Consequently, it was possible to use the familiar read(2) and write(2) functions to perform I/O on those sockets.

When sending and receiving datagrams, however, a different pair of functions is required. This is because each message being sent is potentially sent to a different destination address. The function used for sending a datagram must allow you to specify the address of the intended recipient. Likewise, when you receive a datagram, you need to find out whom it came from. This new function must provide you with a convenient way to determine the address of the sender.

Introducing the sendto(2) Function

The sendto(2) function allows you to write a datagram and specify the destination address of the recipient at the same time. The function synopsis is as follows:

```
#include <sys/types.h>
#include <sys/socket.h>

int sendto(int s,
    const void *msg,
```

```
    int len,
    unsigned flags,
    const struct sockaddr *to,
    int tolen);
```

Don't let the number of arguments intimidate you about this function. They are quite easy to understand, after they are described:

1. The first argument s is the socket number. You received this value from the socket(2) function.

2. Argument msg is a pointer to the buffer holding the datagram message that you wish to send.

3. Argument len is the length, in bytes, of the datagram that starts at the pointer given by msg.

4. The flags argument allows you to specify some option bits. In many cases, you will simply supply a value of zero.

5. The argument to is a pointer to a generic socket address that you have established. This is the address of the recipient of the datagram.

6. Argument tolen is the length of the address argument to.

The value returned by the function sendto(2), when successful, is the number of bytes sent (note that this is no guarantee that they were received at the remote end.) When an error occurs, the function returns a value of –1 and the value errno can be consulted to find out why.

The second-to-last function argument allows you to identify where the datagram must be sent. The argument to must point to a valid socket address, and the argument tolen should contain the correct length of the address. You have become an expert at forming addresses in the preceding chapters, so you should feel right at home here.

Table 6.1 lists the values that the flags argument can have, though most of the time you will simply supply the value zero instead.

Table 6.1: The **flags** *Values for the* **sendto(2)** *Function*

Flag	Hexadecimal	Meaning
0	0x0000	Normal—no special options
MSG_OOB	0x0001	Processes out-of-band data
MSG_DONTROUTE	0x0004	Bypasses routing; uses direct interface
MSG_DONTWAIT	0x0040	Does not block; waiting to write
MSG_NOSIGNAL	0x4000	Does not raise SIGPIPE when the other end has disconnected

---

CAUTION

Always use the macro names, such as MSG_DONTWAIT for example, when specifying constants and flag bits. While Table 6.1 shows the hexadecimal values for each C macro constant, only use the macro name. In this manner, if a change to the constant should be made in a later release of Linux, your program can simply be recompiled and still function correctly without any source code modification.

TIP

The man page for sendto(2) for Red Hat Linux 6.0 lists the value of C macro constant MSG_NOSIGNAL as 0x2000. However, the include/linux/socket.h file within the kernel sources for 2.2.10 lists the value as 0x4000. A comment in this include file also indicates that not all of the flags listed there are supported yet.

Many of the flag values listed in Table 6.1 are for advanced use and won't be covered at this time. They have been listed here for your convenience as a reference. Normally, you will simply supply the value zero.

Later in this chapter, you will put the sendto(2) function to work. Before you do this, however, you should learn about the recvfrom(2) function.

Introducing the recvfrom(2) Function

The companion to the sendto(2) function is the recvfrom(2) function. This function differs from the read(2) function in that it allows you to receive the sender's address at the same time you receive your datagram. The function synopsis is as follows:

```
#include <sys/types.h>
#include <sys/socket.h>

int recvfrom(int s,
    void *buf,
    int len,
    unsigned flags,
    struct sockaddr *from,
    int *fromlen);
```

The list of arguments is very similar to those used in the sendto(2) function. The recvfrom(2) arguments are

1. The socket s to receive the datagram from.

2. The buffer pointer buf to start receiving the datagram into.

3. The maximum length (len) in bytes of the receiving buffer buf.

4. Option flag bits flags.

5. The pointer to the receiving socket address buffer, which will receive the sender's address (pointer argument from).

6. The pointer to the maximum length (fromlen) in bytes of the receiving socket address buffer from. Note that the integer that this pointer points to must be initialized to the maximum size of the receiving address structure from, prior to calling the function.

Like any normal read(2) operation, the receiving buffer buf must be large enough to receive the incoming datagram. The maximum length is indicated to the function by the argument len.

The function returns the value -1 if there was an error, and you should consult the value of errno for the cause of the error. Otherwise, the function returns the number of bytes that were received into your receiving buffer buf. This will be the size of your datagram received.

Note especially, however, that the last argument is a pointer to the length of the receiving address structure. Prior to calling the function recvfrom(2), the int value that this pointer points to must contain the maximum byte size of the receiving address structure from. Upon return from the function, the actual size of the address returned is placed into this int variable. In effect, the value pointed to by fromlen acts as both an input value and a returned value.

TIP

If you are using the function recvfrom(2) to receive datagrams for varying protocols, make certain that you allow sufficient socket address space to receive all address families that you might encounter. For example, the socket address size differs for address families AF_INET and AF_LOCAL (AF_UNIX). Often a C union data type can allow for the maximum size needed.

There are different flag values available for the recvfrom(2) function, which are listed in Table 6.2.

Table 6.2: The **flag** *Values for the* **recvfrom(2)** *Function*

Flag	Hexadecimal	Meaning
0	0x0000	Normal
MSG_OOB	0x0001	Processes out-of-band data
MSG_PEEK	0x0002	Reads a datagram without actually removing it from the kernel's receive queue.
MSG_WAITALL	0x0100	Requests that the operation block until the full request has been satisfied (with some exceptions)
MSG_ERRQUEUE	0x2000	Receives a packet from the error queue
MSG_NOSIGNAL	0x4000	Turns off the raising of SIGPIPE for stream sockets when the other end has become disconnected

Again, the flags shown in Table 6.2 are for your reference only at this point, because many of these options are for more advanced processing. Normally, you will simply provide a value of zero for the `flags` argument.

Writing a UDP Datagram Server

Now you are equipped well enough to write a datagram client and server program. In this section, you'll begin with a datagram server example (remember from Chapter 1, where you saw an example program in Listing 1.4). This program took a `strftime(3)` format string as input and returned the formatted date and time string as a response. You are going to write a datagram server in this section, which will stand by itself, accept format strings as input datagrams. After the server formats a date string using the `strftime(3)` function, it will send the result back to the client program in another datagram as shown in Listing 6.1.

EXAMPLE

Listing 6.1: `dgramsrvr.c`—The Example Datagram Server

```
1:  /* dgramsrvr.c:
2:   *
3:   * Example datagram server:
4:   */
5:  #include <stdio.h>
6:  #include <unistd.h>
7:  #include <stdlib.h>
8:  #include <errno.h>
9:  #include <string.h>
10: #include <time.h>
11: #include <sys/types.h>
12: #include <sys/socket.h>
13: #include <netinet/in.h>
14: #include <arpa/inet.h>
15:
16: /*
17:  * This function reports the error and
18:  * exits back to the shell:
19:  */
20: static void
21: bail(const char *on_what) {
22:     fputs(strerror(errno),stderr);
23:     fputs(": ",stderr);
24:     fputs(on_what,stderr);
25:     fputc('\n',stderr);
26:     exit(1);
27: }
28:
29: int
```

```
30:   main(int argc,char **argv) {
31:       int z;
32:       char *srvr_addr = NULL;
33:       struct sockaddr_in adr_inet;/* AF_INET */
34:       struct sockaddr_in adr_clnt;/* AF_INET */
35:       int len_inet;                /* length  */
36:       int s;                       /* Socket */
37:       char dgram[512];          /* Recv buffer */
38:       char dtfmt[512];    /* Date/Time Result */
39:       time_t td;     /* Current Time and Date */
40:       struct tm tm;       /* Date time values */
41:
42:       /*
43:        * Use a server address from the command
44:        * line, if one has been provided.
45:        * Otherwise, this program will default
46:        * to using the arbitrary address
47:        * 127.0.0.23:
48:        */
49:       if ( argc >= 2 ) {
50:           /* Addr on cmdline: */
51:           srvr_addr = argv[1];
52:       } else {
53:           /* Use default address: */
54:           srvr_addr = "127.0.0.23";
55:       }
56:
57:       /*
58:        * Create a UDP socket to use:
59:        */
60:       s = socket(AF_INET,SOCK_DGRAM,0);
61:       if ( s == -1 )
62:           bail("socket()");
63:
64:       /*
65:        * Create a socket address, for use
66:        * with bind(2):
67:        */
68:       memset(&adr_inet,0,sizeof adr_inet);
69:       adr_inet.sin_family = AF_INET;
70:       adr_inet.sin_port = htons(9090);
71:       adr_inet.sin_addr.s_addr =
72:           inet_addr(srvr_addr);
73:
74:       if ( adr_inet.sin_addr.s_addr == INADDR_NONE )
75:           bail("bad address.");
```

continues

Listing 6.1: continued

```
76:
77:        len_inet = sizeof adr_inet;
78:
79:        /*
80:         * Bind a address to our socket, so that
81:         * client programs can contact this
82:         * server:
83:         */
84:        z = bind(s,
85:            (struct sockaddr *)&adr_inet,
86:            len_inet);
87:        if ( z == -1 )
88:            bail("bind()");
89:
90:        /*
91:         * Now wait for requests:
92:         */
93:        for (;;) {
94:            /*
95:             * Block until the program receives a
96:             * datagram at our address and port:
97:             */
98:            len_inet = sizeof adr_clnt;
99:            z = recvfrom(s,                    /* Socket */
100:                dgram,               /* Receiving buffer */
101:                sizeof dgram,     /* Max recv buf size */
102:                0,                 /* Flags: no options */
103:                (struct sockaddr *)&adr_clnt,/* Addr */
104:                &len_inet);     /* Addr len, in & out */
105:            if ( z < 0 )
106:                bail("recvfrom(2)");
107:
108:            /*
109:             * Process the request:
110:             */
111:            dgram[z] = 0;            /* null terminate */
112:            if ( !strcasecmp(dgram,"QUIT") )
113:                break;                /* Quit server */
114:
115:            /*
116:             * Get the current date and time:
117:             */
118:            time(&td);    /* Get current time & date */
119:            tm = *localtime(&td);  /* Get components */
120:
121:            /*
```

```
122:             * Format a new date and time string,
123:             * based upon the input format string:
124:             */
125:            strftime(dtfmt,        /* Formatted result */
126:                sizeof dtfmt,      /* Max result size */
127:                dgram,       /* Input date/time format */
128:                &tm);        /* Input date/time values */
129:
130:            /*
131:             * Send the formatted result back to the
132:             * client program:
133:             */
134:            z = sendto(s,    /* Socket to send result */
135:                dtfmt, /* The datagram result to snd */
136:                strlen(dtfmt), /* The datagram lngth */
137:                0,                /* Flags: no options */
138:                (struct sockaddr *)&adr_clnt,/* addr */
139:                len_inet); /* Client address length */
140:            if ( z < 0 )
141:                bail("sendto(2)");
142:        }
143:
144:        /*
145:         * Close the socket and exit:
146:         */
147:        close(s);
148:        return 0;
149: }
```

The program might look a little intimidating, but the basic steps are easily understood. They can be described simply as follows:

1. Create a socket, using socket(2).

2. Establish a server address and bind(2) it.

3. Wait for a datagram by calling recvfrom(2).

4. Process the request (format a date string).

5. Send the result back to the client using sendto(2).

6. Repeat step 3, until it is time to exit.

Step 2 is necessary so that the client program is able to contact the server. This is like giving a telephone a number. Step 2 gives a nameless socket an address, so that datagrams can be directed to it by the client program.

The program shown in Listing 6.1 can now be described in detail that is more complete, as follows:

1. Lines 20 to 27 form our simple error-handling function. Its purpose is to report an error, should it occur, and exit out of the program. Real applications would provide better error handling than this.

2. Lines 49 to 55 choose a server address for this server program. If no command-line argument is provided, then the arbitrary address 127.0.0.23 is used. Note that this default address will work for you, even if you do not have any network cards installed.

3. Lines 60 to 62 create a datagram socket. This causes a UDP protocol socket number to be assigned to variable s, when the socket(2) call is successful.

4. Lines 68 to 77 form the address structure adr_inet and establish the address structure length in variable len_inet.

5. Lines 84 to 88 bind the address established in step 4, to the socket s that was created in step 3.

6. A loop begins in line 93.

7. The maximum size of the receiving address buffer is computed in line 98 and assigned to variable len_inet. The receiving address buffer will be the structure adr_clnt.

8. The function recvfrom(2) is called in line 99. This function call will block until the server receives a datagram. Upon return from this function, buffer dgram will contain the datagram, and variable z will contain the size of this datagram (or –1 if there was an error returned). The sender's socket address is returned in structure adr_clnt, and variable len_inet is set to the length of the address in adr_clnt.

9. If step 8 is successful, the variable z is the length of the datagram message that was received. Line 111 places a null byte at the end of the buffer, so that buffer dgram[] may be treated as a null terminated C string.

10. Line 112 tests to see if the datagram contains the string "QUIT". If so, this is a signal for the server to quit, and control breaks out of the loop in line 113.

11. The current date and time are fetched in lines 118 and 119.

12. The datagram received in character array dgram[] is used as a format string for the strftime(3) call in lines 125 to 128. This function call simply formats the date and time according to the datagram message that was received.

13. Lines 134 to 141 send the result back to the client that requested the date and time. Note that lines 138 and 139 simply use the client address and address length that was received in step 8.

14. Repeat the top of the loop, at step 6.

OUTPUT

The program can be compiled as follows:

```
$ make dgramsrvr
gcc -c  -D_GNU_SOURCE -Wall dgramsrvr.c
gcc dgramsrvr.o -o dgramsrvr
$
```

The program dgramsrvr can accept one optional command-line argument. The default server address used is the IP address 127.0.0.23. However, a different one can be specified on the command line. Normally, you will want to run the server in the background, as follows:

```
$ ./dgramsrvr &
[1] 4339
$
```

If you want to run the server with a different IP address, you can specify it on the command line as in the following example:

```
$ ./dgramsrvr 192.168.0.1 &
[1] 4341
$
```

In this case, the server will listen for connections on 192.168.0.1. Note that if you don't have an interface with this number, you will get an error, as shown below:

```
$ ./dgramsrvr 192.168.0.2 &
[1] 4342
Cannot assign requested address: bind()
[1]+  Exit 1              ./dgramsrvr 192.168.0.2
$
```

However, when using the 127.0.0.1 network (your local loopback device), you can specify any class A address, if it starts with 127. The server program example uses 127.0.0.23, but this could have been another number within that same network.

Writing a UDP Datagram Client

In order to make use of the server program just presented, you will need a datagram client program. The client program presented in Listing 6.2 will prompt you for an input line that should contain formatting text for strftime(3). Some input examples will be provided for you, if you don't feel like coming up with your own examples.

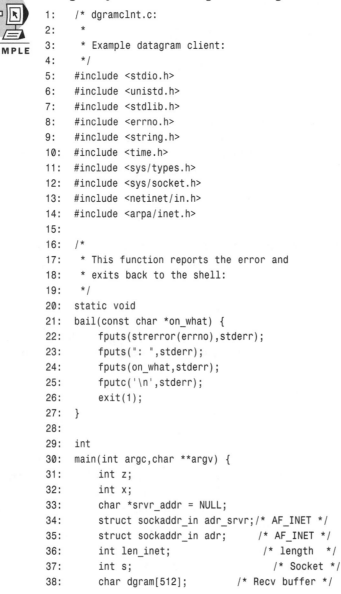

EXAMPLE

Listing 6.2: dgramclnt.c—The Datagram Client Program

```
1:   /* dgramclnt.c:
2:    *
3:    * Example datagram client:
4:    */
5:   #include <stdio.h>
6:   #include <unistd.h>
7:   #include <stdlib.h>
8:   #include <errno.h>
9:   #include <string.h>
10:  #include <time.h>
11:  #include <sys/types.h>
12:  #include <sys/socket.h>
13:  #include <netinet/in.h>
14:  #include <arpa/inet.h>
15:
16:  /*
17:   * This function reports the error and
18:   * exits back to the shell:
19:   */
20:  static void
21:  bail(const char *on_what) {
22:      fputs(strerror(errno),stderr);
23:      fputs(": ",stderr);
24:      fputs(on_what,stderr);
25:      fputc('\n',stderr);
26:      exit(1);
27:  }
28:
29:  int
30:  main(int argc,char **argv) {
31:      int z;
32:      int x;
33:      char *srvr_addr = NULL;
34:      struct sockaddr_in adr_srvr;/* AF_INET */
35:      struct sockaddr_in adr;     /* AF_INET */
36:      int len_inet;                 /* length */
37:      int s;                        /* Socket */
38:      char dgram[512];        /* Recv buffer */
```

```
39:
40:        /*
41:         * Use a server address from the command
42:         * line, if one has been provided.
43:         * Otherwise, this program will default
44:         * to using the arbitrary address
45:         * 127.0.0.23:
46:         */
47:        if ( argc >= 2 ) {
48:            /* Addr on cmdline: */
49:            srvr_addr = argv[1];
50:        } else {
51:            /* Use default address: */
52:            srvr_addr = "127.0.0.23";
53:        }
54:
55:        /*
56:         * Create a socket address, to use
57:         * to contact the server with:
58:         */
59:        memset(&adr_srvr,0,sizeof adr_srvr);
60:        adr_srvr.sin_family = AF_INET;
61:        adr_srvr.sin_port = htons(9090);
62:        adr_srvr.sin_addr.s_addr =
63:            inet_addr(srvr_addr);
64:
65:        if ( adr_srvr.sin_addr.s_addr == INADDR_NONE )
66:            bail("bad address.");
67:
68:        len_inet = sizeof adr_srvr;
69:
70:        /*
71:         * Create a UDP socket to use:
72:         */
73:        s = socket(AF_INET,SOCK_DGRAM,0);
74:        if ( s == -1 )
75:            bail("socket()");
76:
77:        for (;;) {
78:            /*
79:             * Prompt user for a date format string:
80:             */
81:            fputs("\nEnter format string: ",stdout);
82:            if ( !fgets(dgram,sizeof dgram,stdin) )
83:                break;                        /* EOF */
84:
```

continues

Listing 6.2: continued

```
85:            z = strlen(dgram);
86:            if ( z > 0 && dgram[-z] == '\n' )
87:                dgram[z] = 0;    /* Stomp out newline */
88:
89:            /*
90:             * Send format string to server:
91:             */
92:            z = sendto(s,    /* Socket to send result */
93:                dgram, /* The datagram result to snd */
94:                strlen(dgram), /* The datagram lngth */
95:                0,                /* Flags: no options */
96:                (struct sockaddr *)&adr_srvr,/* addr */
97:                len_inet);  /* Server address length */
98:            if ( z < 0 )
99:                bail("sendto(2)");
100:
101:            /*
102:             * Test if we asked for a server shutdown:
103:             */
104:            if ( !strcasecmp(dgram,"QUIT") )
105:                break;            /* Yes, we quit too */
106:
107:            /*
108:             * Wait for a response:
109:             */
110:            x = sizeof adr;
111:            z = recvfrom(s,                  /* Socket */
112:                dgram,              /* Receiving buffer */
113:                sizeof dgram,    /* Max recv buf size */
114:                0,               /* Flags: no options */
115:                (struct sockaddr *)&adr,      /* Addr */
116:                &x);              /* Addr len, in & out */
117:            if ( z < 0 )
118:                bail("recvfrom(2)");
119:
120:            dgram[z] = 0;            /* null terminate */
121:
122:            /*
123:             * Report Result:
124:             */
125:            printf("Result from %s port %u :\n\t'%s'\n",
126:                inet_ntoa(adr.sin_addr),
127:                (unsigned)ntohs(adr.sin_port),
128:                dgram);
129:    }
130:
```

```
131:    /*
132:     * Close the socket and exit:
133:     */
134:    close(s);
135:    putchar('\n');
136:
137:    return 0;
138: }
```

The client program in Listing 6.2 has many similarities to the server program in Listing 6.1. At the most basic level, the steps used in Listing 6.2 are as follows:

1. A server socket address is determined and formed (this is how we identify the socket we want to contact).

2. A socket is created using socket(2).

3. Input is received from the user terminal.

4. The input is sent as a datagram to the server.

5. A response from the server is received.

6. The response is displayed on the terminal and step 3 is repeated until end of file is encountered.

Step 1 does not strictly need to occur first, but it must be done prior to step 4. Otherwise, the program flow is very simple: create a socket, send a datagram, get result, report result, and repeat.

Examining Listing 6.2 in more detail, the steps are as follows:

1. Lines 47 to 53 determine the address of the server to use. The user can supply the server address on the command line or let the default from line 52 prevail.

2. Lines 59 to 68 actually create the socket address that will be used to send datagrams to the server.

3. Lines 73 to 75 create the socket s that is used in the program.

4. The main loop starts in line 77.

5. Input is gathered from the terminal session in lines 81 to 83. If end-of-file is received, the loop is exited in line 83 at the break statement.

6. Lines 85 to 87 remove the annoying newline character that the fgets(3) function leaves in the buffer.

7. Lines 92 to 99 show how the input in array dgram[] is sent to the server. The datagram length is simply the string length of the buffer

dgram[]. Notice also that arguments &adr_srvr and len_inet specify the destination server address and address length, respectively.

8. Lines 104 to 105 test to see if we sent the command "QUIT" to the server. If so, the program exits the for loop at line 105 with the break statement, because the program will not get a response from the server (the server will shut down).

9. Line 110 initializes variable x with the maximum size of the receiving address structure adr.

10. Lines 111 to 118 call upon recvfrom(2) to receive the response from the server.

11. A null byte is placed into array dgram[] in line 120, to allow the program to use the result datagram as a C string.

12. Lines 125 to 128 report the server address that returned the result, as well as the formatted string that it returned in the datagram.

13. The loop repeats with Step 4.

This program doesn't check the returned address in adr, but a production mode program should. While waiting to receive the server's response, another unrelated program could send our client program a message, which should be ignored (the program wants a response from the server—not another process). UDP is quite flexible, but a number of situations like this one, can make your program more complicated. This is something to consider when making a choice between UDP and TCP, for example.

OUTPUT

To compile the program in Listing 6.2, you can perform the following:

```
$ make dgramclnt
gcc -c  -D_GNU_SOURCE -Wall dgramclnt.c
gcc dgramclnt.o -o dgramclnt
$
```

With both a server and a client program at your disposal, you are now ready to test them.

Testing the Datagram Client and Server

The first test that you'll try here is one that should work for everyone, whether you have a network established or just one standalone PC. The only important ingredient will be that you will need to have TCP/IP support compiled into your kernel. If you are running any one of the standard distributions, such as Red Hat Linux 6.0, then you should be all ready to go.

To test these programs out, perform the following:

1. Start the server program (with or without an optional IP number).

2. Start the client program (with or without the optional IP number of the server program).

3. Enter client program input.

4. Enter CTRL+D to close the client program (by signaling end-of-file). Alternatively, you may enter the word QUIT, which will cause both the client and server programs to exit.

In step 4, you might have a different end-of-file character for your terminal session, but CTRL+D is very common.

TIP

If you don't know what your terminal end-of-file character is, you can type the following command:

```
$ stty -a
```

In the output generated, you look for something like eof = ^D; to indicate that your end-of-file character is CTRL+D (the ^ symbol indicates a "control" character).

NOTE

To change your terminal end-of-file character to CTRL+D, for example, you can perform the following command:

```
$ stty eof \^d
```

To start your datagram server, perform the following:

```
$ ./dgramsrvr &
[1] 4405
$
```

The character & places the server program in the background so that you can continue to use your current terminal session to run the client program. In the example, the shell tells us that our server is running now as process ID 4405.

NOTE

The server program permits you to choose the IP number that it will listen for requests from. The port number in this program, however, is hard coded as port number 9090. To change the port number, you will need to change and recompile the server and the client programs.

With the server program up and running, it is now time for you to start up the client program and try it. The following shows how to start the client program and try it out.

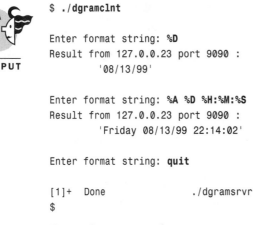

OUTPUT

```
$ ./dgramclnt

Enter format string: %D
Result from 127.0.0.23 port 9090 :
        '08/13/99'

Enter format string: %A %D %H:%M:%S
Result from 127.0.0.23 port 9090 :
        'Friday 08/13/99 22:14:02'

Enter format string: quit

[1]+  Done                  ./dgramsrvr
$
```

From the session shown, you can see that the client program prompts you for input. The first input was just the simple pair of characters %D and a RETURN. The result came back from the server as '08/13/99'. Note that the socket address of the datagram sender was reported, and it agreed with the server address that was expected (the program default). Another input of %A %D %H:%M:%S was tried with the server returning the result of 'Friday 08/13/99 22:14:02'. Finally, the input quit was provided, and both the client program and the server program exited.

Testing with No Server

The following shows what happens when the client program is run, and no server is running:

OUTPUT

```
$ ./dgramclnt

Enter format string: %D
Connection refused: recvfrom(2)
$
```

Note that the client program is able to start up, create the socket, and ask for input. Even the sendto(2) function was reported as successful (the error message came from the recvfrom(2) statement which follows the call to sendto(2)). This confirms the fact that sending a datagram only confirms that it was sent out—not that it was successfully received.

In this particular situation, the program was lucky enough to get an error response to indicate that no server was listening on that address and port. The error indication was picked up by the recvfrom(2) function call. When the client and server are separated by a large network and many routers, this error indication may not always be received.

In practice, you cannot rely on getting the error if the other end is not listening. For this reason, UDP programs often include the use of timers, and assume that no contact was made if no response is received within a certain amount of time.

Testing with Other IP Numbers

In the preceding sections, it was mentioned that an IP number could be given on the command line. If you have your own network set up, you can try running the client and server programs on different hosts. In the next example, the server will be started on host 192.168.0.1, and the client program will be run from 192.168.0.2. The following shows the server startup:

```
$ ./dgramsrvr 192.168.0.1 &
[1] 4416
$
```

OUTPUT

With the server successfully started up, the client program is invoked on the other host. The following session shows the output seen from the client end:

```
$ ./dgramclnt 192.168.0.1

Enter format string: %D
Result from 192.168.0.1 port 9090 :
          '08/13/99'

Enter format string: %A (%D)
Result from 192.168.0.1 port 9090 :
          'Friday (08/13/99)'

Enter format string: QUIT

$
```

OUTPUT

As shown, the client program was told that the server was located at address 192.168.0.1 by providing the address on the command line. A couple of examples were tried, and then the QUIT command was given. The pair of programs demonstrated themselves as working correctly.

While this example shows flawless execution, keep in mind that UDP is unreliable. If the client program fails to get a response from the server, it will hang (at line 111 in Listing 6.2). If you were writing a production mode application, you'd need to provide code for a timeout. This would allow the program to recover from the lack of a response when the original or response datagrams are lost.

Leaving Out `bind(2)` in Client Programs

Some observant readers might have noticed that no call to `bind(2)` was made in the client program for the socket that was created in Listing 6.2. If the `bind(2)` function call can be eliminated, then why bother with it at all?

You'll remember that in Chapter 5, "Binding Addresses to a Socket," there was a section titled "Interfaces and Addressing" which explained that the `bind(2)` function could be used to restrict the interfaces that would be used to perform communications. The example used in Figure 5.1 was a firewall application program that only wished to communicate with a trusted internal network. If this seems vague to you right now, you might want to turn back there and review how `bind(2)` accomplished this.

In Listing 6.2, the call to `bind(2)` was omitted. So what does this omission imply for the sending socket? As you know from Chapter 5, this actually indicates that the program will accept any outgoing interface, as required by the routing of the datagram to its destination. In effect, the socket is said to have a *wild socket address*. Later, when the program waits for a response, it will accept an input datagram from any incoming interface as well. Note also that this socket's port number is also wild. In this particular application, any client port number is acceptable.

You can explicitly request a wild address and port with a call to `bind(2)`. Listing 5.6 showed you how this was done by using the wild address `INADDR_NONE`. To request a wild port number, the port number is given as zero. By combining `INADDR_NONE` for the IP number and a port number of zero, you have requested that `bind(2)` give you the same wild address explicitly that you would have used without a call to `bind(2)`.

Replying to a Wild Address

If the client program's address and port number are wild, you might wonder how the server was able to reply to that particular socket. After all, how do you write a response back to the client without a specific IP address and UDP port number?

The answer to this question lies in the fact that an IP number and port number are assigned at the time the datagram is sent. The previous session shown occurred on the host with an IP number of `192.168.0.2`. When the client program called the `sendto(2)` function, the datagram was known to be destined for host IP number `192.168.0.1`. The routing tables indicated that the Ethernet interface with IP number `192.168.0.2` would be used to send the datagram to that host. Consequently, the sending datagram had a "from" address of `192.168.0.2`. This was the address seen at the server end. The port number, however, was wild and would have been chosen as any one of the free port numbers for the IP number chosen.

If another datagram is destined to a different network, then its "from" IP number will be different again. The "from" address will reflect the IP number of the network interface used to send the datagram.

This is an important concept to grasp and is perhaps one of the most difficult things for the beginner to grapple with. If your understanding is not yet complete on this, you should review Chapter 5 until you have a thorough understanding. As an exercise, you can add the following printf(3) statement to the server in Listing 6.1, immediately after the recvfrom(2) function call (after line 107):

```
printf("Client from %s port %u;\n",
    inet_ntoa(adr_clnt.sin_addr),
    (unsigned)ntohs(adr_clnt.sin_port));
```

EXAMPLE

With this line added, perform the following steps:

1. Kill or take down the existing server(s) if it (they) are still running.

2. Recompile the server dgramsrvr.

3. Restart the server (on 192.168.0.1, for example).

4. Run the client program again (from 192.168.0.2, for example).

The following line was displayed when the client on 192.168.0.2 sent the server on 192.168.0.1 a datagram:

```
Client from 192.168.0.2 port 1026;
```

OUTPUT

This confirms the fact that an IP number was assigned at the client end, and the port number assigned was 1026 in this example. This information enabled the server to direct its response back to the original requesting client.

If you lack a network, you can still perform this experiment on your standalone PC. First, start the server, using its default address:

```
$ ./dgramsrvr &
```

OUTPUT

Now run your client program:

```
$ ./dgramclnt
```

The output of your server program and client program will mix if run from the same terminal window (you can, however, run them from separate windows if you like). The following session shows the server and client output, when they are run on a single standalone PC, within the same terminal window.

```
$ ./dgramsrvr &
[1] 733
$ ./dgramclnt
```

OUTPUT

```
Enter format string: %D
Client from 127.0.0.23 port 1027;
Result from 127.0.0.23 port 9090 :
        '08/15/99'

Enter format string: %A %D
Client from 127.0.0.23 port 1027;
Result from 127.0.0.23 port 9090 :
          'Sunday 08/15/99'

Enter format string: QUIT
Client from 127.0.0.23 port 1027;


[1]+  Done                  ./dgramsrvr
$
```

Notice that for all datagrams sent to the server, the datagram from address was reported as

```
Client from 127.0.0.23 port 1027;
```

Again, this confirms that the correct IP address and a final port number are assigned upon demand, whenever bind(2) is not used on the client's sending socket.

What's Next

This chapter introduced you to the concept of connectionless- and connection-oriented communication. The UDP protocol was used to explore and demonstrate this connectionless mode of communication.

You have demonstrated your ability to write a client and server program using the UDP network protocol. Don't stop here, however, because UDP isn't always the best choice for applications.

The next chapter will show you another mode of communication for client and server. There you will learn about the connection mode of communication using a TCP/IP client program. So, hang onto your red hat!

Connection-Oriented Protocols for Clients

You'll recall from the last chapter that there are two basic modes of communication for sockets. They are connection and connectionless modes of communication. In the last chapter, you also saw how the UDP protocol could be used to communicate in a connectionless fashion. In this chapter, you'll put the TCP/IP protocol to use, using a connection-oriented form of communication.

This chapter will introduce you to

- The advantages of connection-oriented protocols
- The /etc/services file and its support routines
- The /etc/protocols file and its support routines
- The connect(2) function
- How to write a TCP/IP client program

Before you jump in and write your first client program, however, a quick review and an introduction to connection-oriented communications is in order. Additionally, you'll learn about some of the support functions that are often used by TCP/IP programs that locate service and protocol information.

Reviewing the Methods of Communication

It was also noted in the last chapter that connectionless-oriented communication is simpler and more flexible. But you'll see that connection-oriented communication is not really that much more difficult. It does require additional steps, however, and mostly on the server side. A connection is also much more rigid, because after the connection has been established, the socket can only communicate with the connected endpoint.

The selling point in favor of TCP/IP for most application writers is that the communication channel is transparently reliable and that data is delivered in the proper sequence. After the connection has been established, your application can read and write to the socket without worrying about any of the following problems:

- Lost packets

- Timeouts and retransmissions

- Duplicated packets

- Packets received out of sequence

- Flow control

Like opening a file, your program can

1. Establish a TCP/IP connection with a remote socket

2. Transmit large amounts of data

3. Close the socket

These simple steps are all that is necessary to deliver all of your data safely to the remote end. Proven error recovery software will take care of retransmitting lost packets until they can be successfully delivered to the remote host.

TCP/IP Handles Lost Packets

TCP/IP will notice when packets are lost. This does not always happen with UDP. When packet errors are reported, the TCP/IP protocol can immediately respond with retransmissions. However, if an acknowledgement is missing, causing a timeout, the TCP/IP protocol takes steps to ensure that the data is retransmitted to its destination. Carefully crafted algorithms are used to make the transmission of the data nimble, without taxing the network capacity with retransmitted data.

TCP/IP Handles Duplicated Packets

Whenever a retransmission occurs, there is a slight possibility that more than one identical packet can be received at the remote end. If the retransmission occurs too early, for example, this can easily happen. The receiving end must be able to recognize this and discard extraneous packets. This is automatically performed by the TCP/IP protocol.

TCP/IP Handles Sequencing

When the volume of data requires multiple packets to be sent, there is a race to the finish line. The IP packet can be routed in different ways, according to dynamic routing and buffer congestion. This results in a race to the receiving end, where some packets can arrive ahead of other packets. For this reason, the receiving software must recognize this and sequence the data before presenting it to the application. Again, TCP/IP anticipates and corrects this problem.

TCP/IP Handles Flow Control

The `ftp` command uses TCP/IP to send and receive files. When you upload a large file to a remote ftp server, using the `ftp send` command, many data packets are placed on the network. It can happen that the receiving host can end up receiving packets faster than it can process them. The IP way of dealing with this problem is to discard these extra packets.

TCP logically sits on top of the IP protocol like a layer (hence, it is called TCP/IP). It acts as a supervisor of sorts by ensuring that the receiving end is not overloaded with more data than it can handle. When the receiving end feels that it has enough data for the moment, it notifies the sending end not to send more data until further notice. When it catches up, the remote end will signal the sending end to start sending data again. This automatic throttling of data is known as *flow control*.

Understanding the Advantages of TCP/IP

The purpose of this introduction was to show you the advantage of using a connection-oriented protocol. TCP/IP is one such connection-oriented protocol, which you will explore in this chapter. You have seen the number of services it performs for you behind the scenes. This helps you to focus on your application programming, rather than network communication problems. Furthermore, because the same time-tested algorithms are at work for each program that uses TCP/IP, they perform in the same reliable manner. This allows you to focus on application program bugs instead.

Internet Services

Before you have fun working with TCP/IP in this chapter, you need to learn about some additional facilities as TCP/IP pertains to Internet services.

Examining the /etc/services File

Your Linux system has a text file, usually named /etc/services. This file is described in the man page services(5). This file maps the user-friendly names of certain Internet services to a port number and protocol. The precise pathname for this file is given by the C language macro _PATH_SERVICES. A simple example of its use follows:

```
#include <netdb.h>

printf("File is path '%s'\n", _PATH_SERVICES);
```

EXAMPLE The preceding code shows the necessary include file netdb.h and a printf(3) statement, which prints out the pathname for the services file.

Each text line in the /etc/services file describes one Internet service. It has the following general format:

```
service-name    port/protocol    [alias ...]
```

The square brackets shown indicate that the one or more alias entries are optional. The /etc/services text line is described in detail in Table 7.1.

Table 7.1: The /etc/services Fields

Field	Description
service-name	The case-sensitive user-friendly name of the service is described by this table entry.
port	The port number precedes the slash, and is the decimal port number for the service.
/	This separates the port number from the protocol field.
protocol	This specifies the type of the protocol to be used. This should be a protocol that can be found in the protocols(5) file. Common examples are udp or tcp.
alias	Other names for the "service-name." Additional aliases can be separated by tabs or spaces. There is a maximum of 35 aliases permitted, due to restrictions in getservent(3).

Following is a pair of well-known service entries:

```
ftp      21/tcp
telnet   23/tcp
```

The first entry shown lists the ftp service as being available on TCP/IP port 21. The second entry shows the telnet service being available on TCP/IP port 23.

Working with the /etc/services file directly is neither convenient nor wise for your program. Consequently, Linux provides you with some routines to make things easier.

Using Function getservent(3)

If you have used some of the password database functions like getpwent(3) before, the functions about to be described here will seem similar. The synopsis of the getservent(3) function is as follows:

```
#include <netdb.h>

struct servent *getservent(void);
```

For each call to getservent(3), you are returned a pointer to a structure that represents one entry from the /etc/services file. When the end-of-file is reached, a NULL pointer is returned (but see the caution that follows). If an error occurs, a NULL pointer is also returned, with the reason for the error posted to variable errno.

CAUTION

Even when the value of errno is zeroed prior to calling getservent(3), when end-of-file is reached and indicated by a NULL return pointer, the errno value for Red Hat Linux 6.0 is code ENOENT.

Under other UNIX operating systems, such as HP-UX 10.2 and Sun Solaris 5.5.1, the errno value is left at zero when end-of-file is returned. This leads the author to speculate that this behavior is a bug, which might be corrected in a later release of Linux.

When the pointer returned is not NULL, it points to the structure servent, as illustrated in Listing 7.1.

EXAMPLE

Listing 7.1: The struct servent Structure

```
struct servent {
    char    *s_name;  /* official service name */
    char    **s_aliases;        /* alias list */
    int     s_port;             /* port number */
    char    *s_proto;        /* protocol to use */
}
```

CAUTION

Be careful to note that the value in s_port is already in network byte order. To print this value in printf(3), for example, make sure you convert this value back to host order by using ntohs(sp->s_port), for example.

When setting the port number in a socket address, you merely assign this value as-is, since the port number is expected to be in network byte order. Listing 7.7 later in this chapter shows an example of this use.

The structure member s_aliases is actually an array of character pointers. If sp points to the structure, and x is an int subscript, then you can iterate through each alias sp->s_alias[x], until you reach a NULL pointer. A NULL pointer marks the end of this alias list. Listing 7.2 shows a simple program that lists all /etc/services entries and their aliases, if any.

EXAMPLE

Listing 7.2: servent.c—A Program to List All Services

```
1:    /* servent.c:
2:     *
3:     * Example getservent(3) program:
4:     */
5:    #include <stdio.h>
6:    #include <unistd.h>
7:    #include <stdlib.h>
8:    #include <errno.h>
9:    #include <string.h>
10:   #include <netdb.h>
11:   #include <netinet/in.h>
12:
13:   int
14:   main(int argc,char **argv) {
15:       int x;
16:       struct servent *sp;
17:
18:       for (;;) {
19:           errno = 0;
20:           if ( !(sp = getservent()) )
21:               break;
22:
23:           printf("%s:\n"
24:               "\tPort:     %d\n"
25:               "\tProtocol: %s\n"
26:               "\tAliases:  ",
27:               sp->s_name,
28:               ntohs(sp->s_port),
29:               sp->s_proto);
30:           for ( x=0; sp->s_aliases[x] != NULL; ++x )
31:               printf("%s ",sp->s_aliases[x]);
32:           putchar('\n');
33:       }
34:
35:       if ( errno != 0
36:       &&   errno != ENOENT ) /* For RH-6.0 */
37:           fprintf(stderr,
38:               "%s: getservent(3) %d\n",
39:               strerror(errno),errno);
40:
```

```
41:     return 0;
42: }
```

The program in Listing 7.2 uses the following basic steps:

1. Calls getservent(3) to obtain an entry from the /etc/services file.

2. Prints the service name, port, and protocol.

3. In an internal loop, prints all alias names, if any.

4. Repeats step 1, until there are no more entries.

Now looking at the program in more detail:

1. Line 10 shows that netdb.h was included. This defines the function prototype for getservent(3). Line 11 includes netinet/in.h to define ntohs(), which is used in line 28.

2. Line 16 declares a pointer to struct servent, which is named as sp.

3. Line 19 zeros the value of errno. The author suspects that getservent(3) should leave errno as zero when end-of-file is reached. However, Red Hat Linux 6.0 returns with ENOENT in errno at present, when end-of-file is reached. Just be aware that this might be fixed in the future.

4. The pointer is returned from getservent(3) and assigned to variable sp (line 20). If the pointer is NULL, line 21 breaks out of the loop.

5. Lines 23 to 29 display the service name, port, and protocol.

6. Lines 30 and 31 report all aliases, if any.

7. The program repeats step 3 until no more entries remain in the /etc/services file.

8. Lines 35 and 36 try to distinguish between end-of-file and an error. Red Hat Linux 6.0 indicates ENOENT, but zero may be indicated in the future (if this behavior is indeed a bug).

9. Lines 37 to 39 report the error, if step 8 identifies that an error has occurred.

CAUTION

The pointer returned by getservent(3) is only valid until the next call to the same function.

Listing 7.3 shows how to compile and run the program in Listing 7.2. In this example, the output was piped to the head command to show only the first few lines of output.

OUTPUT

Listing 7.3: Compiling and Running `servent.c` from Listing 7.2

```
$ make servent
gcc -c  -D_GNU_SOURCE -Wall servent.c
gcc servent.o -o servent
$ ./servent | head
tcpmux:
        Port:    1
        Protocol: tcp
        Aliases:
echo:
        Port:    7
        Protocol: tcp
        Aliases:
echo:
        Port:    7
Broken pipe
$
```

The error message "Broken pipe" in Listing 7.3 is simply due to the head command being used (it closed the pipe early). There are some companions to the getservent(3) function, and these will be covered next.

Using the `setservent(3)` Function

The setservent(3) function allows you to rewind the file that is opened behind the scenes in the function getservent(3). For example, if you were to try to process entries a second time in Listing 7.2, you would need setservent(3) to rewind to the start of the /etc/services file. Otherwise, you will just continue to receive end-of-file indications. The function synopsis is as follows:

```
#include <netdb.h>

void setservent(int stayopen);
```

This function takes one argument, which is a Boolean value:

- When non-zero (TRUE), the stayopen argument indicates that the file should be rewound instead of re-opened when rereading the /etc/services file is performed. This is preferred for performance reasons.

- When zero (FALSE), the file is closed if it has been previously opened (by getservent(3), for example). Then the function re-opens the file to make ready for the next getservent(3) call.

There is no return value for this function.

Using the endservent(3) Function

The function getservent(3) opens the /etc/services file behind the scenes, before returning a pointer to an entry. If your application has determined that it no longer needs to read more entries, then the endservent(3) function can be used to cause the file to be closed. This is especially important in server programs where the number of open file descriptors may be at a premium. The function synopsis is as follows:

```
#include <netdb.h>

void endservent(void);
```

There is no argument, no return value, and no errors to test.

Looking Up a Service by Name and Protocol

The previously introduced functions enable you to scan the /etc/services file one entry at a time. Often, however, this still proves to be inconvenient because of the amount of code involved. Instead, it would be more convenient to supply the service name and protocol, and have a function return the required entry. The getservbyname(3) function does just that. The function synopsis is as follows:

```
#include <netdb.h>

struct servent *getservbyname(const char *name, const char *proto);
```

The arguments to the function are as follows:

1. The service name to look up. For example, "telnet" could be used.

2. The protocol to be used (proto). Often a service will be available using UDP or TCP/IP. Consequently, you must specify the protocol that you are willing to use in order to contact that service. An example would be "tcp."

The value returned is NULL if the service cannot be found. Otherwise, a pointer to a structure servent is returned. An example of its use is shown as follows:

EXAMPLE

```
struct servent *sp;

sp = getservbyname("telnet","tcp");
if ( !sp )
    abort(); /* No such service! */
```

If the function call is successful, the structure pointer sp will point to all of the pertinent details, including the port number.

CAUTION

The pointer returned by getservbyname(3) is only valid until the next call to the same function.

Looking Up a Service by Port and Protocol

You saw in the last section that it was possible to look up a service by name and protocol. The function getservbyport(3) allows you to also perform a lookup by port and protocol. The function synopsis is as follows:

```
#include <netdb.h>

struct servent *getservbyport(int port, const char *proto);
```

The function arguments are as follows:

1. The port number for this Internet protocol.

2. The protocol proto to be looked up for port.

The function returns a NULL pointer if no service entry can be found to match your input parameters. Otherwise, a pointer is returned to the structure containing information, such as the service name, for example.

CAUTION

The pointer returned by getservbyport(3) is only valid until the next call to the same function.

Consulting the /etc/protocols File

Earlier, in Table 7.1, there was mention made that the protocol used there must appear in the protocols(5) table. The text file /etc/protocols acts as a mini-database of various defined Internet protocol values. There is a set of functions, which perform in a very similar manner to the service entry functions that were just covered. These act as convenience functions, should you need them. These functions are so similar, in fact, that they do not need to be covered in detail. The function synopsis of getprotoent(3) is as follows:

```
#include <netdb.h>

struct protoent *getprotoent(void);
```

The getprotoent(3) function returns one /etc/protocols entry with each call. A NULL pointer is returned when end-of-file or an error has been encountered. Listing 7.4 shows the protoent structure that is returned by the function call.

EXAMPLE

Listing 7.4: The struct protoent Structure

```
struct protoent {
    char    *p_name; /* official protocol name */
    char    **p_aliases;          /* alias list */
    int     p_proto;         /* protocol number */
}
```

The structure members are more fully described as follows:

- The structure member p_name contains a pointer to a C string that names the protocol (for example "tcp").

- The member p_aliases is a pointer to an array of C string pointers, of which the last entry is a NULL pointer. If pp points to this structure, then pp->p_aliases[0] contains the first C string (or is NULL when there are no aliases). An example of an alias might be "TCP" (the uppercase name of the protocol is often specified as an alias).

- The member p_proto contains the protocol number. For example, the protocol number found in /etc/protocols for entry "tcp" should agree with the C macro constant IPPROTO_TCP. If you check with /usr/include/netinet/in.h and with the value in /etc/protocols, you will indeed see that they both have the value 6.

The getprotoent(3) function returns a NULL pointer when end-of-file is reached or when an error has been encountered.

Listing 7.5 shows a demonstration program that iterates through all of the /etc/protocols database entries.

Listing 7.5: protoent.c—The getprotoent(3) Demo Program

```
1:   /* protoent.c:
2:    *
3:    * Example getprotoent(3) program:
4:    */
5:   #include <stdio.h>
6:   #include <unistd.h>
7:   #include <stdlib.h>
8:   #include <errno.h>
9:   #include <string.h>
10:  #include <netdb.h>
11:
12:  int
13:  main(int argc,char **argv) {
14:      int x;
15:      struct protoent *pp;
16:
17:      for (;;) {
18:          errno = 0;
19:          if ( !(pp = getprotoent()) )
20:              break;
21:
22:          printf("%s:\n"
23:              "\tProtocol: %d\n"
24:              "\tAliases:  ",
25:              pp->p_name,
26:              pp->p_proto);
27:          for ( x=0; pp->p_aliases[x] != NULL; ++x )
28:              printf("%s ",pp->p_aliases[x]);
29:          putchar('\n');
30:      }
31:
32:      if ( errno != 0
33:      &&   errno != ENOENT ) /* For RH-6.0 */
34:          fprintf(stderr,
35:              "%s: getprotoent(3) %d\n",
36:              strerror(errno),errno);
37:
38:      return 0;
39:  }
```

The program code in Listing 7.5 is so similar to the program in Listing 7.2 that only the basic steps need to be repeated here. They are

1. Call getprotoent(3) to obtain an entry from the /etc/protocols file.

2. Print the protocol name and the protocol number.

3. In an internal loop, print all protocol alias names, if any.

4. Repeat step 1 until there are no more protocol entries.

Listing 7.6 shows how to compile and run the demonstration program.

Listing 7.6: Compiling and Running the protoent.c Program

```
$ make protoent
gcc -c  -D_GNU_SOURCE -Wall protoent.c
gcc protoent.o -o protoent
$ ./protoent | head
ip:
        Protocol: 0
        Aliases:  IP
icmp:
        Protocol: 1
        Aliases:  ICMP
igmp:
        Protocol: 2
        Aliases:  IGMP
ggp:
$
```

The example command session in Listing 7.6 had its output piped to the head command to keep the listing short. Notice the protocol name of the first entry shown was "ip" and its one and only alias was the uppercase name "IP".

Using the setprotoent(3) Function

The file that is opened implicitly for getprotoent(3) can be rewound by calling the setprotoent(3) function. The function synopsis for it is as follows:

```
#include <netdb.h>

void setprotoent(int stayopen);
```

This function accepts one argument, stayopen, which is interpreted as a Boolean value:

- When stayopen is non-zero (TRUE), this indicates that the implicitly opened file is left opened and merely rewound to the start of the file.

- When stayopen is zero (FALSE), this indicates that the implicitly opened file is closed and then re-opened, effectively rewinding the file.

Best performance is obtained by setting stayopen as TRUE.

Using the `endprotoent(3)` Function

When your program is finished consulting with the `/etc/protocols` file, it can request that the implicitly opened file be closed. This is especially important for server programs to do, because file descriptors are often scarce. The function prototype for `endprotoent(3)` is given as follows:

```
#include <netdb.h>

void endprotoent(void);
```

There are no arguments to this function, and there are no return value or errors to check.

Looking Up a Protocol by Name

Sometimes it is necessary for an application program or utility program, which can work with multiple protocols, to look up a protocol by name. While this can be done by using the previous functions, `getprotobyname(3)` saves the programmer some effort. The function prototype is as follows:

```
#include <netdb.h>

struct protoent *getprotobyname(const char *name);
```

The one input argument is a C string containing the protocol name (`"udp"`, for example). The value returned is a pointer to the `protoent` structure, or is a `NULL` pointer, indicating that it could not be found.

CAUTION

The pointer returned by `getprotobyname(3)` is only valid until the next call to the same function.

Looking Up a Protocol by Number

When your application has the protocol number, and it needs to display it in human readable terms, the `getprotobynumber(3)` routine is used. The function prototype is as follows:

```
#include <netdb.h>

struct protoent *getprotobynumber(int proto);
```

This function accepts the protocol number as the input argument, and returns the pointer to a `protoent` structure if a match is found. Otherwise, the `NULL` pointer is returned to indicate that the protocol is not known by the mini-database. For example, if the input argument is 6 (or the C macro constant `IPPROTO_TCP`), then you should get a structure pointer returned that has the value `"tcp"` in the member p_name.

CAUTION

The pointer returned by getprotobynumber(3) is only valid until the next call to the same function.

This brings you to the end of the getservent(3) and the getprotoent(3) function families. Now that you know how to look up Internet-related services and protocols, it is time to write a connection-oriented client program using TCP/IP.

Writing a TCP/IP Client Program

Using TCP/IP for a connected pair of sockets requires that a slightly different procedure be used from the one you used when using the UDP protocol in the previous chapter. From the client program's point of view, you must perform the following general steps:

1. Create a socket.

2. Optionally bind the socket (to restrict which interface will be used, or to explicitly indicate a wild socket address).

3. Connect to the remote socket (client connects to the server).

4. Communicate with reads and writes.

5. Shut down or close the socket.

When you used the UDP protocol, you performed all of the above steps except for step 3. You never had to connect to anything, because you were using a connectionless protocol. The next section will describe a new socket function for you.

Introducing the connect(2) Function

In order to establish a connection with sockets, you call upon the connect(2) function. Its function synopsis is as follows:

```
#include <sys/types.h>
#include <sys/socket.h>

int connect(int sockfd, struct sockaddr *serv_addr, int addrlen);
```

This function takes three arguments. They are

1. The socket file descriptor sockfd that was returned by a former call to socket(2).

2. The server address serv_addr that the program is connecting to.

3. The length addrlen of the server address in bytes.

The server address and the server address length are the same socket address values that you would have supplied in a call to the sendto(2) function, if you were using UDP. The difference with connection-oriented protocols, however, is that you only establish the destination address *once*. After this function succeeds, all future communications will be with the socket addressed here.

When the function call is successful, the return value is zero. Otherwise, -1 is returned to indicate that an error has occurred, and the nature of the error is recorded in the variable errno.

Preparing to Write the Client Program

To keep the client program short and allow you to focus upon the basic principles, the demonstration program is going to connect to an existing service you have running on your system. The client program will connect to your daytime service to retrieve the current date and time string.

Before the program is presented, however, you should make sure that this service is enabled and operational on your system. As a first step, perform the following:

OUTPUT

```
$ grep daytime /etc/services
daytime         13/tcp
daytime         13/udp
$
```

You should see that your system recognizes the daytime Internet service and that it is available on port 13 using tcp. The first line of grep output confirms this for you.

TIP

The telnet program can often be used to perform simple tests with TCP/IP servers. It is very important, however, to remember to specify the port number after the IP number (or hostname) on the command line. Otherwise, the port number will default to 23, which is the telnet service!

To test the daytime service, for example, you must specify the port number 13 after the IP number on the command line.

The next step is to make sure it is operational. The telnet program is a program that is often usable for simple tests when TCP/IP is used. To test that the daytime service is running, you should be able to perform the following:

OUTPUT

```
$ telnet 127.0.0.1 13
Trying 127.0.0.1...
Connected to 127.0.0.1.
Escape character is '^]'.
Tue Aug 17 17:59:30 1999
```

```
Connection closed by foreign host.
$
```

Make sure you specify the protocol number 13 after the IP number 127.0.0.1 (you can use a remote IP number, but for this testing procedure stick to 127.0.0.1). If your daytime service is running, you should get a date and time string displayed, which is followed by the message "Connection closed by foreign host."

If the service is not available, you will see output similar to this:

```
$ telnet 127.0.0.1 13
Trying 127.0.0.1...
telnet: Unable to connect to remote host: Connection refused
$
```

If you do, then this indicates that your daytime service is not running. To troubleshoot this problem, examine your /etc/inetd.conf file:

```
$ grep daytime /etc/inetd.conf
# Echo, discard, daytime, and chargen are used
#daytime stream  tcp  nowait  root     internal
#daytime dgram   udp  wait    root     internal
$
```

As shown in this case, the daytime service entry in the file has a # character in the first column. This effectively "comments out" the service, which makes it unavailable. This may have been done as a precaution against attacks from the Internet or other hostile users in your network (it's a general principle to disable any Internet service that you do not deem as necessary). To try out the client example program, you will need to enable the tcp daytime service entry (the udp service entry can be left commented out if it is already).

To fix the service, edit the file /etc/inetd.conf by removing the leading # character for the daytime entry that includes the protocol tcp in it. Check it with grep again, and you should see something like the following:

```
$ grep daytime /etc/inetd.conf
# Echo, discard, daytime, and chargen are used
daytime stream  tcp  nowait  root     internal
#daytime dgram   udp  wait    root     internal
$
```

After making changes to the /etc/inetd.conf file, you must tell the inetd daemon to re-read and reprocess the changed file. This is done as follows:

```
$ su -
Password:
# ps ax | grep inetd
  313 ?        S      0:00 inetd
  828 pts/1    S      0:00 grep inetd
# kill -1 313
#
```

CAUTION

Symbolic signal names in commands such as the kill command are being promoted these days. One reason to use these symbolic symbol names is for safety against typing errors. For example, the command "kill -1 313" can be typed as:

kill -HUP 313

Some users (author included) prefer to live dangerously and have resisted making this change.

The above session accomplishes the following:

1. The su command is used to change to the root account.

2. Then you find out what the process ID of the inetd daemon is. The ps command indicates in the example that the process ID is 313 for the inetd daemon process (your process ID may be different).

3. The kill -1 313 command is used to send the signal SIGHUP to process ID 313 (your process ID may be different). Be sure to not forget the -1 (or -HUP) argument on the command line. Otherwise, you'll kill off your inetd daemon!

Having done all of this, you should now be able to repeat the telnet test and verify that it works.

The daytime Client Program

The program shown in Listing 7.7 performs the following simple steps:

1. Looks up the daytime service for the tcp protocol.

2. Connects to your PC's daytime server, using tcp.

3. Reads the server date and time string that it sends back to your socket.

4. Reports the data and time string to your terminal session.

5. Closes the socket and exits back to the shell.

The client program in Listing 7.7 is presented next.

EXAMPLE

Listing 7.7: daytime.c—The Client daytime Demo Program

```
1:   /* daytime.c:
2:    *
3:    * Example daytime client:
4:    */
5:   #include <stdio.h>
6:   #include <unistd.h>
7:   #include <stdlib.h>
```

```
8:    #include <errno.h>
9:    #include <string.h>
10:   #include <sys/types.h>
11:   #include <sys/socket.h>
12:   #include <netinet/in.h>
13:   #include <arpa/inet.h>
14:   #include <netdb.h>
15:
16:   /*
17:    * This function reports the error and
18:    * exits back to the shell:
19:    */
20:   static void
21:   bail(const char *on_what) {
22:       fputs(strerror(errno),stderr);
23:       fputs(": ",stderr);
24:       fputs(on_what,stderr);
25:       fputc('\n',stderr);
26:       exit(1);
27:   }
28:
29:   int
30:   main(int argc,char **argv) {
31:       int z;
32:       char *srvr_addr = NULL;
33:       struct sockaddr_in adr_srvr;/* AF_INET */
34:       int len_inet;                /* length  */
35:       int s;                        /* Socket */
36:       struct servent *sp;   /* Service entry */
37:       char dtbuf[128];      /* Date/Time info */
38:
39:       /*
40:        * Use a server address from the command
41:        * line, if one has been provided.
42:        * Otherwise, this program will default
43:        * to using the arbitrary address
44:        * 127.0.0.1:
45:        */
46:       if ( argc >= 2 ) {
47:           /* Addr on cmdline: */
48:           srvr_addr = argv[1];
49:       } else {
50:           /* Use default address: */
51:           srvr_addr = "127.0.0.1";
52:       }
53:
```

continues

Listing 7.7: continued

```
54:      /*
55:       * Lookup the daytime tcp service:
56:       */
57:      sp = getservbyname("daytime","tcp");
58:      if ( !sp ) {
59:          fputs("Unknown service: daytime tcp\n",
60:                  stderr);
61:          exit(1);
62:      }
63:
64:      /*
65:       * Create a server socket address:
66:       */
67:      memset(&adr_srvr,0,sizeof adr_srvr);
68:      adr_srvr.sin_family = AF_INET;
69:      adr_srvr.sin_port = sp->s_port;
70:      adr_srvr.sin_addr.s_addr =
71:          inet_addr(srvr_addr);
72:
73:      if ( adr_srvr.sin_addr.s_addr == INADDR_NONE )
74:          bail("bad address.");
75:
76:      len_inet = sizeof adr_srvr;
77:
78:      /*
79:       * Create a TCP/IP socket to use:
80:       */
81:      s = socket(PF_INET,SOCK_STREAM,0);
82:      if ( s == -1 )
83:          bail("socket()");
84:
85:      /*
86:       * Connect to the server:
87:       */
88:      z = connect(s,&adr_srvr,len_inet);
89:      if ( z == -1 )
90:          bail("connect(2)");
91:
92:      /*
93:       * Read the date/time info:
94:       */
95:      z = read(s,&dtbuf,sizeof dtbuf-1);
96:      if ( z == -1 )
97:          bail("read(2)");
98:
99:      /*
```

```
100:        * Report the Date & Time:
101:        */
102:       dtbuf[z] = 0;    /* null terminate string */
103:
104:       printf("Date & Time is: %s\n",dtbuf);
105:
106:       /*
107:        * Close the socket and exit:
108:        */
109:       close(s);
110:       putchar('\n');
111:
112:       return 0;
113: }
```

The program can be described in more detail, as follows:

1. The program will use an IP number on the command line if provided (line 48), but otherwise defaults to your local host (also known as localhost) by using the local loopback address 127.0.0.1 (line 51). The IP number on the command line allows the user to test the daytime service on another remote host. This is particularly useful if it is turned off on the local host and the service is available somewhere else.

2. Line 57 looks up the daytime Internet service for use over TCP/IP. If this service is not found, the problem is reported in lines 59 to 61.

3. The server's address and the length of the address are established in lines 67 to 76. Note especially line 69 where the service port number is established for the daytime service.

4. The socket is created in line 81. Note especially the argument SOCK_STREAM that specifies that we want a TCP/IP socket (when used with PF_INET).

5. The program connects to the server in line 88. If this fails, the error is handled in line 90.

6. Line 95 shows a read(2) call that retrieves the output from the server. The return value indicates the number of bytes read. Otherwise, the error is dealt with in line 97.

7. Line 102 makes certain that we have a terminating null byte, so that the buffer dtbuf[] can be treated like a C string.

8. Line 104 reports the value returned by the server.

9. The socket is closed in line 109.

Listing 7.8 shows an example compile and run session for this demo program.

EXAMPLE

Listing 7.8: Compiling and Running the daytime Client Program

```
$ make daytime
gcc -c  -D_GNU_SOURCE -Wall daytime.c
gcc daytime.o -o daytime
$ ./daytime
Date & Time is: Tue Aug 17 18:41:42 1999

$
```

There is an extra newline emitted by the program, because the server places a '\n' at the end of the date and time information that is sent to the client program.

Using connect(2) on SOCK_DGRAM Sockets

The connect(2) function was introduced to you in this chapter for use with connection-oriented protocols. Before moving onto the next chapter, however, it should be noted that there is an exception to this rule.

The connect(2) function can be used with UDP sockets (SOCK_DGRAM for protocol family PF_INET). This does not actually imply a connection, however, but instead imposes some restrictions upon how the UDP socket will be used. This function call should be made

1. After the bind(2) function is called, if used.

2. Before any datagrams are read or written on the socket.

When connect(2) is used on a UDP socket, this indicates that all packets written will be addressed to the destination indicated in the server address specified (argument 2). This also implies that this socket is only interested in receiving datagrams from the same server. This prevents stray datagrams from being received from other sockets, which is otherwise possible with UDP. The kernel will eliminate unwanted UDP datagrams from being received by your UDP socket.

One other advantage to this technique is that it permits the caller to use the read(2) and write(2) system calls instead of the sendto(2) and recvfrom(2) functions. This saves the programmer from having to provide socket address structures and lengths for each I/O operation.

What's Next

This chapter introduced you to the concept of a connection-oriented form of communication. The client program demonstrated that it must connect to its server before performing any I/O.

The next chapter will introduce you to the server's point of view and the different steps that it must perform. You'll also learn about two new important socket functions that you have yet to see in this book.

8

Connection-Oriented Protocols for Servers

The last chapter showed you how to write a connection-oriented client program. The server program that the client connects to must use a different procedure, however. This chapter will teach you about the role of the server, including the following topics:

- The basic steps used by connection-oriented servers
- Why the bind(2) function is necessary for servers
- The listen(2) function and its role
- The accept(2) function and its role
- How to write a connection-oriented server program

With these topics mastered, you will be equipped to program your own custom server programs.

Understanding the Role of the Server

In the last chapter you saw how a client program connected to a server process. Compared to connectionless communication, from the client's point of view, the only new step was the "connect" step. The connection was established by use of the connect(2) function.

You will recall that the client program required five basic steps. In their simplest form, these are shown in Figure 8.1 on the left side of the figure, as steps C1 through C5. Steps S1 through S6 depict the six basic steps that a server program will use. The steps shown flow from top to bottom. Two dotted horizontal lines with arrows in the center of the figure show how these events form a relationship between the client and server programs. Figure 8.1 represents the simplest form that a server can take. This model will be further enhanced as you progress through this chapter.

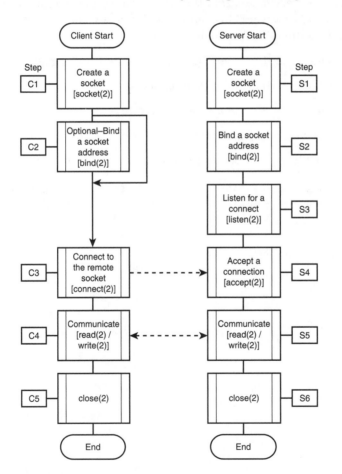

Figure 8.1: *Study and compare these connection steps for client and server connections.*

The basic steps of the server can now be summarized as follows:

1. Create a socket.

2. Bind a socket address (mandatory).

3. Listen for a connection.

4. Accept a connection.

5. Communicate with the client program.

6. Close the socket.

Notice that, for the server, the `bind(2)` step 2 (S2 in Figure 8.1) is not optional. The server cannot be contacted by clients unless the client has an address for connecting. On the other hand, the client `bind(2)` step C2 is optional. In order for a server to be contacted, then, a server address cannot be completely wild.

Notice also that step 3 (S3 in Figure 8.1) is something new. The server must express its interest in accepting connections to the kernel for its socket. This will be discussed further when the `listen(2)` function is covered.

The process of accepting a connection in step 4 (S4 in Figure 8.1) is another new socket concept. Once a client has connected to the server, the server must then accept the connection. This will be covered in detail when the `accept(2)` function is covered later in this chapter.

Briefly, the server differs from the client in the following ways:

- The server must bind a server address to the socket.

- The server listens for a connection.

- The server accepts connections.

The `listen(2)` Function

The `listen(2)` function is how the server is able to express its interest in listening for connections. The function is very simple to call, and its function prototype is given as follows:

```
#include <sys/socket.h>

int listen(int s,int backlog);
```

The two input arguments are the following:

- The socket s to use as the listening socket.

- The `backlog`, which specifies the connect queue length in entries.

The function returns zero when it is successful. Otherwise –1 is returned, and the reason for the error is posted to errno.

Understanding the Connect Queue

It might seem odd that the application programmer would have to supply something apparently so cryptic as a backlog parameter value in the call to the listen(2) function. However, there is a sound reason for it. Figure 8.2 shows the general activity of the very popular www.woohoo.com Web server.

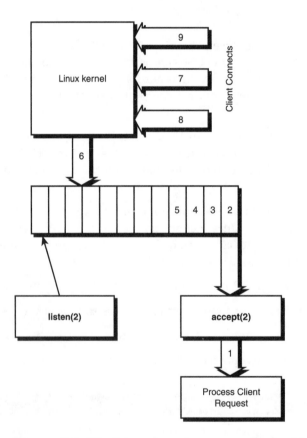

Figure 8.2: *The Linux kernel manages the backlog queue when accepting new connections.*

Notice the block in Figure 8.2 that is labeled listen(2). This block represents the call to listen(2), which establishes a listening queue. A small arrow points up to the queue it established, which resides within the Linux kernel. The length of this queue is determined by the backlog argument of the listen(2) call.

Now look at the block at the bottom right of Figure 8.2. This block is labeled "Process Client Request." The arrow labeled as number one represents the very first connection into your server. In Figure 8.2, this connection has just been accepted by the accept(2) function call and is currently being processed by your server code.

However, while server processing is taking place on the first client connection, more connection requests are coming into your server from all over the world. Within the queue that listen(2) established, you have connect requests two through five pending and waiting to be accepted.

Figure 8.2 shows another connect request being inserted into the tail end of the queue as request number six by the Linux kernel. Even as that is happening, connect requests seven, eight, and nine are being received. A busy server indeed!

The thrust of Figure 8.2 has been to demonstrate the purpose of the backlog argument, within the listen(2) function call. As you have seen, this parameter sets the length of the incoming queue. Now that you understand its purpose, let's discuss what practical values should be used in this parameter.

Specifying a Value for backlog

Historically, the value of backlog in the listen(2) call has been less than precise. In the early days of UNIX, the value 5 was commonly used. However, with the faster and busier systems of today, this value might not be suitable for your server application. So how does one determine a reasonable value?

UNIX literature advises not to use a value of 0 in the backlog argument. This is good advice to programmers writing applications that must be ported to various flavors of UNIX, including Linux. The reason is that for some platforms this means no connections are accepted. For others, it means that at least one connection can be pending in accept(2). A negative value does not make sense, and so it should not be used.

The man page for listen(2) indicates that the behavior of the backlog argument changed at Linux kernel release 2.2. Previously, this count included connections that were still establishing communications with the listening socket. As of 2.2 and later, this backlog count only pertains to those connections that have been established with the listening socket, but are waiting to be accepted by the server.

It would seem that for small servers, the queue length should be specified as 5 or more. For Web servers, however, you might need to experiment with larger numbers. Some tests published by Richard Stevens suggest that for a Web server that is receiving approximately 45,000 connects per hour, you might want to use a backlog length of 16 or more.

The final value chosen for the backlog parameter depends largely upon the amount of elapsed time between each accept(2) function call. If your server accepts one connection and then completely processes this request before accepting the next connection, you'll want to use a larger backlog value. The longer each request takes to process in this scenario, the more critical the backlog queue length becomes.

If, on the other hand, your server can concurrently process several client connections, the backlog parameter value will be lower. This is true because the server will loop back and accept the next pending connect, within the limits of a very efficient processing loop. Processing multiple clients concurrently within a server will be covered in Chapter 11, "Concurrent Client Servers."

The accept(2) Function Call

You have seen the accept(2) function call mentioned several times in this chapter. It is now appropriate to fully discuss this function, so that you will have a clear idea of its role. The function synopsis is shown as follows:

```
#include <sys/types.h>
#include <sys/socket.h>

int accept(int s, struct sockaddr *addr, int *addrlen);
```

The accept(2) function takes three arguments. They are

- The input socket s, which is listening for connections.

- The pointer (addr) to a socket address structure, which will receive the client socket address.

- The pointer to the maximum length (addrlen) of the receiving socket address buffer addr. The int value that this pointer is pointing to is both an input value and an output value. Upon input, it specifies the maximum length of addr. After the function returns, this value contains the actual length of the address that was returned.

CAUTION

Note that argument three of accept(2) is a pointer to an integer data type. The integer that it points to is both an input and output value. Always initialize this value with the maximum length of the address prior to calling accept(2).

The return value from the accept(2) function is a new socket when successful. Otherwise the value –1 is returned, and the value of errno contains the reason for the failure.

Understanding the Role of accept(2)

It might seem strange for accept(2) to return yet another socket. After all, wouldn't it be better to use the original socket? The answer lies in the nature of most server designs. A server, upon accepting one client connection, must be willing to accept additional connections from clients. Any individual socket, however, can only be connected to one client. Where would the www.woohoo.com server be if it could only service one client at one time?

Figure 8.1, which was presented earlier, was an oversimplification of server responsibilities. Figure 8.3 is an improvement, showing the steps that a simple server would use.

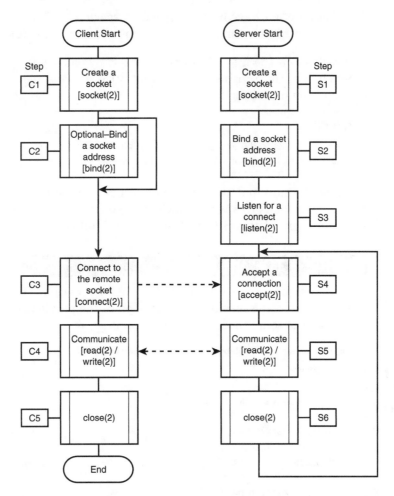

Figure 8.3: *Here is an improved diagram explaining the connection steps for client and server (note the repetition of steps S4 to S6).*

Figure 8.3 shows how the server will repeat steps S4 through S6 for each client that connects. The server finishes processing each client's request with a close(2) function call in step S6. However, to continue to receive new connections, the server needs its original socket that is able to listen for additional requests.

To summarize, there are two types of sockets used by the server program. They are

- Sockets that are being used for listening (passed to the listen(2) function call at one point). No reading or writing of data to these sockets is permitted.

- Sockets that have been returned by accept(2). These are connected to a client process, and can be used to read and write data.

The socket is made into a "listening socket" by passing it to the listen(2) function. A socket returned from accept(2) is a connected socket, which can be read from or written to.

NOTE

The input socket to the accept(2) call must be a listening socket. Any attempt to use a non-listening socket will cause the function to return an error.

You must be sure to understand these concepts in order to write a TCP/IP server program. If this is still unclear to you, the example program presented later in Listing 8.1 will help to clarify all of this.

Writing a TCP/IP Server

This section presents a simple TCP/IP server program. This server will replace the daytime service that was used in the previous chapter. Listing 8.1 shows the source code for the program.

EXAMPLE

Listing 8.1: server.c—The Replacement Daytime Server

```
1:   /* server.c:
2:    *
3:    * Example daytime server:
4:    */
5:   #include <stdio.h>
6:   #include <unistd.h>
7:   #include <stdlib.h>
8:   #include <errno.h>
9:   #include <string.h>
10:  #include <time.h>
11:  #include <sys/types.h>
12:  #include <sys/socket.h>
```

```
13:    #include <netinet/in.h>
14:    #include <arpa/inet.h>
15:    #include <netdb.h>
16:
17:    /*
18:     * This function reports the error and
19:     * exits back to the shell:
20:     */
21:    static void
22:    bail(const char *on_what) {
23:        if ( errno != 0 ) {
24:            fputs(strerror(errno),stderr);
25:            fputs(": ",stderr);
26:        }
27:        fputs(on_what,stderr);
28:        fputc('\n',stderr);
29:        exit(1);
30:    }
31:
32:    int
33:    main(int argc,char **argv) {
34:        int z;
35:        char *srvr_addr = NULL;
36:        char *srvr_port = "9099";
37:        struct sockaddr_in adr_srvr;/* AF_INET */
38:        struct sockaddr_in adr_clnt;/* AF_INET */
39:        int len_inet;                /* length  */
40:        int s;                        /* Socket */
41:        int c;                    /* Client socket */
42:        int n;                         /* bytes */
43:        time_t td;         /* Current date&time */
44:        char dtbuf[128];     /* Date/Time info */
45:
46:        /*
47:         * Use a server address from the command
48:         * line, if one has been provided.
49:         * Otherwise, this program will default
50:         * to using the arbitrary address
51:         * 127.0.0.1:
52:         */
53:        if ( argc >= 2 ) {
54:            /* Addr on cmdline: */
55:            srvr_addr = argv[1];
56:        } else {
57:            /* Use default address: */
58:            srvr_addr = "127.0.0.1";
59:        }
```

continues

Listing 8.1: continued

```
60:
61:        /*
62:         * If there is a second argument on the
63:         * command line, use it as the port #:
64:         */
65:        if ( argc >= 3 )
66:            srvr_port = argv[2];
67:
68:        /*
69:         * Create a TCP/IP socket to use:
70:         */
71:        s = socket(PF_INET,SOCK_STREAM,0);
72:        if ( s == -1 )
73:            bail("socket()");
74:
75:        /*
76:         * Create a server socket address:
77:         */
78:        memset(&adr_srvr,0,sizeof adr_srvr);
79:        adr_srvr.sin_family = AF_INET;
80:        adr_srvr.sin_port = htons(atoi(srvr_port));
81:        if ( strcmp(srvr_addr,"*") != 0 ) {
82:            /* Normal Address */
83:            adr_srvr.sin_addr.s_addr =
84:                inet_addr(srvr_addr);
85:            if ( adr_srvr.sin_addr.s_addr
86:                == INADDR_NONE )
87:                bail("bad address.");
88:        } else {
89:            /* Wild Address */
90:            adr_srvr.sin_addr.s_addr =
91:                INADDR_ANY;
92:        }
93:
94:        /*
95:         * Bind the server address:
96:         */
97:        len_inet = sizeof adr_srvr;
98:        z = bind(s,(struct sockaddr *)&adr_srvr,
99:                len_inet);
100:       if ( z == -1 )
101:           bail("bind(2)");
102:
103:       /*
104:        * Make it a listening socket:
105:        */
106:       z = listen(s,10);
```

```
107:     if ( z == -1 )
108:         bail("listen(2)");
109:
110:     /*
111:      * Start the server loop:
112:      */
113:     for (;;) {
114:         /*
115:          * Wait for a connect:
116:          */
117:         len_inet = sizeof adr_clnt;
118:         c = accept(s,
119:             (struct sockaddr *)&adr_clnt,
120:             &len_inet);
121:
122:         if ( c == -1 )
123:             bail("accept(2)");
124:
125:         /*
126:          * Generate a time stamp:
127:          */
128:         time(&td);
129:         n = (int) strftime(dtbuf,sizeof dtbuf,
130:             "%A %b %d %H:%M:%S %Y\n",
131:             localtime(&td));
132:
133:         /*
134:          * Write result back to the client:
135:          */
136:         z = write(c,dtbuf,n);
137:         if ( z == -1 )
138:             bail("write(2)");
139:
140:         /*
141:          * Close this client's connection:
142:          */
143:         close(c);
144:     }
145:
146:     /* Control never gets here */
147:     return 0;
148: }
```

The basic steps for the program in Listing 8.1 can be listed as follows:

1. Decide on the server network address for the server (lines 53 to 59). The default is the local loopback address of 127.0.0.1 (line 58).

2. Decide on a server port number (lines 65 to 66). Note that the default is port 9099 (line 36).

3. Create a socket (lines 71 to 73).

4. Create the server socket address (lines 78 to 92).

5. Bind the socket address (lines 97 to 101).

6. Mark the socket as a listening socket (lines 106 to 108).

7. Start the client service loop (line 113).

8. Accept a client connection (lines 117 to 123).

9. Generate a date and time string (lines 128 to 131).

10. Write the date and time string back to the client (lines 136 to 138).

11. Close the client connection (line 143).

Some steps require a bit of further explanation. In step 2, the program accepts a port number as an optional command-line argument two. This is necessary, because you don't want to run your version of the server on the standard port 13 (remember from the last chapter, your daytime server listens on that port). Instead, you'll use port 9099 by default, which does not require root privileges to run, and it won't disrupt your standard services. The command-line parameter permits you to use different port numbers if you prefer.

NOTE

TCP/IP ports 1 to 1023 are reserved for privileged programs (running as root). Non-privileged programs use ports 1024 or greater.

Note also that a port value of zero is a wild port number. An unassigned port number will be assigned when bind(2) is called, if the port number is specified as zero.

Step 4 is different from previous programs. Line 81 has a call to strcmp(3) to see if the value "*" was given for the server address. If so, then a wild address is provided in lines 90 and 91. Now this might raise your eyebrow, because it was mentioned earlier that server addresses couldn't be completely wild. The important word to notice is "completely." The port and IP number cannot both be wild. The port number is not wild in this example, but it is permitted for the IP number to be wild in the server address. This allows the server to accept connections on any IP interface. This becomes important for systems that have several network cards.

TIP

A server address cannot completely wild. However, with a specified port number, the IP number portion of a TCP/IP address can be wild (INADDR_ANY). This allows your server to accept connections from any valid IP interface on that host.

Step 8 is the point where the server program calls the function accept(2). This is where the server control "blocks." The server will not execute any further instructions unless a client connects. After a connection has taken place, the accept(2) call will return in line 122. Note that variable c holds the client socket that has been returned by the accept(2) function call.

Client request processing continues in steps 9 to 11. Then the server repeats step 8 to await the next client connection.

The following shows how to make and invoke the server program:

OUTPUT

```
$ make server
gcc -c  -D_GNU_SOURCE -Wall -Wreturn-type server.c
gcc server.o -o server
$ ./server &
[1] 1049
$ telnet 127.0.0.1 9099
Trying 127.0.0.1...
Connected to 127.0.0.1.
Escape character is '^]'.
Sunday Aug 22 21:18:24 1999
Connection closed by foreign host.
$
```

The output shows the server being run in the background, without any command-line parameters. The telnet command connects to it to test it out. Notice that port 9099 is specified on the telnet command line.

The returned output from the server is purposely different from the standard daytime server. The standard daytime server abbreviates the weekday name. Because the session output shows the full weekday name, you can be confident that you contacted your server instead of the standard server.

Before proceeding to the next section, bring down your server. The server is designed to loop forever until you kill it. So you can simply list your jobs and kill it off as follows:

OUTPUT

```
$ jobs
[1]+  Running                 ./server &
$ kill %1
[1]+  Terminated              ./server
$
```

The jobs command is the bash shell built-in that enables you to see which processes you started and left to run in the background. The %1 in the kill command causes the shell to substitute the real process ID (PID) before invoking the kill command. If you leave the server running on port 9099, and you attempt to start another on the same port, you will see something like this:

OUTPUT

```
$ ./server &
Address already in use: bind(2)
[2] 1057
[2]   Exit 1                    ./server
$
```

TIP

Sometimes you will get the "Address already in use" error, even though the server is not running. The Linux kernel will make the server address unavailable for a short period after the server has terminated. This behavior is controlled by the socket option SO_LINGER, which has not been covered yet. This is covered in Chapter 12, "Socket Options."

Running a Wild Server

The server, as started by using the command ./server &, is using a socket bound to the IP address 127.0.0.1 (the program's default). This means that only processes on that local host will be able to contact that server. An alternative is to run the server with an external IP number as follows:

EXAMPLE

```
$ ./server 192.168.0.1 &
```

The problem with this is that your server will only accept connections from the one network interface, which has the matching IP number. What you really need is a wild IP number for this server. This can be accomplished as follows:

```
$ ./server '*' &
```

CAUTION

Be sure to enclose the asterisk character within a pair of single quotes. Otherwise, the shell will expand it into a list of filenames before starting the server.

While a port number was not specified on the command line, the port number used in this program is port number 9099, by default. Having started the server just shown, you may now connect to it locally or from a remote location. The following shows two connects from the host pepper where the server was started:

OUTPUT

```
@pepper
$ ./server '*' &
[1] 1078
@pepper
$ telnet 127.0.0.1 9099
Trying 127.0.0.1...
Connected to 127.0.0.1.
Escape character is '^]'.
Sunday Aug 22 21:40:19 1999
Connection closed by foreign host.
```

```
@pepper
$ telnet 192.168.0.1 9099
Trying 192.168.0.1...
Connected to 192.168.0.1.
Escape character is '^]'.
Sunday Aug 22 21:40:27 1999
Connection closed by foreign host.
@pepper
$
```

The session shown demonstrates the following:

1. The first command in the session output shows the server being started on pepper with a wild server address (but also using the default port number of 9099).

2. The telnet to address 127.0.0.1 port 9099 provoked a response successfully from our server. This contact was made with the server using the local loopback interface.

3. The telnet to address 192.168.0.1 port 9099 also provoked a successful response from our server. This proved that the server could be reached from yet a different IP address.

As further proof of the wild nature of the server address, you can try contacting the server from another host. The following shows a connect attempt from host slug:

OUTPUT

```
@slug
$ telnet 192.168.0.1 9099
Trying 192.168.0.1...
Connected to 192.168.0.1.
Escape character is '^]'.
Sunday Aug 22 21:47:52 1999
Connection closed by foreign host.
@slug
$
```

The telnet command used on host slug still contacts the server on interface address 192.168.0.1 in this example. This proves that the connection attempt went through the network card via the Ethernet link and was able to contact the server. Had the server address been bound only to 127.0.0.1, host slug would not be able to reach the server on pepper.

Modifying the Client Program

To provide a more convincing demonstration, you will dispense with the telnet command. Instead, the client program from the previous chapter will be used with a few modifications applied. Listing 8.2 shows the modified client program.

EXAMPLE

Listing 8.2: `daytime.c`—Modified Client Program for Daytime Service

```
1:  /* daytime.c:
2:   *
3:   * Example daytime client, modified
4:   * to accept different port numbers:
5:   */
6:  #include <stdio.h>
7:  #include <unistd.h>
8:  #include <stdlib.h>
9:  #include <errno.h>
10: #include <string.h>
11: #include <sys/types.h>
12: #include <sys/socket.h>
13: #include <netinet/in.h>
14: #include <arpa/inet.h>
15: #include <netdb.h>
16:
17: /*
18:  * This function reports the error and
19:  * exits back to the shell:
20:  */
21: static void
22: bail(const char *on_what) {
23:     if ( errno != 0 ) {
24:         fputs(strerror(errno),stderr);
25:         fputs(": ",stderr);
26:     }
27:     fputs(on_what,stderr);
28:     fputc('\n',stderr);
29:     exit(1);
30: }
31:
32: int
33: main(int argc,char **argv) {
34:     int z;
35:     char *srvr_addr = NULL;
36:     char *srvr_port = "9099";
37:     struct sockaddr_in adr_srvr;/* AF_INET */
38:     int len_inet;                   /* length */
39:     int s;                          /* Socket */
40:     char dtbuf[128];     /* Date/Time info */
41:
42:     /*
43:      * Use a server address from the command
44:      * line, if one has been provided.
45:      * Otherwise, this program will default
46:      * to using the arbitrary address
47:      * 127.0.0.1:
```

```
48:          */
49:         if ( argc >= 2 ) {
50:             /* Addr on cmdline: */
51:             srvr_addr = argv[1];
52:         } else {
53:             /* Use default address: */
54:             srvr_addr = "127.0.0.1";
55:         }
56:
57:         /*
58:          * If the port number is given, use it:
59:          */
60:         if ( argc >= 3 )
61:             srvr_port = argv[2];
62:
63:         /*
64:          * Create a TCP/IP socket to use:
65:          */
66:         s = socket(PF_INET,SOCK_STREAM,0);
67:         if ( s == -1 )
68:             bail("socket()");
69:
70:         /*
71:          * Create a server socket address:
72:          */
73:         memset(&adr_srvr,0,sizeof adr_srvr);
74:         adr_srvr.sin_family = AF_INET;
75:         adr_srvr.sin_port = htons(atoi(srvr_port));
76:         adr_srvr.sin_addr.s_addr =
77:             inet_addr(srvr_addr);
78:         if ( adr_srvr.sin_addr.s_addr == INADDR_NONE )
79:             bail("bad address.");
80:
81:         /*
82:          * Connect to the server:
83:          */
84:         len_inet = sizeof adr_srvr;
85:
86:         z = connect(s,&adr_srvr,len_inet);
87:         if ( z == -1 )
88:             bail("connect(2)");
89:
90:         /*
91:          * Read the date/time info:
92:          */
93:         z = read(s,&dtbuf,sizeof dtbuf-1);
94:         if ( z == -1 )
```

continues

Listing 8.2: continued

```
95:            bail("read(2)");
96:
97:        /*
98:         * Report the Date & Time:
99:         */
100:       dtbuf[z] = 0;    /* NULL terminate string */
101:
102:       printf("Date & Time is: %s\n",dtbuf);
103:
104:       /*
105:        * Close the socket and exit:
106:        */
107:       close(s);
108:       putchar('\n');
109:
110:       return 0;
111: }
```

The minor changes made to the program are

1. The program now accepts an optional port number on the command line as argument two (lines 60 and 61).

2. The call to getservbyname(3) was removed, because the port number now defaults to 9099 or is given explicitly on the command line.

The following session shows how to compile and test the client program, against a wild addressed server:

OUTPUT

```
@pepper
$ make daytime
gcc -c  -D_GNU_SOURCE -Wall -Wreturn-type daytime.c
gcc daytime.o -o daytime
@pepper
$ ./daytime 127.0.0.1 9099
Date & Time is: Sunday Aug 22 22:02:19 1999


@pepper
$ ./daytime 192.168.0.1 9099
Date & Time is: Sunday Aug 22 22:02:30 1999


@pepper
$
```

The session demonstrates how the client program successfully invoked the same server from both IP addresses that were possible on host pepper. If you have a remote host in your network, be sure to try the program out remotely.

What's Next

In this chapter, you looked at the role played by the server. You saw how it differed from the client because it was required to call upon the functions `listen(2)` and `accept(2)`.

The next chapter is going to discuss hostname lookups. Up to this point in this book, you have confined your Internet addresses to specific IP numbers. The next chapter will show you how to use hostnames in addition to IP numbers.

9

Hostname and Network Name Lookups

It is the noon hour and the battle of your morning meetings and issues has been subdued for the moment. The silence of the cubicles is maligned by the rattle of your brown-bag lunch. Your Netscape browser springs to life, after an entire morning of standing by in a minimized state. You tap out a few keystrokes `http://206.43.198.67` and press ENTER. Huh?

What's wrong with this picture? It was the IP number `206.43.198.67`, wasn't it? After all, what site is that? You likely know this as the site `www.lwn.net` instead, where you get your Linux Weekly News (at least at the time of this writing).

Your associate at work won't ask you to ftp some source code from ftp site `152.2.254.81`, will he? Instead, he'll ask you to ftp from `sunsite.unc.edu`. As you know, IP numbers are simply not easy to remember. In this chapter, you will learn

- How to determine your local hostname

- How to resolve a hostname into an IP number

- How to resolve an IP number into a hostname

Once you have completed this chapter, you will be able to use hostnames or IP numbers in your client and server programs.

Understanding the Need for Names

Humans prefer to use and remember names instead of IP numbers. Names actually solve a number of problems for us in the networked world:

- They provide a human-friendly reference for a site.
- They allow the IP number to change, while the name remains constant.
- They allow multiple IP numbers to be given as possibilities for the same host or service.

You already understand that names provide an easier reference to IP numbers. The second point, however, is that the name can remain fixed but allow the IP number of the host to be changed. IP numbers often change because of network changes, ISP changes, equipment changes, and so on. As long as you remember the name of the Internet site, you are unconcerned about what the actual IP number is that takes you there.

The last point is one that is easily overlooked. Looking up `ftp.redhat.com` (at the time of writing) produced two IP numbers:

- `208.178.165.228`
- `206.132.41.212`

It doesn't matter whether these two IP numbers refer to the same `ftp` host or two different mirror sites for load-balancing purposes. The fact is that, by using either of these IP numbers, you can obtain the same files that you were after.

This introduction leads you into the topic of resolving names in this chapter. First, you will learn how to query the local system for information about itself. Then you will learn how to use remote host names, look them up, and turn them into IP numbers.

Using the `uname(2)` Function

One useful function to know about is the `uname(2)` function. This function tells your program a little bit about the system in which it is executing. The function prototype for this function is as follows:

```
#include <sys/utsname.h>

int uname(struct utsname *buf);
```

The function returns information into the structure `buf`. The value returned is zero when successful, or –1 when an error is reported. External variable `errno` will contain the reason for the error.

The struct `utsname` is defined as follows:

```
#include <sys/utsname.h>  /* defines the following structure */

struct utsname {
    char    sysname[SYS_NMLN];
    char    nodename[SYS_NMLN];
    char    release[SYS_NMLN];
    char    version[SYS_NMLN];
    char    machine[SYS_NMLN];
    char    domainname[SYS_NMLN];
};
```

The structure members are described in detail in Table 9.1.

Table 9.1: The **utsname** *Structure Members*

Member	Description
sysname	This represents the operating system being used. For Linux, this value is the C string `"Linux"`.
nodename	This represents the machine's network node hostname.
release	The operating system release. For example, the C string `"2.2.10"` is returned for kernel release 2.2.10.
version	The operating system version. For Linux, this represents the version number, date, and time stamp of the kernel build.
machine	This represents the hardware type of the host. For example, `"i686"` represents a Pentium CPU.
domainname	This returns the NIS/YP domain name for the host.

NOTE

NIS/YP (Network Information Service) is beyond the scope of this book. NIS provides centralized information management for a group of hosts in a network. It permits a centralized management of users, groups, and passwords, for example.

A simple program to permit you to test the values returned by `uname(2)` is shown in Listing 9.1. This program invokes `uname(2)` and then displays the contents of the information it has returned in the structure `utsname`.

Listing 9.1: `uname.c`—A Simple Test Program for `uname(2)`

```
1:    /* uname.c:
2:     *
3:     * Example of uname(2):
4:     */
5:    #include <stdio.h>
6:    #include <unistd.h>
7:    #include <stdlib.h>
8:    #include <errno.h>
9:    #include <string.h>
```

continues

Listing 9.1: continued

```
10:   #include <sys/utsname.h>
11:
12:   int
13:   main(int argc,char **argv) {
14:        int z;
15:        struct utsname u_name;
16:
17:        z = uname(&u_name);
18:
19:        if ( z == -1 ) {
20:             fprintf(stderr,"%s: uname(2)\n",
21:                  strerror(errno));
22:             exit(1);
23:        }
24:
25:        printf("   sysname[] = '%s';\n",
26:             u_name.sysname);
27:        printf("  nodename[] = '%s';\n",
28:             u_name.nodename);
29:        printf("   release[] = '%s';\n",
30:             u_name.release);
31:        printf("   version[] = '%s';\n",
32:             u_name.version);
33:        printf("   machine[] = '%s';\n",
34:             u_name.machine);
35:        printf("domainname[] = '%s';\n",
36:             u_name.domainname);
37:
38:        return 0;
39:   }
```

The steps used in Listing 9.1 are as follows:

1. Allocate a structure u_name to receive the data from uname(2) (line 15).

2. Call upon uname(2) in line 17.

3. Check for and report errors (lines 19 to 23).

4. Report the values returned (lines 25 to 36).

The following session output shows how to compile and run the program. The output from the program on the example system tux is also included as an example (note that this system is not configured to use NIS):

OUTPUT

```
@tux
$ make uname
gcc -c  -D_GNU_SOURCE -Wall -Wreturn-type uname.c
gcc uname.o -o uname
```

```
@tux
$ ./uname
   sysname[] = 'Linux';
  nodename[] = 'tux';
   release[] = '2.2.10';
   version[] = '#1 Sun Jul 4 00:28:57 EDT 1999';
   machine[] = 'i686';
domainname[] = '';
@tux
$
```

NOTE

Your values might differ substantially from the example shown, depending upon how your system is configured. For example, the domain name might show an NIS domain name instead of an empty string. Many hobby Linux systems that are not configured to use NIS might show an empty domain name string instead.

If you check back with Table 9.1, you can see that the values reported make sense. The value of sysname is reported as "Linux" and the kernel release is reported as "2.2.10" at the time this snapshot was taken. Also, note that the version and time of the kernel build is provided in the member version.

Obtaining Hostnames and Domain Names

The functions gethostname(2) and getdomainname(2) are two other functions which can be used to inquire about the current system.

Using Function gethostname(2)

The gethostname(2) function can be used to determine your current hostname. Its function synopsis is given as follows:

```
#include <unistd.h>

int gethostname(char *name, size_t len);
```

This function takes two arguments:

- The receiving buffer name, which must be len bytes in length or longer.

- The maximum length (len) of the receiving buffer name in bytes.

The return value is the value zero if it is successful. A value of –1 is returned if an error occurs. The error is described by the external variable errno.

TIP

The len argument of gethostname(2) must include the total length of the hostname to be returned and the terminating null byte.

Using the `getdomainname(2)` Function

The `getdomainname(2)` function is another convenience function to allow the programmer to inquire about the host's NIS domain name, where the program is executing. The following is the function synopsis:

```
#include <unistd.h>

int getdomainname(char *name,size_t len);
```

This function is identical in use to the `gethostname(2)` function. The two arguments are

- The buffer `name`, which is to receive the domain name and is at least `len` bytes in length.

- The buffer length (`len`), in bytes, of the buffer `name`.

Again, the function returns zero when successful. The value –1 is returned when there is an error. External variable `errno` contains the error code for the failure.

The Linux man page indicates that the `getdomainname(2)` function internally uses the `uname(2)` function to obtain and return the NIS domain name.

Testing `gethostname(2)` and `getdomainname(2)`

These two functions are demonstrated in a program provided in Listing 9.2. This program simply calls upon the functions and reports their results.

EXAMPLE

Listing 9.2: gethostn.c—The `gethostname(2)` and `getdomainname(2)` Demo Program

```
1:    /* gethostn.c:
2:     *
3:     * Example of gethostname(2):
4:     */
5:    #include <stdio.h>
6:    #include <unistd.h>
7:    #include <stdlib.h>
8:    #include <errno.h>
9:    #include <string.h>
10:
11:   int
12:   main(int argc,char **argv) {
13:       int z;
14:       char buf[32];
15:
16:       z = gethostname(buf,sizeof buf);
17:
18:       if ( z == -1 ) {
19:           fprintf(stderr,"%s: gethostname(2)\n",
```

```
20:                     strerror(errno));
21:             exit(1);
22:         }
23:
24:         printf("host name = '%s'\n",buf);
25:
26:         z = getdomainname(buf,sizeof buf);
27:
28:         if ( z == -1 ) {
29:             fprintf(stderr,"%s: getdomainname(2)\n",
30:                     strerror(errno));
31:             exit(1);
32:         }
33:
34:         printf("domain name = '%s'\n",buf);
35:
36:         return 0;
37:     }
```

The steps used are

1. Define an adequately sized buffer (line 14).

2. Call gethostname(2) to obtain the hostname into the character array buf[] (line 16).

3. Check for and report errors (lines 18 to 22).

4. Report the hostname (line 24).

5. Call getdomainname(2) to obtain the NIS/YP domain name into the same character array buf[] (line 26).

6. Check for and report errors (lines 28 to 32).

7. Report the domain name (line 34).

The following output session shows a compile and run session for the program on the hypothetical system tux:

OUTPUT

```
@tux
$ make gethostn
gcc -c  -D_GNU_SOURCE -Wall -Wreturn-type gethostn.c
gcc gethostn.o -o gethostn
@tux
$ ./gethostn
host name = 'tux'
domain name = ''
@tux
$
```

In the example run, you see that the host and domain values were reported successfully (although the domain name was reported as an empty string due to the fact that no NIS domain was configured). Your values will vary from the example shown, especially if you have an NIS domain configured.

Having learned how to inquire the local system, it is now time to turn your attention to resolving remote hostnames. This will be the focus of the remainder of this chapter.

Resolving Remote Addresses

The process of turning a name like www.lwn.net into an IP number is quite complex. It involves a number of files in your local system's /etc directory, including files such as /etc/resolv.conf, /etc/hosts, and /etc/nsswitch.conf, to name a few of them. Depending upon how your local system is configured, other files and daemon processes might come into play as well. For example, after these files have been consulted, a name server can be queried, which itself can forward queries to other name servers. All of this complexity represents detail that you really don't want to think about when writing your application program.

Fortunately, the application writer is able to play the part of an ostrich and stick his head in the sand. If the system is properly configured, a few system function calls will be all that is required on the part of the programmer. Covered next is a related set of functions, which hide this complexity of remote name lookups for you.

NOTE

It will be assumed in this book that you have a Linux system that is properly configured. Entire books have been written on system and network administration. Consequently, the focus of this book is to teach you how to program with sockets, and not how to set up domains and name servers.

Error Reporting

The functions that are about to be described use a different variable for error reporting. In normal C library functions, the error code is reported to the variable errno (declared by including errno.h). The functions in this section however, report their errors to variable h_errno. Its synopsis is given as follows:

```
#include <netdb.h>

extern int h_errno;
```

The h_errno variable is an external integer variable. Errors are posted to h_errno by the following functions:

- gethostbyname(3)

- gethostbyaddr(3)

The following functions use the value of h_error as input:

- herror(3)

- hstrerror(3)

CAUTION

Note that the h_errno value suffers from the flaw that it cannot be shared between different threads in the same process. While the newer glibc library has made errno thread safe, the h_errno value is not thread safe.

Reporting an h_errno Error

As you probably know, the strerror(3) function conveniently converts an errno value into a human-readable error message. Likewise, there exist two methods for reporting the h_errno value:

```
#include <netdb.h>
extern int h_errno;

void herror(const char *msg);

const char *hstrerror(int err);
```

The function herror(3) is much like the perror(3) function. The herror(3) function is now considered obsolete, but you might find it in existing source code. It prints the message msg and follows that by the text of the error. This is written to the standard error (stderr) output stream.

The hstrerror(3) function mirrors the functionality that the familiar strerror(3) function performs. Accepting as input the h_errno input value, it returns a pointer to a text message describing the error. The pointer returned is only valid until the next call to this function.

UNDERSTANDING THE ERROR CODES

The C macros used for the h_errno variable differ substantially from the errno values. Table 9.2 lists the error codes that you are likely to encounter when calling gethostbyname(3) and gethostbyaddr(3).

Table 9.2: The **h_errno** *Codes*

Error Macro	Description
HOST_NOT_FOUND	The specified hostname is unknown.
NO_ADDRESS	The specified hostname is valid, but does not have an IP address.
NO_DATA	Same as NO_ADDRESS.
NO_RECOVERY	A non-recoverable name server error occurred.
TRY_AGAIN	A temporary error occurred on the authoritative name server. Try this operation again later.

Notice that the TRY_AGAIN error code listed in Table 9.2 represents a condition that might be overcome with retry attempts. The NO_RECOVERY error, on the other hand, represents a name server error that should not be retried, since no recovery is possible for that condition. The NO_ADDRESS (or NO_DATA) error indicates that the name that was queried is known but that there is no IP address defined for it. Finally, the error code HOST_NOT_FOUND indicates that the name queried is unknown.

Using the `gethostbyname(3)` Function

This is the most important function to learn about in this chapter. This function accepts the name of the host that you want to resolve, and it returns a structure identifying it in various ways. The function synopsis is as follows:

```
#include <netdb.h>
extern int h_errno;

struct hostent *gethostbyname(const char *name);
```

The function gethostbyname(3) accepts one input argument that is a C string representing the hostname that you want to resolve into an address. The value returned is a pointer to the hostent structure if the call is successful (see Listing 9.3). If the function fails, then a NULL pointer is returned, and the value of h_errno contains the reason for the failure.

EXAMPLE

Listing 9.3: The `struct hostent` Structure

```
struct hostent {
    char  *h_name;    /* official name of host */
    char  **h_aliases;          /* alias list */
    int   h_addrtype; /* host address type */
    int   h_length;   /* length of address */
    char  **h_addr_list; /* list of addresses */
};

/* for backward compatibility */
#define h_addr  h_addr_list[0]
```

Become familiar with the hostent structure as you will use it often when doing socket programming.

THE hostent h_name MEMBER

The h_name entry within the hostent structure is the official name of the host that your are looking up. It is also known as the *canonical* name of the host. If you provided an alias, or a hostname without the domain name, then this entry will describe the proper name for what you have queried. This entry is useful for displaying or logging your result to a log file.

THE hostent h_aliases MEMBER

The hostent h_aliases member of the returned structure is an array of alias names for the hostname that you have queried. The end of the list is marked by a NULL pointer. As an example, the entire list of aliases for www.lwn.net could be reported as follows:

EXAMPLE

```
struct hostent *ptr;
int x;

ptr = gethostbyname("www.lwn.net");

for ( x=0; ptr->h_aliases[x] != NULL; ++x )
    printf("alias = '%s'\n", ptr->h_aliases[x]);
```

No error checking was shown in the preceding example. If ptr is NULL, this indicates that no information was available.

THE hostent h_addrtype MEMBER

The value presently returned in the member h_addrtype is AF_INET. However, as IPv6 becomes fully implemented, the name server will also be capable of returning IPv6 addresses. When this happens, h_addrtype will also return the value AF_INET6 when it is appropriate.

The purpose of the h_addrtype value is to indicate the format of the addresses in the list h_addr_list, which will be described next.

THE hostent h_length MEMBER

This value is related to the h_addrtype member. For the current version of the TCP/IP protocol (IPv4), this member always contains the value of 4, indicating 4-byte IP numbers. However, this value will be 16 when IPv6 is implemented, and IPv6 addresses are returned instead.

THE hostent h_addr_list MEMBER

When performing a name-to-IP-number translation, this member becomes your most important piece of information. When member h_addrtype contains the value of AF_INET, each pointer in this array of pointers points to a 4-byte IP address. The end of the list is marked by a NULL pointer.

Applying the gethostbyname(3) Function

A short demonstration program for the function gethostbyname(3) has been provided in Listing 9.4. This program accepts multiple hostnames on the command line and then queries the name server for each. All available information is reported to standard output, or an error is reported if the name cannot be resolved.

EXAMPLE

Listing 9.4: lookup.c—Demonstration Program for gethostbyname(3)

```
1:    /* lookup.c:
2:     *
3:     * Example of gethostbyname(3):
4:     */
5:    #include <stdio.h>
6:    #include <unistd.h>
7:    #include <stdlib.h>
8:    #include <string.h>
9:    #include <errno.h>
10:   #include <sys/socket.h>
11:   #include <netinet/in.h>
12:   #include <arpa/inet.h>
13:   #include <netdb.h>
14:
15:   extern int h_errno;
16:
17:   int
18:   main(int argc,char **argv) {
19:       int x, x2;
20:       struct hostent *hp;
21:
22:       for ( x=1; x<argc; ++x ) {
23:           /*
24:            * Look up the hostname:
25:            */
26:           hp = gethostbyname(argv[x]);
27:           if ( !hp ) {
28:               /* Report lookup failure */
29:               fprintf(stderr,
30:                   "%s: host '%s'\n",
31:                   hstrerror(h_errno),
32:                   argv[x]);
33:               continue;
34:           }
35:
```

```
36:              /*
37:               * Report the findings:
38:               */
39:              printf("Host %s :\n",argv[x]);
40:              printf("  Officially:\t%s\n",
41:                  hp->h_name);
42:              fputs("  Aliases:\t",stdout);
43:              for ( x2=0; hp->h_aliases[x2]; ++x2 ) {
44:                  if ( x2 )
45:                      fputs(", ",stdout);
46:                  fputs(hp->h_aliases[x2],stdout);
47:              }
48:              fputc('\n',stdout);
49:              printf("  Type:\t\t%s\n",
50:                  hp->h_addrtype == AF_INET
51:                      ? "AF_INET"
52:                      : "AF_INET6");
53:              if ( hp->h_addrtype == AF_INET ) {
54:                  for ( x2=0; hp->h_addr_list[x2]; ++x2 )
55:                      printf("  Address:\t%s\n",
56:                          inet_ntoa( *(struct in_addr *)
57:                              hp->h_addr_list[x2]));
58:              }
59:              putchar('\n');
60:          }
61:
62:      return 0;
63: }
```

The basic program steps employed are as follows:

1. A loop that iterates through all command-line arguments is started in line 22.

2. The hostname command-line argument is queried by calling upon gethostbyname(3) in line 26.

3. If the returned pointer is NULL, the error is reported in lines 29 to 33. The continue statement in line 33 causes the loop to continue with line 22.

4. Report the name that we queried (line 39).

5. Report the official name of the host (lines 40 and 41).

6. All of the alias names for the host are reported in lines 42 to 48.

7. The address type is reported as AF_INET or AF_INET6 in lines 49 to 52.

8. If the address type in step 7 is AF_INET, the IPv4 addresses are reported in lines 54 to 57.

9. An extra line is written to standard output (line 59).

10. The `for` loop repeats with step 1.

Note lines 56 and 57 in the program listing. The pointer value in `hp->h_addr_list[x2]` is a (`char *`) pointer. This pointer type is used because it may point to different address types, depending upon the value in `hp->h_addrtype`. To report this pointer value as an IPv4 (`AF_INET`) address, the following steps were used:

1. The character pointer `hp->h_addr_list[x2]` is referenced (line 57).

2. The pointer is cast to pointer type `struct in_addr` (line 56).

3. The `struct in_addr` value is fetched by using the * indirection operator (in front of the cast in line 56).

4. The fetched `struct in_addr` value is converted by the function `inet_ntoa(3)` to a string value, which can be printed with `printf(3)`.

The following output shows a terminal session that compiles and runs this sample program:

OUTPUT

```
$ make lookup
gcc -c  -D_GNU_SOURCE -Wall -Wreturn-type lookup.c
gcc lookup.o -o lookup
$ ./lookup www.lwn.net sunsite.unc.edu ftp.redhat.com
Host www.lwn.net :
    Officially:   lwn.net
    Aliases:      www.lwn.net
    Type:         AF_INET
    Address:      206.168.112.90

Host sunsite.unc.edu :
    Officially:   sunsite.unc.edu
    Aliases:
    Type:         AF_INET
    Address:      152.2.254.81

Host ftp.redhat.com :
    Officially:   ftp.redhat.com
    Aliases:
    Type:         AF_INET
    Address:      206.132.41.212
    Address:      208.178.165.228

$
```

When the program was run, notice that the hostname `www.lwn.net` was reported officially as `lwn.net`. This name had one alias, which was `www.lwn.net`, and it had one IP address of `206.168.112.90`.

The name sunsite.unc.edu reported no alias entries and had one IP address.

The hostname ftp.redhat.com reported its official name to be the same as what was provided. There were no alias names reported, but notice that two possible IP addresses were provided. Either of the IP numbers 206.132.41.212 or 208.178.165.228 can be used to reach this host.

The gethostbyaddr(3) Function

There are times where you have an Internet address, but you need to report the hostname instead of the IP number. A server might want to log the hostname of the client that has contacted it, instead of the IP number alone. The function synopsis for gethostbyaddr(3) is as follows:

```
#include <sys/socket.h> /* for AF_INET */

struct hostent *gethostbyaddr(
    const char *addr, /* Input address */
    int len,          /* Address length */
    int type);        /* Address type */
```

The gethostbyaddr(3) function accepts three input arguments. They are

1. The input address (addr) to be converted into a hostname. For address type AF_INET, this is the pointer to the sin_addr member of the address structure.

2. The length of the input address (len). For type AF_INET, this will be the value 4 (4 bytes). For type AF_INET6, this value will be 16.

3. The type of the input address (type), which is the value AF_INET or AF_INET6.

Notice that the first argument is a character pointer, allowing it to potentially accept many forms of addresses. You will need to cast your address pointer to (char *) to satisfy the compiler. The second argument indicates the length of the supplied address.

The third argument is the type of the address being passed. It is AF_INET for an IPv4 Internet address, or in the future, it will be the value AF_INET6 for an IPv6 format address.

Listing 9.5 shows a modified version of the server that was demonstrated in the previous chapter. This server opens a log file named srvr2.log in the current directory and logs each connect request it receives. The server logs both the IP number and the name if possible, of the connecting client.

Listing 9.5: srvr2.c—The Modified Server Using gethostbyaddr(3)

```
1:    /* srvr2.c:
2:     *
3:     * Example daytime server,
4:     * with gethostbyaddr(3):
5:     */
6:    #include <stdio.h>
7:    #include <unistd.h>
8:    #include <stdlib.h>
9:    #include <errno.h>
10:   #include <string.h>
11:   #include <time.h>
12:   #include <sys/types.h>
13:   #include <sys/socket.h>
14:   #include <netinet/in.h>
15:   #include <arpa/inet.h>
16:   #include <netdb.h>
17:
18:   /*
19:    * This function reports the error and
20:    * exits back to the shell:
21:    */
22:   static void
23:   bail(const char *on_what) {
24:       if ( errno != 0 ) {
25:           fputs(strerror(errno),stderr);
26:           fputs(": ",stderr);
27:       }
28:       fputs(on_what,stderr);
29:       fputc('\n',stderr);
30:       exit(1);
31:   }
32:
33:   int
34:   main(int argc,char **argv) {
35:       int z;
36:       char *srvr_addr = NULL;
37:       char *srvr_port = "9099";
38:       struct sockaddr_in adr_srvr;/* AF_INET */
39:       struct sockaddr_in adr_clnt;/* AF_INET */
40:       int len_inet;                /* length */
41:       int s;                       /* Socket */
42:       int c;                  /* Client socket */
43:       int n;                        /* bytes */
44:       time_t td;        /* Current date&time */
45:       char dtbuf[128];    /* Date/Time info */
46:       FILE *logf; /* Log file for the server */
```

```
47:        struct hostent *hp;   /* Host entry ptr */
48:
49:        /*
50:         * Open the log file:
51:         */
52:        if ( !(logf = fopen("srvr2.log","w")) )
53:            bail("fopen(3)");
54:
55:        /*
56:         * Use a server address from the command
57:         * line, if one has been provided.
58:         * Otherwise, this program will default
59:         * to using the arbitrary address
60:         * 127.0.0.1:
61:         */
62:        if ( argc >= 2 ) {
63:            /* Addr on cmdline: */
64:            srvr_addr = argv[1];
65:        } else {
66:            /* Use default address: */
67:            srvr_addr = "127.0.0.1";
68:        }
69:
70:        /*
71:         * If there is a second argument on the
72:         * command line, use it as the port #:
73:         */
74:        if ( argc >= 3 )
75:            srvr_port = argv[2];
76:
77:        /*
78:         * Create a TCP/IP socket to use:
79:         */
80:        s = socket(PF_INET,SOCK_STREAM,0);
81:        if ( s == -1 )
82:            bail("socket()");
83:
84:        /*
85:         * Create a server socket address:
86:         */
87:        memset(&adr_srvr,0,sizeof adr_srvr);
88:        adr_srvr.sin_family = AF_INET;
89:        adr_srvr.sin_port = htons(atoi(srvr_port));
90:        if ( strcmp(srvr_addr,"*") != 0 ) {
91:            /* Normal Address */
92:            adr_srvr.sin_addr.s_addr =
93:                inet_addr(srvr_addr);
94:            if ( adr_srvr.sin_addr.s_addr
```

continues

Listing 9.5: continued

```
95:                    == INADDR_NONE )
96:                bail("bad address.");
97:        } else {
98:            /* Wild Address */
99:            adr_srvr.sin_addr.s_addr =
100:               INADDR_ANY;
101:        }
102:
103:        /*
104:         * Bind the server address:
105:         */
106:        len_inet = sizeof adr_srvr;
107:        z = bind(s,(struct sockaddr *)&adr_srvr,
108:               len_inet);
109:        if ( z == -1 )
110:            bail("bind(2)");
111:
112:        /*
113:         * Make it a listening socket:
114:         */
115:        z = listen(s,10);
116:        if ( z == -1 )
117:            bail("listen(2)");
118:
119:        /*
120:         * Start the server loop:
121:         */
122:        for (;;) {
123:            /*
124:             * Wait for a connect:
125:             */
126:            len_inet = sizeof adr_clnt;
127:            c = accept(s,
128:                (struct sockaddr *)&adr_clnt,
129:                &len_inet);
130:
131:            if ( c == -1 )
132:                bail("accept(2)");
133:
134:            /*
135:             * Log the address of the client
136:             * who connected to us:
137:             */
138:            fprintf(logf,
139:                "Client %s:",
140:                inet_ntoa(adr_clnt.sin_addr));
141:
142:            hp = gethostbyaddr(
```

```
143:                (char *)&adr_clnt.sin_addr,
144:                sizeof adr_clnt.sin_addr,
145:                adr_clnt.sin_family);
146:
147:        if ( !hp )
148:            fprintf(logf," Error: %s\n",
149:                hstrerror(h_errno));
150:        else
151:            fprintf(logf," %s\n",
152:                hp->h_name);
153:        fflush(logf);
154:
155:        /*
156:         * Generate a time stamp:
157:         */
158:        time(&td);
159:        n = (int) strftime(dtbuf,sizeof dtbuf,
160:            "%A %b %d %H:%M:%S %Y\n",
161:            localtime(&td));
162:
163:        /*
164:         * Write result back to the client:
165:         */
166:        z = write(c,dtbuf,n);
167:        if ( z == -1 )
168:            bail("write(2)");
169:
170:        /*
171:         * Close this client's connection:
172:         */
173:        close(c);
174:    }
175:
176:    /* Control never gets here */
177:    return 0;
178: }
```

The changes made to the program consist of the following:

1. The FILE variable logf is declared in line 46.

2. The log file is opened in lines 52 and 53.

3. Immediately after each connect (line 127), the connecting client's IP number is logged (lines 138 to 140).

4. A reverse lookup of the IP number is performed in lines 142 to 145. If successful, the pointer hp that is returned will indicate the official name of the client that has connected.

5. Check for a failed lookup in the `if` statement in line 147. If the pointer is null, the program simply logs the lookup failure.

6. When the lookup is successful, the `hp` pointer will not be null. This value is used to report the official client hostname (lines 151 and 152).

7. Flush the log file out to disk (line 153).

In all other respects, this server program remains the same. Note a few things about the `gethostbyaddr(3)` call in lines 142 to 145, however:

1. Note that the address given in argument one is the address of the `adr_clnt.sin_addr` member, not the address of the structure `adr_clnt`.

2. The length argument is the size of `adr_clnt.sin_addr`, which is 4 bytes. Do not supply the size of the structure `adr_clnt`.

3. The value in argument three was taken from `adr_clnt.sin_family`. This allows the program to be flexible for the possibility of `AF_INET6` support in the near future, instead of hard coding `AF_INET` (line 145).

Compiling and running this program is shown as follows:

OUTPUT

```
$ make srvr2
gcc -c  -D_GNU_SOURCE -Wall -Wreturn-type srvr2.c
gcc srvr2.o -o srvr2
@tux
$ ./srvr2 '*' &
[1] 1175
@tux
$ telnet localhost 9099
Trying 127.0.0.1...
Connected to localhost.
Escape character is '^]'.
Thursday Sep 02 23:29:51 1999
Connection closed by foreign host.
@tux
$ telnet tux 9099
Trying 192.168.0.1...
Connected to tux.penguins.org.
Escape character is '^]'.
Thursday Sep 02 23:30:01 1999
Connection closed by foreign host.
@tux
$ cat srvr2.log
Client 127.0.0.1: localhost
Client 192.168.0.1: tux.penguins.org
@tux
$
```

The server here is started and put into the background, using a wild server address '*'. This allows the server to be tested, in this example, from two different IP addresses:

- 127.0.0.1, which is named as localhost (as it is on most Linux systems)

- 192.168.0.1, which is named tux in the example penguins.org network

After starting the server with its wild address, a telnet to the address localhost on default port 9099 is performed. Later, another telnet is performed using the name tux. In the example, this causes telnet to use 192.168.0.1 to contact the server.

After both of those tests are performed, the log file is inspected using the cat command on the file srvr2.log. Notice that the log entries show 127.0.0.1 as localhost and 192.168.0.1 as tux.penguins.org. The server demonstrated that it was able to convert the client's IP numbers back into names for logging purposes.

Using the sethostent(3) Function

The sethostent(3) function permits you, as the application designer, to control how name server queries are performed. This function can improve the overall network performance of your application. The function synopsis is as follows:

```
#include <netdb.h>

void sethostent(int stayopen);
```

There is one input argument to sethostent(3). The argument stayopen is treated as a Boolean input parameter:

- When TRUE (non-zero), the name server queries are to be performed with a TCP/IP socket, which will remain open with the name server.

- When FALSE (zero), the name server queries will be performed using UDP datagrams as required.

The first case (TRUE) is useful when your application will make frequent name server requests. This is the higher-performance option for many queries. However, if your application only performs one query at startup, then the FALSE setting is more appropriate, because UDP has less network overhead.

Previously, Listing 9.4 showed how the function gethostbyname(3) could be used to perform name server lookups. To cause this program to use a connected TCP socket instead of UDP datagrams, you can add one call to sethostent(3) in the program. Rather than list the entire program again, Listing 9.6 shows a *context* diff of the differences between lookup.c and lookup2.c. This listing highlights the simple changes that were made.

Listing 9.6: Changes Required to lookup.c to Use a TCP Socket for Name Server Lookups

```
$ diff -c lookup.c lookup2.c
*** lookup.c    Sat Sep  4 14:58:35 1999
--- lookup2.c   Sat Sep  4 14:59:50 1999
***************
*** 14,23 ****
--- 15,29 ----

  extern int h_errno;

+ #define TRUE    1
+ #define FALSE   0
+
  int
  main(int argc,char **argv) {
      int x, x2;
      struct hostent *hp;
+
+     sethostent(TRUE);

      for ( x=1; x<argc; ++x ) {
          /*
$
```

In Listing 9.6, the context diff output shows lines added by preceding the line with a + character. From this, you can see that the only instrumental change that was made was that sethostent(TRUE) was called prior to entering the program's for loop. For clarity, macro definitions for TRUE and FALSE were also added, but these were not required.

Using the endhostent(3) Function

After calling upon sethostent(3) with a value of TRUE, your application might enter a phase of processing where it is known that no further name queries will be required. To use resources in a frugal manner, you need a method to end the connection to the name server, thus freeing the TCP/IP socket that is currently in use. This is the purpose of the endhostent(3) function. Its function synopsis is as follows:

```
#include <netdb.h>

void endhostent(void);
```

As you can see, this function takes no arguments and returns no values.

The endhostent(3) function can be of significant value to servers, particularly Web servers, where file descriptors are at a premium. You will recall that a socket uses a file descriptor and that one socket is required for each connected client. Server capacity is often restricted by the number of file descriptors that the server can have open. This makes it vitally important for servers to close file descriptors (and sockets) when they are no longer required.

What's Next

Having come this far with sockets, you might wonder what could possibly be next. The next chapter will show you how to apply those familiar standard I/O routines on sockets. These techniques will make writing client and server code much easier for certain applications. So keep those Linux terminal sessions open as you venture into the next chapter.

Part 2

Advanced Socket Programming

Using Standard I/O on Sockets

Concurrent Client Servers

Socket Options

Broadcasting with UDP

Out-of-Band Data

Using the `inetd` Daemon

Network Security Programming

Passing Credentials and File Descriptors

A Practical Network Project

Using Standard I/O on Sockets

The example code in the previous chapters have all used the read(2) or write(2) system calls to perform read and write operations on sockets. The only exception to this rule was recvfrom(2) and sendto(2) function calls, which were used to read and write datagrams. There are application disadvantages to using the simple read(2) and write(2) calls, however.

This chapter will explore

- How to associate a socket with a FILE stream using fdopen(3)

- How to create and apply read and write FILE streams

- Issues concerning closing streams associated sockets

- Choosing and establishing the correct buffering technique for your FILE streams

- The interrupted system call issue

Mastery of these topics will give you additional ways to solve your network programming assignments, and avoid surprises.

Understanding the Need for Standard I/O

The stdio(3) facility in Linux conforms to the ANSI C3.159-1989 standard. This standardization of the interface helps programs to be portable to many platforms. This might be useful to you, when porting source code from other UNIX systems to your own Linux platform, for example.

The stdio(3) package will itself issue read(2) and write(2) calls, "under the hood," so to speak. You, however, use the standard I/O calls instead, because they will offer you the convenience of getting a line or character at a time, according to your application needs. The read(2) call, for example, cannot return to your application one text line. Instead, it will return as much data as it can, even multiple text lines.

When writing to the socket, the standard I/O routines allow your application to write characters out one at a time, for example, without incurring large overhead. On the other hand, calling write(2) to write one character at a time is much more costly. The standard I/O functions permit your application to work with convenient units of data.

The stdio(3) package also provides the capability to buffer your data, both for input and for output. When buffering can be used, it can significantly improve the I/O performance of your application. Unfortunately, buffering creates difficulties for some forms of communication, and so it cannot always be used.

It will be assumed in this text that you are already familiar with the basics of stdio(3). This is usually taught in C programming texts, along with the C language itself. Consequently, this text will focus on things you need to watch out for, and other subtleties that might not be obvious, as it applies to socket programming.

NOTE

Linux introduces the standard I/O routines in its stdio(3) man page. Perform the following command to display this introductory text:

```
$ man 3 stdio
```

This will provide a list of standard I/O functions. If these all seem new to you, then you might want to review some of them. You should be acquainted with at least fopen(3), fread(3), fgets(3), fwrite(3), fflush(3), and fclose(3).

Associating a Socket with a Stream

The stdio(3) stream is managed through the FILE control block. For example, you've probably already written code that looks something like this many times:

```
FILE *in;

in = fopen(pathname,"r");
if ( in == NULL ) {
    fprintf(stderr,"%s: opening %s for read.\n",strerror(errno),pathname);
    exit(1);
}
```

In the example presented, the file known as variable `pathname` is opened for reading. If the open call succeeds, the variable `in` receives a pointer to the `FILE` structure, which manages the stream I/O for you. Otherwise, variable `in` receives a null pointer, and your application must handle or report the error.

For socket programming, however, there is no `stdio(3)` call available to open a socket. How then does a programmer accomplish associating a stream with a socket? Read the next section to find out.

Using `fdopen(3)` to Associate a Socket with a Stream

The function call `fopen(3)` should be quite familiar to you. However, for many, the `fdopen(3)` call is new or unfamiliar. Because this function is likely to be new to some of you, let's introduce its function synopsis and describe it:

```
#include <stdio.h>

FILE *fdopen(int fildes,const char *mode);
```

This function takes two arguments:

1. An integer file descriptor (`fildes`) to use for performing I/O.

2. The standard I/O mode to use. This will be an open mode, which is the same as the familiar `fopen(3)` mode argument. For example, `"r"` indicates that the stream is to be opened for reading, whereas `"w"` indicates the stream is to be opened for writing.

Like the `fopen(3)` call, if the function is successful, a pointer to the controlling `FILE` structure is returned. Otherwise, a null pointer indicates that a problem developed, and external variable `errno` will contain the nature of the error.

Note that the first argument was a file descriptor. You will recall that the socket returned from the `socket(2)` function is also a file descriptor. This then makes it possible to associate any existing socket to a stream. Listing 10.1 shows a short example of associating a socket to a stream that can be read or written.

Listing 10.1: Associating a Socket with a Stream

```
int s;      /* socket */
FILE *io;   /* stream */

s = socket(PF_INET,SOCK_STREAM,0);
...
io = fdopen(s,"r+");
if ( io == NULL ) {
    fprintf(stderr,"%s: fdopen(s)\n",strerror(errno));
    exit(1);
}
```

Listing 10.1 demonstrates how the socket number, which was held in variable s, was associated with a FILE stream named io. The mode argument of the fdopen(3) call in this example established a stream for input and output. After this open call has been successfully accomplished, the other standard I/O functions such as fgetc(3), for example, can be employed.

Closing a Socket Stream

Listing 10.1 showed how to associate the socket with a standard I/O stream. The application writer might well ask, "How should this socket or stream be closed?"

Reading the man page for fdopen(3) reveals that the file descriptor passed to the function is "not dup'ed." What this means is that the argument fildes is the descriptor actually used for the physical reads and writes. No duplicate is made of the file descriptor with the dup(2) function call. Consequently, in Listing 10.1, you do not want to call close(s) after successfully performing a fdopen(3) call. This would close the very file descriptor that the stream variable io is using.

If, however, you call fclose(io) in Listing 10.1, you will in effect end up closing the socket s. This is understood by examining the internal steps that are used by the fclose(3) function:

1. Flush any buffered data out to the file descriptor (whether file or socket). This results in a call to write(2) to the file descriptor, if there is any outstanding buffered data.

2. Close the underlying file descriptor used by the stream, using close(2).

3. Release the storage occupied by the buffers (if any), and the FILE structure itself. These are performed by calling the free(3) function.

You can visualize in step 2 that the socket s of Listing 10.1 would be closed by the normal procedure used by fclose(3).

Using Separate Read and Write Streams

Listing 10.1 showed how you could associate a socket with a stream that allows both input and output. Although this might be conceptually appealing, it is actually a safer practice to open separate streams for input and output. The reason for this is the fact that the buffering of the stream plays a more complex role on one stream than it does for two separate streams. The Linux fdopen(3) man page indicates that for I/O streams it is often necessary for a fgetpos(3) call to be performed between switching from write to read modes and vice versa.

Rather than try to explain why and when these special circumstances apply to an I/O stream, I'll just advise you to use two separate streams for reading and writing instead. This technique has very little overhead and provides better overall buffering performance in many cases.

Listing 10.2 shows how to create a separate read and write stream from one file descriptor.

EXAMPLE

Listing 10.2: Creating a Read and Write Stream

```
int s;      /* socket */
FILE *rx;   /* read stream */
FILE *tx    /* write stream */

s = socket(PF_INET,SOCK_STREAM,0);
…
rx = fdopen(s,"r");
if ( rx == NULL ) {
    fprintf(stderr,"%s: fdopen(s,'r')\n",strerror(errno));
    exit(1);
}

tx = fdopen(dup(s),"w");
if ( tx == NULL ) {
    fprintf(stderr,"%s: fdopen(s,'w')\n",strerror(errno));
    exit(1);
}
```

Examine Listing 10.2 carefully. Although the listing looks simple, there is one subtle function call included, which must not be overlooked. Can you find it?

Look at the statement where the variable tx is assigned. Then, examine the first argument to the fdopen(3) call in that statement. Did you notice the dup(2) call when you first looked at Listing 10.2? This is very important, because different streams should use different file descriptors. One simple reason for this is so that when fclose(tx) is called, it will not close the same file descriptor being used by the rx stream.

Duplicating a Socket

To understand why Listing 10.2 works, the dup(2) function will be reviewed here in case some readers are unfamiliar with its use:

```
#include <unistd.h>

int dup(int oldfd);
```

UNIX systems, like Linux, allow multiple file descriptors to refer to the same open file (or, in this case, a socket). By calling dup(2) with the socket s as an input argument, you are returned a new file descriptor. This new descriptor also refers to the original socket s. After this duplication has been performed, however, the socket itself will be shut down by the kernel only when the last of these two file descriptors are closed (assuming shutdown(2) is not used).

Numbers always help to clarify an example. Assume that, in Listing 10.2, socket s is created on file descriptor 3. Assume also that the socket s is duplicated as follows:

```
int s2;   /* dup'ed socket */

s2 = dup(s);   /* duplicate */
```

If file descriptor 4 is not currently in use, the Linux kernel will return 4 in the example shown. This allows the file descriptor 3 (variable s) and the file descriptor 4 (variable s2) to both refer to the same socket.

Closing the Dual Streams

After you have two streams established, as shown in Listing 10.2, you can safely use functions such as fgetc(3) or fgets(3) on your rx stream. Write calls using fputs(3) or fputc(3), for example, can use the output stream tx instead. Use of the separate streams eliminates buffer interaction and removes the need to call fgetpos(3) at various points in your program flow.

However, when you are finished with these streams, you must perform the following:

- fclose(rx) to close the input stream.
- fclose(tx) to close the output stream.

The preceding procedure accomplishes the following:

- Flushes any buffered writes for the writing stream.
- Closes the underlying file descriptor.
- Releases the buffers, if any.
- Releases the stream managed by the FILE object.

CAUTION

A failure to `fclose(3)` all streams created will lead to a very bad memory leak. This will also create a failure to properly close the underlying sockets. In a server, this failure will become readily apparent as the server continues to accept new clients and exhausts file descriptors and memory.

Winding Up Communications

The astute reader might have been wondering about the `shutdown(2)` call that was introduced earlier. How should this function call be exercised when it is needed?

With the dual stream approach, you might be tempted to misuse the `shutdown(2)` function, based on a bad assumption. For example, because there are actually two underlying file descriptors being used in Listing 10.2, it might be tempting to call `shutdown(2)` on each of the file descriptors. On one, you might shut down the read side, whereas on the other file descriptor, you might shut down the write side. Do not do this!

Recall from Chapter 1, "Introducing Sockets," that the `shutdown(2)` function was described. There, it was stated that one of the advantages of its use was that "it disregards the number of open references on the socket." Consequently, calling `shutdown(2)` on duplicated sockets will affect all references to the same socket. Consequently, it also affects all existing streams you have connected with that socket!

✔ A discussion of the `shutdown(2)` function can be found in Chapter 1, "Introducing Sockets," page 6.

When winding up communications between your process and the remote process over a socket, there are three basic scenarios to be considered:

- The process is not going to write any further data, but is expecting to receive more data (shutdown of the write side only).

- The process is not going to receive any further data, but is expecting to write more data (shutdown of the read side only).

- The process is not going to read or write any further data (shutdown of reading and writing).

Using the two streams shown in Listing 10.2, the scenarios will be described in the following sections.

Shutting Down the Write Side Only

The `shutdown(2)` function is called upon to indicate to the Linux kernel that the calling process intends no further writes of data, in this particular case.

Because the shutdown(2) call affects the socket and not the file descriptor, either file descriptor could actually be used. However, for program clarity, I would encourage you to use the writing stream to accomplish this task.

The procedure for this task consists of the following steps:

1. Flush any data that might exist in the stream buffers using fflush(3).

2. Shut down the write side of the socket using shutdown(2).

3. Close the stream, using fclose(3).

Before shutting down the write side, you must always flush the output stream. This is important because there might be some unwritten data that is sitting in a buffer. This can be accomplished as follows:

EXAMPLE

```
fflush(tx);   /* Flush buffer out */
```

To accomplish the shutdown(2) step, you need to obtain the underlying file descriptor of the stream tx. To access it, you can use the following C language macro:

```
#include <stdio.h>

int fileno(FILE *stream);
```

You simply pass the stream pointer to the macro as input, and it returns the underlying integer file descriptor that it is using. This is a portable and the only acceptable way of doing this. Applying this macro, you can perform the shutdown step as follows:

```
shutdown(fileno(tx),SHUT_WR);
```

The last step of this procedure is to simply fclose(3) the tx stream that you no longer need:

EXAMPLE

```
fclose(tx);
```

Putting the procedure all together, the shutdown procedure looks like this in C code:

```
fflush(tx);
shutdown(fileno(tx),SHUT_WR);
fclose(tx);
```

EXAMPLE

This sequence will leave the rx stream intact for reading, but forces all buffered data in the tx stream to be written out to the socket. The shutdown(2) call tells the kernel to expedite the sending of the socket data because there will be no more data to send. Finally, the fclose(3) call on the tx stream closes the file descriptor and releases the memory resources associated with the stream.

Shutting Down the Read Side Only

This procedure is similar to shutting down the write side only. The procedure does vary slightly:

1. Call shutdown(2) to indicate that there is no more receive data expected.

2. Close the stream using fclose(3).

You'll notice that there is no fflush(3) step required in this case. The procedure can be summarized in code as follows:

EXAMPLE

```
shutdown(fileno(rx),SHUT_RD);
fclose(rx);
```

Note again the portable use of the fileno(3) macro to fetch the underlying file descriptor for the stream rx. Although Listing 10.2 shows the original socket number is available in variable s, for program clarity it is probably preferred to use the fileno(3) macro after the rx stream has been created.

This procedure accomplishes the indication of no further reads to the Linux kernel, as well as the closing and releasing of all stream resources for rx. However, the application will still be able to write to stream tx unhindered.

Shutting Down Both Read and Write Sides

This procedure might be perceived as being more complex, but it actually turns out to be quite simple:

1. Close the write stream by calling fclose(3).

2. Close the read stream by calling fclose(3).

No fflush(3) is required in step 1 because the fclose(3) function for the write stream will implicitly ensure that this flush takes place. Closing the read stream in step 2 closes the last open file descriptor for the socket, so the socket is implicitly shut down for both reading and writing.

One exception to the rule, which might prove to be a sticking point, depends upon your application design. If your process has forked, then there might be other open file descriptors to your socket. You'll recall that only when the last close(2) takes place will the socket actually be shut down. If there is some doubt about this, you might want to follow a more elaborate procedure as follows:

1. Close the write stream using fclose(3). This will force unwritten data out to the socket, and release the write stream's resources.

2. Call shutdown(2) to terminate both reading and writing to this socket.

3. Close the read stream using fclose(3) to close the read file descriptor, and to release the stream's buffer and FILE structure.

The only real change to the procedure is that the shutdown(2) function is called as follows:

```
shutdown(fileno(rx),SHUT_RDWR);
```

The entire procedure boils down to this:

EXAMPLE

```
fclose(tx);
shutdown(fileno(rx),SHUT_RDWR);
fclose(rx);
```

I will submit to you that this procedure is the best one to use, even if you do not expect to have problems with the two-step procedure. This procedure will always accomplish your task, regardless of any future program modifications that might otherwise impact the other procedure.

Handling Interrupts

Reading the Linux man page for fread(3) or fwrite(3) doesn't reveal much about the possible errors that can be returned. Only the return value is described, which indicates that if the returned count is short, or the count is zero, an error has occurred.

The fread(3) and fwrite(3) functions are described in more detail within the AT&T System V Interface Definition documentation. What is interesting about this UNIX documentation is the fact that the error code EINTR can be returned.

NOTE

The AT&T System V Interface Definition (SVID) was one attempt to specify a UNIX operating system environment that allowed applications to be created, which was independent of the computer hardware used. The SVID standard was stated as compliant with the POSIX 1003.1 Full Use Standard and the ANSI C X3J11 industry standard.

The EINTR error indicates that an interrupted system call has occurred. This error is returned when your process has been signaled, and a signal handler has been called to process it, and that handler has returned from its call. This error code is not returned by all function calls, but it is returned in instances in which the function call might block for a long period of time. Certainly, a read(2) call waiting for incoming data on a socket fits in this category.

You'll recall that the fread(3) function call is simply a functional layer over the underlying read(2) function call that is invoked as required by buffering. Consequently, it follows that the fread(3) might be susceptible to the EINTR error code, if signals have been received by your process.

The same is also true of the fwrite(3) function call. If a large volume of data is written to a socket, the underlying write(2) call might also block for a long time. If, while it is blocked, a signal is received and handled, the write(2) function will return an EINTR error, which might cause the fwrite(3) function to return this error.

The word "might" was used because this depends upon the design of the stdio(3) library that you are using. I have seen some UNIX implementations hide this error from the caller, whereas others return EINTR. Given that Linux has generally been moving from the libc5 library to the newer glibc2 version of the C libraries, your mileage might vary.

Some simple testing for this under Red Hat Linux 6.0 suggests that EINTR will not be returned. However, as the GNU C library code moves with standards, which themselves are undergoing revision and further clarification, this might change. If your application must run on other UNIX platforms in addition to Linux, then you should test for EINTR in your code.

If you must allow for EINTR in your code, then the following code fragment represents a template that you might use:

EXAMPLE

```
int ch;

do  {
    clearerr(rx);
    ch = fgetc(rx);
} while ( ferror(rx) && errno == EINTR );
```

The basic procedure used here is

1. Call clearerr(3) to clear any pending error that might have occurred on this stream.

2. Perform your input/output operation.

3. If the operation failed and the errno value was set to EINTR, then repeat step 1.

After the code has exited the loop, this indicates that the operation either succeeded, or it failed with a different error code other than EINTR. The general principle at work here is that you *retry* the operation when the error EINTR is returned.

NOTE

Simple tests that were performed by the author suggested that the Red Hat Linux 6.0 distribution included a C library that hides the EINTR error from the application code. This can be both a blessing and a curse to the programmer. It is a blessing in the sense that you do not have to code to handle the error condition. It is a curse if you need to test to see whether a signal was processed by the signal handler while execution was blocked in the function call.

Include code to handle EINTR if any of the following applies to your situation:

- The source code might be ported to other UNIX platforms in addition to Linux.

- You are experiencing sporadic EINTR errors in your application (this is always a strong indication).

- The GNU C library has changed direction on its policy of hiding the EINTR error from the application.

If your application does not process signals, or it has established signals that are to be ignored, you might never need to be concerned about the EINTR error code.

Handling EINTR for Other Functions

It should be noted at this point that EINTR is potentially a problem for a host of other functions that you might use for socket programming. The functions affected by signals include

- connect(2)
- accept(2)
- read(2)
- write(2)
- readv(2)

- writev(2)
- recvfrom(2)
- sendto(2)
- select(2)
- poll(2)

The list presented is not meant to be an exhaustive list, and some of these functions have not been covered yet. It is a list of commonly used functions, however, which are affected by signal handling.

The examples that are shown in this text will largely ignore this issue of EINTR, in favor of keeping the example programs small and easier to understand. However, you must allow for the occurrence of EINTR for any production-level code.

CAUTION

Always test for the EINTR error when calling functions affected by signal handling in production-level code.

Defining Buffer Operation

When you make use of the stdio(3) facilities, you generally make use of some buffering behind the scenes. Buffered writes, for example, reduce the frequency that the system function write(2) is called. This increases the overall system output efficiency. Likewise, read requests are also buffered.

For example, fgetc(3) will fetch one character from a buffer. Only when the input buffer is empty will it request more data to be read in using the read(2) system call. This, again, is done to improve the I/O efficiency.

When the underlying file descriptor of a stream is a terminal device, the I/O under Linux will be line buffered. Files, on the other hand, are usually fully buffered (buffered in large blocks).

There are three basic modes of buffering to choose from using FILE streams under Linux. These are

- Fully buffered (or "block" buffered)
- Line buffered
- Unbuffered

Choosing "unbuffered" mode might be appropriate for some socket programs, although no efficiency from buffering can be gained this way. This does save you, however, from worrying about when to call fflush(3).

TIP

If your network application is experiencing hangs, the cause might be output buffering. Change the buffering on your output streams to "unbuffered mode" for testing. If the problem vanishes, then you need some calls to fflush(3) added to the appropriate places. Alternatively, you could reconsider the buffering mode being used by the application.

Line buffered mode is often useful when your socket interaction is text line based. Using line buffered mode means that you are never forced to call upon fflush(3) to force the last text line to be written to the socket.

If you choose to use the "fully" buffered mode, then you must apply fflush(3) at the point where you want a physical write to take place to the socket. Otherwise, your data might sit in an output buffer, while your application waits in vain for a response, because the output data was never sent.

The function synopses of the buffer control functions are shown in Listing 10.3.

EXAMPLE

Listing 10.3: Stream I/O Buffer Functions

```
#include <stdio.h>

int setbuf(FILE *stream,char *buf);

int setbuffer(FILE *stream, char *buf, size_t size);

int setlinebuf(FILE *stream);

int setvbuf(FILE *stream, char *buf, int mode, size_t size);
```

The functions in Listing 10.3 permit the caller to change the buffering mode of the specified stream. The Linux documentation indicates that these functions might be called at any time to change the buffering characteristics of the stream. The non-setvbuf(3) calls are aliases to the function setvbuf(3), which performs the operation.

CAUTION

If your code must be portable to other UNIX platforms, then you must only call the buffer adjustment functions before I/O calls have been made on the streams affected.

The arguments, by argument name, are described as follows:

- Argument stream is the FILE pointer of the stream that is to be affected.

- Argument buf is the pointer to the buffer being supplied. This pointer can be NULL. If a buffer is required, and NULL is supplied, then an internal buffer is allocated instead.

- Argument size is the size in bytes of the buffer provided (by argument buf), or the size of the internal buffer to be allocated.

- Argument mode is the buffering mode to be used.

A suggested buffer size is defined by the include file stdio.h as the macro BUFSIZ. Table 10.1 shows the list of mode values that can be supplied to setvbuf(3).

Table 10.1: The Mode Values for **setvbuf(3)**

C Macro	Description
_IOFBF	Input and/or output on the stream will be fully buffered.
_IOLBF	Input and/or output will be line buffered.
_IONBF	Input and/or output will not be buffered at all.

As an example of how to use the function to change the socket stream tx to use line buffered mode, you could code the following function call after the fdopen(3) call:

```
setlinebuf(tx); /* Line Buffered Mode */
```

Alternatively, you could accomplish the same thing by using the setvbuf(3) function directly:

EXAMPLE

```
setvbuf(tx,NULL,_IOLBF,BUFSIZ);
```

In this example, you allow the software to allocate its own internal buffer of BUFSIZ bytes. The buffering mode for the stream, however, is set to line buffered mode, due to the use of the macro _IOLBF in the function call.

Applying FILE Streams to Sockets

Now it is time to introduce some source code that makes use of the concepts that have been discussed so far. The server program that will be presented next implements a Reverse Polish Notation (abbreviated RPN) calculator. It accepts arbitrarily long integer values, stacks them, and then permits operations to be performed upon the stacked numbers. The result of the operation is placed on the top of the stack.

The integer arithmetic will be performed by the GNU Multi-Precision (GMP) library. This library permits virtually unlimited sized integer numbers to be evaluated. Space does not permit the GMP library to be described here. The purpose of this code is simply to illustrate some server concepts using FILE streams. This same server will help illustrate some advanced topics that will be covered in the nextchapter.

Presenting the mkaddr() Function

The mkaddr.c subroutine function will be presented here, to make this project easier to read. The mkaddr() function being presented, accepts an input string that consists of an IP number and an optional port number, or a hostname and optional port number. The port number can also be a symbolic Internet service name such as "telnet" or "ftp." The function synopsis of the function is as follows:

EXAMPLE

```
int mkaddr(void *addr, int *addr_len, char *str_addr, char *protocol);
```

The function arguments can be described as follows:

1. The argument addr points to the receiving socket address structure. This is the socket address, which is being returned. This value must not be null.

2. The argument addr_len is a pointer to an integer value, which will be filled with the length of the address created in addr when the function returns. The input value that is pointed to must contain the maximum size in bytes of the area pointed to by addr.

3. Argument str_addr is the symbolic hostname and optional port number (or service). This will be more fully described later. A null pointer implies a string value of "*".

4. The protocol argument specifies the protocol that this service will be using. A null pointer implies the protocol string "tcp".

The str_addr input string is designed to be as flexible as possible. It contains two components, separated by a colon character:

```
host_name:service
```

The host_name portion of the string can be one of the following:

- An IP number such as 127.0.0.1, for example.

- A hostname such as sunsite.unc.edu, for example.

- An asterisk, which indicates that the IP address should be the value INADDR_ANY.

The colon character and the service portion of the string are optional within str_addr. When not omitted, this component can be one of the following:

- A port number such as 8080, for example.

- A service name, such as telnet, for example.

- An asterisk, implying port zero. The bind(2) function call will assign a port number when this value is used.

The following examples show valid string values for the argument str_addr in the mkaddr() function call:

- www.lwn.net:80

- 127.0.0.1:telnet

- sunsite.unc.edu:ftp

The mkaddr() function returns the following possible values:

- Zero indicates that the conversion was successful.

- -1 indicates that the host part of the string was invalid, or that the hostname was unknown.

- -2 indicates that the port number was invalid, or that the service name was unknown.

The code for the mkaddr() subroutine is presented in Listing 10.4. This subroutine may be useful to use in projects that you might write. The instructions for compiling the code for mkaddr.c will be provided later, when the whole server is compiled.

EXAMPLE

Listing 10.4: mkaddr.c—The mkaddr() Subroutine

```
1:    /* mkaddr.c
2:     *
3:     * Make a socket address:
4:     */
5:    #include <stdio.h>
6:    #include <unistd.h>
7:    #include <stdlib.h>
```

```
8:    #include <errno.h>
9:    #include <ctype.h>
10:   #include <string.h>
11:   #include <sys/types.h>
12:   #include <sys/socket.h>
13:   #include <netinet/in.h>
14:   #include <arpa/inet.h>
15:   #include <netdb.h>
16:
17:   /*
18:    * Create an AF_INET Address:
19:    *
20:    * ARGUMENTS:
21:    *  1.  addr    Ptr to area
22:    *              where address is
23:    *              to be placed.
24:    *  2.  addrlen Ptr to int that
25:    *              will hold the final
26:    *              address length.
27:    *  3.  str_addr The input string
28:    *              format hostname, and
29:    *              port.
30:    *  4.  protocol The input string
31:    *              indicating the
32:    *              protocol being used.
33:    *              NULL implies "tcp".
34:    * RETURNS:
35:    *  0    Success.
36:    *  -1   Bad host part.
37:    *  -2   Bad port part.
38:    *
39:    * NOTES:
40:    *  "*" for the host portion of the
41:    *  address implies INADDR_ANY.
42:    *
43:    *  "*" for the port portion will
44:    *  imply zero for the port (assign
45:    *  a port number).
46:    *
47:    * EXAMPLES:
48:    *  "www.lwn.net:80"
49:    *  "localhost:telnet"
50:    *  "*:21"
51:    *  "*:*"
52:    *  "ftp.redhat.com:ftp"
53:    *  "sunsite.unc.edu"
```

continues

Listing 10.4: continued

```
54:     *   "sunsite.unc.edu:*"
55:     */
56:     int
57:     mkaddr(void *addr,
58:       int *addrlen,
59:       char *str_addr,
60:       char *protocol) {
61:
62:         char *inp_addr = strdup(str_addr);
63:         char *host_part = strtok(inp_addr,":");
64:         char *port_part = strtok(NULL,"\n");
65:         struct sockaddr_in *ap =
66:             (struct sockaddr_in *) addr;
67:         struct hostent *hp = NULL;
68:         struct servent *sp = NULL;
69:         char *cp;
70:         long lv;
71:
72:         /*
73:          * Set input defaults:
74:          */
75:         if ( !host_part )
76:             host_part = "*";
77:         if ( !port_part )
78:             port_part = "*";
79:         if ( !protocol )
80:             protocol = "tcp";
81:
82:         /*
83:          * Initialize the address structure:
84:          */
85:         memset(ap,0,*addrlen);
86:         ap->sin_family = AF_INET;
87:         ap->sin_port = 0;
88:         ap->sin_addr.s_addr = INADDR_ANY;
89:
90:         /*
91:          * Fill in the host address:
92:          */
93:         if ( strcmp(host_part,"*") == 0 )
94:             ;   /* Leave as INADDR_ANY */
95:         else if ( isdigit(*host_part) ) {
96:             /*
97:              * Numeric IP address:
98:              */
99:             ap->sin_addr.s_addr =
```

```
100:                 inet_addr(host_part);
101:         if ( ap->sin_addr.s_addr
102:             == INADDR_NONE )
103:             return -1;
104:     } else {
105:         /*
106:          * Assume a hostname:
107:          */
108:         hp = gethostbyname(
109:             host_part);
110:         if ( !hp )
111:             return -1;
112:         if ( hp->h_addrtype != AF_INET )
113:             return -1;
114:         ap->sin_addr =
115:             * (struct in_addr *)
116:             hp->h_addr_list[0];
117:     }
118:
119:     /*
120:      * Process an optional port #:
121:      */
122:     if ( !strcmp(port_part,"*") )
123:         ; /* Leave as wild (zero) */
124:     else if ( isdigit(*port_part) ) {
125:         /*
126:          * Process numeric port #:
127:          */
128:         lv = strtol(port_part,&cp,10);
129:         if ( cp != NULL && *cp )
130:             return -2;
131:         if ( lv < 0L || lv >= 32768 )
132:             return -2;
133:         ap->sin_port = htons(
134:             (short)lv);
135:     } else {
136:         /*
137:          * Lookup the service:
138:          */
139:         sp = getservbyname(
140:             port_part,
141:             protocol);
142:         if ( !sp )
143:             return -2;
144:         ap->sin_port =
145:             (short) sp->s_port;
```

continues

Listing 10.4: continued

```
146:      }
147:
148:      /* Return address length */
149:      *addrlen = sizeof *ap;
150:
151:      free(inp_addr);
152:      return 0;
153: }
```

The basic steps employed by the mkaddr() function in Listing 10.4 are as follows:

1. Duplicate the input string using strdup(3) in line 62 (this is necessary to enable the use of strtok(3) later).

2. Parse the host string out using strtok(3) in line 63.

3. Parse the port string out using strtok(3) in line 64.

4. Substitute default string values when NULL arguments are provided (lines 75 to 80).

5. Initialize the caller's address structure (lines 85 to 88).

6. Leave the value as INADDR_ANY if the host string matches the string "*" (line 94).

7. Otherwise, if the hostname starts with a digit, convert the numeric IP address in lines 99 to 103.

8. Otherwise, assume the hostname is a name. Look it up and place the first IP number returned into the address (lines 108 to 116).

9. Leave the port number as zero if the string matches "*" (line 123).

10. Otherwise, if the port number starts with a digit, extract the numeric value and use it as the port number (lines 128 to 134).

11. Otherwise, assume the port number is a service name. Look it up and assign it to the address (lines 139 to 145).

12. Return the constructed address length (line 149).

13. Free the string created by strdup(3) in step 1 (line 151).

14. Return zero to indicate a successful address conversion.

This routine reviews the concepts that were covered in earlier chapters. This subroutine is flexible enough that you might choose to use it in your own programs.

The RPN Calculator Engine Code

The RPN calculator engine code will be presented next. It is not expected that you will understand all of the GMP function calls because they have not been presented. However, if you have Red Hat Linux 6.0 installed, you can find out more about the GMP calls by performing the following command:

```
$ info GMP
```

This will bring up the info viewer with documentation about the GMP function library. Listing 10.5 lists the RPN calculator code. Note especially the standard I/O calls in the functions rpn_dump() and rpn_process().

Listing 10.5: rpneng.c—The RPN Calculator Code

```
1:    /* rpneng.c:
2:     *
3:     * RPN Engine:
4:     */
5:    #include <stdio.h>
6:    #include <stdlib.h>
7:    #include <errno.h>
8:    #include <string.h>
9:    #include <limits.h>
10:   #include <gmp.h>
11:
12:   typedef void (*mpz_func)(mpz_t,
13:       const mpz_t,const mpz_t);
14:   typedef void (*mpz_unary)(mpz_t,const mpz_t);
15:   typedef int (*rpn_spec)(void);
16:
17:   /*
18:    * RPN Stack:
19:    */
20:   #define MAX_STACK        32
21:   static mpz_t *stack[MAX_STACK];
22:   static int sp = 0;
23:
24:   /*
25:    * Allocate a new mpz_t value:
26:    */
27:   static mpz_t *
28:   rpn_alloc(void) {
29:       mpz_t *v = malloc(sizeof(mpz_t));
30:       mpz_init(*v);
31:       return v;
32:   }
```

continues

Listing 10.5: continued

```
33:
34:   /*
35:    * Duplicate a mpz_t value:
36:    */
37:   static mpz_t *
38:   rpn_duplicate(mpz_t *value) {
39:       mpz_t *v = rpn_alloc();
40:
41:       mpz_set(*v,*value);
42:       return v;
43:   }
44:
45:   /*
46:    * Free an allocated mpz_t value:
47:    */
48:   static void
49:   rpn_free(mpz_t **v) {
50:       mpz_clear(**v);
51:       free(*v);
52:       *v = NULL;
53:   }
54:
55:   /*
56:    * Push an mpz_t value onto the stack:
57:    */
58:   static int
59:   rpn_push(mpz_t *value) {
60:       if ( sp >= MAX_STACK )
61:           return -1;
62:       stack[sp] = value;
63:       return sp++;
64:   }
65:
66:   /*
67:    * Pop a mpz_t value from the stack:
68:    */
69:   static int
70:   rpn_pop(mpz_t **value) {
71:       if ( sp <= 0 )
72:           return -1;
73:       *value = stack[--sp];
74:       return sp;
75:   }
76:
77:   /*
78:    * Duplicate the top value on the stack:
```

```
79:    */
80:    static int
81:    rpn_dup(void) {
82:        mpz_t *opr2;
83:
84:        if ( sp <= 0 )
85:            return -1;
86:
87:        opr2 = rpn_alloc();
88:        mpz_set(*opr2,*stack[sp-1]);
89:        return rpn_push(opr2);
90:    }
91:
92:    /*
93:     * Swap the top two values on the stack:
94:     */
95:    static int
96:    rpn_swap(void) {
97:        mpz_t *opr1, *opr2;
98:
99:        if ( sp < 2 )
100:           return -1;
101:
102:       rpn_pop(&opr1);
103:       rpn_pop(&opr2);
104:       rpn_push(opr1);
105:       return rpn_push(opr2);
106: }
107:
108: /*
109:  * Dump the stack:
110:  */
111: static void
112: rpn_dump(FILE *tx) {
113:     int sx;
114:
115:     for ( sx=sp-1; sx >= 0; --sx ) {
116:         fprintf(tx,"%d:",sx);
117:         mpz_out_str(tx,10,*stack[sx]);
118:         fputc('\n',tx);
119:     }
120:     fputs("E:end of stack dump\n",tx);
121: }
122:
123: /*
124:  * Operation "seed":
```

continues

Listing 10.5: continued

```
125:  *
126:  * OPERANDS:
127:  *  1:  the least significant 32 bits
128:  *       will seed the random number
129:  *       generator via srand(3):
130:  * RESULTS:
131:  *  none.
132:  */
133: static int
134: rpn_seed(void) {
135:     int z;
136:     mpz_t *opr;
137:     long lv;
138:
139:     if ( (z = rpn_pop(&opr)) < 0 )
140:         /* No operand available */
141:         return -1;
142:
143:     /*
144:      * Get long value, ignoring errors.
145:      * Then seed the random number
146:      * generator:
147:      */
148:     lv = mpz_get_si(*opr);
149:     srand((int)lv);
150:
151:     rpn_free(&opr);
152:     return z;
153: }
154:
155: /*
156:  * Operation "random":
157:  *
158:  * OPERANDS:
159:  *  1.  A modulo value to apply after
160:  *       the random number is generated.
161:  * RESULTS:
162:  *  1.  A random value: 0 < modulo value.
163:  */
164: static int
165: rpn_random(void) {
166:     mpz_t *opr, *res;
167:     mpz_t r;
168:     size_t limbs;
169:
170:     if ( rpn_pop(&opr) < 0 )
```

```
171:          /* No operand available */
172:          return -1;
173:
174:    mpz_init(r);
175:    res = rpn_alloc();
176:
177:    /*
178:     * Pop the top to use as the modulo
179:     * operand. Generate a random number
180:     * r. Then compute r % opr as the
181:     * final result:
182:     */
183:    limbs = mpz_size(*opr);
184:    mpz_random(r,limbs);
185:    mpz_tdiv_r(*res,r,*opr);
186:
187:    mpz_clear(r);
188:    rpn_free(&opr);
189:
190:    return rpn_push(res);
191: }
192:
193: /*
194:  * Operation "tprime":
195:  *
196:  * Test for probability of being
197:  * a prime number:
198:  *
199:  * OPERANDS:
200:  *  1.  Number to test
201:  *  2.  Number of tests to try
202:  *      (typically 25)
203:  * RESULTS:
204:  *  1.  Number tested is probably
205:  *      prime when value = 1.
206:  *      Number tested is not prime
207:  *      when result is zero.
208:  */
209: static int
210: rpn_test_prime(void) {
211:    mpz_t *opr1, *opr2;
212:    long reps;
213:    int z;
214:
215:    if ( sp < 2 )
216:        /* Insufficient operands */
```

continues

Listing 10.5: continued

```
217:          return -1;
218:
219:    rpn_pop(&opr1);
220:    rpn_pop(&opr2);
221:
222:    if ( mpz_size(*opr2) > 1 )
223:          /* Too many limbs in size */
224:          return -1;
225:
226:    reps = mpz_get_si(*opr2);
227:    if ( reps < 1L || reps > 32768L )
228:          /* Too large for opr2 */
229:          return -1;
230:
231:    z = mpz_probab_prime_p(*opr1,reps);
232:    mpz_set_si(*opr1,(long)z);
233:    rpn_free(&opr2);
234:
235:    return rpn_push(opr1);
236: }
237:
238: /*
239:  * Operation "genprime":
240:  *
241:  * Generate a random prime number.
242:  *
243:  * OPERANDS:
244:  * 1.  The modulo value to apply
245:  *      to the randomizing value
246:  *      (see "random").
247:  * 2.  The number of primality
248:  *      tests to perform (typically
249:  *      this value is 25).
250:  * RESULTS:
251:  * 1.  The randomly generated prime
252:  *      number (actually, only a high
253:  *      probability of being prime).
254:  */
255: static int
256: rpn_genprime(void) {
257:    mpz_t *opr1;
258:    mpz_t *opr2;
259:    mpz_t *res;
260:
261:    if ( sp < 2 )
262:          return -1;
```

```
263:
264:      rpn_pop(&opr1);
265:      rpn_pop(&opr2);
266:
267:      for (;;) {
268:          rpn_push(rpn_duplicate(opr1));
269:          rpn_random();
270:          rpn_dup();
271:          rpn_push(rpn_duplicate(opr2));
272:          rpn_swap();
273:          rpn_test_prime();
274:          rpn_pop(&res);
275:          if ( mpz_cmp_si(*res,0L) != 0 )
276:              break;
277:          rpn_free(&res);
278:          rpn_pop(&res);
279:          rpn_free(&res);
280:      }
281:
282:      rpn_free(&res);
283:      rpn_free(&opr2);
284:      rpn_free(&opr1);
285:
286:      return sp - 1;
287: }
288:
289: /*
290:  * Standard binary arithmetic operations:
291:  *
292:  * OPERANDS:
293:  *   1.  Operand 2
294:  *   2.  Operand 1
295:  *
296:  * RESULTS:
297:  *   1.  Operand 1 op Operand 2
298:  */
299: static int
300: rpn_binoper(mpz_func f) {
301:      mpz_t *res, *opr1, *opr2;
302:
303:      if ( sp < 2 )
304:          /* Insufficient operands */
305:          return -1;
306:
307:      res = rpn_alloc();
308:      rpn_pop(&opr2);
```

continues

Listing 10.5: continued

```
309:     rpn_pop(&opr1);
310:
311:     f(*res,*opr1,*opr2);
312:
313:     rpn_free(&opr1);
314:     rpn_free(&opr2);
315:     return rpn_push(res);
316: }
317:
318: /*
319:  * Standard Unary Operations:
320:  *
321:  * OPERANDS:
322:  * 1.  Operand 1
323:  *
324:  * RESULTS:
325:  * 1.  Result of unary operation.
326:  */
327: static int
328: rpn_unaryop(mpz_unary f) {
329:     mpz_t *res, *opr1;
330:
331:     if ( sp < 1 )
332:         /* Insufficient operands */
333:         return -1;
334:
335:     res = rpn_alloc();
336:     rpn_pop(&opr1);
337:
338:     f(*res,*opr1);
339:
340:     rpn_free(&opr1);
341:     return rpn_push(res);
342: }
343:
344: /*
345:  * Execute RPN operation:
346:  *
347:  * RETURNS:
348:  * 0    Successful.
349:  * -1   Failed.
350:  */
351: static int
352: rpn_opr(char *oper) {
353:     int x;
354:     static struct {
```

```
355:        char    *oper;
356:        rpn_spec func;
357:    } spec[] = {
358:        { "dup", rpn_dup },
359:        { "swap", rpn_swap },
360:        { "seed", rpn_seed },
361:        { "random", rpn_random },
362:        { "tprime", rpn_test_prime },
363:        { "genprime", rpn_genprime },
364:        { 0 }
365:    };
366:    static struct {
367:        char    *oper;
368:        mpz_func func;
369:    } binops[] = {
370:        { "+", mpz_add },
371:        { "-", mpz_sub },
372:        { "*", mpz_mul },
373:        { "/", mpz_tdiv_q },
374:        { "%", mpz_tdiv_r },
375:        { "gcd", mpz_gcd },
376:        { 0 }
377:    };
378:    static struct {
379:        char    *oper;
380:        mpz_unary func;
381:    } unary[] = {
382:        { "abs", mpz_abs },
383:        { "neg", mpz_neg },
384:        { "sqrt", mpz_sqrt },
385:        { 0 }
386:    };
387:
388:    /*
389:     * Special Cases:
390:     */
391:    for ( x=0; spec[x].oper; ++x )
392:        if ( !strcmp(spec[x].oper,oper) )
393:            return spec[x].func();
394:
395:    /*
396:     * Test for a match on binary operators:
397:     */
398:    for ( x=0; binops[x].oper; ++x )
399:        if ( !strcmp(binops[x].oper,oper) )
400:            return rpn_binoper(binops[x].func);
```

continues

Listing 10.5: continued

```
401:
402:      /*
403:       * Test for a match on unary operators:
404:       */
405:      for ( x=0; unary[x].oper; ++x )
406:          if ( !strcmp(unary[x].oper,oper) )
407:              return rpn_unaryop(unary[x].func);
408:
409:      return -1;   /* Failed: unknown operator */
410: }
411:
412: void
413: rpn_process(FILE *tx,char *buf) {
414:      int z;
415:      mpz_t *t;
416:      char *operation;
417:      char *operand;
418:
419:      operation=strtok(buf,":\n\r");
420:      operand=strtok(NULL,"\n\r");
421:
422:      if ( !strcmp(operation,"dump") ) {
423:          rpn_dump(tx);
424:
425:      } else if ( !strcmp(operation,"=") ) {
426:          /*
427:           * Pop off the result:
428:           */
429:          if ( (z = rpn_pop(&t)) == -1 )
430:              fputs("E:Nothing to pop\n",tx);
431:          else {
432:              fprintf(tx,"%d:",z);
433:              mpz_out_str(tx,10,*t);
434:              fputc('\n',tx);
435:              rpn_free(&t);
436:          }
437:
438:      } else if ( !strcmp(operation,"#") ) {
439:          /*
440:           * Push an operand onto the stack:
441:           */
442:          t = rpn_alloc();
443:          if ( !mpz_set_str(*t,operand,10) )
444:              fprintf(tx,"%d:\n",rpn_push(t));
445:          else {
446:              fputs("E:Invalid number\n",tx);
```

```
447:                   rpn_free(&t);
448:            }
449:
450:      } else {
451:            /*
452:             * Perform an operation:
453:             */
454:            z = rpn_opr(operation);
455:            if ( z == -1 )
456:                   fprintf(tx,
457:                        "E:Operation failed.\n");
458:            else
459:                   fprintf(tx,"%d:\n",z);
460:      }
461:
462:      fflush(tx);
463: }
```

While Listing 10.5 is quite long, only the server concepts within it are important to you here. Consequently, only the rpn_process() function will be described:

1. The rpn_process() function is called with the output stream to write to (argument tx), and the input text line in buf to process (line 413).

2. The variables operation and operand are the parsed operation and operand strings, respectively (lines 419 to 420).

3. If the operation is special operation "dump", the function rpn_dump() is called to list the contents of the stack (lines 422 to 423).

4. If step 3 does not apply, and if the operation is "=", the value is popped off the stack and returned to the client program (lines 425 to 436). Proceed to step 7.

5. If steps 3 and 4 do not apply, and if the operation is "#", the operand value is pushed onto the stack (lines 438 to 448). Proceed to step 7.

6. If steps 3, 4, and 5 do not apply, all other RPN operations are handled by the function rpn_opr(). The result reported back to the client is the stack index value or an error indication (lines 454 to 460).

7. The output is forced to be written to the socket by calling fflush(tx) in line 462.

How the server works from the client side, will be examined after the remainder of the server code is presented. Listing 10.6 shows the remainder of the server source code. This represents the main program segment of the server.

Listing 10.6: `rpnsrv.c`—The RPN Main Server Code

```
1:   /* rpnsrv.c:
2:    *
3:    * Example RPN Server:
4:    */
5:   #include <stdio.h>
6:   #include <unistd.h>
7:   #include <stdlib.h>
8:   #include <errno.h>
9:   #include <string.h>
10:  #include <time.h>
11:  #include <sys/types.h>
12:  #include <sys/socket.h>
13:  #include <netinet/in.h>
14:  #include <arpa/inet.h>
15:  #include <netdb.h>
16:
17:  #ifndef SHUT_RDWR
18:  #define SHUT_RDWR 3
19:  #endif
20:
21:  extern int mkaddr(void *addr,
22:      int *addr_len,
23:      char *input_address,
24:      char *protocol);
25:
26:  extern void rpn_process(FILE *tx,
27:      char *buf);
28:
29:
30:  /*
31:   * This function reports the error and
32:   * exits back to the shell:
33:   */
34:  static void
35:  bail(const char *on_what) {
36:      if ( errno != 0 ) {
37:          fputs(strerror(errno),stderr);
38:          fputs(": ",stderr);
39:      }
40:      fputs(on_what,stderr);
41:      fputc('\n',stderr);
42:      exit(1);
43:  }
44:
45:  int
46:  main(int argc,char **argv) {
```

```
47:        int z;
48:        char *srvr_addr = "127.0.0.1:9090";
49:        struct sockaddr_in adr_srvr;/* AF_INET */
50:        struct sockaddr_in adr_clnt;/* AF_INET */
51:        int len_inet;              /* length   */
52:        int s = -1;                  /* Socket */
53:        int c = -1;            /* Client socket */
54:        FILE *rx = NULL;        /* Read stream */
55:        FILE *tx = NULL;       /* Write stream */
56:        char buf[4096];          /* I/O Buffer */
57:
58:        /*
59:         * Use a server address from the command
60:         * line, otherwise default to 127.0.0.1:
61:         */
62:        if ( argc >= 2 )
63:            srvr_addr = argv[1];
64:
65:        len_inet = sizeof adr_srvr;
66:        z = mkaddr(&adr_srvr,&len_inet,
67:            srvr_addr,"tcp");
68:
69:        if ( z < 0 || !adr_srvr.sin_port ) {
70:            fprintf(stderr,"Invalid server "
71:                "address, or no port number "
72:                "was specified.\n");
73:            exit(1);
74:        }
75:
76:        /*
77:         * Create a TCP/IP socket to use:
78:         */
79:        s = socket(PF_INET,SOCK_STREAM,0);
80:        if ( s == -1 )
81:            bail("socket(2)");
82:
83:        /*
84:         * Bind the server address:
85:         */
86:        z = bind(s,(struct sockaddr *)&adr_srvr,
87:                len_inet);
88:        if ( z == -1 )
89:            bail("bind(2)");
90:
91:        /*
92:         * Make it a listening socket:
```

continues

Listing 10.6: continued

```
93:          */
94:          z = listen(s,10);
95:          if ( z == -1 )
96:                  bail("listen(2)");
97:
98:          /*
99:           * Start the server loop:
100:          */
101:         for (;;) {
102:                 /*
103:                  * Wait for a connect:
104:                  */
105:                 len_inet = sizeof adr_clnt;
106:                 c = accept(s,
107:                     (struct sockaddr *)&adr_clnt,
108:                     &len_inet);
109:                 if ( c == -1 )
110:                         bail("accept(2)");
111:
112:                 /*
113:                  * Create streams:
114:                  */
115:                 rx = fdopen(c,"r");
116:                 if ( !rx ) {
117:                     /* Failed */
118:                     close(c);
119:                     continue;
120:                 }
121:
122:                 tx = fdopen(dup(c),"w");
123:                 if ( !tx ) {
124:                     fclose(rx);
125:                     continue;
126:                 }
127:
128:                 /*
129:                  * Set both streams to line
130:                  * buffered mode:
131:                  */
132:                 setlinebuf(rx);
133:                 setlinebuf(tx);
134:
135:                 /*
136:                  * Process client's requests:
137:                  */
138:                 while ( fgets(buf,sizeof buf,rx) )
```

```
139:              rpn_process(tx,buf);
140:
141:         /*
142:          * Close this client's connection:
143:          */
144:         fclose(tx);
145:         shutdown(fileno(rx),SHUT_RDWR);
146:         fclose(rx);
147:     }
148:
149:     /* Control never gets here */
150:     return 0;
151: }
```

The main features of the server code in Listing 10.6 should be relatively familiar to you now. The basic steps used in this module were as follows:

1. The C macro SHUT_RDWR is defined in line 18, if the macro is not already defined. This makes the source code clearer when shutdown(2) is being called later in the program.

2. The server's address is taken from the command line, if it is present (lines 62 and 63).

3. The mkaddr() subroutine is called to construct a server address for us in lines 65 to 74.

4. A server socket is created (lines 79 to 81).

5. The server address is bound to the socket (lines 86 to 89).

6. The socket is made into a listening socket (lines 94 to 96).

7. The program waits for a client to connect (lines 105 to 110).

8. Input and output file streams are created in lines 115 to 126. Notice that error recovery must ensure that the currently open streams and client socket are closed. The error itself is not reported by this server, if it should occur.

9. The I/O streams are set to line buffered mode (lines 132 to 133).

10. Until EOF is reached, each text line is read from the client and processed by the function rpn_process() (lines 138 to 139).

11. A full shutdown is performed for this client (lines 144 to 146).

12. Repeat step 7 to accommodate the next client connection.

Although limited, you can see that Listing 10.6 is a simple server loop that keeps accepting client connections in single-file fashion. Later, you'll learn how to write a higher-performance server that can concurrently process several clients at one time.

Trying Out the RPN Server

To compile all the related source modules for the RPN server, you can perform the following make command:

OUTPUT

```
$ make rpnsrv
gcc -c  -D_GNU_SOURCE -Wall -Wreturn-type rpnsrv.c
gcc -c  -D_GNU_SOURCE -Wall -Wreturn-type rpneng.c
gcc -c  -D_GNU_SOURCE -Wall -Wreturn-type mkaddr.c
gcc rpnsrv.o rpneng.o mkaddr.o -o rpnsrv -lgmp
$
```

After the executable rpnsrv for the server has been created, you can start the server as follows:

OUTPUT

```
$ ./rpnsrv &
[1] 13321
$
```

In the output shown, the server was started with a process ID of 13321, and run in the background.

To keep things simple at this point, you'll just use the telnet command to try out the server. The next chapter will fully outline this server's functions. For now, just try some simple tests.

CAUTION

The server presented is not a production-grade server. Some forms of incorrect input can provoke the server to abort.

The RPN calculator computes based upon numbers that are pushed onto the stack. To perform the add operation, for example, requires at least two numbers to exist on the stack. To push a number onto the stack, you will enter a line as follows:

```
#:970976453
```

After you press Enter, the server will respond with something like this:

```
0:
```

This tells you that the number has been stacked at the bottom of the stack (entry number zero). To stack another number, simply do the same, as follows:

```
#:2636364
```

The server will respond with

```
1:
```

This indicates that the number 2636364 was stacked at position 1, although the original number 970976453 still sits at the bottom of the stack at position 0. You can list the current contents of the stack by entering the following:

```
dump
```

The following example shows what the session and its output might look like this:

OUTPUT

```
$ telnet localhost 9090
Trying 127.0.0.1...
Connected to localhost.
Escape character is '^]'.
#:970976453
0:
#:2636364
1:
dump
1:2636364
0:970976453
E:end of stack dump
```

To perform a binary operation, you simply enter the name of the operation or its symbol. For example, to add these numbers, you would just enter the + character and press return. The session repeated without entering the dump command would appear as follows if the + operation was performed, and then followed by the = operation:

OUTPUT

```
$ telnet localhost 9090
Trying 127.0.0.1...
Connected to localhost.
Escape character is '^]'.
#:970976453
0:
#:2636364
1:
+
0:
=
0:973612817
^]
telnet> c
Connection closed.
$
```

The + operation caused the two stacked numbers to be added together, and the result replaced the two original values. The = operator here pops the result off the stack and displays it for you.

To exit the server, type CTRL+] and you will be prompted with the prompt:

telnet>

From there, enter a c to indicate that you want the session closed, and press Enter. To terminate the server, just use the kill command.

Take a few minutes now to have some fun with the new RPN calculating server program. Restart the server, and see whether you can figure out how to compute the equation (3 + 2) * (2 + 4) using the calculating server just presented.

After your experiment, you deserve a break. The server will be more fully explored in the next chapter as you look at more advanced server issues. For now, just take stock of the concepts you have mastered in this chapter.

What's Next

This chapter has introduced you to the idea of using FILE streams with your sockets. You can readily appreciate how streams will make certain tasks much simpler for your code, such as the input and output of text lines.

You also learned to be aware of the EINTR problem if the glibc library should change or if your code is ported to another UNIX platform.

The next chapter will teach you how servers can service multiple client connections at the same time. This is not as trivial as you might imagine.

Concurrent Client Servers

All of the servers presented in this text so far have processed one client's request in total before accepting a connection to the next client. This design is effective and simple for servers that reply swiftly. However, if the processing takes a long time, or there are periods of inactivity, then this will prevent other clients from being serviced without lengthy delays. Because servers are usually required to service as many clients as possible, with a minimum of delay, a fundamental design change is needed at the server end of the connection.

In this chapter you will learn how to use the following:

- The fork(2) function in order to handle multiple client connections

- The wait(2) and waitpid(2) functions

- The select(2) function for handling multiple client connections

Mastering these concepts will permit you to write professional-grade servers, which can service large numbers of clients at once.

Understanding the Multiple-Client Problem

Figure 11.1 shows several clients, which have contacted one server. The client connections conceptually form spokes around the central server.

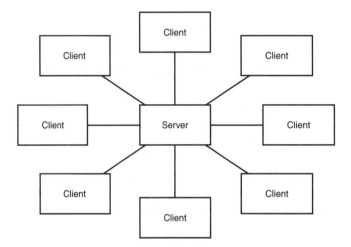

Figure 11.1: *Several clients attached to one server can be graphically represented as spokes attached to a hub.*

The server, acting as the central hub in Figure 11.1, must balance its resources among several connected clients. The server is normally designed to behave such that each client thinks that it has dedicated server access. In reality, however, the server services all clients in a concurrent manner.

There are a few of ways of achieving this. They are

- Forked server processes (multi-process method)
- Threaded server processes (multi-thread method)
- One process and a select(2) call
- One process and a poll(2) call

The first method of using the fork(2) system call is perhaps the simplest way to service multiple-client processes. However, it suffers from the disadvantage that sharing information becomes more complex. This usually requires the use of message queues, shared memory, and semaphores. It also suffers from the disadvantage that it requires more CPU to start and manage a new process for each request.

The threaded server method is relatively new to UNIX, and is now a viable option for Linux. Kernel versions 2.0.0 and later support threads, provided that the appropriate thread-safe libraries are used. Threads offer the light-weight advantages of the multi-process method, without hampering central-ized communication. Threaded processes can be very difficult to debug, however, especially for beginning programmers. For this reason, threads will not be explored in this text.

TIP

Frequently Asked Question (FAQ) documents that describe threads in more detail under Linux are available on the Internet for your viewing. Some references to these are

```
http://metalab.unc.edu/pub/Linux/docs/faqs/Threads-FAQ/html
http://linas.org/linux/threads-faq.html
http://pauillac.inria.fr/~xleroy/linuxthreads
http://www.globenet.it/~ermmau/Threads
```

The last two methods listed involve the use of the select(2) or poll(2) function calls. Each of these functions offer a different way to block execu-tion of the server until an event occurs. The select(2) function will be examined in detail within this chapter. The interested reader is encouraged to read the man pages for poll(2) after completing this chapter.

Overview of Server Functions

Chapter 10, "Using Standard I/0 on Sockets," introduced the Reverse Polish Notation (RPN) calculating server. Only its most primitive functions were described, however. Before you dive into the server's design aspects in this chapter, you should get to know some of the server's capabilities first. In this manner, you'll be able to give the server a better workout.

The most basic functions are listed in Table 11.1. These describe the most rudimentary arithmetic and operating functions available.

Table 11.1: The Rudimentary RPN Server Functions

Function	Argument	Description
#	Integer	An integer value to push onto the stack.
+	N/A	Add the two numbers on the top of the stack. The numeric resulting number replaces these two values on the top of the stack.
–	N/A	Subtract the top number from the next to last number on the stack. The result replaces the two values on the top of the stack.
*	N/A	Multiply the two numbers on the top of the stack. The resulting value replaces the two numbers on the top of the stack.

continues

Table 11.1: continued

Function	Argument	Description
/	N/A	Divide the top number into the next to last number on the top of the stack. The integer result replaces these two numbers on the top of the stack.
%	N/A	Replace the top two numbers on the stack with the modulo result (remainder) of the top number divided into the next to last number.
=	N/A	The top result is popped off of the stack and returned to the client.
dump	N/A	The entire stack is dumped back to the client. The stack is left unmodified.

Listing 11.1 shows a simple calculation being performed. Then the functions dump and = are tested prior to exiting the server.

Listing 11.1: Testing the Basic RPN Server Functions

OUTPUT

```
$ telnet localhost 9090
Trying 127.0.0.1...
Connected to localhost.
Escape character is '^]'.
#:3
0:
#:4
1:
#:7
2:
dump
2:7
1:4
0:3
E:end of stack dump
+
1:
dump
1:11
0:3
E:end of stack dump
*
0:
dump
0:33
E:end of stack dump
=
0:33
dump
E:end of stack dump
```

```
^]
telnet> c
Connection closed.
$
```

The session showed how to compute the following:

```
3 * (4 + 7)
```

The steps performed in Listing 11.1 are as follows:

1. The three values 3, 4, and 7 are first pushed onto the stack.

2. The stack is dumped with the dump operation.

3. The + operation is performed, which causes 4 + 7 to be evaluated and its result 11 to be placed on the stack in place of the inputs.

4. The stack is dumped again using dump. From this, you can see that the values 3 and 11 remain on the stack.

5. The multiplication of 3 * 11 is evaluated when * is entered. The result of 33 replaces the input values on the stack.

6. The dump operation is performed again to show the stack contents. It shows the single result of 33 on the stack.

7. The = operation pops this last value off the stack.

8. The dump operation now shows an empty stack.

9. The telnet session is closed using CTRL+] and then the c character followed by a RETURN.

Unary functions supported by the server are shown in Table 11.2.

Table 11.2: Unary RPN Server Functions

Function	Argument	Description
abs	N/A	The top stack value is replaced with the absolute value of that number.
neg	N/A	The top stack value is replaced with the negated value of that number.
sqrt	N/A	The top stack value is replaced with the integer square root of that number.

Note that the unary functions only require one number to exist on the stack. Table 11.3 lists some more advanced functions that the RPN server supports.

Table 11.3: Advanced RPN Server Functions

Function	Argument	Description
gcd	N/A	Compute the greatest common divisor between the top two numbers on the stack. The result replaces the top two numbers on the stack.
seed	N/A	Use the value on the top of the stack as a random number seed value. There is no result pushed onto the stack.
random	N/A	Use the value on the top of the stack to act as the largest value + 1 for the random number to be generated. The random result replaces the input value on the stack.
tprime	N/A	Test the top stack value to see if it is a prime number. The second-to-last number on the top of the stack indicates how many tests to apply. A typical value is 25. The result replaces the two input values on the stack. A result of 1 indicates that the number is probably prime, while 0 indicates that the number is not prime.
genprime	N/A	Generate a prime number, using the top of the stack as a "maximum random number + 1" value (see random). The second-to-last number on the stack indicates the number of tests to perform (typically 25). The generated result replaces the top two values.
swap	N/A	Swap the top two values on the stack. Useful for exchanging two numbers.
dup	N/A	Duplicate the top value on the stack.

The use of the seed and random functions require a bit of explanation. The seed function allows you to predictably seed a random number generator. This is important if you want to reproduce a set of random numbers for subsequent tests. For example:

OUTPUT

```
#:1000
0:
seed
0:
#:3000
0:
random
0:
dump
0:560
```

This sequence seeds the random number generator with the value 1000. Later, 3000 is input to the function random which produces the random result 560. The value 3000 acts as a maximum value + 1 for the random function. With this as an input value, the random number generated could be between the values of 0 and 2999.

The `genprime` function works similarly. Take for example:

OUTPUT

```
#:25
0:
#:999999999999999999999999999999999
1:
genprime
0:
dump
0:73169466699683312602513089203447
E:end of stack dump
```

This example shows how a large prime number is generated. The value 25 pushed, causing the generated number to be tested 25 times to see if it is a prime number. If you need better assurance that the number is prime, you must use a larger test value. The function `tprime` works the same way, except that it produces a test result of zero or one instead. One indicates the number was tested as probably prime.

NOTE

The prime number tests are implemented in the GMP library function `mpz_probab_prime_p()`. This function implements a "probabilistic primality test" based upon the work by Donald E. Knuth, *The Art of Computer Programming*, vol 2, *Seminumerical Algorithms*, 2nd edition, Addison-Wesley, 1981.

The result of the function indicates a high probability that the number is prime. The probability of returning a false positive indication is $(1/4)^r$, where r represents the number of tests to be performed. The documentation states that the value of 25 is a reasonable number for r.

Using `fork(2)` to Service Multiple Clients

The server that was developed in Chapter 10 has been modified in this section to handle multiple clients by means of a `fork(2)` system call. Listing 11.2 shows the listing of the modified `rpnsrv.c` module. All other source modules remain the same as they appeared in the previous chapter.

EXAMPLE

Listing 11.2: `rpnsrv.c`—The `fork(2)` Modified RPN Server

```
1:    /* rpnsrv.c:
2:     *
3:     * Example RPN Server:
4:     */
5:    #include <stdio.h>
6:    #include <unistd.h>
7:    #include <stdlib.h>
8:    #include <errno.h>
9:    #include <string.h>
```

continues

Listing 11.2: continued

```
10:   #include <time.h>
11:   #include <sys/types.h>
12:   #include <sys/socket.h>
13:   #include <netinet/in.h>
14:   #include <arpa/inet.h>
15:   #include <netdb.h>
16:   #include <sys/wait.h>
17:   #include <signal.h>
18:
19:   #ifndef SHUT_RDWR
20:   #define SHUT_RDWR 3
21:   #endif
22:
23:   extern int mkaddr(void *addr,
24:       int *addr_len,
25:       char *input_address,
26:       char *protocol);
27:
28:   extern void rpn_process(FILE *tx,
29:       char *buf);
30:
31:   /*
32:    * Process Terminated Child processes:
33:    */
34:   static void
35:   sigchld_handler(int signo) {
36:       pid_t PID;
37:       int status;
38:
39:       do  {
40:           PID = waitpid(-1,&status,WNOHANG);
41:       } while ( PID != -1 );
42:
43:       /* Re-instate handler */
44:       signal(SIGCHLD,sigchld_handler);
45:   }
46:
47:   /*
48:    * This function reports the error and
49:    * exits back to the shell:
50:    */
51:   static void
52:   bail(const char *on_what) {
53:       if ( errno != 0 ) {
54:           fputs(strerror(errno),stderr);
55:           fputs(": ",stderr);
```

```
56:         }
57:         fputs(on_what,stderr);
58:         fputc('\n',stderr);
59:         exit(1);
60:     }
61:
62:     int
63:     main(int argc,char **argv) {
64:         int z;
65:         char *srvr_addr = "127.0.0.1:9090";
66:         struct sockaddr_in adr_srvr;/* AF_INET */
67:         struct sockaddr_in adr_clnt;/* AF_INET */
68:         int len_inet;                /* length  */
69:         int s = -1;                   /* Socket */
70:         int c = -1;              /* Client socket */
71:         FILE *rx = NULL;          /* Read stream */
72:         FILE *tx = NULL;        /* Write stream */
73:         char buf[4096];          /* I/O Buffer */
74:         pid_t PID;               /* Process ID */
75:
76:         /*
77:          * Set signal handler for SIGCHLD:
78:          */
79:         signal(SIGCHLD,sigchld_handler);
80:
81:         /*
82:          * Use a server address from the command
83:          * line, otherwise default to 127.0.0.1:
84:          */
85:         if ( argc >= 2 )
86:             srvr_addr = argv[1];
87:
88:         len_inet = sizeof adr_srvr;
89:         z = mkaddr(&adr_srvr,&len_inet,
90:             srvr_addr,"tcp");
91:
92:         if ( z < 0 || !adr_srvr.sin_port ) {
93:             fprintf(stderr,"Invalid server "
94:                 "address, or no port number "
95:                 "was specified.\n");
96:             exit(1);
97:         }
98:
99:         /*
100:          * Create a TCP/IP socket to use:
101:          */
```

continues

Listing 11.2: continued

```
102:     s = socket(PF_INET,SOCK_STREAM,0);
103:     if ( s == -1 )
104:         bail("socket(2)");
105:
106:     /*
107:      * Bind the server address:
108:      */
109:     z = bind(s,(struct sockaddr *)&adr_srvr,
110:             len_inet);
111:     if ( z == -1 )
112:         bail("bind(2)");
113:
114:     /*
115:      * Make it a listening socket:
116:      */
117:     z = listen(s,10);
118:     if ( z == -1 )
119:         bail("listen(2)");
120:
121:     /*
122:      * Start the server loop:
123:      */
124:     for (;;) {
125:         /*
126:          * Wait for a connect:
127:          */
128:         len_inet = sizeof adr_clnt;
129:         c = accept(s,
130:             (struct sockaddr *)&adr_clnt,
131:             &len_inet);
132:         if ( c == -1 )
133:             bail("accept(2)");
134:
135:         /*
136:          * Fork a new server process
137:          * to service this client:
138:          */
139:         if ( (PID = fork()) == -1 ) {
140:             /* Failed to fork: Give up */
141:             close(c);
142:             continue;
143:         } else if ( PID > 0 ) {
144:             /* Parent process: */
145:             close(c);
146:             continue;
147:         }
```

```
148:
149:        /*
150:         * CHILD PROCESS:
151:         * Create streams:
152:         */
153:        rx = fdopen(c,"r");
154:        if ( !rx ) {
155:            /* Failed */
156:            close(c);
157:            continue;
158:        }
159:
160:        tx = fdopen(dup(c),"w");
161:        if ( !tx ) {
162:            fclose(rx);
163:            continue;
164:        }
165:
166:        /*
167:         * Set both streams to line
168:         * buffered mode:
169:         */
170:        setlinebuf(rx);
171:        setlinebuf(tx);
172:
173:        /*
174:         * Process client's requests:
175:         */
176:        while ( fgets(buf,sizeof buf,rx) )
177:            rpn_process(tx,buf);
178:
179:        /*
180:         * Close this client's connection:
181:         */
182:        fclose(tx);
183:        shutdown(fileno(rx),SHUT_RDWR);
184:        fclose(rx);
185:
186:        /*
187:         * Child process must exit:
188:         */
189:        exit(0);
190:    }
191:
192:    /* Control never gets here */
193:    return 0;
194: }
```

The following session shows how to compile and to start the server in the background:

```
$ make rpnsrv
gcc -c  -D_GNU_SOURCE -Wall -Wreturn-type rpnsrv.c
gcc -c  -D_GNU_SOURCE -Wall -Wreturn-type rpneng.c
gcc -c  -D_GNU_SOURCE -Wall -Wreturn-type mkaddr.c
gcc rpnsrv.o rpneng.o mkaddr.o -o rpnsrv -lgmp
$ ./rpnsrv '*:9090' &
 [2] 915
$
```

After the server has been started, you can use telnet from multiple xterm windows to try out the server simultaneously. If you are not running the X Window system, you can use various virtual console sessions to accomplish the same effect.

The principle changes to the module are as follows:

- The <sys/wait.h> and <signal.h> include files were added in lines 16 and 17.

- A signal handler for SIGCHLD was added to lines 34 to 45.

- A process ID variable PID was declared in line 74.

- The SIGCHLD signal handler was installed at line 79.

- A call to fork(2) was added in lines 139 to 147.

- A call to exit(2) was added at line 189.

Understanding the Overall Server Process

The basic main program of the server now functions as follows:

1. A signal handler for SIGCHLD is installed at line 79. This will play a role for terminated processes, which will be discussed later.

2. A server address and socket are created (lines 85 to 112).

3. The socket is converted to a listening socket (lines 117 to 119).

4. The main loop begins (line 124).

5. The server blocks its execution until a client connects (lines 128 to 133).

6. The fork(2) function is called in line 139.

7. If step 6 fails, the value –1 is returned by fork(2) and the server closes the connected socket c (line 141). Then the loop repeats with step 5.

8. If step 6 succeeds, then PID will contain the process ID of the child process in the parent process (lines 144 to 147). The parent process simply closes the accepted connection c and repeats step 5.

The parent process loops between steps 5 to 8 until the server is killed off. Effectively, the parent process only accepts connections. It does no other work.

Understanding the Child Server Process Flow

The child process in Listing 11.2, created by the `fork(2)` process in step 6, follows these steps:

1. Because the `fork(2)` function returns zero for the child process, its code continues execution at line 153.

2. The child process keeps socket c open and associates this socket with FILE streams tx and rx (lines 153 to 164).

3. Processing continues in the child process as normal in lines 170 to 184.

4. At this stage, the child process has finished processing for the client. The `exit(3)` function is called to terminate the child process (line 189). This step will cause the signal SIGCHLD to be raised in the parent server process.

Note that the parent process closes the socket c in line 145. This is important because, after the `fork(2)` call, both parent and client processes have this connected socket open. The parent process is not servicing the client request, so it simply closes the socket. The child process, however, will process the client's requests and uses the open socket in variable c.

With this design, the connected client can take its merry time in submitting requests without making other clients of the same server wait. This is because the parent server process simply accepts new connections. The parent server process performs the following steps:

1. Accept a connection from a client.

2. Fork a new process to service the client.

3. Close its copy of the connected client's socket.

4. Repeat step 1.

The servicing of the connected client is simple, because the server child process only has to worry about one connected socket.

Understanding Process Termination Processing

The one complication that the fork(2) function call inflicts upon the design of the server is that it must process information about terminated processes. This is very important, because when a child process terminates, most of its resources are released. The rest of its resources are released only when the parent process obtains the child process termination status information.

The parent process is notified of a child process termination by means of the signal SIGCHLD. Now examine the steps that the parent server process uses when a child process terminates:

1. The signal SIGCHLD is raised by the kernel to indicate that the child process has terminated.

2. The function sigchld_handler() is called (line 35), because the function was registered for the SIGCHLD signal in line 79.

3. The sigchld_handler() executes a loop calling waitpid(2) until no more exit status information is available.

4. The SIGCHLD handler is re-instated in line 44. This was necessary because the reliable signals interface was not used in order to keep the example program simple.

NOTE

In a production mode server, only the reliable signal functions such as sigaction(2) should be used. This was avoided in the example program to keep the source code simple.

CAUTION

Failure to call wait(2) or waitpid(2) by the parent process after a fork(2) and the child process's subsequent termination will result in *zombie processes* being left around until the parent process terminates. This can tie up valuable system resources.

The reader is encouraged to review the functions fork(2), waitpid(2), and signal(2), if necessary. These are important aspects of this server design.

Designing Servers That Use select(2)

While the server just presented was able to employ the fork(2) function to gainfully serve multiple clients, there are other server designs that might be preferable. A server that must share information between connected clients might find it desirable to keep the server contained within a single process. Another requirement that might dictate a single process server model is the fact that one process does not consume the same amount of system resources as many processes would. For these reasons, it is necessary to consider a new server design philosophy.

Introducing the select(2) Function

The select(2) function permits you to block the execution of your server until there is something for the server to do. More specifically, it permits the caller to know when

- There is something to read from a file descriptor.
- Writing to the file descriptor will not block the execution of the server program.
- An exception has occurred on a file descriptor.

You will recall that the handle to a socket is a file descriptor. The select(2) function will notify the server when something has happened on any one of a specified set of connected client sockets. In effect, this allows the server to process multiple clients in a very efficient manner.

As pointed out previously, the server is interested when any new request data is coming in from a client's socket. To know this, the server needs to know when there is data to be read from a particular client's socket.

When sending data back to the client, it is important for the server to know that it can write the data to the socket without being blocked. If the connected client, for example, requests a large amount of information to be returned, the server will have to write that information to the socket. If the client software is faulty or is slow reading the data at its end, the server will block for a long time, while attempting to write the rest of the result data. This has the consequence that all other clients that are connected to the server must now also wait. This is clearly undesirable, since each client must be serviced as expeditiously as possible.

If your server must also process out-of-band data (to be covered in Chapter 14, "Out-of-Band Data"), then you will be interested in exceptions that might take place on the socket.

Now turn your attention to the synopsis for the select(2) function:

```
#include <sys/time.h>
#include <sys/types.h>
#include <unistd.h>

int select(int n,
    fd_set *readfds,
    fd_set *writefds,
    fd_set *exceptfds,
    struct timeval *timeout);
```

This function requires five input arguments:

1. The maximum number (n) of file descriptors to test. This value is at least the highest file descriptor number plus one, since descriptors start at zero.

2. The set of file descriptors (readfds) that are to be tested for read data.

3. The set of file descriptors (writefds) that are to be tested for writability.

4. The set of file descriptors (exceptfds) that are to be tested for exceptions.

5. The pointer (timeout) to the timeout requirement, which is to be applied to this function call. This pointer may be NULL, indicating that there is no timeout (the function call may block forever).

The return results from the select(2) function can be summarized as follows:

- A return value of -1 indicates that an error in the function call has occurred. The value of errno should be consulted for the nature of the error.

- A return value of zero indicates that a timeout has occurred without anything interesting happening.

- A return value greater than zero indicates the number of file descriptors where something of interest has occurred.

THE timeval STRUCTURE

The last argument, timeout, points to a structure that must be initialized unless a NULL pointer is provided instead. Listing 11.3 shows the definition of the timeval structure.

EXAMPLE

Listing 11.3: The Definition of the timeval Structure

```
struct timeval {
    long  tv_sec;    /* seconds */
    long  tv_usec;   /* microseconds */
};
```

To establish a timeout value of 1.75 seconds, you would code something like this:

EXAMPLE

```
struct timeval tv;

tv.tv_sec = 1;
tv.tv_usec = 750000;
```

The example shows the establishing of a timeout of 1.75 seconds. This is done by setting up a timeout of one second plus 750,000 microseconds.

CAUTION

Note that the timeval structure values are modified by the select(2) call. The timeval structure should be re-initialized prior to each call to select(2), unless the program requires that the time remaining be used as the timeout.

Manipulating File Descriptor Sets

The second, third, and fourth arguments of the select(2) function call require values of type fd_set, which might be new to you. This is an opaque data type, requiring that it be operated upon with macros provided for the purpose. The following is a synopsis of the macros for your use:

EXAMPLE

```
FD_ZERO(fd_set *set);

FD_SET(int fd, fd_set *set);
FD_CLR(int fd, fd_set *set);

FD_ISSET(int fd, fd_set *set);
```

These C macros allow you to manipulate sets of file descriptors. The following subsections will describe these macros in detail.

USING THE FD_ZERO MACRO

This C macro is used to initialize a file descriptor set. Before you can register file descriptors (which includes sockets), you must initialize your set to all zero bits. To initialize a file descriptor set named read_socks and write_socks, you would write the following C language statements:

EXAMPLE

```
fd_set read_socks;
fd_set write_socks;

FD_ZERO(&read_socks);
FD_ZERO(&write_socks);
```

The first two statements declare the storage associated with the file descriptor sets. The last two statements, which use the FD_ZERO macro, initialize these sets to the empty set. In other words, after FD_ZERO has been applied on a set, there are no file descriptors left registered within the set.

USING THE FD_SET MACRO

After you have a file descriptor set initialized with the FD_ZERO macro, the next thing you want to accomplish is to register some file descriptors in it. This can be done with the FD_SET macro. The following example shows how a socket number c can be registered in a set named read_socks:

```
int c;                /* Client socket */
fd_set read_socks;    /* Read set */

...
FD_SET(c,&read_socks);
```

After calling `FD_SET`, a bit has registered interest in the corresponding file descriptor within the referenced set.

USING THE FD_CLR MACRO

This C macro undoes the effect of the `FD_SET` macro. Assuming a socket c once again, if the calling program wants to remove this descriptor from the set, it can perform the following:

```
int c;                /* Client socket */
fd_set read_socks;    /* Read set */

...
FD_CLR(c,&read_socks);
```

The `FD_CLR` macro has the effect that it zeros the corresponding bit representing the file descriptor. Note that this macro differs from `FD_ZERO` in that it only clears one specific file descriptor within the set. The `FD_ZERO` macro, on the other hand, resets all bits to zero in the set.

TESTING FILE DESCRIPTORS WITH FD_ISSET MACRO

It is necessary, at times, to test to see if a particular file descriptor is present within a set (that is, to see if its corresponding bit has been set to one). To test whether socket c is set, you could write the following code:

```
int c;                /* Client socket */
fd_set read_socks;    /* Read set */

...
if ( FD_ISSET(c,&read_socks) ) {
    /* Socket c is in the set */

    ...
} else {
    /* Socket c is not in the set */

    ...
}
```

The `if` statement shown invokes the macro `FD_ISSET` to test if the socket c is present in the file descriptor set `read_socks`. If the test returns true, then the socket c does have its corresponding bit enabled within the set, and the first block of C code is executed. Otherwise, the socket c is not considered part of the set, and the `else` block of statements is executed instead.

Applying `select(2)` to a Server

The preceding text has described the `select(2)` function in some detail. Now it's time to put the function to work in an example. The next modified example of the RPN calculating server will make use of the `select(2)` function call for read events only. This limitation was imposed to keep the programming example relatively short and simple to understand. The limitations of this demonstration will be discussed in more detail later.

The RPN server required a few modifications to the engine module `rpneng.c`, which are reflected in the new source module `rpneng2.c`. Rather than re-list the entire module, only the minor changes are shown in the context `diff` of Listing 11.4.

EXAMPLE

Listing 11.4: rpneng2.c—diff -c rpneng.c rpneng2.c

```
$ diff -c rpneng.c rpneng2.c
*** rpneng.c    Mon Sep 13 22:13:56 1999
--- rpneng2.c   Wed Sep 15 21:55:20 1999
***************
*** 18,25 ****
  * RPN Stack:
  */
  #define MAX_STACK       32
! static mpz_t *stack[MAX_STACK];
! static int sp = 0;

  /*
   * Allocate a new mpz_t value:
--- 18,25 ----
  * RPN Stack:
  */
  #define MAX_STACK       32
! mpz_t **stack;
! int sp = 0;

  /*
   * Allocate a new mpz_t value:
***************
*** 45,51 ****
  /*
   * Free an allocated mpz_t value:
   */
! static void
  rpn_free(mpz_t **v) {
      mpz_clear(**v);
      free(*v);
```

continues

Listing 11.4: continued

```
--- 45,51 ----
  /*
   * Free an allocated mpz_t value:
   */
! void
  rpn_free(mpz_t **v) {
      mpz_clear(**v);
      free(*v);
$
```

The major change that is present in the rpneng2.c module is that the RPN stack array (variable stack) and its stack pointer (variable sp) are declared to be external in scope. Static function rpn_free() is made external also. This allows the variables and the function to be accessed from the main source module, which you'll examine in the example in Listing 11.5.

EXAMPLE

Listing 11.5: rpnsrv2.c—The RPN Server Using select(2)

```
 1:    /* rpnsrv2.c:
 2:     *
 3:     * Example RPN Server
 4:     * using select(2):
 5:     */
 6:    #include <stdio.h>
 7:    #include <unistd.h>
 8:    #include <stdlib.h>
 9:    #include <errno.h>
10:    #include <string.h>
11:    #include <time.h>
12:    #include <sys/time.h>
13:    #include <sys/types.h>
14:    #include <sys/socket.h>
15:    #include <netinet/in.h>
16:    #include <arpa/inet.h>
17:    #include <netdb.h>
18:    #include <sys/wait.h>
19:    #include <gmp.h>
20:
21:    #ifndef SHUT_RDWR
22:    #define SHUT_RDWR 3
23:    #endif
24:
25:    extern int mkaddr(void *addr,
26:        int *addr_len,
27:        char *input_address,
28:        char *protocol);
29:
```

```
30:  extern void rpn_process(FILE *tx,
31:      char *buf);
32:
33:  extern void rpn_free(mpz_t **v);
34:
35:  #define MAX_STACK      32
36:  #define MAX_CLIENTS    64
37:
38:  /*
39:   * Declared in rpneng2.c:
40:   */
41:  extern mpz_t **stack;
42:  extern int sp;
43:
44:  /*
45:   * Client context Info:
46:   */
47:  typedef struct {
48:      mpz_t   **stack;  /* Stack Array */
49:      int     sp;          /* Stack ptr */
50:      FILE    *rx;         /* Recv FILE */
51:      FILE    *tx;         /* Xmit FILE */
52:  } ClientInfo;
53:
54:  ClientInfo client[MAX_CLIENTS];
55:
56:  /*
57:   * This function reports the error and
58:   * exits back to the shell:
59:   */
60:  static void
61:  bail(const char *on_what) {
62:      if ( errno != 0 ) {
63:          fputs(strerror(errno),stderr);
64:          fputs(": ",stderr);
65:      }
66:      fputs(on_what,stderr);
67:      fputc('\n',stderr);
68:      exit(1);
69:  }
70:
71:  /*
72:   * Process client c:
73:   */
74:  static int
75:  process_client(int c) {
```

continues

Listing 11.5: continued

```
76:        char buf[4096];             /* I/O Buffer */
77:        FILE *rx = client[c].rx;
78:        FILE *tx = client[c].tx;
79:
80:        /*
81:         * Install correct RPN stack:
82:         */
83:        stack = client[c].stack;
84:        sp = client[c].sp;
85:
86:        /*
87:         * If not EOF, process one line:
88:         */
89:        if ( !feof(rx)
90:          && fgets(buf,sizeof buf,rx) )
91:            rpn_process(tx,buf);
92:
93:        if ( !feof(rx) ) {
94:            /* Save SP and exit */
95:            client[c].sp = sp;
96:            return 0;
97:        }
98:
99:        /*
100:        * Close this client's connection:
101:        */
102:        fclose(tx);
103:        shutdown(fileno(rx),SHUT_RDWR);
104:        fclose(rx);
105:
106:        client[c].rx = client[c].tx = NULL;
107:
108:        while ( sp > 0 )
109:            rpn_free(&stack[--sp]);
110:        free(stack);
111:
112:        client[c].stack = NULL;
113:        client[c].sp = 0;
114:
115:        return EOF;
116: }
117:
118: /*
119:  * Main program:
120:  */
121: int
```

```
122:  main(int argc,char **argv) {
123:      int z;
124:      char *srvr_addr = "127.0.0.1:9090";
125:      struct sockaddr_in adr_srvr;/* AF_INET */
126:      struct sockaddr_in adr_clnt;/* AF_INET */
127:      int len_inet;               /* length */
128:      int s = -1;                 /* Socket */
129:      int c = -1;            /* Client socket */
130:      int n;    /* return val from select(2) */
131:      int mx;                   /* Max fd + 1 */
132:      fd_set rx_set;            /* Read set */
133:      fd_set wk_set;           /* Working set */
134:      struct timeval tv;    /* Timeout value */
135:
136:      /*
137:       * Initialize client structure:
138:       */
139:      for ( z=0; z<MAX_CLIENTS; ++z ) {
140:          client[z].stack = NULL;
141:          client[z].sp = 0;
142:          client[z].rx = NULL;
143:          client[z].tx = NULL;
144:      }
145:
146:      /*
147:       * Use a server address from the command
148:       * line, otherwise default to 127.0.0.1:
149:       */
150:      if ( argc >= 2 )
151:          srvr_addr = argv[1];
152:
153:      len_inet = sizeof adr_srvr;
154:      z = mkaddr(&adr_srvr,&len_inet,
155:          srvr_addr,"tcp");
156:
157:      if ( z < 0 || !adr_srvr.sin_port ) {
158:          fprintf(stderr,"Invalid server "
159:              "address, or no port number "
160:              "was specified.\n");
161:          exit(1);
162:      }
163:
164:      /*
165:       * Create a TCP/IP socket to use:
166:       */
167:      s = socket(PF_INET,SOCK_STREAM,0);
```

continues

Listing 11.5: continued

```
168:     if ( s == -1 )
169:         bail("socket(2)");
170:
171:     /*
172:      * Bind the server address:
173:      */
174:     z = bind(s,(struct sockaddr *)&adr_srvr,
175:             len_inet);
176:     if ( z == -1 )
177:         bail("bind(2)");
178:
179:     /*
180:      * Make it a listening socket:
181:      */
182:     z = listen(s,10);
183:     if ( z == -1 )
184:         bail("listen(2)");
185:
186:     /*
187:      * Express interest in socket
188:      * s for read events:
189:      */
190:     FD_ZERO(&rx_set);    /* Init. */
191:     FD_SET(s,&rx_set);      /* + s */
192:     mx = s + 1;      /* max fd + 1 */
193:
194:     /*
195:      * Start the server loop:
196:      */
197:     for (;;) {
198:         /*
199:          * Copy the rx_set to wk_set:
200:          */
201:         FD_ZERO(&wk_set);
202:         for ( z=0; z<mx; ++z ) {
203:             if ( FD_ISSET(z,&rx_set) )
204:                 FD_SET(z,&wk_set);
205:         }
206:
207:         /*
208:          * Sample timeout of 2.03 secs:
209:          */
210:         tv.tv_sec = 2;
211:         tv.tv_usec = 30000;
212:
213:         n = select(mx,&wk_set,NULL,NULL,&tv);
```

```
214:        if ( n == -1 ) {
215:            fprintf(stderr,"%s: select(2)\n",
216:                strerror(errno));
217:            exit(1);
218:        } else if ( !n ) {
219:            /* puts("Timeout."); */
220:            continue;
221:        }
222:
223:        /*
224:         * Check if a connect has occured:
225:         */
226:        if ( FD_ISSET(s,&wk_set) ) {
227:            /*
228:             * Wait for a connect:
229:             */
230:            len_inet = sizeof adr_clnt;
231:            c = accept(s,
232:                (struct sockaddr *)&adr_clnt,
233:                &len_inet);
234:            if ( c == -1 )
235:                bail("accept(2)");
236:
237:            /*
238:             * See if we've exceeded server
239:             * capacity. If so, close the
240:             * socket and wait for the
241:             * next event:
242:             */
243:            if ( c >= MAX_CLIENTS ) {
244:                close(c);   /* At capacity */
245:                continue;
246:            }
247:
248:            /*
249:             * Create streams:
250:             */
251:            client[c].rx = fdopen(c,"r");
252:            if ( !client[c].rx ) {
253:                close(c);  /* Failed */
254:                continue;
255:            }
256:
257:            client[c].tx = fdopen(dup(c),"w");
258:            if ( !client[c].tx ) {
259:                fclose(client[c].rx);
```

continues

Listing 11.5: continued

```
260:                     continue;
261:                 }
262:
263:             if ( c + 1 > mx )
264:                 mx = c + 1;
265:
266:             /*
267:              * Set both streams to line
268:              * buffered mode:
269:              */
270:             setlinebuf(client[c].rx);
271:             setlinebuf(client[c].tx);
272:
273:             /*
274:              * Allocate a stack:
275:              */
276:             client[c].sp = 0;
277:             client[c].stack =
278:                 (mpz_t **) malloc(
279:                     sizeof (mpz_t *)
280:                     * MAX_STACK);
281:
282:             FD_SET(c,&rx_set);
283:         }
284:
285:         /*
286:          * Check for client activity:
287:          */
288:         for ( c=0; c<mx; ++c ) {
289:             if ( c == s )
290:                 continue;   /* Not s */
291:             if ( FD_ISSET(c,&wk_set) ) {
292:                 if ( process_client(c) == EOF ) {
293:                     FD_CLR(c,&rx_set);
294:                 }
295:             }
296:         }
297:
298:         /*
299:          * Reduce mx if we are able to:
300:          */
301:         for ( c = mx - 1;
302:               c >= 0 && !FD_ISSET(c,&rx_set);
303:               c = mx - 1 )
304:                 mx = c;
```

```
305:    }
306:
307:    /* Control never gets here */
308:    return 0;
309: }
```

The source module rpnsrv2.c contains quite a number of changes. First, examine the structural overview of the program:

- Include file <sys/time.h> is added to define the data structure timeval (line 12).

- The function prototype is declared for rpn_free() in line 33.

- The MAX_STACK macro is copied from rpnsrv2.c in line 35. The macro MAX_CLIENTS defines the maximum number of client processes supported by this server (line 36).

- The external declarations for stack and sp are defined in lines 41 and 42.

- The information about each client is maintained in this program by the data type ClientInfo, which is declared in lines 47 to 52.

- The ClientInfo array client[] is declared in line 54.

- A new client processing function, process_client(), is defined in lines 74 to 116.

- A number of new declarations are present in the main() program. The first of these is the value n, which is declared in line 130. This variable receives the return value from the select(2) call in line 207.

- Variable mx in line 131 will hold the maximum file descriptor that select(2) is interested in, plus one.

- Two file descriptor sets, rx_set and wk_set, are declared in lines 132 and 133.

- A timeout value structure, tv, is declared in line 134.

There are several significant changes made to the main flow of the main() program, which will be examined now. The following outlines the general steps that are executed by the server program:

1. The ClientInfo array client[] is initialized first, in the for loop of lines 139 to 144.

2. The usual socket creation, the bind(2) call and listen(2) call, are performed in lines 150 to 184.

3. rx_set is zeroed out in line 190. rx_set will function as the master set of sockets for which the server is interested in read events.

4. The FD_SET macro is called to enter socket s into the file descriptor set rx_set (line 191). This is done because a connect to this socket is considered a read event that select(2) will respond to.

5. The variable mx is initialized to s + 1. This variable will hold the maximum file descriptor plus one. At this moment, there is only the one file descriptor s in the set. Hence, the program knows that the value of mx is currently and simply the value s + 1 (line 192).

6. The server for loop begins in line 197.

7. The FD_ZERO macro is called for the wk_set file descriptor set in line 201. This clears all bits in it to the zero (off) state. wk_set will function as the working set for this program, since select(2) will modify the sets that are passed to it.

8. The for loop in lines 202 to 205 copy all file descriptors logged in rx_set to the work set wk_set.

9. The timeout values are established in lines 210 to 211. It is necessary to establish the values each time select(2) is called, because these values are changed upon return from the function.

10. The select(2) function is invoked in line 213. The return value is assigned to the variable n. Note that the wk_set is passed as the read file descriptor set in argument 2. Upon return from the select(2) function, the only bits that will remain in this set will be for the sockets that have data to be read (in the case of socket s, a client has connected).

11. The value of n is tested for -1 in line 214. Lines 215 to 217 report the error and exit if an error should occur. An error here probably indicates a programming error. The error EINTR should be handled, however, if the program is handling signals at all.

12. Lines 218 to 220 show how you can intercept a timeout event. The program shown simply does nothing and restarts the loop at step 6.

13. The FD_ISSET macro is used to test whether socket s is present in set wk_set (line 226). If it is, this indicates that a client has just connected to the server socket s.

14. The client connect is accepted in lines 230 to 235 if the test in step 12 is true. Note that the accept(2) call will not block the execution of the server here, because the select(2) function result guarantees that we have a connected client waiting to be accepted.

15. Client connect processing continues with line 243. If the socket number (file descriptor) is greater than or equal to MAX_CLIENTS, the server

rejects the connection in line 244 by closing the socket and looping back to step 6. In this program, the socket number is used as a subscript into the `client[]` array, and, as such, it must be less than the value of `MAX_CLIENTS` in this program.

16. The usual `FILE` streams `rx` and `tx` are created and the buffering modes set in lines 251 to 271. Note, however, that in lines 263 and 264 the variable `mx` is increased to the new connected socket plus one, if the `mx` value needs increasing. Recall that `mx` must contain the maximum file descriptor value plus one, for the `select(2)` call.

17. The `client[]` entry for this client is further initialized by allocating a stack for the client and resetting its stack pointer `sp` to zero (lines 276 to 280).

18. Finally, `FD_SET` is used on set `rx_set` in line 282 to register the new client in the list of interesting file descriptors.

The steps just shown cover the server initialization and the accepting of new client connections. The following steps are used when clients send data to the server to be processed:

1. Line 226 invokes the `FD_ISSET` macro to test whether the socket s has any input data. If it has, the client accept process just described is executed in lines 227 to 283.

2. A `for` loop in line 288 iterates through all file descriptors less than the maximum value `mx`.

3. Line 289 causes processing to be skipped for socket s, since only `accept(2)` is used on that socket.

4. The `FD_ISSET` macro is called in line 291 to see if socket c has data waiting to be read (by testing descriptor set `wk_set`).

5. If step 4 evaluates as true, then the function `process_client()` is called (line 292) with the socket number c as its input argument.

6. If the function call in step 5 returns the value `EOF` in line 292, then socket c is removed from the `rx_set` in line 293, using the `FD_CLR` macro. This is necessary because the socket has been closed by the `process_client()` function and obviously will no longer return any data to be read.

7. The `for` loop in lines 301 to 304 perform the job of lowering the value of `mx` if it is possible. This is not essential, but it can help the performance of the `select(2)` call and the server when this value is maintained as small as possible.

Now it's time to examine the steps employed by the function process_client(). These steps are as follows:

1. The local variables rx and tx are established in lines 77 and 78 for programming convenience, from the client[c] array member. Note that the socket number c is used as a subscript into the client[] array.

2. The RPN stack is established for the client by assigning values from client[c] into the external variables stack and sp (lines 83 and 84).

3. Line 89 makes certain that end of file has not already been detected. If it has been, this will be handled in code that follows.

4. Line 90 fetches one text line to be processed by the server. If this fgets(3) call should return an end-of-file indication, the code that follows will close things up for this client.

5. The rpn_process() function call is executed to carry out the client request (line 91).

6. End of file is tested in line 93. If this tests false, then the current sp value is saved back into the client[c] array member for future use. Then the function returns zero to indicate that EOF has not yet been seen (line 96).

7. When the execution reaches line 102, it is known that the client has shut down its writing end of the socket. The function fclose(3) is called to force write out any unbuffered data to the client.

8. The shutdown(2) function is called in line 103 to force a socket shutdown (this is not essential in this case, but is used for demonstration purposes).

9. The rx stream is closed in line 104 for this client.

10. Lines 106 to 113 free the client's leftover stack, if any, and clear the client[] array entry.

11. Finally, EOF is returned in line 115.

Notice that step 11 causes source line 293 to remove the socket number c from the list of sockets that select(2) should report on.

TIP

It should be noted that even if no data is sent by the client process to be read, the act of the client closing the socket will cause select(2) to register a read event. Your code should always anticipate an end-of-file event.

Testing the `select(2)`-Based Server

The source code for the `select(2)` version of the RPN calculating server can be compiled as follows:

EXAMPLE

```
$ make rpnsrv2
gcc -c  -D_GNU_SOURCE -Wall -Wreturn-type rpnsrv2.c
gcc -c  -D_GNU_SOURCE -Wall -Wreturn-type rpneng2.c
gcc -c  -D_GNU_SOURCE -Wall -Wreturn-type mkaddr.c
gcc rpnsrv2.o rpneng2.o mkaddr.o -o rpnsrv2 -lgmp
$
```

The server executable `rpnsrv2` will execute as one single process, even when many clients connect to the server. To allow this to be tested, you will first want to start the server itself. The following launch of the server permits it to be contacted on any allowable interface on your system:

```
$ ./rpnsrv2 '*:9099' &
[1] 730
$
```

The server is launched and placed into the background. The command-line argument of `'*:9099'` tells the server to specify a wild IP number, but to listen on TCP/IP port number 9099 for connects.

In order to properly test that this `select(2)` logic is operational, it is necessary to connect to the server with at least two simultaneous sessions. Without X Window sessions, this can be done from multiple console sessions. Using the X Window interface, you can easily start multiple terminal sessions for testing purposes.

Listing 11.6 shows one example `xterm` session using `telnet` to connect to the server. While this session is going on, another session, shown in Listing 11.7, is also created at the same time. It is only important that both sessions be connected to the server at the same time. Switching back and forth between sessions, the server should respond to each session as commands are provided to it.

EXAMPLE

Listing 11.6: First `telnet` Session with `rpnsrv2`

```
$ telnet localhost 9099
Trying 127.0.0.1...
Connected to localhost.
Escape character is '^]'.
#:44
0:
#:7777777777777777
1:
genprime
```

continues

Listing 11.6: continued

```
0:
=
0:3478699960711639
^]
telnet> c
Connection closed.
$
```

The second example `telnet` session is shown in Listing 11.7. Keep in mind that these are example sessions. You are free to exercise any of the functions of the RPN server in your own testing.

EXAMPLE

Listing 11.7: Second Session with `rpnsrv2`

```
$ telnet localhost 9099
Trying 127.0.0.1...
Connected to localhost.
Escape character is '^]'.
#:99
0:
#:9999999999999999
1:
genprime
0:
=
0:3039223729873609
^]
telnet> c
Connection closed.
$
```

While the sessions of Listings 11.6 and 11.7 were in progress, a list of processes were produced in a third session, which is shown in Listing 11.8.

EXAMPLE

Listing 11.8: List of Processes During `rpnsrv2` Access

```
$ ps -af
UID        PID  PPID  C STIME TTY       TIME CMD
wwg        730   629  0 21:51 pts/1  00:00:00 ./rpnsrv2 *:9099
wwg        731   629  0 21:58 pts/1  00:00:00 telnet localhost 9099
wwg        754   752  0 21:59 pts/5  00:00:00 telnet localhost 9099
wwg        757   665  0 21:59 pts/3  00:00:00 ps -af
$
```

The process listing in Listing 11.8 clearly shows that, while the two telnet sessions (PID 731 and 754) were connected to the `rpnsrv2` process, there was only one process representing the server (PID 730). As each input line was entered in the telnet sessions, a response was received after pressing

Enter in either of the two open sessions. This demonstrates the capability of the one process to serve multiple connected clients.

Limitations of the Example

It was noted earlier that only read events were used for this server example. Even accepting this limitation of the demo server, there is still some exposure to difficulty, should a wayward client program decide to play havoc.

Consider what would happen if a client process were to do the following:

1. Send three bytes: '#', ':', and '9'.

2. Wait for a long time or an indefinite period.

The server end would experience the following events:

1. Three bytes would be received at the receiving end of the server socket for the client.

2. The select(2) call would return with an indication that the client socket has data to be read.

3. The fgets(3) function would eventually be called in line 90 of Listing 11.5.

4. The fgets(3) function waits indefinitely because, after reading all available data, there is no linefeed character to indicate that the end of the line has been received.

The server becomes blocked in the fgets(3) call at this point, and now no other client will be serviced either (they will all appear to have a hung connection).

The preceding discussion demonstrates that, while select(2) makes it possible to handle many sockets in one process, the design of the server tends to be complex in order to avoid hangs.

The write side of the operation is equally complex. While the select(2) call can indicate when a write(2) call will not block, it does not indicate how much data can be written without blocking. For servers that might return large amounts of data in a response, this is a serious problem. Again, special buffering techniques must be applied to successfully utilize select(2) in a robust server process.

What's Next

This chapter has covered a number of server design concepts. In the early part of the chapter, you saw how fork(2) and separate processes could handle multiple client connections concurrently. The select(2) function demonstrated how it could service multiple clients within one server process.

The next chapter will take you on a tour of socket options. There you will learn how to enable a socket to broadcast, reuse socket addresses, turn on the TCP/IP "keep alive" feature, and much more.

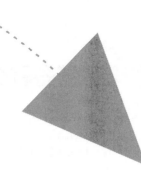

Socket Options

In the heyday of the Model T Ford, it was said that you could have any color you wanted, as long as it was black. This obviously poked fun at the idea that there were no other options. Fortunately, sockets are not so restrictive!

The earlier chapters covered the basics of using sockets. It is now appropriate to examine some of the optional features that are available. After you have mastered this chapter's concepts, you'll be ready for the more advanced socket topics that are covered in the remainder of this book. This chapter will focus on the following topics:

- How to retrieve socket option values with getsockopt(2)
- How to change socket option values with setsockopt(2)
- How to apply the most commonly needed socket options

Getting Socket Options

Oftentimes, an application needs to determine what the current option settings are for a socket. This is especially true of a subroutine library function, which will have no prior knowledge of what was done with the socket, which was passed to it as an argument. The application might also need to know things such as the optimal buffer size to use, which is determined by the system defaults.

The function that permits you to inspect socket option values is the getsockopt(2) function. Its function synopsis is given as follows:

```
#include <sys/types.h>
#include <sys/socket.h>

int getsockopt(int s,
    int level,
    int optname,
    void *optval,
    socklen_t *optlen);
```

The five arguments are described as follows:

1. The socket s from which to inspect the option.

2. The protocol level at which the option is to be inspected.

3. The option optname to inspect.

4. The pointer optval pointing to the receiving buffer for the option value.

5. The pointer optlen pointing to both the input buffer length, and the returned option length values.

The return value from this function returns zero when successful. When an error occurs, −1 is returned and the external variable errno contains the nature of the error.

The protocol level argument indicates where in the protocol stack you want to access an option. Usually, you will use one of these:

- SOL_SOCKET to access socket level options

- SOL_TCP to access TCP level options

The discussion in this chapter will center strictly on the use of SOL_SOCKET level options.

The optname argument is an integer value. The value used here will be determined first by the choice of the level argument value used. Within a specified protocol level, the optname argument will determine which option you want to access. Table 12.1 shows some of the level and option combinations that are possible.

Table 12.1: Protocol Level and Option Names

Protocol Level	Option Name
SOL_SOCKET	SO_REUSEADDR
SOL_SOCKET	SO_KEEPALIVE
SOL_SOCKET	SO_LINGER
SOL_SOCKET	SO_BROADCAST
SOL_SOCKET	SO_OOBINLINE
SOL_SOCKET	SO_SNDBUF
SOL_SOCKET	SO_RCVBUF
SOL_SOCKET	SO_TYPE
SOL_SOCKET	SO_ERROR
SOL_TCP	SO_NODELAY

Most of the options listed in the table are socket level options, where the level was given as SOL_SOCKET. One TCP level socket option was included for comparison purposes, where its level is specified as SOL_TCP.

Many socket options are retrieved into an int data type. When looking at the manual pages, data type int can usually be assumed unless otherwise indicated. When a Boolean value is used, the int value indicates TRUE when the value is nonzero and indicates FALSE when it is zero.

Applying getsockopt(2)

In this section, you'll compile and run a program getsndrcv.c, which will fetch and report the sending and receiving buffer sizes for a socket. The example in Listing 12.1 illustrates the code.

EXAMPLE

Listing 12.1: getsndrcv.c—Get and Report SO_SNDBUF and SO_RCVBUF Options

```
1:   /* getsndrcv.c:
2:    *
3:    * Get SO_SNDBUF & SO_RCVBUF Options:
4:    */
5:   #include <stdio.h>
6:   #include <unistd.h>
7:   #include <stdlib.h>
8:   #include <errno.h>
9:   #include <string.h>
10:  #include <sys/types.h>
11:  #include <sys/socket.h>
12:  #include <assert.h>
```

continues

Listing 12.1: continued

```
13:
14:    /*
15:     * This function reports the error and
16:     * exits back to the shell:
17:     */
18:    static void
19:    bail(const char *on_what) {
20:        if ( errno != 0 ) {
21:            fputs(strerror(errno),stderr);
22:            fputs(": ",stderr);
23:        }
24:        fputs(on_what,stderr);
25:        fputc('\n',stderr);
26:        exit(1);
27:    }
28:
29:    int
30:    main(int argc,char **argv) {
31:        int z;
32:        int s = -1;                    /* Socket */
33:        int sndbuf=0;    /* Send buffer size */
34:        int rcvbuf=0;/* Receive buffer size */
35:        socklen_t optlen;  /* Option length */
36:
37:        /*
38:         * Create a TDP/IP socket to use:
39:         */
40:        s = socket(PF_INET,SOCK_STREAM,0);
41:        if ( s == -1 )
42:            bail("socket(2)");
43:
44:        /*
45:         * Get socket option SO_SNDBUF:
46:         */
47:        optlen = sizeof sndbuf;
48:        z = getsockopt(s,SOL_SOCKET,SO_SNDBUF,
49:            &sndbuf,&optlen);
50:        if ( z )
51:            bail("getsockopt(s,SOL_SOCKET,"
52:                "SO_SNDBUF)");
53:
54:        assert(optlen == sizeof sndbuf);
55:
56:        /*
57:         * Get socket option SO_SNDBUF:
58:         */
```

```
59:        optlen = sizeof rcvbuf;
60:        z = getsockopt(s,SOL_SOCKET,SO_RCVBUF,
61:            &rcvbuf,&optlen);
62:        if ( z )
63:            bail("getsockopt(s,SOL_SOCKET,"
64:                "SO_RCVBUF)");
65:
66:        assert(optlen == sizeof rcvbuf);
67:
68:        /*
69:         * Report the buffer sizes:
70:         */
71:        printf("Socket s : %d\n",s);
72:        printf(" Send buf: %d bytes\n",
73:            sndbuf);
74:        printf(" Recv buf: %d bytes\n",
75:            rcvbuf);
76:
77:        close(s);
78:        return 0;
79:  }
```

The getsockopt(2) steps used were as follows:

1. The options SO_SNDBUF and SO_RCVBUF are received into an int data type. Consequently, storage for these values was declared in lines 33 and 34.

2. The getsockopt(2) function requires an option length argument that acts as both an input value and a return value. Storage for this was allocated in line 35 and named optlen. Note that the data type for this variable is socklen_t.

3. A socket for testing purposes is created in line 40.

4. The length of the receiving option buffer sndbuf is established in variable optlen (line 47).

5. The option is fetched by calling getsockopt(2) in line 48. The socket level was SOL_SOCKET and the option name was specified as SO_SNDBUF. Note the pointer to sndbuf was given as the receiving buffer.

6. The length of the result returned in sndbuf is placed into variable optlen by the function getsockopt(2). Line 54 uses the assert(3) macro to ensure that it matches the return length that was expected.

7. Lines 59 to 66 repeat the process for the option SO_RCVBUF into variable rcvbuf.

8. Lines 71 to 75 report the socket file descriptor, and the corresponding buffer sizes that were retrieved.

The following output shows a compile and execute session for this program on a Red Hat Linux 6.0 distribution, using a 2.2.10 kernel:

OUTPUT

```
$ make getsndrcv
gcc -c  -D_GNU_SOURCE -Wall -Wreturn-type getsndrcv.c
gcc getsndrcv.o -o getsndrcv
$ ./getsndrcv
Socket s : 3
 Send buf: 65535 bytes
 Recv buf: 65535 bytes
$
```

The session shows that the socket was created on file descriptor 3, and that the sending and receiving buffer sizes were 65535 bytes in size.

Setting Socket Options

Knowing that the size of the sending and receiving buffers for the default socket are quite large, you as an application designer might decide that a smaller set of buffers might be more appropriate. This might be especially significant if you are expecting several instances of the program to run on your system.

Options are set on sockets using the setsockopt(2) function. Its function prototype is given as follows:

```
#include <sys/types.h>
#include <sys/socket.h>

int setsockopt(int s,
    int level,
    int optname,
    const void *optval,
    socklen_t optlen);
```

This function closely resembles the getsockopt(2) function discussed earlier. The arguments for setsockopt(2) are listed as follows:

1. The socket s to effect an option change upon.

2. The socket level of the option.

3. The option optname to set.

4. The pointer optval to the value to be used for the new option value.

5. The option value length optlen, in bytes.

The only real difference between this function's arguments and the getsockopt(2) argument list is that the last argument is passed by value only. It is an input value only in this case.

Applying the `setsockopt(2)` Function

Listing 12.2 shows a short program that changes the send and receive buffer sizes for a socket. After setting these options, the program obtains the actual sizes of these buffers and reports them.

EXAMPLE

Listing 12.2: setsndrcv.c—Setting SOL_SOCKET Options SO_SNDBUF and SO_RCVBUF

```
1:   /* setsndrcv.c:
2:    *
3:    * Set SO_SNDBUF & SO_RCVBUF Options:
4:    */
5:   #include <stdio.h>
6:   #include <unistd.h>
7:   #include <stdlib.h>
8:   #include <errno.h>
9:   #include <string.h>
10:  #include <sys/types.h>
11:  #include <sys/socket.h>
12:  #include <assert.h>
13:
14:  /*
15:   * This function reports the error and
16:   * exits back to the shell:
17:   */
18:  static void
19:  bail(const char *on_what) {
20:      if ( errno != 0 ) {
21:          fputs(strerror(errno),stderr);
22:          fputs(": ",stderr);
23:      }
24:      fputs(on_what,stderr);
25:      fputc('\n',stderr);
26:      exit(1);
27:  }
28:
29:  int
30:  main(int argc,char **argv) {
31:      int z;
32:      int s = -1;                 /* Socket */
33:      int sndbuf=0;   /* Send buffer size */
34:      int rcvbuf=0;/* Receive buffer size */
35:      socklen_t optlen;  /* Option length */
36:
37:      /*
38:       * Create a TCP/IP socket to use:
39:       */
```

continues

Listing 12.2: continued

```
40:      s = socket(PF_INET,SOCK_STREAM,0);
41:      if ( s == -1 )
42:          bail("socket(2)");
43:
44:      /*
45:       * Set the SO_SNDBUF Size:
46:       */
47:      sndbuf = 5000;  /* Send buffer size */
48:      z = setsockopt(s,SOL_SOCKET,SO_SNDBUF,
49:          &sndbuf,sizeof sndbuf);
50:      if ( z )
51:          bail("setsockopt(s,SOL_SOCKET,"
52:              "SO_SNDBUF)");
53:
54:      /*
55:       * Set the SO_RCVBUF Size:
56:       */
57:      rcvbuf = 8192;  /* Send buffer size */
58:      z = setsockopt(s,SOL_SOCKET,SO_RCVBUF,
59:          &rcvbuf,sizeof rcvbuf);
60:      if ( z )
61:          bail("setsockopt(s,SOL_SOCKET,"
62:              "SO_RCVBUF)");
63:
64:      /*
65:       * As a check on the above...
66:       * Get socket option SO_SNDBUF:
67:       */
68:      optlen = sizeof sndbuf;
69:      z = getsockopt(s,SOL_SOCKET,SO_SNDBUF,
70:          &sndbuf,&optlen);
71:      if ( z )
72:          bail("getsockopt(s,SOL_SOCKET,"
73:              "SO_SNDBUF)");
74:
75:      assert(optlen == sizeof sndbuf);
76:
77:      /*
78:       * Get socket option SO_SNDBUF:
79:       */
80:      optlen = sizeof rcvbuf;
81:      z = getsockopt(s,SOL_SOCKET,SO_RCVBUF,
82:          &rcvbuf,&optlen);
83:      if ( z )
84:          bail("getsockopt(s,SOL_SOCKET,"
85:              "SO_RCVBUF)");
```

```
86:
87:        assert(optlen == sizeof rcvbuf);
88:
89:        /*
90:         * Report the buffer sizes:
91:         */
92:        printf("Socket s : %d\n",s);
93:        printf(" Send buf: %d bytes\n",
94:            sndbuf);
95:        printf(" Recv buf: %d bytes\n",
96:            rcvbuf);
97:
98:        close(s);
99:        return 0;
100: }
```

The program is similar to the previous one. However, after the initial socket is created, the following steps are used to set the buffer sizes:

1. The value of variable sndbuf is set to the value of the buffer size desired. In this case, line 47 shows the value of 5000 being assigned.

2. The setsockopt(2) function is called, setting the option named SO_SNDBUF at level SOL_SOCKET according to the value of sndbuf. Errors are checked in lines 50 to 52.

3. The SO_RCVBUF option is set in the same manner as step 2, except that the buffer size is chosen as 8192 instead of 5000 bytes.

4. Source code that follows at line 68 to the end of the program will fetch these option values from the kernel and report what has been established.

The following output shows a compile and execute session of this program:

OUTPUT

```
$ make setsndrcv
gcc -c  -D_GNU_SOURCE -Wall -Wreturn-type setsndrcv.c
gcc setsndrcv.o -o setsndrcv
$ ./setsndrcv
Socket s : 3
 Send buf: 10000 bytes
 Recv buf: 16384 bytes
$
```

Notice the results that were reported by the program! They appear as twice the original sizes that were specified. The reason for this can be found in the Linux kernel source code module /usr/src/linux-2.2.10/net/core/sock.c. Look for the case statements for SO_SNDBUF and SO_RCVBUF. Here is a code excerpt for the SO_SNDBUF handling within the kernel module sock.c (this particular code segment appears to have been contributed by Alan Cox based on the source code comments at the top of the module):

```
case SO_SNDBUF:
        /* Don't error on this BSD doesn't and if you think
           about it this is right. Otherwise apps have to
           play 'guess the biggest size' games. RCVBUF/SNDBUF
           are treated in BSD as hints */

        if (val > sysctl_wmem_max)
                val = sysctl_wmem_max;

        sk->sndbuf = max(val*2,2048);

        /*
         *      Wake up sending tasks if we
         *      upped the value.
         */
        sk->write_space(sk);
        break;
```

EXAMPLE

Based upon the code shown, what actually happens for SO_SNDBUF is this (Linux kernel 2.2.10):

1. The SO_SNDBUF option value is checked to see whether it exceeds the maximum buffer size.

2. If the SO_SNDBUF option does exceed the maximum in step 1, the maximum value is used without returning an error to the caller.

3. The value of 2048 bytes or double the value from steps 1 and 2 is used, whichever value is greater.

The message here is that the option value SO_SNDBUF is only a hint value to be used. The kernel will ultimately decide the best buffer size to apply for SO_SNDBUF.

Examination of more kernel source code reveals something similar for the SO_RCVBUF option. See the following code excerpt (this code segment written by Alan Cox):

```
case SO_RCVBUF:
        /* Don't error on this BSD doesn't and if you think
           about it this is right. Otherwise apps have to
           play 'guess the biggest size' games. RCVBUF/SNDBUF
           are treated in BSD as hints */

        if (val > sysctl_rmem_max)
                val = sysctl_rmem_max;
```

EXAMPLE

```
/* FIXME: is this lower bound the right one? */
sk->rcvbuf = max(val*2,256);
break;
```

For kernel release 2.2.10, the value actually used will be a minimum value of 256 bytes or the given value doubled (unless the given value exceeds the kernel maximum). Again, this emphasizes the fact that these option settings are hints to the kernel, and are not absolute.

CAUTION

Note that setting the SOL_SOCKET options SO_SNDBUF or SO_RCVBUF only provides hints to the kernel from the application. The kernel will ultimately decide the final values that will be established.

If it is critical for the application and kernel to precisely agree on these sizes, the application should retrieve the final values established by the kernel. This is done with a subsequent call to the function getsockopt(2).

Retrieving the Socket Type (SO_TYPE)

Some socket options can only be retrieved. The SO_TYPE is one such example. This option allows a subroutine, which is passed a socket (as a file descriptor), to determine what kind of socket it is dealing with.

Listing 12.3 shows an example program that determines the type of the socket s.

EXAMPLE

Listing 12.3: gettype.c—Getting SO_TYPE Value of SOL_SOCKET Level Option

```
1:   /* gettype.c:
2:    *
3:    * Get SO_TYPE Option:
4:    */
5:   #include <stdio.h>
6:   #include <unistd.h>
7:   #include <stdlib.h>
8:   #include <errno.h>
9:   #include <string.h>
10:  #include <sys/types.h>
11:  #include <sys/socket.h>
12:  #include <assert.h>
13:
14:  /*
15:   * This function reports the error and
16:   * exits back to the shell:
17:   */
```

continues

Listing 12.3: continued

```
18:   static void
19:   bail(const char *on_what) {
20:       if ( errno != 0 ) {
21:           fputs(strerror(errno),stderr);
22:           fputs(": ",stderr);
23:       }
24:       fputs(on_what,stderr);
25:       fputc('\n',stderr);
26:       exit(1);
27:   }
28:
29:   int
30:   main(int argc,char **argv) {
31:       int z;
32:       int s = -1;                      /* Socket */
33:       int so_type = -1;     /* Socket type */
34:       socklen_t optlen;   /* Option length */
35:
36:       /*
37:        * Create a TCP/IP socket to use:
38:        */
39:       s = socket(PF_INET,SOCK_STREAM,0);
40:       if ( s == -1 )
41:           bail("socket(2)");
42:
43:       /*
44:        * Get socket option SO_SNDBUF:
45:        */
46:       optlen = sizeof so_type;
47:       z = getsockopt(s,SOL_SOCKET,SO_TYPE,
48:           &so_type,&optlen);
49:       if ( z )
50:           bail("getsockopt(s,SOL_SOCKET,"
51:               "SO_TYPE)");
52:
53:       assert(optlen == sizeof so_type);
54:
55:       /*
56:        * Report the buffer sizes:
57:        */
58:       printf("Socket s : %d\n",s);
59:       printf(" SO_TYPE : %d\n",so_type);
60:       printf(" SOCK_STREAM = %d\n",
61:           SOCK_STREAM);
```

```
62:
63:        close(s);
64:        return 0;
65:   }
```

The salient points of the program are as follows:

1. Variable so_type is declared as an integer to receive the socket type in line 33.

2. The socket of type SOCK_STREAM is created in line 39.

3. The option SO_TYPE is fetched into variable so_type in lines 46 to 53.

4. The socket s is reported in line 58, whereas its socket type in variable so_type is reported in line 59.

5. The value of C macro SOCK_STREAM is reported in lines 60 and 61 for comparison purposes.

The following output shows an example compile and execution session for the program:

OUTPUT

```
$ make gettype
gcc -c  -D_GNU_SOURCE -Wall -Wreturn-type gettype.c
gcc gettype.o -o gettype
$ ./gettype
Socket s : 3
 SO_TYPE : 1
 SOCK_STREAM = 1
$
```

From this output, you can see that socket number 3 was reported to be of type 1 in the following output line. Note that the C macro SOCK_STREAM is the value of 1, also, confirming that the option value is correct. Just for fun, you might want to modify the program to try the value of SOCK_DGRAM in the socket(2) function call and see whether the reported value changes.

Setting the SO_REUSEADDR Option

In the first part of Chapter 11, "Concurrent Client Servers," a server design using the fork(2) system call was presented and tested. Figure 12.1 shows three processes that exist after a telnet command has established contact with the server.

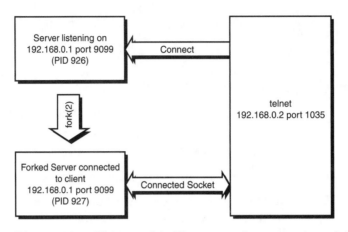

Figure 12.1: *This graphic illustrates the connection of the* telnet *command to a forked server process.*

The steps that take place in Figure 12.1 are as follows:

1. The server process (PID 926) is started. It listens for connections from clients.

2. The client process (a telnet command) is started, and connects to the server process (PID 926).

3. The server process (PID 926) forks by calling fork(2). This leaves the original parent process (PID 926) and a new server child process (PID 927).

4. The connected client socket is closed by the parent server process (PID 926), leaving the connected client socket open only in the child process (PID 927).

5. The telnet command and the child server process (PID 927) converse at will, independently of the parent process (PID 926).

At step 5, there are two socket activities happening:

- The server (PID 926) is listening on 192.168.0.1 port 9099.

- The client is being served by the socket 192.168.0.1 port 9099 (by PID 927), which is connected to the client's address of 192.168.0.2 port 1035.

The client is being serviced by process ID 927. This means that you can kill process ID 926 and the client will continue to be serviced. However, no new connections to the server can be made, because there will be no server listening for new connections (listening server PID 926 was killed).

Now, if you were to restart the server to listen for new connections, a problem would develop. When the new server process attempts to bind the IP address 192.168.0.1 port 9099, the bind(2) function will return the error EADDRINUSE. This error code indicates that the IP address is already in use with port 9099. This occurs because process ID 927 is still engaged in servicing a client. Address 192.168.0.1 port 9099 is still being used by that process (review Figure 12.1).

The solution to this problem is to kill off process 927, which will close that socket and release the IP address and port. However, if the client being serviced is the CEO of the company you work for, this will not be an option (this might be a career-limiting move). In the meantime, you'll be bugged by other departments, wondering why you haven't restarted the server.

A better solution to the problem just presented is to use the SO_REUSEADDR socket option. All servers should make use of this option, unless there is a good reason not to. To make effective use of this option, perform the following in the server, which listens for connections:

1. Create your listening socket as usual with socket(2).

2. Call setsockopt(2) setting SO_REUSEADDR option to TRUE.

3. Now call bind(2) as usual.

The socket will now be marked as reusable. If the listening server process (PID 926 in Figure 12.1) terminates for any reason, you will be able to be restart it. This will be true even when a client has another server process engaged using the same IP address and port number.

In order for SO_REUSEADDR option to be effective, the following conditions must be met:

- No other socket with the same IP address and port can be in a listen mode.

- All sockets with the same IP address and port number must have the SO_REUSEADDR option set to TRUE.

What this means is that there can be only one listener at a specific IP address and port number pair. If one such socket already exists, then setting the option will not accomplish your goal.

Setting SO_REUSEADDR to TRUE can be effective only if all existing sockets with the same address and port number have this option set. If any existing socket does not have this option set, then bind(2) will continue to return an error.

The following code shows how to set the option to TRUE:

EXAMPLE

```
#define TRUE  1
#define FALSE 0

int z;      /* Status code */
int s;    /* Socket number */
int so_reuseaddr = TRUE;

z = setsockopt(s,SOL_SOCKET,SO_REUSEADDR,
    &so_reuseaddr,
    sizeof so_reuseaddr);
```

The SO_REUSEADDR option can be queried with the getsockopt(2) function if required.

Setting the SO_LINGER Option

Another commonly applied socket option is the SO_LINGER option. This option differs from the SO_REUSEADDR option in that the data structure used is not a simple int data type.

The purpose of the SO_LINGER option is to control how the socket is shut down when the function close(2) is called. This option applies only to connection-oriented protocols such as TCP.

The default behavior of the kernel is to allow the close(2) function to return immediately to the caller. Any unsent TCP/IP data will be transmitted and delivered if possible, but no guarantee is made. Because the close(2) call returns control immediately to the caller, the application has no way of knowing whether the last bit of data was actually delivered.

The SO_LINGER option can be enabled on the socket, to cause the application to block in the close(2) call until all final data is delivered to the remote end. Furthermore, this assures the caller that both ends have acknowledged a normal socket shutdown. Failing this, the indicated option timeout occurs and an error is returned to the calling application.

One final scenario can be applied, by use of different SO_LINGER option values. If the calling application wants to abort communications immediately, appropriate values can be set in the linger structure. Then, a call to close(2) will initiate an abort of the communication link, discarding all pending data and immediately close the socket.

The modes of operation for SO_LINGER are controlled by the structure linger:

```
struct linger {
    int    l_onoff;
```

```
    int    l_linger;
};
```

The member l_onoff acts as a Boolean value, where a nonzero value indicates TRUE and zero indicates FALSE. The three variations of this option are specified as follows:

1. Setting l_onoff to FALSE causes member l_linger to be ignored and the default close(2) behavior implied. That is, the close(2) call will return immediately to the caller, and any pending data will be delivered if possible.

2. Setting l_onoff to TRUE causes the value of member l_linger to be significant. When l_linger is nonzero, this represents the time in seconds for the timeout period to be applied at close(2) time (the close(2) call will "linger"). If the pending data and successful close occur before the timeout occurs, a successful return takes place. Otherwise, an error return occur and errno is set to the value of EWOULDBLOCK.

3. Setting l_onoff to TRUE and setting l_linger to zero causes the connection to be aborted and any pending data is immediately discarded upon close(2).

You are probably well advised to write your applications so that the option SO_LINGER is enabled and a reasonable timeout is provided. Then, the return value from close(2) can be tested to see whether the connection was mutually shut down successfully. If an error is returned instead, this tells your application that it is probable that the remote application was unable to receive all the data that you sent. Alternatively, it might just mean that problems occurred when the connection was closed (after the data was successfully received by the peer).

You must be aware, however, that lingering in some server designs will create new problems. When the SO_LINGER option is configured to linger upon close(2), this will prevent other clients from being serviced while your server execution lingers within the close(2) function call. This problem exists if you are serving many clients within one process (usually a server that uses select(2) or poll(2)). Using the default behavior might be more appropriate because it will allow close(2) to return immediately. Any pending written data will still be delivered by the kernel, if it is able to.

Finally, using the abort behavior (mode number 3 listed previously) is appropriate if the application or server knows that the connection should be aborted. This might be applied when the server has determined that someone without access privilege is attempting to gain access. The client in this situation deserves no special care and so minimum overhead is expended in dispensing of the culprit.

The following shows an example of enabling the linger option, using a time-out (linger value) of 30 seconds:

EXAMPLE

```
#define TRUE     1
#define FALSE    0

int z;  /* Status code */
int s;      /* Socket s */
struct linger so_linger;


…
so_linger.l_onoff = TRUE;
so_linger.l_linger = 30;
z = setsockopt(s,
    SOL_SOCKET,
    SO_LINGER,
    &so_linger,
    sizeof so_linger);

if ( z )
    perror("setsockopt(2)");
```

The next example shows how to establish SO_LINGER values to effect an abort of the current connection on socket s:

EXAMPLE

```
#define TRUE     1
#define FALSE    0

int z;  /* Status code */
int s;      /* Socket s */
struct linger so_linger;


…
so_linger.l_onoff = TRUE;
so_linger.l_linger = 0;
z = setsockopt(s,
    SOL_SOCKET,
    SO_LINGER,
    &so_linger,
    sizeof so_linger);

if ( z )
    perror("setsockopt(2)");
close(s);  /* Abort connection */
```

In the prior example, the socket connection s is aborted when the function close(2) is called. The abort semantic is implied by setting the timeout value to zero seconds.

Setting the SO_KEEPALIVE Option

When connections are used, they can sometimes be idle for long periods. For example, a telnet session can be established to access a stock quotation service by a portfolio manager of a mutual fund company. He might perform a few initial inquiries and then leave the connection to the service open in case he wants to go back for more. In the meantime, however, the connection remains idle, possibly for hours at a time.

Any server that thinks it has a connected client must dedicate some resources to it. If the server is of the forking type, then an entire Linux process with its associated memory is dedicated to that client. When things are going well, this scenario does not present any problem. The difficulty arises when a network disruption occurs, and all 578 of your clients become disconnected from your stock quotation service.

After the network service is restored, an additional 578 clients will be attempting to connect to your server, as they re-establish connections. This is a real problem for you because your server has not yet realized that it lost the idle clients earlier—option SO_KEEPALIVE to the rescue!

The following example shows how to enable SO_KEEPALIVE on a socket s so that a disconnected idle connection can eventually be detected:

EXAMPLE

```
#define TRUE    1
#define FALSE   0

int z;  /* Status code */
int s;      /* Socket s */
int so_keepalive;

...
so_keepalive = TRUE;

z = setsockopt(s,
    SOL_SOCKET,
    SO_KEEPALIVE,
    &so_keepalive,
    sizeof so_keepalive);

if ( z )
    perror("setsockopt(2)");
```

The preceding example enables the SO_KEEPALIVE option so that when the socket connection is idle for long periods, a *probe message* is sent to the remote end. This is usually done after two hours of inactivity. There are three possible responses to a keep-alive probe message. They are

1. The peer responds appropriately to indicate that all is well. No indication is returned to the application, because this is the application's assumption to begin with.

2. The peer can respond indicating that it knows nothing about the connection. This indicates that the peer has been rebooted since the last communication with that host. The error ECONNRESET will then be returned to the application with the next socket operation.

3. No response is received from the peer. In this case, the kernel might make several more attempts to make contact. TCP will usually give up in approximately 11 minutes if no response is solicited. The error ETIMEDOUT is returned with the next socket operation when this happens. Other errors such as EHOSTUNREACH can be returned if the network is unable to reach the host any longer, for example (this can happen because of bad routing tables or router failures).

The time frames involved for SO_KEEPALIVE limit its general usefulness. The probe message is sent only after approximately two hours of inactivity. Then, when no response is elicited, it might take another 11 minutes before the connection returns an error. Nevertheless, this facility does eventually allow idle disconnected sockets to be detected, and then closed by the server. Consequently, servers that support potentially long idle connections should enable this feature.

Setting the SO_BROADCAST Option

The topic of broadcasting with UDP has not been covered yet. However, it should be easily appreciated that the use of a broadcasting capability could be misused and cause grief on the affected networks. To avoid broadcasting when broadcasting wasn't intended, the socket is creating with the broadcasting feature disabled. If broadcasting is truly intended, then the C programmer is expected to take the trouble to enable this feature for the socket first.

The topic of broadcasting will be covered in Chapter 13, "Broadcasting with UDP." Consequently, only the option itself will be described here. The SO_BROADCAST option is a Boolean flag option, which is defined, fetched, and set with the int data type. The following example shows how to enable the SO_BROADCAST option:

EXAMPLE

```
#define TRUE    1
#define FALSE   0

int z;  /* Status code */
int s;      /* Socket s */
int so_broadcast;
```

```
...
so_broadcast = TRUE;

z = setsockopt(s,
    SOL_SOCKET,
    SO_BROADCAST,
    &so_broadcast,
    sizeof so_broadcast);

if ( z )
    perror("setsockopt(2)");
```

If the setsockopt(2) function returns zero, the socket s has been enabled to perform broadcasting. Note, however, that the socket type chosen must be one that is capable of broadcasting, such as a UDP socket.

Setting the SO_OOBINLINE Option

The topic of *out-of-band data* will be covered in Chapter 14, "Out-of-Band Data." Here, you can just note that in some circumstances limited amounts of data can be expedited ahead of data that might already be sent. Normally, this out-of-band data is received using a different method from the usual data receiving functions. There are times, however, when it is preferred to receive this out-of-band data in the normal manner. When this method is chosen, the out-of-band data arrives ahead of the normal data as part of the normal data stream.

To enable this feature, you could use the following code:

EXAMPLE

```
#define TRUE    1
#define FALSE   0

int z;   /* Status code */
int s;       /* Socket s */
int so_oobinline;

...
so_oobinline = TRUE;

z = setsockopt(s,
    SOL_SOCKET,
    SO_OOBINLINE,
    &so_oobinline,
    sizeof so_oobinline);

if ( z )
    perror("setsockopt(2)");
```

After the option SO_OOBINLINE has been enabled, the out-of-band data will be received with the normal data. In this manner, the out-of-band data received is indistinguishable from the normal data.

Options SO_PASSCRED and SO_PEERCRED

These options are applicable to PF_UNIX (PF_LOCAL) sockets only. These are used to control and pass credentials on sockets that are local to the current host machine. The discussion of credentials will be deferred until Chapter 17, "Passing Credentials and File Descriptors." This is perhaps the most difficult topic for you to master in this book. For now, simply note that these two options are likely to be of interest to you if you plan to write server programs that serve clients on the same local host.

What's Next

In this chapter, you learned that socket options can be fetched and set using the functions getsockopt(2) and setsockopt(2), respectively. It was shown that socket options have levels and various SOL_SOCKET level options were discussed.

Many options required Boolean values, which are defined in the int data type. It was shown that some other options such as SO_LINGER, for example, required a special structure to be used instead.

A number of socket options relate to advanced uses of sockets, which have not been covered yet. You will see these options again, as the more advanced topics are encountered in the chapters that follow. The next chapter discusses broadcasting with UDP, and consequently you are now prepared to enable the SO_BROADCAST option and use it!

Broadcasting with UDP

Communication would be inefficient if it always had to be accomplished between two individuals. Broadcasting, on the other hand, allows information to be disseminated to many recipients at once.

In this chapter, you will learn how to

- Establish a broadcast UDP socket

- Send broadcast messages with a socket

- Receive broadcast messages with a socket

Upon completion of this chapter, you will know how to write programs using IPv4 socket broadcast facilities.

Understanding Broadcast Addresses

To use broadcasting, you must know about certain IP broadcast address conventions for IPv4. (Review Figure 3.1 in Chapter 3, "Address Conversion Functions.") Recall that the IP address is split between the Network ID portion on the left (the most significant bits) and the Host ID portion on the right (the least significant bits). The convention used for a broadcast address is that the Host ID bits are all set to 1 bits.

When your network card is properly configured, you can display the broadcast address for the interface of your choice by performing the following command (interface eth0 is shown in this example):

OUTPUT

```
# ifconfig eth0
eth0  Link encap:Ethernet  HWaddr 00:A0:4B:06:F4:8D
      inet addr:192.168.0.1  Bcast:192.168.0.255  Mask:255.255.255.0
      UP BROADCAST RUNNING PROMISC MULTICAST  MTU:1500  Metric:1
      RX packets:1955 errors:0 dropped:0 overruns:0 frame:31
      TX packets:1064 errors:0 dropped:0 overruns:0 carrier:0
      collisions:0 txqueuelen:100
      Interrupt:9 Base address:0xe400

#
```

The second line of output shows the broadcast address for the eth0 interface to be 192.168.0.255. The Network ID in this address is the first three octets (bytes) 192.168.0, whereas the Host ID part of this address is the 255 (recall that this address is a class C address). The value 255 is a decimal value representing all 1 bits for the Host ID.

Broadcasting on 255.255.255.255

The special broadcast address 255.255.255.255 can also be used for broadcasting. Although this form of the address might suggest a broadcast to the world, it is much more limited than that. This type of broadcast is never forwarded by a router, whereas a more specific broadcast address (such as 192.168.0.255) might be forwarded, depending upon the router's configuration.

The notion of a general broadcast address like 255.255.255.255 is not very well defined. For example, some flavors of UNIX interpret this to mean that a broadcast should take place on all network interfaces for that host. Other UNIX kernels will choose only one of several interfaces—usually the first one defined. This becomes a serious issue when a host has more than one network interface card (or *NIC* for short). For this reason, the use of the general broadcast address is generally discouraged.

If it becomes necessary to broadcast out of every network interface, then your software should perform the following steps prior to a broadcast:

1. Determine the next (or first) interface name.

2. Determine the interface's broadcast address.

3. Broadcast using that interface's broadcast address.

4. Repeat steps 1 through 3 for all additional network interfaces that are active (that is, "up") in the system.

After these steps have been performed, you can be assured that a broadcast has been made on every interface of your software.

The remainder of this chapter will focus on how to broadcast out of one network interface. After you have mastered this concept, you can then apply the preceding procedure if it becomes necessary to broadcast out of every interface.

Enhancing the `mkaddr.c` Subroutine

One of the limitations of the `mkaddr.c` subprogram that was presented in Chapter 10, "Using Standard I/O on Sockets," was that it was not able to properly handle the `255.255.255.255` broadcast address case. In this section, you'll see the reason for correcting this problem.

The diff output that follows illustrates what to change in the `mkaddr.c` source code to fix this problem. Applying this change will allow you to experiment with the `255.255.255.255` broadcast address, if you choose to do so.

EXAMPLE

```
$ diff ../ch.11/mkaddr.c mkaddr.c
99,102c99,100
<            ap->sin_addr.s_addr =
<                inet_addr(host_part);
<            if ( ap->sin_addr.s_addr
<                == INADDR_NONE )
...
>            if ( !inet_aton(host_part,
>                &ap->sin_addr) )
$
```

The preceding example shows that the routine `inet_aton(3)` function replaces the more limited `inet_addr(3)` function. The problem with `inet_addr(3)` is that it returns the value `INADDR_NONE` when an address is invalid. When the IP address `255.255.255.255` is converted to a 32-bit value, its return value is identical to the constant `INADDR_NONE`. Consequently, it becomes impossible to distinguish between a bad input IP address, and the general broadcast address. Use of the `inet_aton(3)` function avoids this ambiguity.

Broadcasting from a Server

This chapter will demonstrate a simple broadcasting server program and a corresponding client program. The server will be presented and explained first.

To provide a flavor of what could be accomplished with a broadcasting facility, the server being presented will provide a stock market index simulation. The server program will represent a program that obtains a data feed from external quotation suppliers and then rebroadcasts the stock market index quotations to all interested clients. The example in Listing 13.1 shows the stksrv.c server program.

NOTE

The mkaddr.c listing is not repeated in this chapter. If you want to experiment with the 255.255.255.255 general broadcast address, then be sure to make the minor adjustment described in the previous section. The mkaddr.c listing is otherwise identical to that which was used in Chapter 11, "Concurrent Client Servers."

EXAMPLE

Listing 13.1: stksrv.c—The Stock Market Index Broadcasting Server

```
 1:    /* stksrv.c:
 2:     *
 3:     * Example Stock Index Broadcast:
 4:     */
 5:    #include <stdio.h>
 6:    #include <unistd.h>
 7:    #include <stdlib.h>
 8:    #include <errno.h>
 9:    #include <string.h>
10:    #include <time.h>
11:    #include <sys/types.h>
12:    #include <sys/socket.h>
13:    #include <netinet/in.h>
14:    #include <arpa/inet.h>
15:
16:    #ifndef TRUE
17:    #define TRUE    1
18:    #define FALSE   0
19:    #endif
20:
21:    extern int mkaddr(
22:        void *addr,
23:        int *addrlen,
24:        char *str_addr,
25:        char *protocol);
26:
27:    #define MAXQ    4
```

```
28:
29:   static struct {
30:       char    *index;
31:       int     start;
32:       int     volit;
33:       int     current;
34:   } quotes[] = {
35:       { "DJIA",    1030330, 375 },
36:       { "NASDAQ",  276175,  125 },
37:       { "S&P 500", 128331,   50 },
38:       { "TSE 300", 689572,   75 },
39:   };
40:
41:   /*
42:    * Initialize:
43:    */
44:   static void
45:   initialize(void) {
46:       short x;
47:       time_t td;
48:
49:       /*
50:        * Seed the random number generator:
51:        */
52:       time(&td);
53:       srand((int)td);
54:
55:       for ( x=0; x < MAXQ; ++x )
56:           quotes[x].current =
57:               quotes[x].start;
58:   }
59:
60:   /*
61:    * Randomly change one index quotation:
62:    */
63:   static void
64:   gen_quote(void) {
65:       short x;      /* Index */
66:       short v;      /* Volatility of index */
67:       short h;      /* Half of v */
68:       short r;      /* Random change */
69:
70:       x = rand() % MAXQ;
71:       v = quotes[x].volit;
72:       h = (v / 2) - 2;
73:       r = rand() % v;
```

continues

Listing 13.1: continued

```
74:        if ( r < h )
75:            r = -r;
76:        quotes[x].current += r;
77:    }
78:
79:    /*
80:     * This function reports the error and
81:     * exits back to the shell:
82:     */
83:    static void
84:    bail(const char *on_what) {
85:        fputs(strerror(errno),stderr);
86:        fputs(": ",stderr);
87:        fputs(on_what,stderr);
88:        fputc('\n',stderr);
89:        exit(1);
90:    }
91:
92:    int
93:    main(int argc,char **argv) {
94:        short x;      /* index of Stock Indexes */
95:        double I0;       /* Initial index value */
96:        double I;                /* Index value */
97:        char bcbuf[512], *bp;/* Buffer and ptr */
98:        int z;           /* Status return code */
99:        int s;                      /* Socket */
100:       struct sockaddr_in adr_srvr;/* AF_INET */
101:       int len_srvr;              /* length */
102:       struct sockaddr_in adr_bc;  /* AF_INET */
103:       int len_bc;                /* length */
104:       static int so_broadcast = TRUE;
105:       static char
106:           *sv_addr = "127.0.0.1:*",
107:           *bc_addr = "127.255.255.255:9097";
108:
109:       /*
110:        * Form a server address:
111:        */
112:       if ( argc > 2 )
113:           /* Server address: */
114:           sv_addr = argv[2];
115:
116:       if ( argc > 1 )
117:           /* Broadcast address: */
118:           bc_addr = argv[1];
119:
```

```
120:     /*
121:      * Form the server address:
122:      */
123:     len_srvr = sizeof adr_srvr;
124:
125:     z = mkaddr(
126:         &adr_srvr,  /* Returned address */
127:         &len_srvr,  /* Returned length */
128:         sv_addr,    /* Input string addr */
129:         "udp");     /* UDP protocol */
130:
131:     if ( z == -1 )
132:         bail("Bad server address");
133:
134:     /*
135:      * Form the broadcast address:
136:      */
137:     len_bc = sizeof adr_bc;
138:
139:     z = mkaddr(
140:         &adr_bc,    /* Returned address */
141:         &len_bc,    /* Returned length */
142:         bc_addr,    /* Input string addr */
143:         "udp");     /* UDP protocol */
144:
145:     if ( z == -1 )
146:         bail("Bad broadcast address");
147:
148:     /*
149:      * Create a UDP socket to use:
150:      */
151:     s = socket(AF_INET,SOCK_DGRAM,0);
152:     if ( s == -1 )
153:         bail("socket()");
154:
155:     /*
156:      * Allow broadcasts:
157:      */
158:     z = setsockopt(s,
159:         SOL_SOCKET,
160:         SO_BROADCAST,
161:         &so_broadcast,
162:         sizeof so_broadcast);
163:
164:     if ( z == -1 )
165:         bail("setsockopt(SO_BROADCAST)");
```

continues

Listing 13.1: continued

```
166:
167:     /*
168:      * Bind an address to our socket, so that
169:      * client programs can listen to this
170:      * server:
171:      */
172:     z = bind(s,
173:         (struct sockaddr *)&adr_srvr,
174:         len_srvr);
175:
176:     if ( z == -1 )
177:         bail("bind()");
178:
179:     /*
180:      * Now start serving quotes:
181:      */
182:     initialize();
183:
184:     for (;;) {
185:         /*
186:          * Update one quote in the list:
187:          */
188:         gen_quote();
189:
190:         /*
191:          * Form a packet to send out:
192:          */
193:         bp = bcbuf;
194:         for ( x=0; x<MAXQ; ++x ) {
195:             I0 = quotes[x].start / 100.0;
196:             I = quotes[x].current / 100.0;
197:             sprintf(bp,
198:                 "%-7.7s %8.2f %+.2f\n",
199:                 quotes[x].index,
200:                 I,
201:                 I - I0);
202:             bp += strlen(bp);
203:         }
204:
205:         /*
206:          * Broadcast the updated info:
207:          */
208:         z = sendto(s,
209:             bcbuf,
210:             strlen(bcbuf),
211:             0,
```

```
212:                 (struct sockaddr *)&adr_bc,
213:                 len_bc);
214:
215:         if ( z == -1 )
216:             bail("sendto()");
217:
218:         sleep(4);
219:     }
220:
221:     return 0;
222: }
```

The server shown in Listing 13.1 is functionally divided into the following sections:

1. The table of stock market indexes is declared in lines 27 to 39. Four indexes are defined with starting values and a crude form of volatility value, which is used for the simulation.

2. The function `initialize()` in lines 44 to 58 is called once to initialize for the simulation.

3. The function `gen_quote()` is called to randomly change the simulated value of a randomly selected stock market index (lines 63 to 77).

4. The `main()` program, which forms the basis of the server, is contained within lines 92 to 222.

The basic operation of this stock market server is as follows:

1. Default addresses are declared in lines 106 and 107. These are used when no command-line arguments are supplied.

2. If two command-line arguments are supplied, then the server address takes the address from the second argument (line 114).

3. If one or more command-line arguments are supplied, then the broadcast argument is taken from argument one (line 118).

4. The server address is formed (lines 123 to 132).

5. The broadcast address is formed (lines 137 to 146).

6. A socket is created (lines 151 to 153).

7. The `SO_BROADCAST` option is enabled on the socket (lines 158 to 165).

8. The server address is bound (lines 172 to 177).

9. The stock market indices are initialized (line 182).

10. The server loop begins in line 184.

The server loops indefinitely. You will need to kill it to end its execution. The server loop uses the following steps:

1. A randomly selected index is updated (line 188) by calling `gen_quote()`.

2. The quotes from all indices are extracted and formatted into a buffer (lines 193 to 203). This creates a string with four text lines in it, corresponding to each stock market index.

3. The formatted string is sent out using the `sendto(2)` function (lines 208 to 216). This call broadcasts because the address `adr_bc` contains a broadcast address.

4. A `sleep(3)` call of four seconds takes place to simulate some reasonable time delay between quote updates.

5. The loop repeats with step 1.

A couple of points are worth reviewing here:

- The socket must have the `SO_BROADCAST` option enabled. Otherwise, broadcasting would not be permitted from this socket.

- The `sendto(2)` call effected a broadcast because the destination address was a broadcast address.

Both of these conditions are prerequisites for a broadcast. The socket must be enabled for broadcasting and the destination address must be a broadcast IP address.

To compile this program, use the following command:

OUTPUT

```
$ make stksrv
gcc -c  -D_GNU_SOURCE -Wall -Wreturn-type -g stksrv.c
gcc -c  -D_GNU_SOURCE -Wall -Wreturn-type -g mkaddr.c
gcc -g stksrv.o mkaddr.o -o stksrv
$
```

Before the server can be tested, we must compile and understand the client program.

Receiving Broadcasts

The client program that will be presented must listen for the broadcasts that our stock market index program is going to issue. Listing 13.2 illustrates the client program source code that will be used.

Listing 13.2: gquotes.c—The Stock Market Index Client Program

```
1:   /* gquotes.c:
2:    *
3:    * Get datagram stock market
4:    * quotes from UDP broadcast:
5:    */
6:   #include <stdio.h>
7:   #include <unistd.h>
8:   #include <stdlib.h>
9:   #include <errno.h>
10:  #include <string.h>
11:  #include <time.h>
12:  #include <signal.h>
13:  #include <sys/types.h>
14:  #include <sys/socket.h>
15:  #include <netinet/in.h>
16:  #include <arpa/inet.h>
17:
18:  #ifndef TRUE
19:  #define TRUE    1
20:  #define FALSE   0
21:  #endif
22:
23:  extern int mkaddr(
24:      void *addr,
25:      int *addrlen,
26:      char *str_addr,
27:      char *protocol);
28:
29:  /*
30:   * This function reports the error and
31:   * exits back to the shell:
32:   */
33:  static void
34:  bail(const char *on_what) {
35:      fputs(strerror(errno),stderr);
36:      fputs(": ",stderr);
37:      fputs(on_what,stderr);
38:      fputc('\n',stderr);
39:      exit(1);
40:  }
41:
42:  int
43:  main(int argc,char **argv) {
44:      int z;
45:      int x;
```

continues

Listing 13.2: continued

```
46:        struct sockaddr_in adr;      /* AF_INET */
47:        int len_inet;                /* length  */
48:        int s;                       /* Socket */
49:        char dgram[512];             /* Recv buffer */
50:        static int so_reuseaddr = TRUE;
51:        static char
52:            *bc_addr = "127.255.255.255:9097";
53:
54:        /*
55:         * Use a server address from the command
56:         * line, if one has been provided.
57:         * Otherwise, this program will default
58:         * to using the arbitrary address
59:         * 127.0.0.23:
60:         */
61:        if ( argc > 1 )
62:            /* Broadcast address: */
63:            bc_addr = argv[1];
64:
65:        /*
66:         * Create a UDP socket to use:
67:         */
68:        s = socket(AF_INET,SOCK_DGRAM,0);
69:        if ( s == -1 )
70:            bail("socket()");
71:
72:        /*
73:         * Form the broadcast address:
74:         */
75:        len_inet = sizeof adr;
76:
77:        z = mkaddr(&adr,
78:            &len_inet,
79:            bc_addr,
80:            "udp");
81:
82:        if ( z == -1 )
83:            bail("Bad broadcast address");
84:
85:        /*
86:         * Allow multiple listeners on the
87:         * broadcast address:
88:         */
89:        z = setsockopt(s,
90:            SOL_SOCKET,
91:            SO_REUSEADDR,
```

```
92:            &so_reuseaddr,
93:            sizeof so_reuseaddr);
94:
95:      if ( z == -1 )
96:          bail("setsockopt(SO_REUSEADDR)");
97:
98:      /*
99:       * Bind our socket to the broadcast address:
100:      */
101:     z = bind(s,
102:         (struct sockaddr *)&adr,
103:         len_inet);
104:
105:     if ( z == -1 )
106:         bail("bind(2)");
107:
108:     for (;;) {
109:         /*
110:          * Wait for a broadcast message:
111:          */
112:         z = recvfrom(s,              /* Socket */
113:             dgram,         /* Receiving buffer */
114:             sizeof dgram,/* Max rcv buf size */
115:             0,             /* Flags: no options */
116:             (struct sockaddr *)&adr, /* Addr */
117:             &x);           /* Addr len, in & out */
118:
119:         if ( z < 0 )
120:             bail("recvfrom(2)"); /* else err */
121:
122:         fwrite(dgram,z,1,stdout);
123:         putchar('\n');
124:
125:         fflush(stdout);
126:     }
127:
128:     return 0;
129: }
```

The client program presented takes one optional command-line argument.
If none is supplied, the broadcast address that will be assumed will be
127.255.255.255 on port 9097. The default is established by line 52 in
Listing 13.2. When a command-line argument is provided, this will indicate
the IP broadcast address and UDP port number.

The general steps used by the client program are these:

1. The socket is created (lines 68 to 70).

2. The broadcast address is formed (lines 75 to 83).

3. The SO_REUSEADDR option is enabled (lines 89 to 96).

4. Bind the broadcast address to the current socket (lines 101 to 106).

5. Begin a broadcast receiving loop (line 108).

6. Receive a broadcast (lines 112 to 120).

7. Write the broadcast information to the standard output (lines 122 to 125).

8. Repeat step 5.

Pay special attention to step 4. To receive the broadcast, there has to be a client program that has this address bound to the socket. This identifies the client program as the intended recipient of the messages.

There is a problem with this approach, however. If one client program binds this address, then no others on the same host will be able to bind that address. This would defeat the purpose of broadcasting. Enabling SO_REUSEADDR allows multiple client programs to receive from the same broadcast address, on the same host.

To compile the demonstration client program, you can use the following command:

```
$ make gquotes
gcc -c  -D_GNU_SOURCE -Wall -Wreturn-type -g gquotes.c
gcc -g gquotes.o mkaddr.o -o gquotes
$
```

OUTPUT

Demonstrating the Broadcasts

With the server and client programs compiled, you are ready to begin. The first example sessions should work for everyone, with or without a network established. The demonstration will make use of the local loopback interface that every Linux system should have available unless it has been disabled.

The first step is to start the broadcast server:

```
@pepper
$ ./stksrv 127.255.255.255:9097 &
[1] 756
@pepper
$
```

OUTPUT

The session shows the starting of the stksrv server program on the host system pepper. The client session on the same host looked like this:

OUTPUT

```
$ ./gquotes 127.255.255.255:9097
DJIA      10302.06 -1.24
NASDAQ    2766.86 +5.11
S&P 500   1285.48 +2.17
TSE 300   6897.99 +2.27

DJIA      10302.06 -1.24
NASDAQ    2766.86 +5.11
S&P 500   1285.73 +2.42
TSE 300   6897.99 +2.27

DJIA      10302.06 -1.24
NASDAQ    2766.86 +5.11
S&P 500   1286.00 +2.69
TSE 300   6897.99 +2.27

[CTRL+C]
@pepper
$
```

In the client session shown, the program was allowed to provide three quote updates before CTRL+C was typed to end its execution (your interrupt character might be different). Note that the broadcast address and port number must agree for both the client and server.

To prove to yourself that a broadcast is being performed, and not simply a point-to-point communication, you can start multiple instances of the client program. When this is done, they will all update at approximately the same time.

Broadcasting to a Network

If you have a network card installed in your PC and you have a correctly configured network, you should be able to test the broadcast server and client programs successfully. This section will demonstrate the broadcast server broadcasting from a host named pepper, on the interface card eth0 (IP address 192.168.0.1).

Starting Broadcasts

The broadcast server is told to broadcast on interface card 192.168.0.1 by performing the following:

OUTPUT

```
@pepper
$ ./stksrv 192.168.0.255:9097 '192.168.0.1:*' &
[2] 815
@pepper
$
```

Notice that there are two command-line arguments given on the command line. These are

1. The broadcast address and port number to which the messages are directed.

2. The source address and port number, from which the broadcasts will originate.

The second address specifies the local IP address of the socket to be used for the broadcast. This, in effect, chooses the network interface card that the broadcasting will take place on (thus choosing the network for the broadcast). The asterisk that follows the colon character specifies that any local port number is to be used. This is done because the actual port number used in this case does not need to be agreed upon in advance (any port will do).

If you fail to bind the local end of the socket correctly, you will experience something like this:

OUTPUT

```
@pepper
$ ./stksrv 192.168.0.255:9097 &
[3] 816
Invalid argument: sendto()
[3]+  Exit 1     ./stksrv 192.168.0.255:9096
@pepper
$
```

The sendto(2) function fails because the server program binds a default local address of 127.0.0.1 to the socket. This cannot work because no 192.168.0.* address can be reached from the 127.*.*.* network. This is not detected until the sendto(2) function attempts to perform the broadcast.

Three possible solutions to this problem exist:

- Be certain that the local end of the socket is explicitly bound to the correct interface card, which is to be used for the broadcast (192.168.0.1 in the demonstration).

- Use a wild local socket address (INADDR_ANY). In the example program, this can be specified on the command line as '*:*'.

- Don't bind(2) the local address for the socket at all (leave out the call to bind(2) completely).

Omitting the bind(2) function call is effectively the same as binding to INADDR_ANY and specifying a port number of zero (allowing any choice of port number). The choice used depends upon the amount of control that you want to exert over the choice of the network interface card.

Receiving Broadcasts

The most obvious place to begin testing the operation of the broadcast server, is on the same host as the server. This is shown in the following session output:

OUTPUT

```
@pepper
$ ./gquotes 192.168.0.255:9097
DJIA      10304.73 +1.43
NASDAQ    2761.19 -0.56
S&P 500   1283.31 +0.00
TSE 300   6895.82 +0.10

DJIA      10304.73 +1.43
NASDAQ    2761.19 -0.56
S&P 500   1283.31 +0.00
TSE 300   6896.35 +0.63
```

The session demonstrates that indeed, the broadcasts are being received from the server. Now it's time to try the client program on another host and see broadcasts being received over a physical network.

Receiving Broadcasts from a Remote Host

Another host named slug is used in this demonstration, with an IP address of 192.168.0.2. Starting a copy of the client program on that host looks like this:

OUTPUT

```
@slug
$ ./gquotes 192.168.0.255:9097
DJIA      10309.80 +6.50
NASDAQ    2767.29 +5.54
S&P 500   1286.06 +2.75
TSE 300   6897.75 +2.03

DJIA      10309.80 +6.50
NASDAQ    2767.29 +5.54
S&P 500   1286.06 +2.75
TSE 300   6897.67 +1.95

DJIA      10313.18 +9.88
NASDAQ    2767.29 +5.54
S&P 500   1286.06 +2.75
TSE 300   6897.67 +1.95
```

Here, it is demonstrated on host slug that broadcasts were indeed being received over the Ethernet link between these two hosts. The values are different in this output because it was captured much later than the earlier session shown. However, if you were to establish clients that ran on the local and remote hosts at the same time, you would be able to verify that their content was in full agreement.

Troubleshooting Hints

If you fail to achieve similar results on your own personal network, then a large number of things could be involved in the problem. It is not the intention of this book to describe aspects of network administration or design. Nor will this book be a treatise on network troubleshooting. The following simple tips are offered in the hope that it might prove to be useful as a starting point in diagnosis.

If the problem exists over a simple network of your own construction and there is little or no network traffic on it, you might be able to just look at the hub. Many mini-hubs, for example, offer LED indicators that provide indication of packet traffic for the corresponding ports involved. The server program presented should cause a flicker to occur approximately every four seconds when a broadcast occurs. Failure to see this suggests that the broadcast is not occurring.

Another approach is to use the tcpdump command, which is now part of most Linux distributions today. An example of tcpdump(8) output is shown as follows while the server was broadcasting:

OUTPUT

```
@slug
# tcpdump udp port 9097
tcpdump: listening on eth0
21:04:43.967482 pepper.ve3wwg.org.1032 > 192.168.0.255.9097: udp 96
21:04:47.977482 pepper.ve3wwg.org.1032 > 192.168.0.255.9097: udp 96
21:04:51.987482 pepper.ve3wwg.org.1032 > 192.168.0.255.9097: udp 96
```

The command-line arguments used cause only the UDP packets on port 9097 to be displayed. The sample output includes three packet summaries that were displayed. More information about tcpdump(8) can be accessed by reading its manual page.

These are but two very simple methods of checking for broadcast packets. Frequently, however, these simple techniques will be sufficient for the programmer.

What's Next

This chapter has introduced you to the concept of special addresses known as IPv4 broadcast addresses. Additionally, you saw how the socket options SO_REUSEADDR and SO_BROADCAST were applied in a practical manner.

In the next chapter, you will be introduced to the advanced topic of out-of-band data. You will learn why it is needed and about its advantages and limitations. Discover how Linux is schizophrenic and how to determine which personality your system thinks it possesses presently.

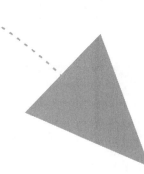

14

Out-of-Band Data

This chapter will bring you into the fray of using out-of-band data with TCP. You will learn why it is provided and about some of its pitfalls. Most important of all however, you will become equipped to properly apply out-of-band modes of communication, with any protocol that supports it.

Here is a summary of what will be covered in this chapter:

- Define what out-of-band data is.
- Why is it needed?
- What are the socket related issues of using it?
- What are the variations in the TCP/IP implementation?
- How do you use it with TCP stream sockets?

Defining Out-of-Band

Imagine a lineup of people at the bank waiting to cash their paychecks. The line forms a queue, in which people eventually move forward to be served by a teller. Now imagine that a person walks into the bank, bypasses the entire lineup, and then engages a teller with a gun. This person would be viewed as being "out-of-band" (or quite possibly out of his head). This "bandit" jumps the queue because the gun gives him priority over the people in the queue. The teller also provides her undivided attention to the bandit because she knows the situation is urgent.

Conceptually, out-of-band data over a connected stream socket works the same way. Normally, data flows from one end of the connection to the other, with precise ordering of all bytes of data guaranteed. No later byte is permitted to arrive ahead of bytes that were written earlier. The socket API, however, provides a facility where, conceptually, a bunch of data bytes can be expedited ahead of the normal data to the receiver. This is known as sending out-of-band data.

Technically speaking, a TCP stream cannot send out-of-band data. What it does support is a concept of "urgent" data, which is mapped to the socket API as out-of-band data. This brings about a number of limitations, which will be discussed later in this chapter.

Understanding the Need for Out-of-Band Data

Although you can immediately appreciate the benefits of bypassing the lineup in a bank, you would also recognize that using a gun for this purpose is considered rather antisocial. A TCP stream is normally expected to send data bytes in perfect sequence and so to send them out of sequence seems counter to what streams are all about. Why then provide out-of-band socket facilities?

As you have probably realized, there are times when data simply becomes "urgent" in some way. A stream socket can have a large amount of data queued waiting to be transmitted to the network. At the remote end, there can be a large amount of data received, which has yet to be read by the application. If the sending client program now has a reason to cancel the request that has already been written to the server, it might want to urgently indicate a cancel request to the server. Failing to issue a cancel request to the remote server unnecessarily wastes the server's resources.

You might answer this design problem by saying that the socket can be prematurely closed, or information can be transmitted on an additional socket connection. Both of these solutions are less than ideal for different reasons:

- Shutting down a socket does not permit recovery if more communication is to be continued.

- The addition of an extra connection can be quite expensive when hundreds or thousands of users are pounding on your server.

- Company firewall restrictions make it even more desirable to perform all your networking needs within the one socket connection.

Practical examples of programs that use of out-of-band data are the `telnet`, `rlogin`, and `ftp` commands. The first two programs send the interrupt character as urgent data to the remote end. This allows the remote end to flush all unprocessed input and to discard with any unsent terminal output. This facilitates a quick interrupt of a running process, which might have been spewing oodles of output to your screen. The `ftp` command uses out-of-band data to abort a file transfer.

Sockets and Out-of-Band Data

It was stated earlier that TCP streams have some pitfalls when using the socket out-of-band concept. It is important to re-emphasize that the socket interface itself is not the limiting factor. The out-of-band concept is actually mapped to the urgent data mode of TCP/IP communications. TCP streams are important to networking today and this chapter will focus only on the socket use of out-of-band data as it applies to TCP urgent data. Consequently, while the two terms are technically different, they will often be used interchangeably.

It is also necessary to point out that the limitations pertaining to TCP urgent data do not necessarily apply to other protocols that might be used with the socket interface. For example, if you look at out-of-band data for infrared communications, you'll need to research the underlying protocol for it before reaching any conclusions about its capabilities.

Variations in Implementation

The implementation of TCP, unfortunately, has two different interpretations of how urgent data should be handled. These differences will be described fully, later in the chapter (the impatient can refer to Table 14.2 later in the chapter). The different interpretations are

- The RFC793 interpretation of the TCP urgent-pointer

- The BSD interpretation of the TCP urgent-pointer

This dichotomy has come about because the original TCP specification permitted both interpretations. Subsequently, a "Host Requirements" RFC identified the correct interpretation. However, most implementations were based upon the BSD (Berkeley) source code and the BSD approach remains in common use today. Linux is schizophrenic in this regard, supporting both interpretations. The Linux default however, is to use the BSD interpretation.

NOTE

The tcp(4) man page indicates that the BSD interpretation is used by default under Linux. This can be changed, but it might not be advisable to do so. The reason for this is that a change in this setting can cause other existing network processes to fail.

Take a moment now and check the current setting of your Linux system. This is critical in order to obtain the same results that the examples in this chapter will produce.

```
$ cat /proc/sys/net/ipv4/tcp_stdurg
0
$
```

OUTPUT

The output presented here shows the value zero. This indicates that the BSD interpretation is in effect at present. If you have some other value shown (such as 1), then you should change this value to zero if you want to achieve the results shown in this chapter.

CAUTION

If you are running a multiuser system, be sure to consider your users before making a change to the interpretation of TCP urgent data.

Table 14.1 summarizes the values for the tcp_stdurg settings. The tcp_stdurg value can be queried and set in shell scripts, including startup and shutdown scripts.

Table 14.1: The **/proc/sys/net/ipv4/tcp_stdurg** *Settings*

Value	Interpretation
0	BSD Interpretation (Linux default)
1	RFC793 interpretation

If you need to change this setting to zero, you'll need to gain root access, and type the following:

```
# echo 0 >/proc/sys/net/ipv4/tcp_stdurg
#
```

EXAMPLE

It is always wise to double-check things, so list the value after establishing a change to see whether the change was accepted by the kernel. You should be able to display the zero value with the cat command as was shown in a previous example.

Using Out-of-Band Data

Although you probably still have many questions about out-of-band data, fret not. Some simple example programs will help illustrate the concepts more clearly than a lot of text. An explanation will be provided as you progress through the demonstrations.

A few more basics about out-of-band I/O must be covered in the next short sections. After that is out of the way, the fun begins.

Writing Out-of-Band Data

A call to write(2) will simply write the normal "in-band" data that you are already accustomed to doing. Consequently, a new function must be used to write out-of-band data. The send(2) function's prototype is shown here for this purpose:

```
#include <sys/types.h>
#include <sys/socket.h>

int send(int s, const void *msg, int len, unsigned int flags);
```

This function requires four arguments, which are

1. The socket s to write to.

2. The message buffer msg to write from.

3. The length (len) of the message.

4. Sending option flags.

The send(2) function is like the write(2) call except that it has the additional flags argument provided. This is the essential ingredient. The send(2) function returns the number of characters written or −1 if an error occurred (check errno for the cause of the error).

To send out-of-band data, you use the first three arguments as you would in a call to write(2). If you supply the C language macro MSG_OOB for the flags argument, the data is sent as out-of-band data instead of the normal "in-band" data, as follows:

EXAMPLE

```
char buf[64]; /* Data */
int len;      /* Bytes */
int s;        /* Socket */

...

send(s,buf,len,MSG_OOB);
```

If the flags argument is supplied without the MSG_OOB flag bit, then the data is written as normal in-band data. This allows you to write both in-band and out-of-band data with the same function call. You simply change the flags argument value under program control to accomplish this.

Reading Out-of-Band Data

Out-of-band data can be read in two different ways:

- Read separately as out-of-band data

- Read intermixed with the in-band data

In order to read out-of-band data separately from the normal stream of data, you need to use the function recv(2). If you guessed that recv(2) is like read(2) with an additional flags argument, then you guessed correctly. The function prototype is shown as follows:

```
#include <sys/types.h>
#include <sys/socket.h>

int recv(int s, void *buf, int len, unsigned int flags);
```

The recv(2) function accepts four arguments, which are

1. The socket s to receive data from (in-band or out-of-band data).

2. The buffer buf to place the received data into.

3. The maximum byte length (len) of the receiving buffer.

4. The option flags to use for this call.

As you can see, recv(2) is a counterpart to the send(2) function call. To receive out-of-band data, supply the C macro MSG_OOB in the flags argument. Without flag bit MSG_OOB, normal in-band data is received by the recv(2) function as if the normal read(2) call were made instead.

The recv(2) function returns the number of bytes received or –1 if an error occurred (check errno for the cause of the error).

The following shows an example of reading out-of-band data:

EXAMPLE

```
char buf[128];   /* Buffer */
int n;       /* No. of bytes */
int s;            /* Socket */
int len;      /* Max bytes */

…
n = recv(s,buf,len,MSG_OOB);
```

Although it was indicated earlier that out-of-band data could optionally be intermixed with normal data, we will defer this discussion until later.

Understanding the Signal SIGURG

The receiving process needs to be notified when out-of-band data has arrived. This is particularly true if it must be read separately from the normal data stream. One such method for doing this is to have the Linux kernel send your process the SIGURG signal when out-of-band data has arrived.

There are two requirements for using SIGURG signal notification:

- You must establish ownership of the socket.
- You must establish a signal handler for SIGURG.

To receive the SIGURG signal, you must establish your process (or process group) as the owner of the socket. To establish this ownership, you use the fcntl(2) function. Its function prototype as it applies to us here is as follows:

```
#include <unistd.h>
#include <fcntl.h>

int fcntl(int fd, int cmd, long arg);
```

The arguments for this function are as follows:

1. The file descriptor fd (or socket) to apply a control function to.
2. The control function cmd to apply.
3. The value arg to set (if any).

The return value depends upon the control function being exercised by fcntl(2). The Linux man page for fcntl(2) describes the cmd operation F_SETOWN in some detail, for those who are interested in additional reading.

To establish your process (or process group) as the owner of a socket, the receiving program could use the following code:

EXAMPLE

```
int z;   /* Status */
int s;   /* Socket */

z = fcntl(s,F_SETOWN,getpid());

if ( z == -1 ) {
    perror("fcntl(2)");
    exit(1);
}
```

The F_SETOWN operation causes the fcntl(2) function to return zero if successful, or −1 if it fails (errno indicates the cause of the failure).

One additional requirement is that the program must be prepared to receive the signal SIGURG, which is done by establishing a signal handler for the signal. You'll see an example of this shortly.

Supporting Subprograms

In order to reduce the amount of duplicated code in the example programs to be presented, several of the mundane functions will be grouped into one source module and presented once here. This will help you later to focus on the important concepts of out-of-band data processing.

The source module bindacpt.c is presented in Listing 14.1, which contains much of the common code for establishing and accepting socket connections.

EXAMPLE

Listing 14.1: The bindacpt.c Source Module for Connecting and Accepting

```
1:   /* bindacpt.c:
2:    *
3:    * socket, bind, listen & accept:
4:    */
5:   #include <stdio.h>
6:   #include <unistd.h>
7:   #include <stdlib.h>
8:   #include <errno.h>
9:   #include <string.h>
10:  #include <time.h>
11:  #include <sys/types.h>
12:  #include <sys/socket.h>
13:  #include <netinet/in.h>
14:  #include <arpa/inet.h>
15:  #include <netdb.h>
16:
17:  extern int
18:     mkaddr(void *addr,
19:     int *addrlen,
20:     char *str_addr,
21:     char *protocol);
22:
23:  /*
24:   * This function reports the error and
25:   * exits back to the shell:
26:   */
27:  void
28:  bail(const char *on_what) {
29:      if ( errno != 0 ) {
30:          fputs(strerror(errno),stderr);
31:          fputs(": ",stderr);
32:      }
33:      fputs(on_what,stderr);
```

```
34:        fputc('\n',stderr);
35:        exit(1);
36:  }
37:
38:  /*
39:   * Call socket(2), bind(2),
40:   * listen(2) and accept(2):
41:   *
42:   * Returns socket.
43:   */
44:  int
45:  BindAccept(char *addr) {
46:      int z;
47:      int s;
48:      struct sockaddr_in adr_srvr;
49:      struct sockaddr_in adr_clnt;
50:      int len_inet;
51:
52:      /*
53:       * Create a TCP/IP socket to use:
54:       */
55:      s = socket(PF_INET,SOCK_STREAM,0);
56:      if ( s == -1 )
57:          bail("socket()");
58:
59:      /*
60:       * Bind the server address:
61:       */
62:      len_inet = sizeof adr_srvr;
63:      z = mkaddr(&adr_srvr,&len_inet,
64:          addr,"tcp");
65:
66:      if ( z != 0 ) {
67:          puts("Bad address/port");
68:          exit(1);
69:      }
70:
71:      /*
72:       * Bind server address:
73:       */
74:      z = bind(s,(struct sockaddr *)&adr_srvr,
75:              len_inet);
76:      if ( z == -1 )
77:          bail("bind(2)");
78:
79:      /*
```

continues

Listing 14.1: continued

```
80:        * Set listen mode:
81:        */
82:       if ( listen(s,10) == -1 )
83:           bail("listen(2)");
84:
85:       /*
86:        * Wait for a connect:
87:        */
88:       len_inet = sizeof adr_clnt;
89:
90:       z = accept(s,
91:           (struct sockaddr *)&adr_clnt,
92:           &len_inet);
93:
94:       if ( z == -1 )
95:               bail("accept(2)");
96:
97:       close(s);   /* No longer needed */
98:       return z;   /* Connected socket */
99:   }
100:
101: int
102: Connect(char *addr) {
103:       int z;
104:       int s;
105:       struct sockaddr_in adr_srvr;
106:       int len_inet;
107:
108:       /*
109:        * Create a TDP/IP socket to use:
110:        */
111:       s = socket(PF_INET,SOCK_STREAM,0);
112:       if ( s == -1 )
113:           bail("socket()");
114:
115:       /*
116:        * Bind the server address:
117:        */
118:       len_inet = sizeof adr_srvr;
119:       z = mkaddr(&adr_srvr,&len_inet,
120:           addr,"tcp");
121:
122:       if ( z != 0 ) {
123:           puts("Bad address/port");
124:           exit(1);
125:       }
```

```
126:
127:     /*
128:      * Connect to server:
129:      */
130:     len_inet = sizeof adr_srvr;
131:
132:     z = connect(s,
133:         (struct sockaddr *)&adr_srvr,
134:         len_inet);
135:
136:     if ( z == -1 )
137:             bail("connect(2)");
138:
139:     return s;   /* Connected socket */
140: }
```

The major components within this module are

- The bail() function for reporting an error and bailing out of the program (lines 27 to 36).

- The BindAccept() function which creates a socket, binds an address to it. Additionally, the listen(2) and accept(2) calls are made to wait for a client connection. The return value is the connected client socket (lines 44 to 99).

- The Connect() function which creates a socket and connects to the remote server (lines 101 to 140).

This source module will not be discussed in detail, because you should now have a good grasp of the operations contained within it.

The mkaddr.c source module is used again without changes from the last chapter, so it is not repeated here.

Receiving with the SIGURG Signal

With the grunt work out of the way, it's time now to have some fun exploring this out-of-band data concept. The program in Listing 14.2 is the program that you will use to receive data and to process out-of-band data when it arrives. It is designed for the BSD interpretation of the out-of-band processing, which is the default for Linux.

Listing 14.2: The oobrecv.c Receiving Main Program

```
1:     /* oobrecv.c:
2:      *
3:      * Example OOB receiver:
```

continues

Listing 14.2: continued

```
 4:      */
 5:     #include <stdio.h>
 6:     #include <unistd.h>
 7:     #include <stdlib.h>
 8:     #include <errno.h>
 9:     #include <string.h>
10:     #include <signal.h>
11:     #include <fcntl.h>
12:     #include <sys/types.h>
13:     #include <sys/socket.h>
14:
15:     extern void bail(char *on_what);
16:     extern int BindAccept(char *addr);
17:
18:     static int s = -1;   /* Socket */
19:
20:     /*
21:      * SIGURG signal handler:
22:      */
23:     static void
24:     sigurg(int signo) {
25:         int n;
26:         char buf[256];
27:
28:         n = recv(s,buf,sizeof buf,MSG_OOB);
29:         if ( n < 0 )
30:             bail("recv(2)");
31:
32:         buf[n] = 0;
33:         printf("URG '%s' (%d)\n",
34:             buf,n);
35:
36:         signal(SIGURG,sigurg);
37:     }
38:
39:     int
40:     main(int argc,char **argv) {
41:         int z;                /* Status */
42:         char buf[256];
43:
44:
45:         /*
46:          * Use a server address from the command
47:          * line, if one has been provided.
48:          * Otherwise, this program will default
49:          * to using the arbitrary address
```

```
50:         * 127.0.0.1:
51:         */
52:        s = BindAccept(argc >= 2
53:              ? argv[1]
54:              : "127.0.0.1:9011");
55:
56:        /*
57:         * Establish ownership:
58:         */
59:        z = fcntl(s,F_SETOWN,getpid());
60:        if ( z == -1 )
61:              bail("fcntl(2)");
62:
63:        /*
64:         * Catch SIGURG:
65:         */
66:        signal(SIGURG,sigurg);
67:
68:        for (;;) {
69:              z = recv(s,buf,sizeof buf,0);
70:              if ( z == -1 )
71:                    bail("recv(2)");
72:              if ( z == 0 )
73:                    break;
74:              buf[z] = 0;
75:
76:              printf("rcv '%s' (%d)\n",
77:                    buf, z);
78:        }
79:
80:        close(s);
81:        return 0;
82:    }
```

The oobrecv.c main program consists of the following main components:

- A SIGURG signal handler (lines 23 to 37)

- The main test program (lines 40 to 82)

Examine the main program's functionality first. The basic steps used by the main program are

1. Create, bind, listen, and accept a connection from the client program (lines 52 to 54). The BindAccept() function handles all the dirty work for us here.

2. Ownership of the socket s is established by the call to fcntl(2) (lines 59 to 61). You can think of this as expressing interest in receiving the SIGURG signal.

3. The default action for signal SIGURG is to ignore it. Consequently, a signal handler must be established in line 66.

4. A receiving for loop is started in line 68.

5. The recv(2) function is called to receive normal data (lines 69 to 71). Note that the flags argument is zero here.

6. Test for end-of-file on the socket (lines 72 and 73). If zero bytes are returned, the break statement breaks out of the for loop.

7. The data content and length is reported (lines 74 to 77).

8. Repeat step 4.

Briefly, the main program initializes and waits for a connection. When a client connects, it simply loops to receive and report each block of data that it is able to receive.

Now, turn your attention to the signal handler. The following steps are used for it:

1. Upon entry into the handler, the code attempts to read some urgent (out-of-band) data (lines 28 to 30).

2. The out-of-band data is reported (lines 32 to 34).

3. The signal handler for SIGURG is re-established. This is necessary because this signal reverts to being ignored when the signal is caught.

CAUTION

Normally, it is unwise to use functions such as printf(3) inside a signal handler. Under contrived conditions, it is safe enough for demonstration purposes as is done here.

Furthermore, it is unwise to modify errno as might be done by the recv(2) call. Production quality code should save and restore the errno value in a signal handler to preserve its re-entrancy status.

NOTE

It should be noted that the use of the signal(2) function is to be discouraged in modern programs. Reliable signal functions such as sigaction(2) should be used instead. The signal(2) function is used here to keep the example programs simple.

Before you can put your receiving program to use, however, you'll need a sending program.

Sending Out-of-Band Data

The program in Listing 14.3 illustrates a short program that will transmit a few small strings, and a short burst of out-of-band data. The program uses a number of calls to sleep(3) in order to manage the timing of the transmission blocks at the receiving end.

Listing 14.3: The oobsend.c Sending Program

```
1:   /* oobsend.c:
2:    *
3:    * Example OOB sender:
4:    */
5:   #include <stdio.h>
6:   #include <unistd.h>
7:   #include <stdlib.h>
8:   #include <errno.h>
9:   #include <string.h>
10:  #include <sys/types.h>
11:  #include <sys/socket.h>
12:
13:  extern void bail(char *on_what);
14:  extern int Connect(char *addr);
15:
16:  /*
17:   * Send in-band data:
18:   */
19:  static void
20:  iband(int s,char *str) {
21:      int z;
22:
23:      z = send(s,str,strlen(str),0);
24:      if ( z == -1 )
25:          bail("send(2)");
26:
27:      printf("ib: '%s' (%d)\n",str,z);
28:  }
29:
30:  /*
31:   * Send out-of-band data:
32:   */
33:  static void
34:  oband(int s,char *str) {
35:      int z;
36:
37:      z = send(s,str,strlen(str),MSG_OOB);
38:      if ( z == -1 )
39:          bail("send(2)");
40:
41:      printf("OOB '%s' (%d)\n",str,z);
42:  }
```

continues

Listing 14.3: continued

```
43:
44:   int
45:   main(int argc,char **argv) {
46:       int s = -1;      /* Socket */
47:
48:       s = Connect(argc >= 2
49:             ? argv[1]
50:             : "127.0.0.1:9011");
51:
52:       iband(s,"In the beginning");
53:       sleep(1);
54:
55:       iband(s,"Linus begat Linux,");
56:       sleep(1);
57:
58:       iband(s,"and the Penguins");
59:       sleep(1);
60:
61:       oband(s,"rejoiced");
62:       sleep(1);
63:
64:       iband(s,"exceedingly.");
65:       close(s);
66:
67:       return 0;
68:   }
```

The sending program is, in fact, much simpler than the receiving program you just looked at. The general components in this source module are

- The iband() function that simply writes and reports the data that was written in-band (lines 19 to 28).

- The oband() function that writes its data string as out-of-band data (lines 33 to 42).

- The main() program, which occupies lines 44 to 68.

The sending functions iband() and oband() are straightforward. They simply write data using the send(2) function call with and without the flag MSG_OOB, respectively.

Now let's examine the steps used by the main program:

1. The main program creates a socket and connects to the receiving program with the use of the Connect() function (lines 48 to 50).

2. Three in-band write and sleep operations are performed as pairs (lines 52 to 59).

3. The string "rejoiced" is sent as out-of-band data in lines 61 and 62.

4. One more in-band write occurs in line 64.

After compiling the sending and receiving programs, you will be ready to apply out-of-band data transmission. To compile these programs, perform the following:

OUTPUT

```
$ make oobrecv oobsend
gcc -c  -D_GNU_SOURCE -Wall -Wreturn-type -g oobrecv.c
gcc -c  -D_GNU_SOURCE -Wall -Wreturn-type -g mkaddr.c
gcc -c  -D_GNU_SOURCE -Wall -Wreturn-type -g bindacpt.c
gcc oobrecv.o mkaddr.o bindacpt.o -o oobrecv
gcc -c  -D_GNU_SOURCE -Wall -Wreturn-type -g oobsend.c
gcc oobsend.o mkaddr.o bindacpt.o -o oobsend
$
```

After the compile is complete, you have two executable programs:

- oobrecv is the receiving program (a server).

- oobsend is the sending program (a client).

Now you are ready to invoke these programs.

Testing the oobrecv and oobsend Programs

It is best to run these programs in two completely different terminal sessions. Use either two different xterm windows, or two different console sessions. Start the receiving program first in the first terminal session:

EXAMPLE

```
$ ./oobrecv
```

Both programs accept an optional address and port number pair if you want to specify your Ethernet address instead of the local loopback address ("127.0.0.1:9011" is assumed by default). For example, the following would work on a system with an NIC card addressed as 192.168.0.1:

EXAMPLE

```
$ ./oobrecv 192.168.0.1:9023
```

This would start the server listening on 192.168.0.1 port number 9023. For the purposes of this demonstration, however, you can just run the program without arguments.

Now start the sending program on the second terminal session, as follows:

OUTPUT

```
$ ./oobsend
ib: 'In the beginning' (16)
ib: 'Linus begat Linux,' (18)
ib: 'and the Penguins' (16)
OOB 'rejoiced' (8)
ib: 'exceedingly.' (12)
$
```

The lines starting with `ib:` indicate in-band data that was written. The line beginning with `OOB` indicates that `'rejoiced'` was written as out-of-band data to the socket.

If you were able to watch both sessions at the same time, you will notice that the receiving program reports the data shortly after it is sent by the sending program. Its session output should look like this:

OUTPUT

```
$ ./oobrecv
rcv 'In the beginning' (16)
rcv 'Linus begat Linux,' (18)
rcv 'and the Penguins' (16)
URG 'd' (1)
rcv 'rejoice' (7)
rcv 'exceedingly.' (12)
$
```

The output lines shown in this terminal session that begin with `rcv` indicate normal in-band data that was received. The line starting with `URG` indicates that `SIGURG` was raised and the signal handler was called. Within the signal handler, the urgent data is read and reported. You should notice something peculiar—only the `d` byte was received as out-of-band data! What gives? Read on to find out.

Understanding the Urgent Pointer

Early in this chapter, it was stated that the socket interface provides a general network interface. This includes how it deals with out-of-band data. The TCP implementation of urgent data, however, falls somewhat short of what a general concept might include for out-of-band data.

Although the entire string `'rejoiced'` was sent as out-of-band data using `send(2)`, the following observations can be made at the receiving end:

- Only the `d` character was received as out-of-band data.

- The `d` character was received ahead of the remaining characters in `'rejoice'`.

The fact that the `d` byte was received ahead of the bytes `'rejoice'` does indeed demonstrate that the `d` byte was more urgent. It shows that the byte ordering has been disturbed by an urgency factor.

Understanding TCP Urgent Mode

The fact that only one byte was received as out-of-band data has to do with the mapping of a TCP protocol concept to a socket concept. The TCP *urgent mode* is mapped to the more general socket concept of out-of-band data.

The TCP protocol itself does not actually provide out-of-band data facilities. The closest concept to this socket idea is TCP's urgent mode of communications. A little bit of discussion of the TCP protocol is necessary in this section in order to provide you with an understanding of how urgent mode works.

When the send(2) socket interface function is used with the flag bit MSG_OOB set, the data is written to the TCP outgoing queue and an *urgent pointer* is established. The precise location of this pointer is determined by the tcp_stdurg setting that was covered earlier. Table 14.2 reviews the two interpretations and indicates where the urgent pointer is placed.

Table 14.2: The TCP Urgent Pointer Based Upon **tcp_stdurg** *Settings*

Value	Interpretation	Urgent Pointer
0	BSD interpretation (Linux)	After urgent byte
1	RFC793 interpretation	Before urgent byte

Figure 14.1 shows how the TCP sending buffer can be visualized after the send(2) call has returned from queuing the string 'rejoiced' as out-of-band data. Although we are most interested in the BSD interpretation (because of Linux), both interpretations are illustrated in the figure.

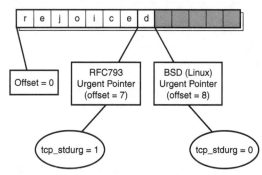

Figure 14.1: *Here is a graphical representation of the TCP urgent pointers.*

The sequence of events that occur from calling send(2) using the MSG_OOB flag are as follows for the BSD interpretation (tcp_stdurg=0):

1. The data is placed into the TCP outgoing queue (in this case, the beginning of the empty TCP buffer).

2. The TCP urgent mode is started (a TCP URG bit is set to true).

3. The urgent pointer is computed to point after the last byte that was entered into the outgoing TCP queue.

In the example program oobsend.c, the send(2) call was followed by a call to sleep(3). This action causes the Linux kernel to perform the following:

1. Send what it has queued so far in the TCP buffer, rather than wait indefinitely for more data.

2. The packet header that is now created by the TCP protocol software now has the URG bit set. This indicates that TCP urgent mode has been used (this is because the send(2) call used the MSG_OOB flag bit).

3. A TCP urgent pointer is computed and placed into the packet header. In this case (tcp_stdurg=0), this pointer points after the last byte of out-of-band data that was queued.

4. The TCP packet header containing the URG bit, urgent pointer, and all packet data that was waiting to be sent is now transmitted to the network interface device as one physical packet.

After these steps take place, the packet speeds on its way to the receiving host over the network. This packet is received at the remote end, conceptually as shown in Figure 14.2 (with protocol details omitted):

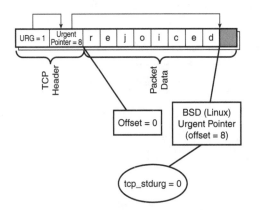

Figure 14.2: *The TCP header bit* URG=1 *indicates that urgent data immediately precedes the byte at offset 8.*

When a packet is received with the URG bit set to true, as shown in Figure 14.2, the Linux kernel will notify the process (or process group) that owns the socket, with the signal SIGURG. This is done because the packet contains an urgent pointer (that is why the URG bit is set in the TCP header).

The application oobrecv.c, upon handling the SIGURG signal, reads the out-of-band data by calling upon recv(2) with the flag bit MSG_OOB set. This causes the Linux kernel to return only the out-of-band data. Because TCP does not record where the out-of-band data starts, the socket API can return only the one byte prior to the urgent pointer within the packet (assuming that tcp_stdurg=0). Consequently, in our example, only the d byte is returned as out-of-band data. Any subsequent read of in-band data will read the remaining bytes 'rejoice', and any data that follows the urgent byte, if any exists.

Even if the out-of-band data was not read in the signal handling function, only the bytes 'rejoice' and subsequent nonurgent data would be read, if any. The d byte would be prevented from being returned in the normal in-band data because it has been identified as out-of-band data.

Urgent Mode When tcp_stdurg=1

Space does not permit us to dwell on this case, but a few comments are worthwhile. When tcp_stdurg=1, a strange thing often happens—urgent mode is often entered and its corresponding urgent pointer is received without any corresponding urgent data to be read. If the urgent pointer happens to be at the end of the last data byte included within the packet, then there might not be any following byte received. The urgent data byte might follow in a subsequent packet. For this reason, when this mode of operation is used, the recv(2) call with the MSG_OOB flag set does not necessarily return an out-of-band byte for TCP when the signal SIGURG is raised.

TIP

When tcp_stdurg=1 under Linux, a recv(2) call will return the errno value EAGAIN when no urgent data is available to read. Some other UNIX implementations (BSD UNIX, for example) return the errno value EWOULDBLOCK instead.

To handle the situation where the urgent data byte was unavailable, you must perform the following (remember this applies only when tcp_stdurg=1):

1. Record the SIGURG event in a flag (say, a variable named urg_mode=1).

2. Return from your signal handler.

3. Continue to read in-band data within your application.

4. When the urg_mode value is true, try to read some out-of-band data by using recv(2) and the MSG_OOB flag bit.

5. If step 4 yields data, then set urg_mode=0 and return to normal processing. Repeat step 3.

6. If step 4 does not yield any out-of-band data, continue processing while leaving urg_mode set true. Repeat step 3.

Again, it must be emphasized that you probably won't use these steps for Linux code, unless a change in direction is made for Linux. Linux uses the BSD (tcp_stdurg=0) mode of urgent data by default, which is easier to cope with.

Receiving Out-of-Band Data Inline

Earlier, it was indicated that it is possible to receive out-of-band data intermixed with the regular in-band data. This is done when it is more convenient for the application to process it this way. To enable this mode of operation for a particular socket, you must set the SO_OOBINLINE socket option:

EXAMPLE

```
int z;                  /* Status */
int s;                  /* Socket */
int oobinline = 1;      /* TRUE */

z = setsockopt(s,
    SOL_SOCKET,         /* Level */
    SO_OOBINLINE,       /* Option */
    &oobinline,         /* Ptr to value */
    sizeof oobinline);  /* Size of value */
```

CAUTION

After you have enabled the option SO_OOBINLINE for a socket, you must not call recv(2) with the MSG_OOB flag. If you do, the function will return an error, with variable errno set to the code EINVAL.

NOTE

It is still possible to use the SIGURG signal if you find it useful. This is established by a call to fcntl(2) using the command F_SETOWN.

Determining the Urgent Pointer

Whether you are receiving your data inline or not, you have at your disposal a function that can tell you when you have reached the urgent pointer within your current data stream. This can be determined by calling ioctl(2) with the correct arguments:

EXAMPLE

```
#include <sys/ioctl.h>
...
int z;   /* Status */
int s;   /* Socket */
int flag; /* True when at mark */

z = ioctl(s,SIOCATMARK,&flag);
if ( z == -1 )
    abort();            /* Error */
if ( flag != 0 )
    puts("At Mark");
else
    puts("Not at mark.");
```

With the preceding functionality in mind, a modified oobrecv program will be demonstrated that receives its data inline, and tests for the urgent data mark as the data is being received.

Using Out-of-Band Data Inline

Listing 14.4 shows a new receiving program oobinline.c, which will receive in-band and out-of-band data inline. A modified SIGURG signal handler is included so that it will report when urgent data arrives. This will allow you to observe a number of events.

EXAMPLE

Listing 14.4: The oobinline.c Receiver Using SO_OOBINLINE

```
1:   /* oobinline.c:
2:    *
3:    * OOB inline receiver:
4:    */
5:   #include <stdio.h>
6:   #include <unistd.h>
7:   #include <stdlib.h>
8:   #include <errno.h>
9:   #include <string.h>
10:  #include <signal.h>
11:  #include <fcntl.h>
12:  #include <sys/ioctl.h>
13:  #include <sys/types.h>
14:  #include <sys/socket.h>
15:
16:  extern void bail(char *on_what);
17:  extern int BindAccept(char *addr);
18:
19:  /*
20:   * SIGURG signal handler:
```

continues

Listing 14.4: continued

```
21:   */
22:   static void
23:   sigurg(int signo) {
24:
25:       write(1,"[SIGURG]\n",9);
26:       signal(SIGURG,sigurg);
27:   }
28:
29:   /*
30:    * Emulate the IEEE Std 1003.1g
31:    * standard function sockatmark(3):
32:    */
33:   static int
34:   Sockatmark(int s) {
35:       int z;
36:       int flag;
37:
38:       z = ioctl(s,SIOCATMARK,&flag);
39:       if ( z == -1 )
40:           return -1;
41:       return flag ? 1 : 0;
42:   }
43:
44:   int
45:   main(int argc,char **argv) {
46:       int z;                 /* Status */
47:       int s;                 /* Socket */
48:       int oobinline=1; /* OOB inline */
49:       char buf[256];
50:
51:
52:       /*
53:        * Use a server address from the command
54:        * line, if one has been provided.
55:        * Otherwise, this program will default
56:        * to using the arbitrary address
57:        * 127.0.0.1:
58:        */
59:       s = BindAccept(argc >= 2
60:           ? argv[1]
61:           : "127.0.0.1:9011");
62:
63:       /*
64:        * Establish ownership:
65:        */
66:       z = fcntl(s,F_SETOWN,getpid());
67:       if ( z == -1 )
```

```
68:            bail("fcntl(2)");
69:
70:        /*
71:         * Catch SIGURG:
72:         */
73:        signal(SIGURG,sigurg);
74:
75:        /*
76:         * Receive the OOB data inline:
77:         */
78:        z = setsockopt(s,
79:            SOL_SOCKET,
80:            SO_OOBINLINE,
81:            &oobinline,
82:            sizeof oobinline);
83:        if ( z == -1 )
84:            bail("setsockopt(2)");
85:
86:        for (;;) {
87:            printf("\n[%s]\n",
88:                Sockatmark(s)
89:                    ? "AT MARK"
90:                    : "No Mark");
91:
92:            z = recv(s,buf,sizeof buf,0);
93:            if ( z == -1 )
94:                bail("recv(2)");
95:            if ( z == 0 )
96:                break;
97:            buf[z] = 0;
98:
99:            printf("rcv '%s' (%d)\n",
100:                buf, z);
101:        }
102:
103:        close(s);
104:        return 0;
105: }
```

This program is very similar to the oobrecv.c module, so only the differences will be highlighted here. They are

1. The include file for sys/ioctl.h is added in line 12 for the benefit of ioctl(2) call later in the program.

2. The signal handler for SIGURG is modified to report only that the signal was raised (lines 22 to 27).

3. A new function Sockatmark() is defined in lines 33 to 42 to emulate the new sockatmark(3) function.

4. The ownership of the socket is set and the signal handler is established as before (lines 66 to 73). Note that this is not a requirement for using SO_OOBINLINE.

5. The socket option SO_OOBINLINE is set true in lines 78 to 84 using the setsockopt(2) function.

6. At the start of the for loop, the function Sockatmark() is called and a report is provided to the terminal session. Either "[AT MARK]" is reported if the socket is at the urgent data mark, or "[No Mark]" is reported to standard output.

7. The data is received as in-band data (lines 92 to 100).

8. The loop repeats with step 6, until end-file is received on the socket (see the break statement in line 96).

Now compile the program:

OUTPUT

```
$ make oobinline
gcc -c  -D_GNU_SOURCE -Wall -Wreturn-type -g oobinline.c
gcc oobinline.o mkaddr.o bindacpt.o -o oobinline
$
```

Use the following procedure for this test:

1. In the first terminal session, start the oobinline program.

2. In the second terminal session, start the oobsend program that you previously used.

The terminal session for the sending program should look like this:

OUTPUT

```
$ ./oobsend
ib: 'In the beginning' (16)
ib: 'Linus begat Linux,' (18)
ib: 'and the Penguins' (16)
OOB 'rejoiced' (8)
ib: 'exceedingly.' (12)
$
```

Effectively, this terminal session should appear the same as before. The receiving terminal session, however, should look like this:

OUTPUT

```
$ ./oobinline

[No Mark]
rcv 'In the beginning' (16)

[No Mark]
rcv 'Linus begat Linux,' (18)
```

```
[No Mark]
rcv 'and the Penguins' (16)

[No Mark]
[SIGURG]
rcv 'rejoice' (7)

[AT MARK]
rcv 'd' (1)

[No Mark]
rcv 'exceedingly.' (12)

[No Mark]
$
```

Notice that, when the string 'rejoiced' was received, the SIGURG signal is raised as it was before. Note, however, that the mark is not reached until the bytes 'rejoice' are read first. Then the mark is reached and one more inline byte is received (the d byte again). A few points are worth noting about this:

- The signal SIGURG arrives as early as possible, as it did when not using inline reads of urgent data.

- The in-band data must be read in sequence before the out-of-band data can be read.

- Although the transmitted packet includes the entire string 'rejoiced' as one unit, the recv(2) call stops at the point where the urgent data byte is located (receiving stops short of the d byte).

- A subsequent call to recv(2) is required to read the urgent data. For TCP, this is a single byte d in the example.

Normally, data is read from a stream socket without implied message boundaries. However, you saw that a boundary does form when urgent data is read inline. Reading will stop short of the urgent data byte. If this were not done, you would easily read past the mark.

Limitations of the Urgent Mode Pointer

So far, it has been demonstrated that TCP really can provide only one byte of out-of-band data. This is because it is implemented using TCP's urgent mode feature of the protocol.

It is tempting to think that the TCP urgent mode and its urgent pointer should make it possible to mark boundaries of urgent data. However, this cannot be accomplished in practice, because subsequent sends of out-of-band data overwrite the receiver's original urgent data mark that might not have been processed yet.

This can be demonstrated if you modify the oobsend.c program. Remove all the sleep(3) function calls and insert one more call to oband(s,"very") after the oband(s,"rejoiced") function call. The main program should now look like this:

EXAMPLE

```
int
main(int argc,char **argv) {
    int s = -1;      /* Socket */

    s = Connect(argc >= 2
        ? argv[1]
        : "127.0.0.1:9011");

    iband(s,"In the beginning");
    iband(s,"Linus begat Linux,");
    iband(s,"and the Penguins");
    oband(s,"rejoiced");
    oband(s,"very");
    iband(s,"exceedingly.");
    close(s);

    return 0;
}
```

When the test is run again, on a fast system, you will receive results like this:

OUTPUT

```
$ ./oobinline

[No Mark]
rcv 'In the beginning' (16)

[No Mark]
rcv 'Linus begat Linux,' (18)

[No Mark]
[SIGURG]
rcv 'and the Penguinsrejoicedver' (27)

[AT MARK]
rcv 'yexceedingly.' (13)

[No Mark]
$
```

Notice a few things here:

- Only one SIGURG signal was received.

- There was only one urgent data mark, although two out-of-band writes were made on the sending end.

- The first byte y in the string `'yexceedingly'`. was the single out-of-band data byte. The following bytes were simply the subsequent in-band data bytes.

Prior testing depended upon the delays provided by `sleep(3)` to concoct a controlled set of physical packets.

NOTE

Some tests, such as the foregoing, might yield different results on different systems and different networks. The performance level of the CPU and the network will determine how and when packets are divided up for the stream of data being sent and received.

As the prior note indicates, your results can vary slightly from the example output shown. Further variance can be demonstrated when sending from a slow 486 system to a fast Pentium III at the receiving end. Another receiving pattern can be observed when sending from the faster CPU to the slower one. When all the `sleep(3)` calls are removed, other factors decide how the packets are divided up.

Processing Out-of-Band Data with `select(2)`

There is insufficient space available in this chapter to explore this particular topic, but some simple advice on the subject seems appropriate.

Out-of-band data notifications arrive as exceptions for the `select(2)` function call. You will recall in Chapter 11, "Concurrent Client Servers," that the `select(2)` call will block until one or more of the following events occur:

- A read event (data to be read has arrived)

- A write event (data can now be written)

- An exception (out-of-band data has arrived)

Your program can express interest in exceptions on the sockets involved in the `select(2)` call. Then, it can subsequently process out-of-band data by the appropriate call to `recv(2)` using the `MSG_OOB` flag when necessary.

What's Next

This chapter has shown you that the socket API provides a general interface to the use of out-of-band data. The limitations of TCP urgent mode were apparent in some of the demonstrations that you ran. However, you know that these limitations do not necessarily extend to other protocols that might support out-of-band data using sockets.

The next chapter will show you how the `inetd` daemon is frugal with system resources. You'll also learn what the requirements are for writing servers, which are launched by `inetd`.

15

Using the `inetd` Daemon

Each server running under UNIX offering a service normally executes as a separate process. When the number of services being offered becomes large, however, this becomes a burden to the system. This is because resources must be allocated to each server process running, even when there are no current requests for the services being offered.

Additionally, it can be observed that most server programs use the same general procedure to create, bind, listen, and accept new client connections. A similar observation can be made for connectionless server operation.

In this chapter, you will learn about

- What the `inetd` daemon is

- How `inetd` solves the server resource utilization issue

- How `inetd` simplifies the writing of servers

Steps Common to Most Servers

If you think back to Chapter 8, "Connection-Oriented Protocols for Servers," you will recall that the basic steps a connection-oriented server used to establish contact with a client were the following:

1. Create a socket.
2. Bind a socket to a well-known address.
3. Listen for a client connect.
4. Accept the client connect.

Figure 8.1 outlined these very steps. Now, imagine two different servers, say telnetd for telnet clients and ftpd for ftp clients. Are steps 1 through 4 going to be any different for either server? The answer is that these steps are exactly the same for both. You will see that the inetd daemon can perform these initial steps for any connection-oriented server, saving the server writer from having to write and debug code for these steps. The inetd daemon idea can be extended to handle connectionless servers as well.

Introducing inetd

When your Linux system is booted for the first time, the inetd daemon is started from one of the startup scripts. On Red Hat Linux 6.0 systems, this daemon is started from the script file:

EXAMPLE

```
/etc/rc.d/init.d/inet
```

This script is symbolically linked from various other places including the following noteworthy links:

```
/etc/rc.d/rc3.d/S50inet
/etc/rc.d/rc5.d/S50inet
```

These links initiate inetd when the system is started in the usual run-level 3 or run-level 5 modes.

NOTE

A run-level is simply a systemwide mode of operation. Linux supports several of these levels. See the init(8) man page for a full discussion of this.

Run-level 3 is normally the run-level used when X Window is not used on a Linux system. Run-level 5 is usually used to automatically invoke the X Window server on the console. Note that this is simply a convention and your system conventions might differ.

Other Linux distributions will have various other clever scripts and filenames to accomplish the same thing.

When the inetd daemon is started for the first time, it must know what Internet services it must listen for and what servers to pass the request off to when a request arrives. This is defined within the startup file /etc/inetd.conf.

NOTE

If you are using a company, university, or other shared Linux host, you might find that the /etc/inetd.conf file has been stripped down for security purposes. Many sites eliminate nonessential services to avoid vulnerabilities in network attacks. Some sites might even eliminate running inetd completely.

If this is the case, you will need to coordinate your efforts with the people looking after the security for the host involved.

The /etc/inetd.conf Configuration File

The general file layout of the /etc/inetd.conf file is organized as a text file, with each text line representing one record, which describes one Internet service. Lines starting with # are simply comment lines and are ignored.

The blank (or tab) separated fields are described in Table 15.1 with some examples (fields are listed in order from left to right).

Table 15.1: The **/etc/inetd.conf** *Configuration Record*

Field #	Description	Example
1.	Internet service name	telnet (this might also be a port number)
2.	Socket type	stream or dgram
3.	Protocol	tcp or udp
4.	Flags	nowait or wait
5.	Userid to use	root or nobody
6.	Pathname of executable	/usr/sbin/in.telnetd
7.	Server arguments	in.telnetd

INTERNET SERVICE NAME FIELD

The Internet service name field within the /etc/inetd.conf record is simply an Internet service name from the /etc/services file, which was covered in Chapter 7, "Connection-Oriented Protocols for Clients." Refer to Table 7.1 for details. You can perform a quick lookup now in the /etc/services file as follows:

OUTPUT

```
# grep telnet /etc/services
telnet          23/tcp
rtelnet         107/tcp      # Remote Telnet
rtelnet         107/udp
#
```

There, you will see that the service labeled telnet is configured as a tcp service on port number 23. This is how the inetd daemon determines the port number it must listen for connects on.

Alternatively, you can simply supply a port number. You will see an example of this later in this chapter.

THE SOCKET TYPE FIELD

Although the Linux inetd daemon can accept a number of socket types here, only the types stream or dgram will be discussed for simplicity's sake. For the more curious reader, the inetd(8) man page also lists socket types raw, rdm, and seqpacket types as additional possibilities.

The stream type corresponds to the SOCK_STREAM socket type for the socket(2) function call. The value dgram requests a SOCK_DGRAM socket type.

THE PROTOCOL FIELD

As you might guess, this selects the protocol to be used for the socket. This value must be a valid entry that appears in the /etc/protocols file (see the section in Chapter 7 titled, "Consulting /etc/protocols File"). Two often-used selections are

- tcp for the TCP protocol
- udp for the UDP protocol

Other possibilities also exist, but these are the most commonly used.

THE FLAGS FIELD

This field is intended for datagram sockets only. Nondatagram sockets (such as stream tcp, for example) should specify the value nowait.

Datagram-oriented servers come in two types. They are

- Servers that keep reading UDP packets until they timeout and exit (specify wait for these).
- Servers that read one packet and exit (specify nowait for these).

This information is needed by inetd because the handling of dgram traffic is more complex than it is for stream-oriented protocols. This helps the daemon determine how it should handle future dgram connects while the server for that service is running. This will be explained in detail later in this chapter.

THE USERID FIELD

The `inetd` daemon runs under the root account. This gives it the capability to change its identity to another user account, if it chooses to do so (see `setuid(2)` for details). It is recommended to run servers with the least amount of privilege necessary to carry out their job, for security purposes. Consequently, servers often run under a more limited userID such as `nobody`, for example.

Some servers, however, must be run as `root`, so you'll sometimes see the userID specified this way.

THE PATHNAME FIELD

This field simply informs `inetd` what the full pathname of the executable file is. This is the executable file that is executed by `exec(2)` after the daemon calls `fork(2)`.

THE SERVER ARGUMENTS FIELD

All remaining fields on the `/etc/inetd.conf` configuration line are provided as command-line arguments to the server being invoked with `exec(2)`. One common source of confusion is that these arguments start with the argument `argv[0]`. This allows the command name to differ from the pathname. This is useful when one executable exhibits different personalities depending upon its name.

The Design Parameters of `inetd` Servers

One of the advantages of using `inetd` as the front end for servers is that the server writer's job is made easier. There is no longer the burden of writing the same `socket(2)`, `bind(2)`, `listen(2)`, and `accept(2)` calls for stream tcp servers, for example. Similar code savings can be had for dgram udp servers, also. How then, does the `inetd` server hand off the connected socket to the server process when the process is started?

Using the simple elegance of UNIX, the started server is handed the client socket on the following file units (file descriptors):

- File unit 0 has client socket for standard input
- File unit 1 has client socket for standard output
- File unit 2 has client socket for standard error

With this design in place, it is possible that some servers will not require a single socket function call. All of the server I/O can be performed on the normal standard inputs, output, and error file units. Later, a simple demonstration program will show how standard output is used in this manner.

Implementing a Simple stream tcp Server

You will recall that in Chapter 8 a small program was introduced in Listing 8.1. Take a moment now to review that program. Listing 15.1 shows new code for the very same server, except that it is designed for use by the inetd daemon.

EXAMPLE

Listing 15.1: inetdserv.c—The inetd Version of the Listing 8.1 Server

```
1:   /* inetdserv.c:
2:    *
3:    * Example inetd daytime server:
4:    */
5:   #include <stdio.h>
6:   #include <unistd.h>
7:   #include <stdlib.h>
8:   #include <errno.h>
9:   #include <string.h>
10:  #include <time.h>
11:  #include <sys/types.h>
12:
13:  /*
14:   * This function reports the error and
15:   * exits back to the shell:
16:   */
17:  static void
18:  bail(const char *on_what) {
19:      if ( errno != 0 ) {
20:          fputs(strerror(errno),stderr);
21:          fputs(": ",stderr);
22:      }
23:      fputs(on_what,stderr);
24:      fputc('\n',stderr);
25:      exit(1);
26:  }
27:
28:  int
29:  main(int argc,char **argv) {
30:      int z;
31:      int n;
32:      time_t td;          /* Current date&time */
33:      char dtbuf[128];      /* Date/Time info */
34:
35:      /*
36:       * Generate a time stamp:
37:       */
38:      time(&td);
39:      n = (int) strftime(dtbuf,sizeof dtbuf,
```

```
40:            "%A %b %d %H:%M:%S %Y\n",
41:            localtime(&td));
42:
43:      /*
44:       * Write result back to the client:
45:       */
46:      z = write(1,dtbuf,n);
47:      if ( z == -1 )
48:            bail("write(2)");
49:
50:      return 0;
51:  }
```

Notice how simple this program is compared to the one in Listing 8.1. Note the following differences (line number references refer to Listing 15.1):

- No socket include files were necessary (lines 5 through 11).

- No socket address structures were needed (lines 30 to 33).

- No socket calls whatsoever. Note that the program immediately starts the task at hand (lines 38 to 48 generate a date and time string).

Because this program no longer uses socket functions, it can be easily tested from the shell as follows:

OUTPUT

```
$ make inetdserv
gcc -c  -D_GNU_SOURCE -Wall -Wreturn-type inetdserv.c
gcc inetdserv.o -o inetdserv
$ ./inetdserv
Tuesday Nov 02 16:29:45 1999
$
```

Recall that this is similar to the daytime service on port 13:

OUTPUT

```
$ telnet 192.168.0.1 13
Trying 192.168.0.1...
Connected to 192.168.0.1.
Escape character is '^]'.
Tue Nov  2 16:31:09 1999
Connection closed by foreign host.
$
```

The only real difference in format is that our program shows the full weekday name. It is time now to demonstrate how this program functions with the help of the inetd daemon.

Configuring /etc/inetd.conf to Invoke a New Server

To make our simple new server useful (or at least as useful as the daytime server), we must alter the configuration file that is used by the inetd daemon. Now might be a good time to review Table 15.1 if you need to.

ESTABLISHING THE EXECUTABLE

It has been assumed here that you compiled the inetdserv program earlier.
To keep the steps simple here, enter the following commands:

```
$ cp inetdserv /tmp/inetdserv
$ chmod a+rx /tmp/inetdserv
```

EXAMPLE

The previous two steps copy the server executable to a known location, and
ensure that it is executable.

ESTABLISHING THE SERVICE

For this test, add one line to the /etc/inetd.conf file (make this the last
line of the file). After this is accomplished with vi or your favorite editor,
you should be able to list it as follows:

```
$ tail -1 /etc/inetd.conf
9099 stream tcp nowait root /tmp/inetdserv inetdserv
```

OUTPUT

NOTE

You will need to su to root to modify your /etc/inetd.conf file.

CAUTION

You should exercise extreme caution when editing a system file such as
/etc/inetd.conf. As a precaution, make a backup copy of this file as follows:

```
# cp /etc/inetd.conf /tmp/inetd.bak
```

If you need to restore the contents of your configuration file, you can restore it as
follows:

```
# cp /tmp/inetd.bak /etc/inetd.conf
```

Also be extra careful to remove any test entries you have added later, when you no
longer need them. This should be done to avoid leaving ports available, which might be
exploited by hackers from the Internet.

Now, let's review what this last line means to inetd:

- Because your new service does not have a name in the /etc/services
  file, the first field simply contains the port number you want to use.
  Port 9099 was chosen here.

- The second field contains stream so that TCP stream sockets will be
  used.

- The third field contains tcp to indicate that we want a TCP stream, as
  opposed to some other protocol stream.

- The fourth field is specified as nowait, which is what is required for
  TCP stream entries.

- The fifth field is given as root in this example. Your normal userID could be used here (but be sure that appropriate permission to execute /tmp/inetdserv exists, however).

- The pathname /tmp/inetdserv is given as the sixth field. This is the pathname of the executable that will be executed when a connect arrives on the socket.

- The seventh field is specified as inetdserv in this example. In this particular case, our server program pays no attention to the value of argv[0], and just about any value would do here.

Now, before we actually connect to this service, perform one more test to be certain things are ready:

```
$ /tmp/inetdserv
Tuesday Nov 02 16:52:33 1999
$
```

OUTPUT

If you fail to receive the output shown, then check to be certain that you have copied the file with the correct filename. Additionally, make certain that the file has appropriate execute permissions. After this functionality has been demonstrated as shown, you are ready to let inetd know that a change has been made to its configuration.

ALERTING inetd TO CONFIGURATION CHANGES

To indicate to inetd that changes have occurred, you must change to root and perform the following:

```
# ps -ax | grep inetd
  314 ?         S      0:00 inetd
# kill -HUP 314
#
```

EXAMPLE

Your process ID might not be 314 as shown—in fact, it's likely to be different. The steps that were used were as follows:

1. List the process ID of the inetd daemon with the ps command filtered by the grep command.

2. Send a SIGHUP signal to inetd to tell it to reread its /etc/inetd.conf configuration file. This does not terminate the process.

After the inetd has been signaled, you might want to check whether your configuration change has been accepted. One way of checking this is to perform the following:

OUTPUT

```
# lsof -i
COMMAND  PID USER  FD   TYPE DEVICE SIZE NODE NAME
portmap  238 root   3u  inet   369       UDP *:sunrpc
portmap  238 root   4u  inet   370       TCP *:sunrpc (LISTEN)
inetd    314 root   4u  inet   474       TCP *:ftp (LISTEN)
inetd    314 root   5u  inet   475       TCP *:telnet (LISTEN)
inetd    314 root   6u  inet   476       TCP *:login (LISTEN)
inetd    314 root   8u  inet   477       TCP *:exec (LISTEN)
inetd    314 root  10u  inet   478       TCP *:auth (LISTEN)
inetd    314 root  11u  inet  1124       TCP *:9099 (LISTEN)
inetd    314 root  12u  inet  1163       TCP *:daytime (LISTEN)
named    342 root   4u  inet   531       UDP *:1024
...
```

The line in the output showing the node name TCP *:9099 indicates the new service that was added for the new server. Note that the left side shows that inetd is the process listening for connects on this port 9099. The TCP *:9099 tells you that TCP port 9099 will accept connects from any port (the asterisk indicates a wild server address).

TESTING THE NEW SERVICE

Test out the new inetd service by trying the localhost address:

OUTPUT

```
$ telnet localhost 9099
Trying 127.0.0.1...
Connected to localhost.
Escape character is '^]'.
Tuesday Nov 02 17:10:37 1999
Connection closed by foreign host.
$
```

You will recall that localhost is usually configured to be your local loop-back address of 127.0.0.1 (try that, too). If you have an Ethernet card installed, try its interface address. Your output should look similar to this:

OUTPUT

```
$ telnet 192.168.0.1 9099
Trying 192.168.0.1...
Connected to 192.168.0.1.
Escape character is '^]'.
Tuesday Nov 02 17:13:28 1999
Connection closed by foreign host.
$
```

This output confirms the fact that connects are permitted from any interface. Now compare to your existing daytime service (if you have it enabled). Don't forget to add the port 13 argument on the command line:

OUTPUT

```
$ telnet 192.168.0.1 13
Trying 192.168.0.1...
Connected to 192.168.0.1.
Escape character is '^]'.
Tue Nov  2 17:16:57 1999
Connection closed by foreign host.
$
```

Note that the weekday name is abbreviated, unlike your server's output.

Disabling the New Service

Now su to root again, and remove your custom server entry from the
/etc/inetd.conf file (assuming that you are now finished with it). Then,
resignal the daemon as follows:

EXAMPLE

```
# ps -ax | grep inetd
  314 ?           S        0:00 inetd
# kill -HUP 314
#
```

Your process ID might not be 314 as shown—in fact, it's likely to be different. Substitute the one that you see instead.

CAUTION

Be sure to remove your inetd entry now, if you are finished with it. Be sure to signal
inetd with SIGHUP (kill -HUP) after you have removed the entry. This is recommended to avoid having someone attempt to exploit your little demonstration server
from the Internet.

Datagram Servers with `inetd`

This chapter has focused so far on the use of TCP stream sockets for inetd.
When datagram server ports are established by inetd, a special consideration is added. This was hinted at by the description of the wait and nowait
flag values earlier in this chapter.

Let's review the inetd steps used as they apply to UDP servers:

1. The inetd server listens on the UDP port that your UDP server will
   service requests on.

2. The select(2) call used by inetd indicates that a datagram has
   arrived on the socket (note that inetd does not read this datagram).

3. The inetd server calls fork(2) and exec(2) to start your UDP server.

4. Your UDP server uses file unit zero (stdin) to read one UDP packet.

Steps 1 to 4 are identical to our TCP stream scenario. However, after processing the first (single) UDP packet received in step 4, the UDP server has two basic choices:

- Exit (terminate)

- Wait for more UDP packets (and exit only after a timeout occurs).

A little careful thought suggests that starting a new process for each UDP packet might be somewhat taxing on the system if the UDP packets arrive frequently. For this reason, rather than immediately exit, some UDP servers loop back and attempt to read subsequent UDP packets after servicing the first one. A timeout is used so that the process will give up and exit if nothing further arrives. When that happens, the inetd daemon takes over the watch again, for new UDP packets.

Understanding wait and nowait

A datagram server that simply processes one datagram and then exits should use the nowait flag word. This tells inetd that it may launch additional server processes when additional datagrams arrive. This is necessary because each process started is going to process only one datagram.

For other datagram servers that attempt to read more datagrams, you should use the wait flag word. This is necessary because the server process that inetd starts is going to process subsequent datagrams until it terminates. The wait flag word tells inetd not to launch any more servers for that port until the wait(2) system call informs inetd (with the help of signal SIGCHLD) that your datagram server has terminated. Otherwise, inetd would start additional server processes that are unnecessary. Let's restate this in a systematic fashion:

1. The inetd server starts your looping UDP server process because of an incoming datagram.

2. The inetd server waits for other unrelated events based upon its configuration: It will currently ignore the present UDP port because your datagram server has been started to process those. Note that this behavior is being used because the service was configured with the wait flag word (inetd cannot determine what kind of server the executable represents).

3. Your datagram server finishes processing the first UDP datagram.

4. Your datagram server attempts to read another UDP datagram from the standard input (the datagram socket).

5. A timeout eventually occurs in your datagram server because no more datagrams are arriving—your datagram server process terminates by calling exit(3).

6. The signal SIGCHLD is raised in inetd (remember that inetd is the parent process of your server).

7. The inetd server calls wait(2) to determine the process ID and termination status of your server process.

8. The inetd daemon notes that the process ID returned by wait(2) belonged to your datagram server. It notes the fact that it must now watch for any new datagrams because there is currently no process waiting to service them.

Remember the following important points about inetd when defining datagram services:

- The inetd daemon cannot determine whether the configured datagram server requires the wait or nowait parameter. You must know and provide the correct flag word for the server.

- The wait flag word means that another server process will not be started unless the previously started process (if any) has terminated.

- Specifying nowait for a wait datagram server will unnecessarily duplicate server processes.

- Specifying wait for a nowait datagram server will hurt the server performance for that service. This happens because additional processes will not be started until the present process completes.

Also, remember that stream services should always use the nowait flag word. This allows multiple clients to be serviced at the same time (one server process for each connecting client). If the wait flag word is used instead for stream services, only one client connection will be serviced at one time (this is seldom desirable).

What's Next

This chapter has been a brief introduction to the inetd daemon. You have learned how to install a test stream service. You saw how the simple server program simply used file unit 1 (stdout) to write its reply back to the client. Additionally, it was shown in that example that there was no socket code required at all. Although this is not always the case, you saw how the inetd daemon takes care of a lot of networking detail for you.

You also learned that datagram servers have special needs. This is due to the connectionless mode of operation that datagram servers use.

The next chapter continues to discuss inetd as it applies to network security. There, you will learn about the TCP wrapper concept that was pioneered by Wietse Venema. Additionally, you will learn that the wait type of datagram server poses even more challenges.

Network Security Programming

Up to this point in the book, you have focused on learning how to write socket-enabled programs, whether they be client or server programs. No consideration has been given to securing your programs against external threats, which can come from the Internet or from hostile users within your own local area network (at a university, for example). This chapter will introduce you to

- How the inetd daemon can be used with the TCP wrapper concept to provide screening of clients

- How the TCP wrapper concept works

- How the TCP wrapper concept falls short in some areas

When you complete this chapter, you will fully understand how the TCP wrapper concept works and know how to apply it to servers that you might administer or write yourself.

Defining Security

The Merriam Webster's Collegiate Dictionary defines security in a number of ways. There are two definitions which are of particular interest to you here:

- The quality or state of being secure as freedom from danger.

- Measures taken to guard against espionage or sabotage, crime, attack, or escape.

When network security is discussed, certainly the first point applies: You want to be free from any perceived threat. Secondly, you must guard your system resources from being examined without permission, sabotaged in some manner, stolen, or otherwise attacked. Your written works that are not public must not "escape" from your system without permission.

The complexity of this task and the broadness of its application make it impossible to fully treat this subject in one chapter. However, some aspects of network security apply directly to socket programming, and you should not ignore the dangers that exist. A few simple measures presented in this chapter will help prevent your servers from being exploited or attacked. You will learn where vulnerabilities exist and what you can do about them.

The Challenges of Security

If you review all the everyday situations in which security is at work, you boil down the common elements to locks. Locks take different forms:

- Hired armed guards

- Key- and card-based locks

- Combination locks, passwords, and PIN numbers

- Retina, fingerprint, and voice print scans

Armed guards are given conditions to enforce and the means to apply force if it becomes necessary. This form does not apply to our discussion well, because these are human agents applying a screening process.

Key- and card-based locks require access to physical tokens to grant access. The key might be a car or house key, for example. Card locks use a magnetic stripe, which provides the identification.

Combination locks, passwords, and PIN numbers identify the person by the knowledge of a secret. Some security systems combine a physical token with a secret: ATM bank cards, for example, require both the bank card and the PIN number.

The retina, fingerprint, and voice print scan methods all rely on the principle that each person has unique features. Consequently, people are directly identified by these characteristics.

Every one of these methods can be foiled. Table 16.1 provides a sample of ways in which these security methods can be defeated.

Table 16.1: Security Methods and Weaknesses

Security Method	Weakness
Key lock	Keys can be copied and locks can be picked.
Card lock system	Magnetic stripes from one card can be copied to a new plastic card.
Combination lock	Combinations can be shared, or left written down somewhere. Safe-crackers can exploit weaknesses (sound) in a mechanical combination lock.
Password, PIN number	Passwords can be shared, or left written down somewhere. Simple passwords can be guessed by chance, brute force, or by knowing information about the owner. Software can try dictionary attacks, using common words and names. Passwords can also be obtained by force.
Retina, fingerprints, and so on	The person can be forced at gunpoint to identify himself to a machine. Sometimes these "prints" might be copied and presented in a manner that will fool the identification machinery.

You can probably think of more ways these systems can suffer breaches of security. The point of this exercise is to point out one fundamental truth about security:

> Any system that permits one person to gain access is potentially able to permit other persons access as well.

This leads us to consider the possible corollary that

> The only completely secure system is to which no one can gain access.

This situation is unfruitful to take seriously and is difficult to prove. This leads to a conclusion:

> One must always be concerned about security as it applies to proper and safe access to resources.

Granting or denying access to resources on a computer is a simple matter when the identity has been established. Network security, however, poses some additional challenges because it is even more difficult to establish a remote identity. This is akin to verifying the author of a letter from some remote location of our planet.

With that as the backdrop, let's now dive into network security as it applies to socket programming.

Identifying Friend or Foe

Chapter 17, "Passing Credentials and File Descriptors," will show you that you can identify a local user of your server with a high degree of confidence using credentials. When the user of your server is remote, however, this same level of confidence is not easy to achieve.

In this chapter, we'll be relying on the peer's network address to identify the user of a resource. This is not a bulletproof technique, however, because the peer's address can be spoofed under the right conditions. Nevertheless, it does provide a simple first-level defense against attacks.

After you have the IP number, you can also look up the client's registered host and domain name. This provides an extra level of screening that requires more effort on the attacker's part.

Resolved host and domain names allow your server to apply the following types of access policies:

- Grant access to specific hostnames
- Grant access to specific domains
- Deny access to specific hostnames
- Deny access to specific domains
- Deny access to IP numbers that do not resolve to a name

The following section will discuss aspects of these different policies.

Securing by Hostname or Domain Name

When a client connects to your server, you will recall that the server receives the socket address of the client from the function call to accept(2). The following code fragment extracted from Listing 8.1 shows an example of this:

EXAMPLE

```
struct sockaddr_in adr_clnt;/* AF_INET */
int len_inet;                   /* length   */
int c;                  /* Client socket */
...
len_inet = sizeof adr_clnt;
c = accept(s,
    (struct sockaddr *)&adr_clnt,
    &len_inet);
```

Datagram servers obtain the client's address from the recvfrom(2) function. The following is a code excerpt from Listing 6.1:

EXAMPLE

```
int z;
struct sockaddr_in adr_clnt;/* AF_INET */
int len_inet;              /* length  */
int s;                     /* Socket */
char dgram[512];        /* Recv buffer */

len_inet = sizeof adr_clnt;
z = recvfrom(s,                   /* Socket */
    dgram,              /* Receiving buffer */
    sizeof dgram,    /* Max recv buf size */
    0,                  /* Flags: no options */
    (struct sockaddr *)&adr_clnt,/* Addr */
    &len_inet);    /* Addr len, in & out */
```

After the client's address has been obtained in either type of server, you then apply the techniques from Chapter 9, "Hostname and Network Name Lookups," using the gethostbyaddr(3) function. Here is another code excerpt from Listing 9.8 to review how a client's IP number is resolved to a hostname:

EXAMPLE

```
struct sockaddr_in adr_clnt;/* AF_INET */
struct hostent *hp;  /* Host entry ptr */

hp = gethostbyaddr(
    (char *)&adr_clnt.sin_addr,
    sizeof adr_clnt.sin_addr,
    adr_clnt.sin_family);

if ( !hp )
    fprintf(logf," Error: %s\n",
        hstrerror(h_errno));
else
    fprintf(logf," %s\n",
        hp->h_name);
```

After the server has the fully qualified hostname in hp->h_name, it is able to apply any grant or deny policy that the program designer wants.

Identifying by IP Number

Although it is convenient for humans to work with system hostnames and domain names, there are security problems associated with this method of identification. When the IP number is received by the server, it must then use another network process (initiated by gethostbyaddr(3)) to resolve that number into a hostname. It is quite conceivable that the attacker has set up his private name server to lie about his IP number. For this reason, it is sometimes preferable to base security decisions upon IP number alone.

Another compromise that can be used is to grant access based upon IP number alone, but log both the IP number and the resolved name together in the log file for your server. This provides good security while providing some measure of convenience when viewing the history logs. When mysterious activity occurs, you can then check both the IP number and the apparent name that was resolved at that time.

Using IP numbers for security provides additional challenges for the server's administrator. The administrator must update IP numbers if your client changes his IP number, although his hostname and domain name remain unchanged.

Another challenge that awaits the administrator when securing by IP number is that he might end up dealing with users who do not know what their IP number is. You might be able to get the hostname and domain name information from them, however. With this information, you can use the nslookup(1) command to determine the client's IP number and then configure that number. Then, contact the client and have them confirm that it works.

Finally, some clients will use different IP numbers every time they start their workstation—when they use DHCP, for example. Their IP number is assigned from a pool of available IP numbers that are determined by their administrator. The best you can do in this situation is to get in touch with their administrator to find out more about the pool of IP numbers that they will be drawing from. In these cases, you will often just restrict access at a network ID level (review Figure 3.1 in Chapter 3, "Address Conversion Functions," if necessary).

Securing inetd Servers

So far, the discussion has been around customized code within each server to carry out your security policy. This has a number of disadvantages:

- Code to manage security must be built in to each server that is exposed to hostilities.

- Each server must go through rigorous testing to verify its accuracy and resilience against attack.

- Multiple points of access allow additional points of weakness to be exploited.

The first two points speak well for themselves. The last point is illustrated by the problem of securing many doors when a shopping mall closes. When several doors must be locked, it is far easier to overlook one of them. Additionally, it is far more likely that one door will be found with weaknesses that can be exploited. For all these reasons, it is desirable to put security policy into a centralized module.

Centralized Network Policy

In the last chapter, you saw how the inetd daemon made server design simpler. The inetd daemon provides all the server code necessary to listen for client requests and start the server only when it is necessary to do so. The inetd daemon provides one additional level of convenience: It allows a centralized network security model to be installed.

If you are using one of the newer Linux distributions such as Red Hat Linux 6.0, then you already have Wietse Venema's TCP wrapper program being invoked by inetd. To verify this, grep for the entry for telnetd, as follows:

```
# grep telnet /etc/inetd.conf
telnet stream tcp nowait root /usr/sbin/tcpd in.telnetd
#
```

OUTPUT

From the example output, you see that inetd invokes the executable /usr/sbin/tcpd when a telnet request arrives. If you also grep for ftp, you will see that /usr/sbin/tcpd (hereafter simply referred to as tcpd) is also invoked for that service. So, what does this tcpd program do?

It should be emphasized that this tcpd program inserts itself between inetd and the server (telnetd, for example). This is done in a transparent way, because it does not perform any input or output on the socket. The tcpd program simply applies its network security rules and then invokes the intended server if access is granted.

From the grep example shown earlier, the tcpd program is provided the string in.telnetd as its command name (its argv[0] value). This tells tcpd what server to invoke if access is to be granted. If access is denied for any reason, the attempt is logged and the socket is closed (when tcpd exits), without invoking the server.

Understanding the TCP Wrapper Concept

Figure 16.1 shows how you can visualize the role of tcpd as it interacts with inetd and the resulting server.

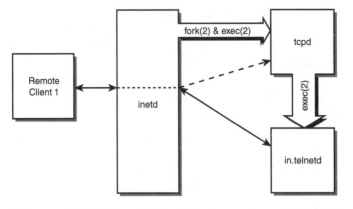

Figure 16.1: *This graphical representation of the TCP wrapper concept illustrates the relationship of the processes involved.*

Let's review the process of a remote client connecting to your in.telnetd server:

1. The client uses his telnet client command to issue a connect request to your machine's telnet daemon.

2. Your Linux host is using inetd, which has been configured to listen on port 23 for telnet requests. It accepts the connection request from step 1.

3. The /etc/inetd.conf configuration file directs your inetd server to fork(2) a new process. The parent process goes back to listening for more connects.

4. The child process from step 3 now calls exec(2) to execute the /usr/sbin/tcpd TCP wrapper program.

5. The tcpd program determines whether the client should be given access or not. This is determined by the combination of the socket addresses involved and the configuration files /etc/hosts.deny and /etc/hosts.allow.

6. If access is to be denied, tcpd simply terminates (this causes file units 0, 1, and 2 to be closed, which are the socket file descriptors).

7. If access is to be granted, the executable that is to be started is determined by tcpd's argv[0] value. In this example, the name is in.telnetd. This specifies the executable pathname /usr/sbin/in.telnetd, which is passed to the exec(2) function to load and execute.

8. The server now runs in place of tcpd with the same process ID that tcpd formerly had. The server now performs input and output on the sockets (file units 0, 1, and 2).

Step 7 is important—it is where the server process is started by the exec(2) function call from within tcpd. This maintains the important parent/child relationship between inetd and the (child) server process. When the wait flag word is used, the inetd daemon can start the next server only when it detects that the current child process has ended. This works correctly only when the server process is a direct child process of the parent inetd. Numbers might help make this easier to digest:

1. The inetd daemon has process ID 124 for this example.

2. The inetd daemon calls fork(2) to start a child process. This child process ID is now 1243 for this example.

3. The inetd child process (PID 1243) now calls exec(2) to start /usr/sbin/tcpd.

4. Note that tcpd is now running as PID 1243 (recall that exec(2) uses the same process resources to start a new program, while discarding the original program that called exec(2)).

5. The tcpd eventually calls exec(2) again, when access is to be granted. This starts the new server, which is /usr/sbin/in.telnetd in this example.

6. Note that the server /usr/sbin/in.telnetd still is PID 1243 because exec(2) does not create a new process (see notes in step 4).

7. Server in.telnetd eventually exits (PID 1243 terminates).

8. Parent process inetd (PID 124) receives a SIGCHLD signal to indicate that its child process ID 1243 has terminated. This will cause inetd to call upon wait(2) to determine which child process has terminated.

From this list of steps, you can see how cleverly inserted the tcpd wrapper program is. This program never actually performs I/O on the sockets—this would disturb the protocol being used (telnet or otherwise).

Determining Access

You might still have two questions at this point:

1. How does the TCP wrapper program determine what service it is securing (telnet, ftp, and so on)?

2. How does it determine who the client is?

Now, let's briefly state each solution in the following sections.

DETERMINING THE SERVICE

The tcpd program can determine the service it is protecting by calling upon the getsockname(2) function. Remember that function? It not only returns the socket address that the client was connecting to, but it indicates the port number of the service. In the previous examples, the port number was 23 (the telnet service).

DETERMINING THE CLIENT IDENTITY

Because the tcpd program was not the one that executed the accept(2) function call (this was done by inetd), it must determine who the client is. As you've probably guessed, this is done with the getpeername(2) function. You will recall that this function retrieves the address and port number of the remote client, in the same manner as getsockname(2).

DETERMINING THE DATAGRAM CLIENT IDENTITY

Determining the identity of a datagram client is a bit trickier. The astute reader might have wondered about this in the previous section, because datagrams do not use the accept(2) function call. It is also not possible to use getpeername(2) on datagram sockets because each datagram can potentially come from different clients. The client's address is returned by the recvfrom(2) function call. How, then, can tcpd determine the client's identity without actually reading the server's datagram?

It turns out that tcpd is able to cheat. The client's address and port number can be determined by calling recvfrom(2) using the flag option MSG_PEEK. Example code is shown as follows:

EXAMPLE

```
int z;
struct sockaddr_in adr_clnt;/* AF_INET */
int len_inet;                    /* length  */
int s;                           /* Socket */
char dgram[512];        /* Recv buffer */

len_inet = sizeof adr_clnt;
z = recvfrom(s,                     /* Socket */
    dgram,              /* Receiving buffer */
    sizeof dgram,    /* Max recv buf size */
    MSG_PEEK,      /* Flags: Peek at data */
    (struct sockaddr *)&adr_clnt,/* Addr */
    &len_inet);      /* Addr len, in & out */
```

Notice the flag option MSG_PEEK. This option directs the kernel to carry out the recvfrom(2) call as normal except that the datagram is not to be removed from the queue as "read." This allows the tcpd program to "peek" at the datagram that the server will subsequently read, if access is granted.

Notice that the data itself is not important here. What this MSG_PEEK operation accomplishes is that it returns the client's IP address (in the example, this is placed into adr_clnt). The wrapper program can determine from the variable adr_clnt whether this datagram should be processed by the server or not.

So far, you have digested the theory behind the TCP wrapper concept. Next, you'll see this idea illustrated in the concrete form of example programs.

Installing Wrapper and Server Programs

This section will present a simple datagram server and a corresponding TCP wrapper program. The wrapper program implements a very simple security policy.

Examining Server and Wrapper Logging Code

The server and wrapper program share a few functions for logging purposes. These logging functions are presented in Listing 16.1.

EXAMPLE

Listing 16.1: log.c—Logging Functions Used by Server and Wrapper

```
1:   /* log.c
2:    *
3:    * Logging Functions:
4:    */
5:   #include <stdio.h>
6:   #include <unistd.h>
7:   #include <stdlib.h>
8:   #include <string.h>
9:   #include <stdarg.h>
10:  #include <errno.h>
11:
12:  static FILE *logf = NULL;       /* Log File */
13:
14:  /*
15:   * Open log file for append:
16:   *
17:   * RETURNS:
18:   *   0    Success
19:   *  -1    Failed.
20:   */
21:  int
22:  log_open(const char *pathname) {
23:
24:      logf = fopen(pathname,"a");
25:      return logf ? 0 : -1;
```

continues

Listing 16.1: continued

```
26:    }
27:
28:    /*
29:     * Log information to a file:
30:     */
31:    void
32:    log(const char *format,...) {
33:        va_list ap;
34:
35:        if ( !logf )
36:            return;          /* No log file open */
37:
38:        fprintf(logf,"[PID %ld] ",(long)getpid());
39:
40:        va_start(ap,format);
41:        vfprintf(logf,format,ap);
42:        va_end(ap);
43:        fflush(logf);
44:    }
45:
46:    /*
47:     * Close the log file:
48:     */
49:    void
50:    log_close(void) {
51:
52:        if ( logf )
53:            fclose(logf);
54:        logf = NULL;
55:    }
56:
57:    /*
58:     * This function reports the error to
59:     * the log file and calls exit(1).
60:     */
61:    void
62:    bail(const char *on_what) {
63:
64:        if ( logf ) {              /* Is log open? */
65:            if ( errno )           /* Error? */
66:                log("%s: ",strerror(errno));
67:            log("%s\n",on_what);   /* Log msg */
68:            log_close();
69:        }
70:        exit(1);
71:    }
```

The major components present in Listing 16.1 are the following:

- A `log_open()` function to open the log file (lines 21 to 26).

- A `printf(3)` styled logging function `log()` (lines 31 to 44). This function provides the convenience of `printf(3)`, while ensuring that the process ID is always part of the log message (see line 38).

- A `log_close()` function to close the log file (lines 49 to 55).

- A modified version of the `bail()` function that writes its output to the log file instead of `stderr` (lines 61 to 71).

The include file that is used by the referencing programs is shown in Listing 16.2.

EXAMPLE

Listing 16.2: `log.h`—The `log.h` Header File

```
1:    /* log.h
2:     *
3:     * log.c externs:
4:     */
5:    extern int log_open(const char *pathname);
6:    extern void log(const char *format,...);
7:    extern void log_close(void);
8:    extern void bail(const char *on_what);
```

Listing 16.2 simply defines the function prototypes for the logging functions shown previously in Listing 16.1.

Examining the Datagram Server Code

This section illustrates a datagram server that processes the first datagram and then loops back for more. If no further datagrams arrive within eight seconds, the server times out and exits. The `inetd` daemon will not start another server until it is notified of this server's termination (the `/etc/inetd.conf` entry must use the `wait` flag word).

Listing 16.3 shows the code used for the datagram server program.

EXAMPLE

Listing 16.3: `dgramisrvr.c`—The `inetd` Datagram Server

```
1:    /* dgramisrvr.c:
2:     *
3:     * Example inetd datagram server:
4:     */
5:    #include <stdio.h>
6:    #include <unistd.h>
7:    #include <stdlib.h>
8:    #include <stdarg.h>
```

continues

Listing 16.3: continued

```
9:   #include <errno.h>
10:  #include <string.h>
11:  #include <sys/types.h>
12:  #include <sys/time.h>
13:  #include <sys/socket.h>
14:  #include <netinet/in.h>
15:  #include <arpa/inet.h>
16:
17:  #include "log.h"
18:
19:  #define LOGPATH "/tmp/dgramisrvr.log"
20:
21:  int
22:  main(int argc,char **argv) {
23:      int z;
24:      int s;                          /* Socket */
25:      int alen;         /* Length of address */
26:      struct sockaddr_in adr_clnt; /* Client */
27:      char dgram[512];      /* Receive buffer */
28:      char dtfmt[512];   /* Date/Time Result */
29:      time_t td;     /* Current Time and Date */
30:      struct tm dtv;       /* Date time values */
31:      fd_set rx_set;    /* Incoming req. set */
32:      struct timeval tmout; /* Timeout value */
33:
34:      /*
35:       * Open a log file for append:
36:       */
37:      if ( log_open(LOGPATH) == -1 )
38:          exit(1);               /* No log file! */
39:
40:      log("dgramisrvr started.\n");
41:
42:      /*
43:       * Other initialization:
44:       */
45:      s = 0;   /* Our socket is on std input */
46:      FD_ZERO(&rx_set);          /* Initialize */
47:      FD_SET(s,&rx_set);       /* Notice fd=0 */
48:
49:      /*
50:       * Now wait for incoming datagrams:
51:       */
52:      for (;;) {
53:          /*
54:           * Block until a datagram arrives:
```

```
55:           */
56:         alen = sizeof adr_clnt;
57:
58:         z = recvfrom(s,              /* Socket */
59:             dgram,       /* Receiving buffer */
60:             sizeof dgram, /* Max recv size */
61:             0,           /* Flags: no options */
62:             (struct sockaddr *)&adr_clnt,
63:             &alen);   /* Addr len, in & out */
64:
65:         if ( z < 0 )
66:             bail("recvfrom(2)");
67:
68:         dgram[z] = 0; /* NULL terminate dgram */
69:
70:         /*
71:          * Log the request:
72:          */
73:         log("Got request '%s' from %s port %d\n",
74:             dgram,
75:             inet_ntoa(adr_clnt.sin_addr),
76:             ntohs(adr_clnt.sin_port));
77:
78:         /*
79:          * Get the current date and time:
80:          */
81:         time(&td);   /* current time & date */
82:         dtv = *localtime(&td);
83:
84:         /*
85:          * Format a new date and time string,
86:          * based upon the input format string:
87:          */
88:         strftime(dtfmt, /* Formatted result */
89:             sizeof dtfmt,       /* Max size */
90:             dgram,       /* date/time format */
91:             &dtv);             /* Input values */
92:
93:         /*
94:          * Send the formatted result back to the
95:          * client program:
96:          */
97:         z = sendto(s,              /* Socket */
98:             dtfmt,       /* datagram result */
99:             strlen(dtfmt),       /* length */
100:            0,          /* Flags: no options */
```

continues

Listing 16.3: continued

```
101:                 (struct sockaddr *)&adr_clnt,
102:                 alen);
103:
104:         if ( z < 0 )
105:                 bail("sendto(2)");
106:
107:         /*
108:          * Wait for next packet or timeout:
109:          *
110:          * This is easily accomplished with the
111:          * use of select(2).
112:          */
113:         do {
114:             /* Establish Timeout = 8.0 secs */
115:             tmout.tv_sec = 8;   /* 8 seconds */
116:             tmout.tv_usec = 0;  /* + 0 usec */
117:
118:             /* Wait for read event or timeout */
119:             z = select(s+1,&rx_set,NULL,NULL,&tmout);
120:
121:         } while ( z == -1 && errno == EINTR );
122:
123:         /*
124:          * Exit if select(2) returns an error
125:          * or if it indicates a timeout:
126:          */
127:         if ( z <= 0 )
128:             break;
129:     }
130:
131:     /*
132:      * Close the socket and exit:
133:      */
134:     if ( z == -1 )
135:         log("%s: select(2)\n",strerror(errno));
136:     else
137:         log("Timed out: server exiting.\n");
138:
139:     close(s);
140:     log_close();
141:     return 0;
142: }
```

The server code is organized simply as one main() program. The basic steps used by this server can be described as follows:

1. The log file is opened, and the process ID and the startup message is logged to the log file (lines 37 to 40).

2. The socket given to this server from inetd is on file units 0, 1, and 2. The server will use file unit 0 for this purpose (line 45).

3. The variable rx_set is initialized for use with select(2) by the macro calls in lines 46 and 47.

4. The server loop starts in line 52. This server loops, and so the flag word wait must be specified in the /etc/inetd.conf file.

5. The server reads a datagram from the socket (s=0) in lines 56 to 66.

6. The received datagram has a terminating null byte stuffed into the buffer dgram[] (line 68).

7. The server processes the request by formatting a date/time string according to the received format string (lines 81 to 91).

8. The server responds back to the client with the formatted result (lines 97 to 105).

9. The server waits for another datagram in the select(2) call (lines 113 to 121). This will be described in more detail later.

10. If an error has occurred, or a timeout has occurred, the control exits the for loop at line 128 (the break statement).

11. Finally, the server logs the error message (line 135) or it logs the fact that it timed out (line 137).

Now, examine the segment of code that implements the timeout code:

1. A do while loop is entered starting in line 113. This is necessary because you should always allow for the possibility of an interrupted system call. This is indicated after a signal handler returns from handling a signal, by returning an error indication and setting errno to the value EINTR. Consequently, the while statement repeats this call if −1 is returned from select(2) and the error value is EINTR.

2. The timeout value is established in lines 115 and 116. Here, the timeout is established at eight seconds.

3. The variable rx_set is initialized in lines 46 and 47 so that the select(2) call will report when datagrams arrive on file unit 0 (its socket). Normally, this should be established prior to each entry to select(2) because this function updates the contents of rx_set. However, in this case, this is unnecessary because the for loop is repeated only if select(2) returns with the rx_set bit set for unit 0 set (indicating that a datagram has arrived).

4. The select(2) call returns with 1 if a datagram has arrived, 0 if a timeout occurred instead, or –1 if some other error has occurred.

5. If a timeout or error occurs, the for loop is exited (line 128).

6. Otherwise, rx_set still has bit 0 set, and the for loop is repeated (line 52).

This server program shows how a UDP server can loop back, and read more datagrams until a timeout occurs. There are other ways to accomplish a timeout, but this is perhaps one of the simplest ways it can be done.

Examining the Simple TCP Wrapper Program

Now, it is time to introduce the source code for the simple TCP wrapper program that will be used. This program is illustrated in Listing 16.4.

EXAMPLE

Listing 16.4: wrapper.c—The Simple TCP Wrapper Program

```
1:    /* wrapper.c:
2:     *
3:     * Simple wrapper example:
4:     */
5:    #include <stdio.h>
6:    #include <unistd.h>
7:    #include <stdlib.h>
8:    #include <errno.h>
9:    #include <string.h>
10:   #include <sys/types.h>
11:   #include <sys/socket.h>
12:   #include <netinet/in.h>
13:   #include <arpa/inet.h>
14:
15:   #include "log.h"
16:
17:   #define LOGPATH "/tmp/wrapper.log"
18:
19:   int
20:   main(int argc,char **argv,char **envp) {
21:       int z;
22:       struct sockaddr_in adr_clnt; /* Client */
23:       int alen;                /* Address length */
24:       char dgram[512];        /* Receive buffer */
25:       char *str_addr; /* String form of addr */
26:
27:       /*
28:        * We must log denied attempts:
29:        */
30:       if ( log_open(LOGPATH) == -1 )
```

```
31:          exit(1);   /* Can't open log file! */
32:
33:      log("wrapper started.\n");
34:
35:      /*
36:       * Peek at datagram using MSG_PEEK:
37:       */
38:      alen = sizeof adr_clnt;       /* length */
39:
40:      z = recvfrom(0, /* Socket on std input */
41:          dgram,             /* Receiving buffer */
42:          sizeof dgram,      /* Max recv size */
43:          MSG_PEEK,       /* Flags: Peek!!!!!! */
44:          (struct sockaddr *)&adr_clnt,
45:          &alen);        /* Addr len, in & out */
46:
47:      if ( z < 0 )
48:          bail("recvfrom(2), peeking at client"
49:              " address.");
50:
51:      /*
52:       * Convert IP address to string form:
53:       */
54:      str_addr = inet_ntoa(adr_clnt.sin_addr);
55:
56:      if ( strcmp(str_addr,"127.7.7.7") != 0 ) {
57:          /*
58:           * Not our special 127.7.7.7 address:
59:           */
60:          log("Address %s port %d rejected.\n",
61:              str_addr, ntohs(adr_clnt.sin_port));
62:
63:          /*
64:           * We must read this packet now without
65:           * the MSG_PEEK option to discard dgram:
66:           */
67:          z = recvfrom(0,            /* Socket */
68:              dgram,       /* Receiving buffer */
69:              sizeof dgram,  /* Max rcv size */
70:              0,                   /* No flags!! */
71:              (struct sockaddr *)&adr_clnt,
72:              &alen);
73:
74:          if ( z < 0 )
75:              bail("recvfrom(2), eating dgram");
76:          exit(1);
```

continues

Listing 16.4: continued

```
77:      }
78:
79:      /*
80:       * Accept this dgram request, and
81:       * launch the server:
82:       */
83:      log("Address %s port %d accepted.\n",
84:          str_addr, ntohs(adr_clnt.sin_port));
85:
86:      /*
87:       * inetd has provided argv[0] from the
88:       * config file /etc/inetd.conf: we have
89:       * used this to indicate the server's
90:       * full pathname for this example. We
91:       * simply pass any other arguments and
92:       * environment as is.
93:       */
94:      log("Starting '%s'\n",argv[0]);
95:      log_close();     /* No longer need this */
96:
97:      z = execve(argv[0],argv,envp);
98:
99:      /*
100:      * If control returns, then execve(2)
101:      * failed for some reason:
102:      */
103:     log_open(LOGPATH);     /* Re-open log */
104:     bail("execve(2), starting server");
105:     return 1;
106: }
```

The wrapper program shown in Listing 16.4 implements the following very simple security policy:

- If the client's address is 127.7.7.7, his request is allowed to go to the datagram server. No restriction upon client's port number is applied.

- If the client's address is any other IP address, the request is logged and denied.

NOTE

The policy address of 127.7.7.7 was chosen as an example that all readers should be able to test (even those readers without an actual network established). The reader is encouraged to modify the program if he does have a network, in order to try out additional policy rules.

The TCP wrapper program presented uses the following basic steps:

1. To log denied and granted attempts, a separate log file /tmp/wrapper.log is opened in lines 30 to 31. The wrapper program's process ID and start banner are also logged for demonstration purposes in line 33.

2. A datagram wrapper program cannot use getpeername(2) function to determine the datagram address. Instead, it must call upon recvfrom(2) using the MSG_PEEK flag bit (lines 40 to 49). The MSG_PEEK flag allows the client address to be returned into the address structure adr_clnt (line 44) without actually removing the datagram from the input queue for this socket.

3. For demonstration purposes, this simple program converts the client's address into a string for easier comparison (line 54). This is probably not recommended for a secure wrapper program.

4. The client's address is tested in line 56. If the client's IP address is not the magic 127.7.7.7 IP number that the wrapper program insists upon, the code in lines 60 to 77 is executed (the request is denied).

5. If the request is accepted, the code in lines 83 to 97 is executed.

Now, examine what happens when an incoming request is rejected by this wrapper program:

1. First, the rejection of the request is logged in lines 60 to 61.

2. The datagram must be discarded (or "eaten") by the wrapper program. This is done by receiving it in lines 67 to 72 (note that no MSG_PEEK flag is used here). If this is not done, the datagram remains waiting to be processed for this socket.

3. Finally, errors are reported, if required, and the wrapper program terminates (lines 74 to 76).

When the datagram request is accepted by the wrapper program, the following steps are carried out:

1. The log() function is called to log this request (lines 83 to 84).

2. For demonstration reasons, the executable being started (the server) is logged in line 94. This can aid debugging if you decide to modify this code.

3. The log file is closed (line 95). This should be done because the log file unit will remain open after the call to execve(2) if this is not done.

4. The wrapper program is replaced with the server by calling execve(2) (line 97). The current wrapper program is abandoned as the server

program is brought into memory to replace it. For this reason, the wrapper and the server programs keep the same process ID (this is important to inetd, the parent process).

If all goes well, the server begins to execute. If for some reason the server does not execute, then the execve(2) function will return control. The following error recovery steps are then carried out:

1. The log file is reopened (line 103) because it was closed prior to calling execve(2) in line 95.

2. The error is reported to the log file (line 104).

Introducing the Client Program

A modified version of an earlier client program is presented here. This client program requires two command-line arguments: the server address and the client address to use. The specification of the additional client IP address permits you to perform more experimentation with your TCP wrapper program. Listing 16.5 shows the modified datagram client program.

EXAMPLE

Listing 16.5: dgramcln2.c—The Modified Datagram Client Program

```
1:    /* dgramcln2.c:
2:     *
3:     * Modified datagram client:
4:     */
5:    #include <stdio.h>
6:    #include <unistd.h>
7:    #include <stdlib.h>
8:    #include <errno.h>
9:    #include <string.h>
10:   #include <time.h>
11:   #include <sys/types.h>
12:   #include <sys/socket.h>
13:   #include <netinet/in.h>
14:   #include <arpa/inet.h>
15:
16:   /*
17:    * This function reports the error and
18:    * exits back to the shell:
19:    */
20:   static void
21:   bail(const char *on_what) {
22:
23:       if ( errno ) {
24:           fputs(strerror(errno),stderr);
25:           fputs(": ",stderr);
```

```
26:        }
27:        fputs(on_what,stderr);
28:        fputc('\n',stderr);
29:        exit(1);
30:    }
31:
32:    int
33:    main(int argc,char **argv) {
34:        int z;
35:        char *srvr_addr = NULL;    /* Srvr addr */
36:        char *clnt_addr = NULL;    /* Clnt addr */
37:        struct sockaddr_in adr_srvr; /* Server */
38:        struct sockaddr_in adr_clnt; /* Client */
39:        struct sockaddr_in adr;      /* AF_INET */
40:        int alen;          /* Socket addr length */
41:        int s;                       /* Socket */
42:        char dgram[512];         /* Recv buffer */
43:
44:        /*
45:         * Insist on two command-line arguments
46:         * (without port numbers):
47:         *
48:         * dgramcln2 <server_addr> <client_addr>
49:         */
50:        if ( argc != 3 ) {
51:            fputs("Usage: dgramclnt <server_ipaddr> "
52:                "<client_ipaddr>\n",stderr);
53:            return 1;
54:        }
55:
56:        srvr_addr = argv[1]; /* 1st arg is srv */
57:        clnt_addr = argv[2]; /* 2nd arg is cln */
58:
59:        /*
60:         * Create a server socket address:
61:         */
62:        memset(&adr_srvr,0,sizeof adr_srvr);
63:        adr_srvr.sin_family = AF_INET;
64:        adr_srvr.sin_port = htons(9090);
65:        adr_srvr.sin_addr.s_addr =
66:            inet_addr(srvr_addr);
67:
68:        if ( adr_srvr.sin_addr.s_addr == INADDR_NONE )
69:            bail("bad server address.");
70:
71:        /*
```

continues

Listing 16.5: continued

```
72:          * Create a UDP socket:
73:          */
74:         s = socket(AF_INET,SOCK_DGRAM,0);
75:         if ( s == -1 )
76:             bail("socket()");
77:
78:         /*
79:          * Create the specific client address:
80:          */
81:         memset(&adr_clnt,0,sizeof adr_clnt);
82:         adr_clnt.sin_family = AF_INET;
83:         adr_clnt.sin_port = 0;        /* Any port */
84:         adr_clnt.sin_addr.s_addr =
85:             inet_addr(clnt_addr);
86:
87:         if ( adr_clnt.sin_addr.s_addr == INADDR_NONE )
88:             bail("bad client address.");
89:
90:         /*
91:          * Bind the specific client address:
92:          */
93:         z = bind(s, (struct sockaddr *)&adr_clnt,
94:             sizeof adr_clnt);
95:
96:         if ( z == -1 )
97:             bail("bind(2) of client address");
98:
99:         /*
100:          * Enter input client loop:
101:          */
102:         for (;;) {
103:             /*
104:              * Prompt user for a date format string:
105:              */
106:             fputs("\nEnter format string: ",stdout);
107:             if ( !fgets(dgram,sizeof dgram,stdin) )
108:                 break;                    /* EOF */
109:
110:             z = strlen(dgram);
111:             if ( z > 0 && dgram[--z] == '\n' )
112:                 dgram[z] = 0;   /* Stomp out newline */
113:
114:             /*
115:              * Send format string to server:
116:              */
117:             z = sendto(s,               /* Socket */
118:                 dgram,        /* datagram to snd */
```

```
119:            strlen(dgram), /* dgram length */
120:            0,          /* Flags: no options */
121:            (struct sockaddr *)&adr_srvr,
122:            sizeof adr_srvr);
123:
124:        if ( z < 0 )
125:            bail("sendto(2)");
126:
127:        /*
128:         * Wait for a response:
129:         *
130:         * NOTE: Control will hang here if the
131:         * wrapper decides we lack access (no
132:         * response will arrive).
133:         */
134:        alen = sizeof adr;
135:
136:        z = recvfrom(s,          /* Socket */
137:            dgram,       /* Receiving buffer */
138:            sizeof dgram, /* Max recv size */
139:            0,          /* Flags: no options */
140:            (struct sockaddr *)&adr,
141:            &alen);  /* Addr len, in & out */
142:
143:        if ( z < 0 )
144:            bail("recvfrom(2)");
145:
146:        dgram[z] = 0;      /* NULL terminate */
147:
148:        /*
149:         * Report Result:
150:         */
151:        printf("Result from %s port %u :"
152:            "\n\t'%s'\n",
153:            inet_ntoa(adr.sin_addr),
154:            (unsigned)ntohs(adr.sin_port),
155:            dgram);
156:    }
157:
158:    /*
159:     * Close the socket and exit:
160:     */
161:    close(s);
162:    putchar('\n');
163:
164:    return 0;
165: }
```

The client program will not be covered in much detail, because it is very similar to the program dgramclnt.c presented in Listing 6.2 in Chapter 6, "Connectionless-Oriented Protocols." Aside from some cosmetic differences, the primary modifications added were

- Lines 50 to 54 now insist that two command-line arguments be supplied.

- The local socket is bound to the IP address specified in argv[2] with bind(2) (lines 81 to 97). This will be instrumental in your testing later.

Note that the program dgramcln2 will hang if the wrapper program decides that it should not gain access to the server. This occurs because the recvfrom(2) function never receives a reply from the server (lines 136 to 144). When this happens, you will need to interrupt out of the program (usually Ctrl+C is the interrupt character, but yours might be different).

Installing and Testing the Wrapper

You have now examined all the code that will be used. To start your wrapper experiments, first compile all the code as follows:

OUTPUT

```
$ make
gcc -c  -D_GNU_SOURCE -Wall -Wreturn-type dgramisrvr.c
gcc -c  -D_GNU_SOURCE -Wall -Wreturn-type log.c
gcc dgramisrvr.o log.o -o dgramisrvr
gcc -c  -D_GNU_SOURCE -Wall -Wreturn-type wrapper.c
gcc wrapper.o log.o -o wrapper
gcc -c  -D_GNU_SOURCE -Wall -Wreturn-type dgramcln2.c
gcc dgramcln2.o -o dgramcln2
$
```

Normally, you would require root access to install your server permanently. However, for simple testing purposes, you can perform this experiment without root access. To establish your files in the /tmp directory, perform the following:

OUTPUT

```
$ make install
rm -f /tmp/wrapper.log /tmp/dgramisrvr.log
rm -f /tmp/inetd.conf /tmp/wrapper /tmp/dgramisrvr
cp dgramisrvr wrapper /tmp/.
chmod 500 /tmp/wrapper /tmp/dgramisrvr
chmod 600 /tmp/inetd.conf
- - - - - - - - - - - - - - - - - - - - - - - - - - - -
Now do:

 /usr/sbin/inetd /tmp/inetd.conf

to start the server.
$
```

The make command places a number of files into the /tmp directory, including a simple /tmp/inetd.conf file. Take a moment to inspect it now:

```
$ cat /tmp/inetd.conf
9090 dgram udp wait studnt1 /tmp/wrapper /tmp/dgramisrvr
$
```

You might want to double check that your other files are installed correctly in /tmp, as follows:

```
$ ls -ltr /tmp | tail
-rw-r-----  1 stdnt1   class1       29454 Feb 19 22:59 xprnKg3RSc
-rw-r--r--  1 root     root            11 Feb 21 23:18 lpq.0002621c
-r-x------  1 stdnt1   class1       14202 Feb 22 22:48 wrapper
-rw-------  1 stdnt1   class1          53 Feb 22 22:48 inetd.conf
-r-x------  1 stdnt1   class1       15237 Feb 22 22:48 dgramisrvr
$
```

In the output, you can see that the TCP wrapper program wrapper is installed, and that the dgramisrvr executable program is also installed into the /tmp directory.

Monitoring the Log Files

If you are using X Window sessions, it is recommended that you start in one terminal session, the following command:

```
$ >/tmp/wrapper.log
$ tail -f /tmp/wrapper.log
```

This creates and then monitors the wrapper log file (the log file does not exist yet). You will see this window update as the wrapper program writes log entries to this file.

In a new window start

```
$ >/tmp/dgramisrvr.log
$ tail -f /tmp/dgramisrvr.log
```

This will establish and monitor the server log file. Again, you will see entries displayed as they are written to the server log file.

If you are not using X Window sessions, you can accomplish the same thing by using multiple console sessions. This procedure is recommended only for your convenience. You can always examine the logs upon demand later, instead, if this is your preference.

Starting Your inetd Daemon

Before starting up the clients, you must ready your copy of the inetd daemon. This daemon will run under your own userID and not require any special root privileges. However, you must be careful to give it the correct configuration file on the command line, as follows:

EXAMPLE

```
$ /usr/sbin/inetd /tmp/inetd.conf
$
```

If you are using a distribution different from the Red Hat Linux distribution, then the executable program /usr/sbin/inetd might be located in a different directory.

The single command-line argument tells your inetd daemon to use the configuration that you have provided in file /tmp/inetd.conf instead of the /etc/inetd.conf file that the system normally uses. The program will automatically place itself into the background (daemons like to do that), and you should be able to see it executing as follows:

OUTPUT

```
$ ps -ef | grep inetd
root        313     1  0 Feb15 ?       00:00:00 inetd
studnt1   12763     1  0 23:04 ?       00:00:00 /usr/sbin/inetd /tmp/inetd.conf
studnt1   12765 11739  0 23:08 pts/3   00:00:00 grep inetd
$
```

The example output shown illustrates that there are now two copies of the inetd daemon running: the system daemon (PID 313) running as root, and your nonprivileged daemon process (PID 12763). With the inetd daemon started, you are ready to perform some testing.

Testing the Wrapper Program

With the logs being monitored in separate windows, it is now appropriate to start the client command and try something. First let's attempt something that the wrapper program should accept:

OUTPUT

```
$ ./dgramcln2 127.0.0.1 127.7.7.7

Enter format string: %A %B %D
Result from 127.7.7.7 port 9090 :
        'Tuesday November 11/09/99'


Enter format string:
```

This starts the client program with the client's end of the socket bound to the IP address 127.7.7.7, which the wrapper program is programmed to find acceptable. The wrapper log file should look like this:

OUTPUT

```
$ tail -f /tmp/wrapper.log
[PID 1279] wrapper started.
[PID 1279] Address 127.7.7.7 port 1027 accepted.
[PID 1279] Starting '/tmp/dgramisrvr'
```

These log records indicate the process ID was 1279 and that the request came from 127.7.7.7 port number 1027. Because the request was accepted, the server /tmp/dgramisrvr was executed to carry out the request.

Listing the server's log now should reveal something like this:

OUTPUT

```
$ tail -f /tmp/dgramisrvr.log
[PID 1279] dgramisrvr started.
[PID 1279] Got request '%A %B %D' from 127.7.7.7 port 1027
[PID 1279] Timed out: server exiting.
```

Notice that the server's process ID remained the same as the wrapper's (the wrapper process started the server with execve(2)). The log records tell us that the server started and processed the request. The last record shows that the server timed out waiting for further datagrams.

DENYING A REQUEST

Cancel your client program now with end-file (usually Ctrl+D) or interrupt it (usually Ctrl+C). Start it again with a new address, such as this:

OUTPUT

```
$ ./dgramcln2 127.0.0.1 127.13.13.13

Enter format string: %D (%B %A)
```

You will note that your client program will not get a response this way. It will "hang" because the wrapper program has denied this request from reaching the server. You can interrupt (Ctrl+C) to get out.

The wrapper log file should now look like this:

OUTPUT

```
$ tail -f /tmp/wrapper.log
[PID 1279] wrapper started.
[PID 1279] Address 127.7.7.7 port 1027 accepted.
[PID 1279] Starting '/tmp/dgramisrvr'
[PID 1289] wrapper started.
[PID 1289] Address 127.13.13.13 port 1027 rejected.
```

You see that the next datagram request was handled by a new wrapper process ID 1289 this time. The last log line shows that the address 127.13.13.13 is rejected. The client program hangs because this wrapper program eats the datagram to prevent it from being processed by a server. The wrapper program then exits.

Testing the Server Timeout

To test out the looping capability of the server, you must quickly enter two date format requests (within eight seconds). An example session is provided as follows:

OUTPUT

```
$ ./dgramcln2 127.0.0.1 127.7.7.7

Enter format string: %x
Result from 127.7.7.7 port 9090 :
        '11/09/99'
```

```
Enter format string: %x %X
Result from 127.7.7.7 port 9090 :
        '11/09/99 19:11:32'

Enter format string: CTRL+D
$
```

If you did this quickly enough, the server should have been able to process both of these requests within one single server process. To see whether this worked, check the server log:

OUTPUT

```
$ tail -f /tmp/dgramisrvr.log
[PID 1279] dgramisrvr started.
[PID 1279] Got request '%A %B %D' from 127.7.7.7 port 1027
[PID 1279] Timed out: server exiting.
[PID 1294] dgramisrvr started.
[PID 1294] Got request '%x' from 127.7.7.7 port 1027
[PID 1294] Got request '%x %X' from 127.7.7.7 port 1027
[PID 1294] Timed out: server exiting.
```

The last four log lines confirm that server process ID 1294 was able to process both date requests before it timed out.

Uninstalling the Demonstration Programs

To uninstall the demonstration programs, perform the following:

OUTPUT

```
$ make clobber
rm -f *.o core a.out
rm -f /tmp/wrapper.log /tmp/dgramisrvr.log
rm -f /tmp/inetd.conf /tmp/wrapper /tmp/dgramisrvr
rm -f dgramisrvr wrapper dgramcln2

studnt1 12763    1    0 23:04 ?    00:00:00 /usr/sbin/inetd /tmp/inetd.conf

If you see your inetd process running above, you may
want to kill it now.

$
```

The clobber target of the Makefile provided will remove all of the files created in the /tmp directory and attempt to display the process ID of your inetd daemon. In the example output shown, the daemon is running as PID 12763. This should be terminated with the kill command as follows:

```
$ kill 12763
$
```

EXAMPLE

Datagram Vulnerability

There is vulnerability in this wrapper design for datagram servers. Did you spot the problem? Hint: It has to do with the server looping.

Datagram servers that loop, as in the one shown, have a vulnerability to attack, using the wrapper concept. When no server process is running, the wrapper program is always able to screen the datagram before the server reads it. However, if the server waits for more datagrams and exits only after it times out, the wrapper program is not used to screen out those extra datagrams. This exposure can be summarized as follows:

1. A datagram arrives, alerting inetd.
2. The inetd daemon starts the wrapper program.
3. The wrapper program allows the datagram, and calls exec(2) to start the datagram server.
4. The datagram server reads and processes the datagram.
5. The server waits for another datagram.
6. If a datagram arrives, then step 4 is repeated.
7. Otherwise, the server times out and exits.
8. Repeat step 1.

While the server continues to run, the process repeats at step 4. This leaves out the security check in step 3. If you are quick enough, you can demonstrate this for yourself with the example programs provided earlier.

For better security, you have only a few options:

- Use only nowait-styled datagram servers (these servers process one datagram and exit). This forces all requests to be scrutinized by the wrapper program.

- Use custom code within your datagram server to test each datagram before it is accepted for processing.

A compromise method is to run shorter timeout periods, but this still leaves some exposure.

For these reasons, many sites will choose to disable the datagram service if a TCP version of the same service exists (the TCP request is always checked by the wrapper program). Where the datagram service must be offered, secure sites will not allow their datagram servers to loop. This requires source code changes to the server or a custom server program is written instead. Alternatively, the server program itself checks every access of the requesting client and does not rely on the TCP wrapper concept for this.

What's Next

This chapter has given you a working knowledge of the TCP wrapper concept. Applying the wrapper concept, you can now use it on servers that you write to provide your system with greater network security. You have also learned that it has a weakness in the datagram case, which requires special consideration.

In the next chapter, you will be introduced to one more security-related concept. There, you will learn how to receive credentials from a PF_UNIX/PF_LOCAL socket. Additionally, you will learn how a server can open a file on your behalf and pass the opened file descriptor to you, by means of a PF_UNIX/PF_LOCAL socket.

Passing Credentials and File Descriptors

If you share your Linux host with other users, you might have had reason to struggle with certain resource access issues. In this chapter, you will see how credentials can be obtained from a local socket and how file descriptors can be transmitted by sockets as well. These two important features open an entirely new avenue of security access solutions for your users, while keeping your machine secure.

These features are provided for by the use of socket ancillary data. This is an advanced topic, which might be beyond what many beginning programmers want to tackle. Beginners might want to simply skim this chapter or skip to the next.

The intermediate to advanced readers, however, will want to study this chapter carefully, as an introduction to the processing of ancillary data. Emphasis has been placed on a practical example that can be studied and experimented with.

This chapter covers the following topics:

- How to send user credentials to a local server process

- How to receive and interpret user credentials

- How to send a file descriptor to another process on the local host

- How to receive a file descriptor from another process on the local host

Problem Statement

Assume that you have a user on your Linux system who has been entrusted to maintain and care for your Web server. For security purposes, your Web server does not run with the root account privilege (to protect your system against intrusion). Yet, you want the Web server to be available on port 80 where all normal Web servers live. The problem is that Linux (and UNIX in general) treats all ports under port 1024 as privileged port numbers. This means that the Web server needs root access in order to start up (after that, root is not required). Finally, we're going to assume that the inetd daemon will not be used.

Although you like the work that your friend does for the Web server, you prefer not to give him root access. This lets you sleep better at night. Last of all, you don't want to resort to a setuid solution if it can be avoided.

The challenge is to offer a solution that provides

- The ability for a specific user to start the Web server up on port 80 (normally, this requires root).

- The program must not use setuid permission bits.

- The inetd daemon cannot be used.

This chapter will provide a solution to this problem by making use of the following:

- A simple socket server.

- The credentials received by the server will identify the requesting user without doubt.

- The server will create and bind a socket on port 80 and pass it back to the authorized requesting user process.

After some initial theory, the remainder of this chapter will show you how this works by means of a hands-on demonstration.

Introducing Ancillary Data

Although it is very difficult to prove the identity of a remote user over the Internet, it is a simple matter for the Linux kernel to identify another user on the same host. This makes it possible for PF_LOCAL/PF_UNIX sockets to provide credentials to the receiving end about the user at the other end. The only way for these credentials to be compromised would be for the kernel itself to be compromised in some way (perhaps by a rogue kernel loadable module).

Credentials can be received as part of ancillary data that is received with a communication. Ancillary data is supplementary or auxiliary to the normal data. This brings up some points that are worth emphasizing here:

- Credentials are received as part of ancillary data.

- Ancillary data must accompany normal data (it cannot be transmitted on its own).

- Ancillary data can also include other information such as file descriptors.

- Ancillary data can include multiple ancillary items together (such as credentials and file descriptors at the same time).

The credentials are provided by the Linux kernel. They are never provided by the client application. If they were, the client would be allowed to lie about its identity. Because the kernel is trusted, the credentials can be trusted by the process that is interested in the credentials.

As noted in the list, you now know that file descriptors are also transmitted and received as ancillary data. However, before you can start writing socket code to use these elements of ancillary data, you need to be introduced to some new programming concepts.

TIP

Ancillary data is referred to by several different terms. Other names for ancillary data include auxiliary or control data. In the context of PF_LOCAL/PF_UNIX sockets, these all refer to the same thing.

Introducing I/O Vectors

Before you are introduced to the somewhat complex functions that work with ancillary data, you should become familiar with I/O vectors as used by the readv(2) and writev(2) system calls. Not only might you find these functions useful, but the way they work is also carried over into some of the ancillary data functions. This will make understanding them easier later.

The I/O Vector (struct iovec)

The functions readv(2) and writev(2) both use a concept of an I/O vector. This is defined by including the file:

```
#include <sys/uio.h>
```

EXAMPLE

The sys/uio.h include file defines the struct iovec, which is defined as follows:

EXAMPLE

```
struct iovec {
    ptr_t  iov_base; /* Starting address */
    size_t iov_len;  /* Length in bytes */
};
```

The struct iovec defines one vector element. Normally, this structure is used as an array of multiple elements. For each transfer element, the pointer member iov_base points to a buffer that is receiving data for readv(2) or is transmitting data for writev(2). The member iov_len in each case determines the maximum receive length and the actual write length, respectively.

The readv(2) and writev(2) Functions

These functions are known as scatter read and write functions. They are designated that way because these functions can read into or write from many buffers in one atomic operation. The function prototypes for these functions are provided as follows:

EXAMPLE

```
#include <sys/uio.h>

int readv(int fd, const struct iovec *vector, int count);

int writev(int fd, const struct iovec *vector, int count);
```

These functions take three arguments, which are

- The file descriptor fd to read or write upon.
- The I/O vector (vector) to use for reading or writing.
- The number of vector elements (count) to use.

The return value for these functions are the number of bytes read for readv(2) or the number of bytes written for writev(2). If an error occurs, −1 is returned and errno holds the error code for the failure. Note that like other I/O functions, the error EINTR can be returned to indicate that it was interrupted by a signal.

Example Using writev(2)

The program in Listing 17.1 shows how writev(2) is used to scatter write three physically separate C strings as one physical write to standard output.

EXAMPLE

Listing 17.1: writev.c—The writev(2) Example Program

```
1:   /* writev.c
2:    *
3:    * Short writev(2) demo:
```

```
4:      */
5:      #include <sys/uio.h>
6:
7:      int
8:      main(int argc,char **argv) {
9:          static char part2[] = "THIS IS FROM WRITEV";
10:         static char part3[] = "]\n";
11:         static char part1[] = "[";
12:         struct iovec iov[3];
13:
14:         iov[0].iov_base = part1;
15:         iov[0].iov_len = strlen(part1);
16:
17:         iov[1].iov_base = part2;
18:         iov[1].iov_len = strlen(part2);
19:
20:         iov[2].iov_base = part3;
21:         iov[2].iov_len = strlen(part3);
22:
23:         writev(1,iov,3);
24:
25:         return 0;
26:     }
```

This program uses the following basic steps:

1. Three physically separate C string arrays are defined in lines 9 to 11.

2. The I/O vector iov[3] is defined in line 12. This particular vector can hold up to three scattered buffer references.

3. The pointer to the first string to be written is assigned to the first I/O vector in line 14.

4. The length of the first string to be written is determined in line 15.

5. The I/O vectors iov[1] and iov[2] are established in lines 17 to 21.

6. The writev(2) system call is invoked in line 23. Notice that file unit 1 is used (standard output), and the I/O vector array iov is supplied. The number of elements to be used in iov[] is defined by the third argument, which has the value 3.

Compile and run the program shown as follows:

OUTPUT

```
$ make writev
gcc -g -c  -D_GNU_SOURCE -Wall -Wreturn-type writev.c
gcc writev.o -o writev
$ ./writev
[THIS IS FROM WRITEV]
$
```

When the program is run, you will see that despite how scattered the buffer references were, all the buffers were written out to form the final string, [THIS IS FROM WRITEV], complete with a trailing linefeed character.

You might want to take some time to modify this program and try other variations. Be sure to allocate the array iov[] large enough.

The sendmsg(2) and recvmsg(2) Functions

These functions provide the programmer with advanced features not found in other socket I/O interfaces. The next section will introduce the topic by looking at sendmsg(2) first. And then recvmsg(2) will be presented for completeness, because their functional interfaces are so similar. Subsequently, the complex structure msghdr will be described.

The sendmsg(2) Function

Now it's time to move into the big leagues. The sendmsg(2) function is conceptually the foundation for all the write functions, as it pertains to sockets. Table 17.1 lists the write functions available, in increasing complexity. At each level, the features that are added are listed also.

Table 17.1: Write Functions in Increasing Complexity

Function	Features Added
write(2)	The simplest socket write function
send(2)	Adds the flags argument
sendto(2)	Adds socket address and socket length arguments
writev(2)	No flags or socket address, but has scatter write capabilities
sendmsg(2)	Adds flags, socket address and length, scatter write, and ancillary data capabilities

Given the expanded capabilities of the sendmsg(2) function, you can expect it to require more effort to program. The function prototype for sendmsg(2) is provided as follows:

```
#include <sys/types.h>
#include <sys/socket.h>

int sendmsg(int s, const struct msghdr *msg, unsigned int flags);
```

The function's arguments are described as follows:

- The socket s to send a message on.

- The message header structure pointer msg, which will control the operation of this function call.

- The optional flag bits argument flags. These are the same flags that are valid for send(2) or sendto(2) function calls.

The return value from this function is the number of bytes sent. Otherwise, -1 indicates an error occurred and `errno` indicates the reason for it.

The `recvmsg(2)` Function

The `recvmsg(2)` function is the natural counterpart to the `sendmsg(2)` function. The function prototype for it is as follows:

EXAMPLE

```
#include <sys/types.h>
#include <sys/socket.h>

int recvmsg(int s, struct msghdr *msg, unsigned int flags);
```

The function arguments are as follows:

- The socket s to receive a message from.

- The message header structure pointer `msg`, which will control the operation of this function call.

- The optional flag bits argument `flags`. These are the same flags that are valid for `recv(2)` or `recvfrom(2)` function calls.

The return value from this function is the number of bytes received. Otherwise, -1 indicates an error occurred and `errno` indicates the reason for it.

Understanding `struct msghdr`

This appears to be a formidable structure to establish when seeing it for the first time. But don't fear the penguins! Examine the following structure definition:

EXAMPLE

```
struct msghdr {
    void          *msg_name;
    socklen_t     msg_namelen;
    struct iovec  *msg_iov;
    size_t        msg_iovlen;
    void          *msg_control;
    size_t        msg_controllen;
    int           msg_flags;
};
```

NOTE

Prior to the Posix.1g standard, the `msg_name` and `msg_control` members were typically defined as C data type (`char *`). Additionally, members `msg_namelen` and `msg_controllen` were previously declared as `int` types.

The structure members can be divided into four groups. These are

- Socket address members msg_name and msg_namelen.
- I/O vector references msg_iov and msg_iovlen.
- Ancillary data buffer members msg_control and msg_controllen.
- Received message flag bits msg_flags.

After you divide this structure into the preceding categories, the structure becomes less intimidating.

MEMBERS msg_name AND msg_namelen

These members are required only when your socket is a datagram socket. The msg_name member points to the socket address that you are sending to or receiving from. The member msg_namelen indicates the length of this socket address.

When calling recvmsg(2), msg_name will point to a receiving area for the address being received. When calling sendmsg(2), this will point to the destination address that the datagram is being addressed to.

Note that msg_name is defined as a (void *) data type. You will not have to cast your socket address to (struct sockaddr *).

MEMBERS msg_iov AND msg_iovlen

These members specify where your I/O vector array is and how many entries it contains. The msg_iov member points to the struct iovec array. You'll remember that the I/O vector points to your buffers (review the source Listing 17.1 if you need to). The member msg_iovlen indicates how many elements are in your I/O vector array.

MEMBERS msg_control AND msg_controllen

These members will point to your ancillary data buffer and indicate the buffer size (recall that ancillary data is also known as control data). The member msg_control points to the ancillary data buffer whereas msg_controllen indicates the size of that buffer.

MEMBER msg_flags

This member is used for receiving special flag bits when recvmsg(2) is used (it is not used for sendmsg(2)). The flag bits that can be received in this location are listed in Table 17.2.

Table 17.2: `struct msghdr msg_flags` *Values*

Flag Bit	Description
MSG_EOR	This flag bit is set when the end of a record has been received. This is generally useful with SOCK_SEQPACKET socket types.
MSG_TRUNC	This flag bit indicates that the trailing end of the datagram was truncated because the receiving buffer was too small to accommodate it.
MSG_CTRUNC	This bit indicates that some control (ancillary) data was truncated because the buffer was too small.
MSG_OOB	This bit indicates that expedited or out-of-band data was received.
MSG_ERRQUEUE	This flag bit indicates that no data was received, but an extended error was returned.

More information can be located in the man pages for recvmsg(2) and sendmsg(2) for those who are curious.

Ancillary Data Structures and Macros

The recvmsg(2) and sendmsg(2) functions permit the programmer to send and receive ancillary data. However, this supplementary information is subject to certain format rules. This section will introduce to you the control message header and the macros that the programmer should use to manage this information.

Introducing the `struct cmsghdr` Structure

Ancillary information can include zero, one, or more separate ancillary data objects. Each of these objects is preceded by a struct cmsghdr. This header is followed possibly by pad bytes and then the object itself. Finally, the ancillary data object itself might be followed by still more pad bytes before the next cmsghdr follows. In this chapter, the only ancillary data objects that you'll be concerned about will be the file descriptor and a credentials structure.

Figure 17.1 illustrates how a buffer containing ancillary data is structured.

Note the following additional points about Figure 17.1:

- The value of cmsg_len is equivalent to the length shown as the macro value for CMSG_LEN() in Figure 17.1.

- The macro CMSG_SPACE() computes the total necessary space required for one ancillary data object.

- The value of msg_controllen is the sum of the CMSG_SPACE() lengths, and is computed for each ancillary data object.

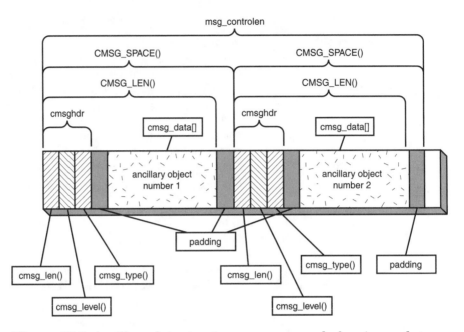

Figure 17.1: *Ancillary data structures are composed of various substructures, data zones, and pad bytes.*

The control message header itself is defined as the following C structure:

```
struct cmsghdr {
    socklen_t  cmsg_len;
    int        cmsg_level;
    int        cmsg_type;
/*  u_char     cmsg_data[]; */
};
```

EXAMPLE

Table 17.3 describes the members of this structure in detail.

Table 17.3: The **struct cmsghdr** *Members*

Member	Description
cmsg_len	This is the byte count of the ancillary data, which includes the size of this structural header. This value is computed by the CMSG_LEN() macro.
cmsg_level	This value indicates the originating protocol level (for example, SOL_SOCKET).
cmsg_type	This value indicates the control message type (for example, SCM_RIGHTS).
cmsg_data	This member does not actually exist. It is shown in comments to illustrate where additional ancillary data is located physically.

The example programs used in this chapter will use only a `cmsg_level` value of `SOL_SOCKET`. The control message types that are of interest to you in this chapter are shown in Table 17.4.

Table 17.4: `cmsg_type` *Types for* `cmsg_level=SOL_SOCKET`

cmsg_level	Description
SCM_RIGHTS	The ancillary data object is a file descriptor.
SCM_CREDENTIALS	The ancillary data object is a structure containing credential information.

Introducing the `cmsg(3)` Macros

Due to the complexity of structuring the ancillary data, a number of C macros were provided to make this easier for you. Additionally, these macros enable much greater portability between different UNIX platforms and provide some insulation against changes that might occur in the future. These macros are described by the man page `cmsg(3)` and the synopsis for them are as follows:

EXAMPLE

```
#include <sys/socket.h>

struct cmsghdr *CMSG_FIRSTHDR(struct msghdr *msgh);
struct cmsghdr *CMSG_NXTHDR(struct msghdr *msgh, struct cmsghdr *cmsg);
size_t CMSG_ALIGN(size_t length);
size_t CMSG_SPACE(size_t length);
size_t CMSG_LEN(size_t length);
void *CMSG_DATA(struct cmsghdr *cmsg);
```

TIP

Some of the macros presented in this chapter are not available on other UNIX platforms. For example, FreeBSD UNIX lacks the `CMSG_ALIGN()`, `CMSG_SPACE()`, and `CMSG_LEN()` macros. This should be borne in mind if you are writing code that must compile on other UNIX platforms in addition to Linux.

THE `CMSG_LEN()` MACRO

This macro accepts as an input parameter the size of the object that you want to place into the ancillary data buffer. If you review Figure 17.1, you see that this macro computes the byte length of the `cmsghdr` header structure plus any pad characters that might be required, added to the length of the data object. This value is used to set the `cmsg_len` member of the `cmsghdr` object.

The following example shows how you would compute the value for the `cmsg_len` member, if the ancillary object is a file descriptor (this example just prints the value):

```
int fd;    /* File descriptor */

printf("cmsg_len = %d\n",CMSG_LEN(sizeof fd));
```

EXAMPLE

THE CMSG_SPACE() MACRO

This macro is used to compute the total space required for the ancillary data object and its header. Although the CMSG_LEN() macro computes a similar length, the CMSG_LEN() value does not include possible trailing pad bytes (refer to Figure 17.1). The CMSG_SPACE() macro is useful for determining the buffer size requirements, as shown in the following example:

```
int fd;   /* File Descriptor */
char abuf[CMSG_SPACE(sizeof fd)];
```

EXAMPLE

This example declares enough buffer space in abuf[] to hold the header, pad bytes, the ancillary data object itself, and any final pad bytes. If multiple ancillary data objects are being constructed in the buffer, be sure to add multiple CMSG_SPACE() macro calls together to arrive at the total space required.

THE CMSG_DATA() MACRO

This macro accepts a pointer to the cmsghdr structure. The pointer value returned points to the first byte of ancillary data that follows the header and pad bytes, if any. If the pointer mptr points to a valid ancillary data message header that describes a file descriptor, the file descriptor can be extracted with the following example code:

```
struct cmsgptr *mptr;
int fd; /* File Descriptor */
...
fd = *(int *)CMSG_DATA(mptr);
```

EXAMPLE

THE CMSG_ALIGN() MACRO

This is a Linux extension macro that is not part of the Posix.1g standard. Given a byte length as input, this macro computes a new length, which includes any additional pad bytes that are required to maintain alignment.

THE CMSG_FIRSTHDR() MACRO

This macro is used to return a struct cmsghdr pointer to the first ancillary object within the ancillary data buffer. The input value is the pointer to the struct msghdr structure (do not confuse this with the struct cmsghdr). This macro evaluates the msghdr members msg_control and msg_controllen to determine whether any ancillary objects exist in the buffer. Then, it computes the pointer to be returned.

The pointer value returned is a NULL pointer if there is no ancillary data objects present. Otherwise, the pointer points to the first struct cmsghdr present. This macro is used at the start of a for loop, to start iterating through the ancillary data objects present.

THE CMSG_NXTHDR() MACRO

This macro is used to return the struct cmsghdr pointer of the next ancillary data object. This macro accepts two input arguments:

- The pointer to the struct msghdr structure

- The pointer to the current struct csmghdr

This macro returns a NULL pointer if there is no next ancillary data object.

Iterating Through Ancillary Data

When ancillary data is received, the CMSG_FIRSTHDR() and CMSG_NEXTHDR() macros are used to iterate through the ancillary data objects. The following example code shows the general form that the for loop and macros should take:

EXAMPLE

```
struct msghdr msgh;       /* Message Hdr */
struct cmsghdr *cmsg;     /* Ptr to ancillary hdr */
int *fd_ptr;              /* Ptr to file descript.*/
int received_fd;          /* The file descriptor */

for ( cmsg=CMSG_FIRSTHDR(&msgh); cmsg!=NULL; cmsg=CMSG_NXTHDR(&msgh,cmsg) ) {
    if ( cmsg->cmsg_level == SOL_SOCKET && cmsg->cmsg_type == SCM_RIGHTS ) {
        fd_ptr = (int *) CMSG_DATA(cmsg);
        received_fd = *fd_ptr;
        break;
    }
}

if ( cmsg == NULL ) {
    /* Error: No file descriptor recv'd */
}
```

The general procedure is as follows:

1. The for loop initializes by obtaining the first ancillary data header (struct cmsghdr) using the macro CMSG_FIRSTHDR().

2. The for loop tests whether the pointer cmsg is NULL. The body of the for loop is executed if this pointer is not NULL.

3. The if statement applies two tests to the struct cmsghdr header structure: The program is interested only in messages that are at the

cmsg_level equal to SOL_SOCKET and is of the message type SCM_RIGHTS. This identifies an ancillary data object that represents a file descriptor.

4. If the test in step 3 succeeds, the pointer to the file descriptor is stored in pointer variable fd_ptr.

5. The pointer fd_ptr is then used to extract the file descriptor out of the ancillary data buffer into the variable received_fd.

6. The control leaves the for loop with the break statement, because the program has located the information it was interested in.

7. The if statement test that follows the for loop tests the cmsg pointer variable to see whether the ancillary data object was found. If the pointer cmsg is NULL, this indicates the for loop ran until completion without finding the file descriptor. When it is not NULL, this indicates that the break statement was executed, indicating that the file descriptor was indeed extracted.

This covers the general outline for extracting data from an ancillary data buffer.

Creating Ancillary Data

The process that wants to send a file descriptor must create an ancillary data buffer with the correctly formatted data within it. The following code outlines the general procedure:

EXAMPLE

```
struct msghdr msg;              /* Message header   */
struct cmsghdr *cmsg; /* Ptr to ancillary hdr  */
int fd;              /* File descriptor to send */
char buf[CMSG_SPACE(sizeof fd)];  /* Anc. buf   */
int *fd_ptr;         /* Ptr to file descriptor  */

msg.msg_control = buf;
msg.msg_controllen = sizeof buf;

cmsg = CMSG_FIRSTHDR(&msg);
cmsg->cmsg_level = SOL_SOCKET;
cmsg->cmsg_type = SCM_RIGHTS;
cmsg->cmsg_len = CMSG_LEN(sizeof fd);

/* Initialize the payload: */
fd_ptr = (int *)CMSG_DATA(cmsg);
*fd_ptr = fd;

/*
 * Sum of the length of all control
 * messages in the buffer:
 */
msg.msg_controllen = cmsg->cmsg_len;
```

The general procedure used is as follows:

1. The ancillary data buffer was declared to make room to format an ancillary data object (array variable buf[ ]). Notice that the CMSG_SPACE() macro is used to compute the size of the buffer that is required.

2. The message header members msg_control and msg_controllen are initialized to point to the ancillary buffer and assign its maximum length, respectively.

3. The pointer cmsg is initialized to point at the first ancillary data object within the buffer using the CMSG_FIRSTHDR() macro. Note that the input argument to the macro is the pointer to the message header (&msg) and is not the pointer to the ancillary data buffer.

4. The ancillary data object's header is initialized by setting cmsg->cmsg_level and cmsg->cmsg_type.

5. The length of the ancillary data object is established by using the CMSG_LEN() macro with the size of the file descriptor as the input value.

6. The pointer to the file descriptor within the ancillary data buffer is determined by using the CMSG_DATA() macro.

7. The file descriptor fd is then copied into the ancillary data buffer using the pointer fd_ptr.

8. Finally, the total ancillary message length is computed and assigned to msg.msg_controllen.

NOTE

If there is more than one ancillary data object included, you must be sure that msg.msg_controllen is the sum of all of the parts. Additionally, be certain to sum the total requirements needed for the buffer (buf[ ] in the example shown).

Presenting an Ancillary Data Example

Now, it is time to present the software in order to tie all of the concepts together into a concrete example pair of programs. Two programs will be presented:

- A socket server
- A very simple Web server

The Web server will serve one, and only one, simple demonstration HTML page. The socket server will be used to gain access to a port 80 socket without requiring root access or root setuid.

NOTE

If you have a Web server running already, you will need to terminate it, if it uses port 80. For Red Hat Linux 6.0 users, you can stop your Web server from the root account as follows:

```
# /etc/rc.d/init.d/httpd stop
Shutting down http:              [   OK   ]
#
```

The following sections will present the various source code components.

The Common Header File `common.h`

This file simply lists all function prototypes and other common definitions and include files (see Listing 17.2).

EXAMPLE

Listing 17.2: common.h—The common.h Header File

```
1:    /* common.h
2:     *
3:     * Source common to all modules:
4:     */
5:    #include <stdio.h>
6:    #include <unistd.h>
7:    #include <stdlib.h>
8:    #include <errno.h>
9:    #include <string.h>
10:   #include <fcntl.h>
11:   #include <time.h>
12:   #include <sys/types.h>
13:   #include <sys/socket.h>
14:   #include <netinet/in.h>
15:   #include <sys/un.h>
16:   #include <sys/uio.h>
17:
18:   #ifndef TRUE
19:   #define TRUE    1
20:   #define FALSE   0
21:   #endif
22:
23:   extern void bail(const char *on_what);
24:
25:   extern int recv_fd(int s);
26:
27:   extern int reqport(int port);
28:
29:   extern int send_fd(
30:       int s,int fd,
31:       void *addr,socklen_t alen);
```

```
32:
33:   extern int recv_cred(
34:       int s,struct ucred *credp,
35:       void *buf,unsigned bufsiz,
36:       void *addr,socklen_t *alen);
```

The `misc.c` Module

This module lists a small error-handling function that is in common with both programs. This self-explanatory module is shown in Listing 17.3.

EXAMPLE

Listing 17.3: `misc.c`—The `misc.c` Module

```
1:    /* misc.c:
2:     *
3:     * Misc. Functions:
4:     */
5:    #include "common.h"
6:
7:    /*
8:     *
9:     * This function reports the error to
10:    * the log file and calls exit(1).
11:    */
12:   void
13:   bail(const char *on_what) {
14:
15:       if ( errno != 0 )
16:           fprintf(stderr,"%s: ",strerror(errno));
17:       fprintf(stderr,"%s\n",on_what);
18:
19:       exit(1);
20:   }
```

The `recvcred.c` Module

Listing 17.4 shows the source module `recvcred.c`, which is used by our example programs. The `recv_cred()` function centralizes much of the work of receiving data and user credentials.

Listing 17.4: `recvcred.c`—The `recvcred.c` source module

```
1:    /* recvcred.c
2:     *
3:     * Send a file descriptor:
4:     */
5:    #include "common.h"
6:
7:    /*
```

continues

Listing 17.4: continued

```
 8:     * Receive Data & Credentials:
 9:     *
10:     * ARGUMENTS:
11:     *  s        Socket to read from
12:     *  credp    Ptr to receiving area for cred.
13:     *  buf      Ptr to receiving buffer for data
14:     *  bufsiz   Maximum # of bytes for buffer
15:     *  addr     Ptr to buffer to receive peer
16:     *           address (or NULL)
17:     *  alen     Ptr to Maximum byte length
18:     *           (updated with actual length
19:     *           upon return.)
20:     *
21:     * RETURNS:
22:     *  >=0   ·   Data bytes read
23:     *  -1       Failed: check errno
24:     *
25:     * NOTES:
26:     *  The value -1 is returned with errno set
27:     *  to ENOENT, if data is returned without
28:     *  any credentials.
29:     */
30:    int
31:    recv_cred(
32:       int s,                              /* Socket */
33:       struct ucred *credp, /* Credential buffer   */
34:       void *buf,        /* Receiving Data buffer  */
35:       unsigned bufsiz,   /* Recv. Data buf size   */
36:       void *addr,        /* Received Peer address  */
37:       socklen_t *alen) {  /* Ptr to addr length    */
38:
39:        int z;
40:        struct msghdr msgh;   /* Message header */
41:        struct iovec iov[1];       /* I/O vector */
42:        struct cmsghdr *cmsgp = NULL;
43:        char mbuf[CMSG_SPACE(sizeof *credp)];
44:
45:        /*
46:         * Zero out message areas:
47:         */
48:        memset(&msgh,0,sizeof msgh);
49:        memset(mbuf,0,sizeof mbuf);
50:
51:        /*
52:         * Establish datagram address (if any):
53:         */
```

```
54:        msgh.msg_name = addr;
55:        msgh.msg_namelen = alen ? *alen : 0;
56:
57:        /*
58:         * Point to our I/O vector of 1 element:
59:         */
60:        msgh.msg_iov = iov;
61:        msgh.msg_iovlen = 1;
62:
63:        /*
64:         * Initialize our 1 I/O element vector:
65:         */
66:        iov[0].iov_base = buf;
67:        iov[0].iov_len = bufsiz;
68:
69:        /*
70:         * Initialize control structure:
71:         */
72:        msgh.msg_control = mbuf;
73:        msgh.msg_controllen = sizeof mbuf;
74:
75:        /*
76:         * Receive a message:
77:         */
78:        do  {
79:            z = recvmsg(s,&msgh,0);
80:        } while ( z == -1 && errno == EINTR );
81:
82:        if ( z == -1 )
83:            return -1;   /* Failed: check errno */
84:
85:        /*
86:         * If ptr alen is non-NULL, return the
87:         * returned address length (datagrams):
88:         */
89:        if ( alen )
90:            *alen = msgh.msg_namelen;
91:
92:        /*
93:         * Walk the list of control messages:
94:         */
95:        for ( cmsgp = CMSG_FIRSTHDR(&msgh);
96:            cmsgp != NULL;
97:            cmsgp = CMSG_NXTHDR(&msgh,cmsgp) ) {
98:
99:            if ( cmsgp->cmsg_level == SOL_SOCKET
```

continues

Listing 17.4: continued

```
100:          && cmsgp->cmsg_type == SCM_CREDENTIALS ) {
101:
102:              /*
103:               * Pass back credentials struct:
104:               */
105:              *credp = *
106:                  (struct ucred *) CMSG_DATA(cmsgp);
107:
108:              return z; /* # of data bytes read */
109:          }
110:      }
111:
112:      /*
113:       * There were no credentials found. An error
114:       * is returned here, since this application
115:       * insists on getting credentials.
116:       */
117:      errno = ENOENT;
118:      return -1;
119: }
```

The highlights of this source module are as follows:

- The arguments used by the function recv_cred() are described in the program comments in lines 11 to 19.

- Lines 39 to 43 define the various variables and control structures needed.

- The function body is defined in lines 44 to 119.

The general procedure used by the recv_cred() function is as follows:

1. Lines 48 to 73 perform all of the initialization required in preparation for the recvmsg(2) function call.

2. Lines 78 to 83 accomplish the read function by calling upon recvmsg(2). This function reads both data and ancillary data at the same time.

3. Lines 92 to 110 extract the user credentials from the ancillary data. If the credentials are found, the number of data bytes received is returned in line 108.

4. When no credentials are received, this recv_cred() function returns –1 with errno set to ENOENT (lines 112 to 118). This tells the calling program that no user credentials were returned.

TIP

The struct ucred used in line 33 of Listing 17.4 is not portable to all UNIX platforms. For example, FreeBSD uses the struct cmsgcred instead.

The Simple Web Server web80

This very simple Web server is designed to operate two ways:

- Without the socket server
- With the socket server

This will help illustrate the problem and how the problem was solved. Listing 17.5 shows the web80.c module.

Listing 17.5: web80.c—The Simple Web Server Module web80.c

```
1:   /* web80.c:
2:    *
3:    * This is an extremely simple Web server:
4:    *
5:    * This program runs in two modes:
6:    *
7:    * 1. Standalone Mode:
8:    *    $ ./web80 standalone
9:    *
10:   *    In this mode, this program functions
11:   *    as a very simple standalone Web server.
12:   *    However, it must run as root to bind
13:   *    to the Web port 80.
14:   *
15:   * 2. Sock Server Mode:
16:   *    $ ./web80
17:   *
18:   *    In this mode, this program contacts
19:   *    the sockserv server to request a
20:   *    socket bound to port 80. If sockserv
21:   *    allows the request, it returns
22:   *    a port 80 socket. This allows this
23:   *    program to run without root and
24:   *    with no setuid requirement.
25:   */
26:  #include "common.h"
27:
28:  int
29:  main(int argc,char **argv) {
30:      int z;
```

continues

Listing 17.5: continued

```
31:      int s;              /* Web Server socket */
32:      int c;                /* Client socket */
33:      int alen;            /* Address length */
34:      struct sockaddr_in a_web; /* Web Server   */
35:      struct sockaddr_in a_cln;/* Client addr   */
36:      int b = TRUE;        /* For SO_REUSEADDR  */
37:      FILE *rx;              /* Read Stream */
38:      FILE *tx;              /* Write Stream */
39:      char getbuf[2048];       /* GET buffer   */
40:      time_t td;        /* Current date & time  */
41:
42:      /*
43:       * If any arguments are present on the
44:       * command line, obtain the socket
45:       * without help from the server (run
46:       * in simple standalone mode):
47:       */
48:      if ( argc > 1 ) {
49:          /*
50:           * Standalone mode:
51:           */
52:          s = socket(PF_INET,SOCK_STREAM,0);
53:          if ( s == -1 )
54:              bail("socket(2)");
55:
56:          /*
57:           * Web address on port 80:
58:           */
59:          memset(&a_web,0,sizeof a_web);
60:          a_web.sin_family = AF_INET;
61:          a_web.sin_port = ntohs(80);
62:          a_web.sin_addr.s_addr =
63:              ntohl(INADDR_ANY);
64:
65:          /*
66:           * Bind the Web server address-
67:           * we need to be root to succeed
68:           * at this:
69:           */
70:          z = bind(s,
71:              (struct sockaddr *)&a_web,
72:              sizeof a_web);
73:          if ( z == -1 )
74:              bail("binding port 80");
75:
76:          /*
```

```
77:                 * Turn on SO_REUSEADDR:
78:                 */
79:                z = setsockopt(s,SOL_SOCKET,
80:                    SO_REUSEADDR,&b,sizeof b);
81:                if ( z == -1 )
82:                    bail("setsockopt(2)");
83:
84:        } else  {
85:            /*
86:             * Run in sockserv mode:  Request
87:             * a socket bound to port 80:
88:             */
89:            s = reqport(80);
90:            if ( s == -1 )
91:                bail("reqport(80)");
92:        }
93:
94:        /*
95:         * Now make this a listening socket:
96:         */
97:        z = listen(s,10);
98:        if ( z == -1 )
99:            bail("listen(2)");
100:
101:        /*
102:         * Perform a simple, Web server loop for
103:         * demonstration purposes. Here we just
104:         * accept one line of input text, and
105:         * ignore it. We provide one simple
106:         * HTML page back in response:
107:         */
108:        for (;;) {
109:            /*
110:             * Wait for a connect from browser:
111:             */
112:            alen = sizeof a_cln;
113:            c = accept(s,
114:                (struct sockaddr *)&a_cln,
115:                &alen);
116:            if ( c == -1 ) {
117:                perror("accept(2)");
118:                continue;
119:            }
120:
121:            /*
122:             * Create streams for convenience, and
```

continues

Listing 17.5: continued

```
123:              * just eat any Web command provided:
124:              */
125:             rx = fdopen(c,"r");
126:             tx = fdopen(dup(c),"w");
127:             fgets(getbuf,sizeof getbuf,rx);
128:
129:             /*
130:              * Now serve a simple HTML response.
131:              * This includes this Web server's
132:              * process ID and the current date
133:              * and time:
134:              */
135:             fputs("<HTML>\n"
136:                 "<HEAD>\n"
137:                 "<TITLE>Test Page for this little "
138:                     "web80 server</TITLE>\n"
139:                 "</HEAD>\n"
140:                 "<BODY>\n"
141:                 "<H1>web80 Worked!</H1>\n",tx);
142:
143:             time(&td);
144:             fprintf(tx,
145:                 "<H2>From PID %ld @ %s</H2>\n",
146:                 (long)getpid(),
147:                 ctime(&td));
148:
149:             fputs("</BODY>\n"
150:                 "</HTML>\n",tx);
151:
152:             fclose(tx);
153:             fclose(rx);
154:         }
155:
156:     return 0;
157: }
```

The very simple Web server in Listing 17.5 uses the following basic procedure:

1. If command-line arguments are provided, a socket is created and bound with bind(2) if it can (lines 49 to 83). This allows you to prove that you need root access to obtain such a port under Linux.

2. If no command line arguments are provided, the code between lines 89 and 91 is executed instead. Line 89 calls upon a function reqport() to obtain a socket on port 80.

3. The function listen(2) is called to allow connections to this socket (lines 97 to 99).

4. The for loop allows for a continuous number of client connections to take place to this Web server (line 108).

5. Lines 112 to 154 form the body of the for loop, which simply waits for one text line of input and then sends some formatted HTML back to the client in return. The client's socket is closed at lines 152 and 153.

Note in lines 144 to 147 that the process ID of the Web server is reported back to the browser so that you can have confirmation of where this information came from.

The reqport() Function

In the web80.c program of Listing 17.5, you saw that there was a call to the function reqport(). This function is responsible for contacting the socket server and obtaining a socket on port 80. Listing 17.6 shows the listing of this function.

EXAMPLE

Listing 17.6: reqport.c—The reqport() Function

```
 1:    /* reqport.c
 2:     *
 3:     * Request a port from the sockserv:
 4:     */
 5:    #include "common.h"
 6:
 7:    /*
 8:     * Request a INADDR_ANY socket on the
 9:     * port number requested:
10:     *
11:     * ARGUMENTS:
12:     *  s       Socket to send request on
13:     *  port    Port (host order) being requested
14:     *
15:     * RETURNS:
16:     *  >= 0    Socket to use
17:     *  -1      Failed: check errno
18:     */
19:    int
20:    reqport(int port) {
21:        int z;
22:        int s;                          /* socket */
23:        struct sockaddr_un a_srvr;/* serv. adr */
24:
25:        /*
```

continues

Listing 17.6: continued

```
26:        * Create a Unix Socket:
27:        */
28:       s = socket(PF_LOCAL,SOCK_STREAM,0);
29:       if ( s == -1 )
30:           return -1;   /* Failed: check errno */
31:
32:       /*
33:        * Create the abstract address of
34:        * the socket server:
35:        */
36:       memset(&a_srvr,0,sizeof a_srvr);
37:       a_srvr.sun_family = AF_LOCAL;
38:       strncpy(a_srvr.sun_path,
39:           "zSOCKET-SERVER",
40:           sizeof a_srvr.sun_path-1);
41:       a_srvr.sun_path[0] = 0;
42:
43:       /*
44:        * Connect to the sock server:
45:        */
46:       z = connect(s,&a_srvr,sizeof a_srvr);
47:       if ( z == -1 )
48:           return -1;   /* Failed: check errno */
49:
50:       /*
51:        * Now issue our request:
52:        */
53:       do  {
54:           z = write(s,&port,sizeof port);
55:       } while ( z == -1 && errno == EINTR );
56:
57:       if ( z == -1 )
58:           return -1;     /* Failed: see errno */
59:
60:       /*
61:        * Now wait for a reply:
62:        */
63:       z = recv_fd(s);
64:       close(s);
65:
66:       return z;                 /* z == fd or -1 */
67:   }
```

The procedure that function reqport() implements is as follows:

1. The function accepts as input the port number being requested (line 20). The web80.c program calls this function with the argument 80.

2. A PF_LOCAL (PF_UNIX) socket is created in lines 28 to 30. This socket must be a PF_LOCAL socket in order that credentials be available to the receiving server.

3. An abstract server address is formed in lines 36 to 41. This will be used to contact the socket server.

4. A call to connect(2) is made to contact the socket server (lines 46 to 48).

5. A write(2) call is used to send the port number that is being requested.

6. The function recv_fd() is called to obtain the server response (line 63). The return value will be >= 0 if a socket was received, or -1 if an error was received instead.

7. The socket or the value -1 is returned in line 66.

Now you must investigate the workings of recv_fd() to see how the file descriptor was received.

The recv_fd() Function

Listing 17.7 shows the code for the function recv_fd().

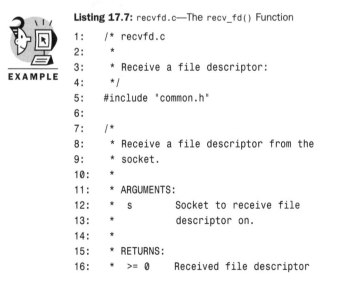

EXAMPLE

Listing 17.7: recvfd.c—The recv_fd() Function

```
1:    /* recvfd.c
2:     *
3:     * Receive a file descriptor:
4:     */
5:    #include "common.h"
6:
7:    /*
8:     * Receive a file descriptor from the
9:     * socket.
10:    *
11:    * ARGUMENTS:
12:    *   s         Socket to receive file
13:    *             descriptor on.
14:    *
15:    * RETURNS:
16:    *   >= 0      Received file descriptor
```

continues

Listing 17.7: continued

```
17:   *   -1         Failed: See errno
18:   */
19:  int
20:  recv_fd(int s) {
21:      int z;
22:      struct msghdr msgh;   /* Message header */
23:      struct iovec iov[1];      /* I/O vector */
24:      struct cmsghdr *cmsgp = NULL;
25:      char buf[CMSG_SPACE(sizeof(int))];
26:      char dbuf[80];     /* Small data buffer */
27:
28:      /*
29:       * Initialize structures to zero bytes:
30:       */
31:      memset(&msgh,0,sizeof msgh);
32:      memset(buf,0,sizeof buf);
33:
34:      /*
35:       * No socket addresses are used here:
36:       */
37:      msgh.msg_name = NULL;
38:      msgh.msg_namelen = 0;
39:
40:      /*
41:       * Install our I/O vector:
42:       */
43:      msgh.msg_iov = iov;
44:      msgh.msg_iovlen = 1;
45:
46:      /*
47:       * Initialize I/O vector to read data
48:       * into our dbuf[] array:
49:       */
50:      iov[0].iov_base = dbuf;
51:      iov[0].iov_len = sizeof dbuf;
52:
53:      /*
54:       * Load control data into buf[]:
55:       */
56:      msgh.msg_control = buf;
57:      msgh.msg_controllen = sizeof buf;
58:
59:      /*
60:       * Receive a message:
61:       */
62:      do  {
```

```
63:            z = recvmsg(s,&msgh,0);
64:        } while ( z == -1 && errno == EINTR );
65:
66:        if ( z == -1 )
67:            return -1;      /* Failed: see errno */
68:
69:        /*
70:         * Walk the control structure looking for
71:         * a file descriptor:
72:         */
73:        for ( cmsgp = CMSG_FIRSTHDR(&msgh);
74:            cmsgp != NULL;
75:            cmsgp = CMSG_NXTHDR(&msgh,cmsgp) ) {
76:
77:            if ( cmsgp->cmsg_level == SOL_SOCKET
78:            && cmsgp->cmsg_type == SCM_RIGHTS ) {
79:                /*
80:                 * File descriptor found:
81:                 */
82:                return *(int *) CMSG_DATA(cmsgp);
83:            }
84:        }
85:
86:        /*
87:         * No file descriptor was received:
88:         * If we received 4 bytes, assume we
89:         * received an errno value... then
90:         * set errno from our received data.
91:         */
92:        if ( z == sizeof (int) )
93:            errno = *(int *)dbuf; /* Rcvd errno */
94:        else
95:            errno = ENOENT;      /* Default errno */
96:
97:        return -1; /* Return failure indication */
98: }
```

The function recv_fd() implements the following procedure:

1. The input argument s is the socket that the server response is to come from (line 20).

2. This function expects to receive only one ancillary data object containing a file descriptor. This allows the buffer size to be simply stated as shown in line 25. Note that if multiple ancillary objects might be received, you will need to declare a larger buffer than the one shown on line 25.

3. Ancillary data can be received only with data. Hence, a small data buffer is declared in line 26 to receive some data.

4. The message header msgh and buffer buf are cleared to zero bytes (lines 31 and 32). This step can be omitted for efficiency if you like, but is recommended while you are debugging.

5. The message header members msg_name and msg_namelen are nulled out because no socket address is required (a stream socket is being used). If you are using a datagram socket, you will want to receive the socket address so that you know where the datagram came from.

6. The pointer to the I/O vector is established in lines 43 and 44. Additionally, it is established that it has exactly one entry.

7. The I/O vector itself is established in lines 50 and 51. The first I/O vector entry iov[0] is set to receive data into buffer dbuf (line 50) for a maximum size indicated in line 51.

8. The recvmsg(2) function is called in lines 62 to 64. If an error occurs, this function exits with the return statement in line 67.

9. The ancillary data is iterated through using the CMSG_FIRSTHDR() and CMSG_NXTHDR() macros (lines 73 to 84). If an ancillary data object of level SOL_SOCKET and of type SCM_RIGHTS is found, the function returns the file descriptor in line 82.

10. If the socket server denied the request or failed, the data buffer contains the (int) value of the server's errno value. This function stores this errno value into the calling process' errno variable in line 93. If received data is not sizeof(int), then the function sets the errno value to ENOENT (line 95). This should never happen unless the wrong server was contacted, or the server had a bug.

11. The return value is -1 when the error has been stuffed into errno (line 97).

In the following sections, you will look at the code behind the socket server.

The socksexv Server Program

The socket server is the server program that will run as root. This gives it the capability to create and bind a socket on port 80. However, this is the only component that runs with this privilege, and you will have full control over who gets what by having the server examine the credentials of the request. Listing 17.8 shows the source code for the socket server.

Listing 17.8: sockserv.c—The Socket Server

```
1:   /* sockserv.c:
2:    *
3:    * This simple server will serve up a socket
4:    * to a valid recipient:
5:    */
6:   #include "common.h"
7:   #include <pwd.h>
8:
9:   /*
10:   * Check user's access:
11:   *
12:   * RETURNS:
13:   *   ptr      To (struct passwd *) if granted.
14:   *   NULL     Access is to be denied.
15:   */
16:  static struct passwd *
17:  check_access(
18:    int port,          /* Port being requested */
19:    struct ucred *pcred, /* User credentials */
20:    char **uidlist) { /* List of valid users */
21:      int x;
22:      struct passwd *pw; /* User passwd entry */
23:
24:      /*
25:       * Look the user's uid # up in the
26:       * /etc/password file:
27:       */
28:      if ( (pw = getpwuid(pcred->uid)) != 0 ) {
29:          /*
30:           * Make sure request is coming from
31:           * one of the acceptable users:
32:           */
33:          for ( x=0; uidlist[x]; ++x )
34:              if ( !strcmp(uidlist[x],pw->pw_name) )
35:                  break;
36:          if ( !uidlist[x] )
37:              pw = 0;         /* Access denied */
38:      }
39:
40:      /*
41:       * Screen the port #. For this demo,
42:       * only port 80 is permitted.
43:       */
44:      if ( port != 80 )
45:          pw = 0;             /* Access denied */
```

continues

Listing 17.8: continued

```
46:
47:      return pw;    /* NULL or ptr if granted */
48:  }
49:
50:  /*
51:   * Access has been granted: send socket
52:   * to client.
53:   *
54:   * ARGUMENTS:
55:   *  c        Client socket
56:   *  port     Port requested
57:   *
58:   * RETURNS:
59:   *  0        Success
60:   *  -1       Failed: check errno
61:   */
62:  static int
63:  grant_access(int c,int port) {
64:      int z;
65:      int fd = -1;             /* New socket fd */
66:      int b = TRUE;            /* Boolean TRUE */
67:      struct sockaddr_in addr;/* work address  */
68:
69:      /*
70:       * Create a new TCP/IP socket:
71:       */
72:      fd = socket(PF_INET,SOCK_STREAM,0);
73:      if ( fd == -1 ) {
74:          perror("socket(2)");
75:          goto errxit;
76:      }
77:
78:      /*
79:       * Turn on SO_REUSEADDR:
80:       */
81:      z = setsockopt(fd,SOL_SOCKET,
82:          SO_REUSEADDR,&b,sizeof b);
83:      if ( z == -1 )
84:          bail("setsockopt(2)");
85:
86:      /*
87:       * Create the address to bind:
88:       */
89:      memset(&addr,0,sizeof addr);
90:      addr.sin_family = AF_INET;
91:      addr.sin_port = ntohs(port);
```

```
 92:        addr.sin_addr.s_addr = ntohl(INADDR_ANY);
 93:
 94:        /*
 95:         * Bind the requested address:
 96:         */
 97:        z = bind(fd,
 98:            (struct sockaddr *)&addr,
 99:            sizeof addr);
100:        if ( z == -1 ) {
101:            fprintf(stderr,"%s: binding port %d\n",
102:                strerror(errno),port);
103:            goto errxit;
104:        }
105:
106:        /*
107:         * Send the fd back to the
108:         * requesting client:
109:         */
110:        z = send_fd(c,fd,NULL,0);
111:        if ( z == -1 ) {
112:            perror("send_fd()");
113:            goto errxit;
114:        }
115:
116:        close(fd);          /* finished with fd */
117:        return 0;                   /* Success*/
118:
119: errxit:
120:        z = errno;                  /* Save errno */
121:        if ( fd )
122:            close(fd);        /* Release socket */
123:        errno = z;                /* Restore errno */
124:        return -1;
125: }
126:
127: /*
128:  * Process a connected client's request:
129:  */
130: void
131: process_client(
132:    int c,                       /* Client socket */
133:    char **uidlist      /* List of valid users   */
134:    ) {
135:        int z;
136:        int er;             /* Captured errno value */
137:        int b = TRUE;            /* Boolean: True */
```

continues

Listing 17.8: continued

```
138:     struct ucred cred;  /* Clnt credentials */
139:     short port;     /* Port being requested */
140:     struct passwd *pw; /* User passwd entry */
141:
142:     /*
143:      * Now make certain that we can receive
144:      * credentials on this socket:
145:      */
146:     z = setsockopt(c,
147:         SOL_SOCKET,
148:         SO_PASSCRED,
149:         &b,
150:         sizeof b);
151:     if ( z )
152:         bail("setsockopt(2)");
153:
154:     /*
155:      * Receive a request with the
156:      * user credentials:
157:      */
158:     z = recv_cred(c,          /* socket */
159:         &cred, /* Returned credentials */
160:         &port,       /* Returned port # */
161:         sizeof port,   /* Size of data */
162:         NULL, 0); /* no socket address */
163:
164:     if ( z == -1 )
165:         perror("recv_cred()");
166:
167:     /*
168:      * Now check access. If pw is returned
169:      * as non-NULL, the request is OK.
170:      */
171:     pw = check_access(port,&cred,uidlist);
172:
173:     if ( pw ) {
174:         if ( !grant_access(c,port) ) {
175:             close(c);
176:             return;   /* request sucessful */
177:         }
178:         /* Failed */
179:         er = errno;       /* Capture reason */
180:     } else {
181:         /*
182:          * Userid was not known, or not in
183:          * the privileged list:
```

```
184:         */
185:         er = EACCES;          /* Perm denied */
186:     }
187:
188:     /*
189:      * Control reaches here if the
190:      * request failed or is denied:
191:      *
192:      * Here we simply send the error
193:      * code back without a file
194:      * descriptor. This lack of a fd
195:      * will be detected by the client.
196:      */
197:     do  {
198:         z = write(c,&er,sizeof er);
199:     } while ( z == -1 && errno == EINTR );
200:
201:     if ( z == -1 )
202:         perror("write(2)");
203: }
204:
205: /*
206:  * Main program:
207:  */
208: int
209: main(int argc,char **argv) {
210:     int z;
211:     int s;                 /* Server UDP socket */
212:     int c;                    /* Client socket */
213:     int alen;              /* Address length */
214:     struct sockaddr_un a_srvr;  /* Server @  */
215:     struct sockaddr_un a_clnt;  /* Client @  */
216:
217:     /*
218:      * Make sure we have a userid specified:
219:      */
220:     if ( argc < 2 ) {
221:         fputs("Must have at least 1 userid.\n",
222:             stderr);
223:         exit(1);
224:     }
225:
226:     /*
227:      * Create a Unix Socket:
228:      */
229:     s = socket(PF_LOCAL,SOCK_STREAM,0);
```

continues

Listing 17.8: continued

```
230:    if ( s == -1 )
231:        bail("socket(2)");
232:
233:    /*
234:     * Create abstract address:
235:     */
236:    memset(&a_srvr,0,sizeof a_srvr);
237:    a_srvr.sun_family = AF_LOCAL;
238:    strncpy(a_srvr.sun_path,
239:        "zSOCKET-SERVER",
240:        sizeof a_srvr.sun_path-1);
241:    a_srvr.sun_path[0] = 0;
242:
243:    /*
244:     * Bind the server address:
245:     */
246:    z = bind(s,
247:        (struct sockaddr *)&a_srvr,
248:        sizeof a_srvr);
249:    if ( z == -1 )
250:        bail("bind(2)");
251:
252:    /*
253:     * Now make this a listening socket:
254:     */
255:    z = listen(s,10);
256:    if ( z == -1 )
257:        bail("listen(2)");
258:
259:    /*
260:     * Now process requests:
261:     */
262:    for (;;) {
263:        /*
264:         * Wait for a connect:
265:         */
266:        alen = sizeof a_clnt;
267:        c = accept(s,&a_clnt,&alen);
268:        if ( c == -1 )
269:            bail("accept(2)");
270:
271:        /*
272:         * Process this request:
273:         */
274:        process_client(c,argv+1);
275:        close(c);
```

```
276:     }
277:
278:     return 0;
279: }
```

The listing for the socket server is quite long, so let's break up the study of it into smaller segments. The procedure used by the main() program is as follows:

1. The socket server program insists on at least one command-line argument. Each argument is the name of a userID that is permitted to request a socket on port 80 (lines 220 to 224).

2. A PF_LOCAL (PF_UNIX) streams socket is created, and bound to an abstract socket address (lines 229 to 250).

3. The listen(2) function is called to allow connects to this socket (lines 255 to 257).

4. The top of the server loop starts with the for statement in line 262.

5. The connection is accepted in lines 266 to 269.

6. The client program's request is serviced by calling process_client() in line 274, and then the client's socket is closed (line 275).

7. The server continues with step 4 until the server is terminated.

Now, examine the process_client() function's steps:

1. This function accepts as input (lines 131 to 134) the client socket c and the list of userIDs that are granted permission to make requests (this argument comes from argv[]).

2. The socket must have option SOL_SOCKET SO_PASSCRED enabled before credentials can be received. Lines 146 to 152 enable this socket feature.

3. The function recv_cred() (Listing 17.4) is called to receive the request and the client's credentials (lines 158 to 165). The request is returned in variable port which is the port number. The credentials will be returned in variable cred, which is declared in line 138. The recv_cred() program is designed to return -1 if no credentials were received.

4. With the value port being requested, and the credentials cred available, the request for access is tested in function check_access() (line 171). If the pointer value pw is returned without being NULL, the access is to be granted. Otherwise, access is to be denied.

5. Line 173 tests the pointer pw for NULL. If not NULL, the function grant_access() is called to comply with the request. When the request

is granted successfully, the function returns to the caller in line 176. If, however, it fails (and it can), the error is captured in variable er in line 179.

6. If the access has been denied, er is set to the error code EACCES (line 185).

7. The write(2) call in lines 197 to 202 is executed if the access was denied or the granting of the request failed. This response simply sends the error code captured in variable er back to the caller as normal data.

Now, examine the code for check_access():

1. The input values accepted are the port number, the credentials pointer pcred and the privileged userID list uidlist (lines 16 to 20).

2. The function getpwuid(3) is called to look up the userID number found in the credentials. If the value is not found in the /etc/passwd database, it is immediately rejected by not executing lines 29 to 38. The pointer pw will be NULL when this happens.

3. When step 2 succeeds, the for loop in lines 33 to 37 are executed to see whether the requesting user is a member of the privileged list. If so, the break statement in line 35 is executed.

4. Lines 44 to 45 perform one further test: This module insists that only port 80 is available. If any other port is requested, the request is denied by line 45. This area can be customized if you want to experiment with making other ports available.

5. The return statement in line 47 returns the pointer pw. If the pointer managed not to be set to NULL by some condition in this function, then the user and the request were considered valid.

Now, you must look at the code for function grant_access(). This function implements the following steps:

1. The function grant_access() accepts as input the client socket c and the port number being granted (lines 62 and 63).

2. A PF_INET SOCK_STREAM socket is created in lines 72 to 76.

3. The socket option SO_REUSEADDR is enabled in lines 81 to 84. This is especially useful if you don't like having to wait to restart your servers that use this socket.

4. The socket address is bound to INADDR_ANY for the port requested (lines 89 to 92). The port is established in line 91.

5. The socket is bound by calling bind(2) in lines 97 to 104. This is where root access is required, which the server possesses.

6. The bound socket now must be sent back to the client over socket c. This is accomplished by calling send_fd() in lines 110 to 114.

7. Because the socket fd has been sent to the client on socket c, the server closes it in line 116 (it is not required by the server).

8. If any errors occur in granting the request in this function, control passes to label errxit (lines 119 to 124). Here, the error is captured and the socket fd is closed if it was created. The return value is -1 from this function if it fails, with a corresponding error code established in errno (line 123).

That ends the tour of the socket server module. The next section examines the send_fd() function code.

The send_fd() Function

The socket server calls upon the send_fd() function to send the created and bound socket back to the requesting process. Listing 17.9 shows the source code listing for this function.

EXAMPLE

Listing 17.9: sendfd.c—The send_fd() Function

```
1:    /* sendfd.c
2:     *
3:     * Send a file descriptor:
4:     */
5:    #include "common.h"
6:
7:    /*
8:     * Send a file descriptor via socket:
9:     *
10:    * ARGUMENTS:
11:    *   s       Socket to send on
12:    *   fd      Open file descriptor to send
13:    *   addr    Ptr to UDP address or NULL
14:    *   alen    Size of addr or zero
15:    *
16:    *
17:    * RETURNS:
18:    *   0       Successful
19:    *   -1      Failed: check errno
20:    */
21:   int
22:   send_fd(int s,int fd,void *addr,socklen_t alen) {
```

continues

Listing 17.9: continued

```
23:        int z;
24:        struct msghdr msgh;   /* Message header */
25:        struct iovec iov[1];      /* I/O vector */
26:        struct cmsghdr *cmsgp = NULL;
27:        char buf[CMSG_SPACE(sizeof fd)];
28:        int er=0;   /* "No error" code of zero */
29:
30:        /*
31:         * Clear message areas:
32:         */
33:        memset(&msgh,0,sizeof msgh);
34:        memset(buf,0,sizeof buf);
35:
36:        /*
37:         * Supply socket address (if any):
38:         */
39:        msgh.msg_name = addr;
40:        msgh.msg_namelen = alen;
41:
42:        /*
43:         * Install our I/O vector:
44:         */
45:        msgh.msg_iov = iov;
46:        msgh.msg_iovlen = 1;
47:
48:        /*
49:         * Initialize the I/O vector to send
50:         * the value in "er" (which is zero).
51:         * This is done because data must be
52:         * transmitted to send the fd.
53:         */
54:        iov[0].iov_base = &er;
55:        iov[0].iov_len = sizeof er;
56:
57:        /*
58:         * Establish control buffer:
59:         */
60:        msgh.msg_control = buf;
61:        msgh.msg_controllen = sizeof buf;
62:
63:        /*
64:         * Configure the message to send
65:         * a file descriptor:
66:         */
67:        cmsgp = CMSG_FIRSTHDR(&msgh);
68:        cmsgp->cmsg_level = SOL_SOCKET;
```

```
69:        cmsgp->cmsg_type = SCM_RIGHTS;
70:        cmsgp->cmsg_len = CMSG_LEN(sizeof fd);
71:
72:        /*
73:         * Install the file descriptor value:
74:         */
75:        *((int *)CMSG_DATA(cmsgp)) = fd;
76:        msgh.msg_controllen = cmsgp->cmsg_len;
77:
78:        /*
79:         * Send it to the client process:
80:         */
81:        do  {
82:            z = sendmsg(s,&msgh,0);
83:        } while ( z == -1 && errno == EINTR );
84:
85:        return z == -1 ? -1 : 0;
86:    }
```

The procedure used by the send_fd() function is broken down into the
following steps:

1. The function accepts several input arguments: the socket s to send the
   file descriptor on; the file descriptor fd itself to be sent; NULL or the
   address of the destination; and the address length (lines 10 to 22).
   Because the server uses a stream socket, NULL is supplied for the
   address and zero for the address length.

2. The message header msgh and the ancillary data buffer buf[] are initialized to zero by the memset(3) calls in lines 33 and 34. This is
   optional, but useful when debugging.

3. The socket address and length are established in lines 39 and 40. The
   server in this example does not use them, but this serves as an example of how to establish them.

4. The I/O vector is determined by lines 45 and 46. The I/O vector length
   is specified as being one element long in line 46.

5. The I/O vector itself is established in lines 54 and 55. The iov[0]
   entry points to the er variable so that the errno value can be transmitted as data (it is zero when no error is being transmitted).

6. The pointer to and the size of the ancillary data buffer are established
   in lines 60 and 61. The ancillary data will reside in array buf[].

7. The cmsgp pointer is established in line 67.

8. The ancillary message level, type, and length are established in lines
   68 to 70. This message describes a file descriptor ancillary data object.

9. The file descriptor being sent is copied into the ancillary data buffer in line 75. Note the careful use of the CMSG_DATA() macro and the type cast.

10. The final ancillary data length is established in line 76. Note that if you send multiple ancillary data objects, this value must be the sum total of them all.

11. The message is sent by calling upon sendmsg(2) in lines 81 to 83.

12. The success or failure of the call is returned in line 85 (zero is success and -1 represents failure).

Now, you fully understand all the source code involved in this example. The next section will put the code to the test.

Testing the Socket Server

First, compile the modules as follows:

OUTPUT

```
$ make
gcc -g -c  -D_GNU_SOURCE -Wall -Wreturn-type web80.c
gcc -g -c  -D_GNU_SOURCE -Wall -Wreturn-type misc.c
gcc -g -c  -D_GNU_SOURCE -Wall -Wreturn-type reqport.c
gcc -g -c  -D_GNU_SOURCE -Wall -Wreturn-type recvfd.c
gcc web80.o misc.o reqport.o recvfd.o -o web80
gcc -g -c  -D_GNU_SOURCE -Wall -Wreturn-type sockserv.c
gcc -g -c  -D_GNU_SOURCE -Wall -Wreturn-type recvcred.c
gcc -g -c  -D_GNU_SOURCE -Wall -Wreturn-type sendfd.c
gcc sockserv.o misc.o recvcred.o sendfd.o -o sockserv
$
```

This make procedure leaves you with two executables:

- The socket server program sockserv
- The simple Web server web80

Now, test out the simple little Web server without any root privileges (make sure to provide a command-line argument):

OUTPUT

```
$ ./web80 stand_alone
Permission denied: binding port 80
$
```

Any command-line argument like the stand_alone argument shown causes web80 to try to create its own socket on port 80. As you can see, the Linux kernel does not permit this without root privileges.

Testing `sockserv`

Now, start up the socket server under your `root` account in one terminal session or window. Supply as command-line arguments the one or more userIDs that are going to be permitted to request a port 80 socket. The following example allows userID `fred` access:

```
$ su root
Password:
# ./sockserv fred &
[1] 1077
#
```

OUTPUT

Now that you have the socket server executing, start another terminal session or window to run your Web server in. Do this with the proper login account (userID `fred` in this example):

```
$ ./web80 &
[1] 1079
$
```

OUTPUT

In this example, the process ID was 1079. Keep this fact in the back of your mind for later verification. The fact that `web80` started up without reporting any errors is a good indication that it successfully got a socket from the socket server already. To prove this beyond all doubt now, start your Web browser and contact it with the URL `http://127.0.0.1` if you are running `netscape` on the same host. If you are connecting from another host on your network, you will need to supply the correct hostname or IP number. Your browser should report something like this:

web80 Worked!

From PID 1079 @ Sat Nov 20 12:26:00 1999

OUTPUT

The preceding output shows the simple HTML response that your Web browser should receive. Notice how the reported process ID matches that of your `web80` process that you started.

TIP

If you cannot start `netscape` on your host because you lack X Window capabilities, you can use the following `lynx` command:

```
$ lynx http://127.0.0.1
```

You can also use the `telnet` procedure outlined in this section as another alternative.

Another effective and simple way you can test the web80 server is to try the following (make special note of the additional argument 80 on the telnet command line):

OUTPUT

```
$ telnet 127.0.0.1 80
Trying 127.0.0.1...
Connected to 127.0.0.1.
Escape character is '^]'.
GET /something
<HTML>
<HEAD>
<TITLE>Test Page for this little web80 server</TITLE>
</HEAD>
<BODY>
<H1>web80 Worked!</H1>
<H2>From PID 1079 @ Sat Nov 20 12:39:26 1999
</H2>
</BODY>
</HTML>
Connection closed by foreign host.
$
```

Using the telnet procedure, you will need to supply one line of input (see the line GET /something).

What's Next

This has been a long and perhaps difficult chapter for some of you. However, it has been presented in the interest of completeness for those of you who need to design local servers where credentials are essential. For example, a local RDBMS database server uses credentials to establish the ID of the user connecting to the database.

Now, you have covered all the material to be learned in this book. But don't close it yet! The next chapter is going to show you how to apply what you know. A working example of a server that uses TCP/IP to obtain stock quotes from the Internet will be presented. After the stock quotes are obtained from the Internet, they will be rebroadcast to your local area network. The penguins are already gathering in the next chapter to see how all those Linux IPOs have been doing lately!

18

A Practical Network Project

Whether your brain is smarting from the last chapter or whether it got
smarter, it's time to take a rest. Rather than cover new material in this
chapter, you are going to have some fun applying the knowledge that you
have learned throughout this book. It's important to have a little fun after
so much learning effort has been expended.

In this chapter, you will

- Apply TCP/IP stream sockets to download stock quotations from the
  Internet
- Apply UDP broadcasting to deliver stock quotes to your LAN
- Use a UDP client program to receive the LAN broadcast stock quota-
  tions

Problem Statement

It is always a good practice to state the problem before a solution is presented. So, here is the problem that you are going to solve in this chapter.

You have a small company office of full- or part-time day traders. Your office is small, cheap, or both, so obtaining quotes without fees is important. Additionally, you are concerned about network traffic between your host and your Internet provider because you need the available bandwidth for other purposes. Meanwhile, your office staff insists on obtaining the best free quote service possible.

Solving the Quote Service Problem

It is clear from the problem statement that it is desirable to get one set of quotes from the quote provider. There is no point in having all your office workers using separate TCP/IP connections to the same quote server, for the same information. This would use up valuable bandwidth to your Internet service provider. From the free quotation provider's point of view, this is also less than desirable.

One local server program could continually fetch updated stock market quotes for everyone. This information could then be broadcast to the local network for all interested parties. This is the solution that you will apply in this chapter. This application will also give you the chance to review the use of both stream sockets and datagram sockets.

Obtaining Stock Market Quotes

The data source that you'll use for market quotations will be the fine service at finance.yahoo.com. In this section, you'll learn how the program manages to fetch the quotation information from finance.yahoo.com.

NOTE

The programs being presented in this chapter worked at the time of writing. It is possible, however, that the Internet service being used might have changed by the time you read this. Notes are provided later in this chapter to help you adjust these programs should this become necessary.

To determine how to obtain stock quotes, you can use your Web browser to visit http://finance.yahoo.com (Netscape will be assumed here). There, you will be presented with a page that lets you enter a ticker symbol and press the Get Quotes button. Entering RHAT and pressing the button leads you to another page giving you the details about Red Hat Inc. Underneath the quote information, you will find a link that reads Download Spreadsheet Format. This is the gold mine!

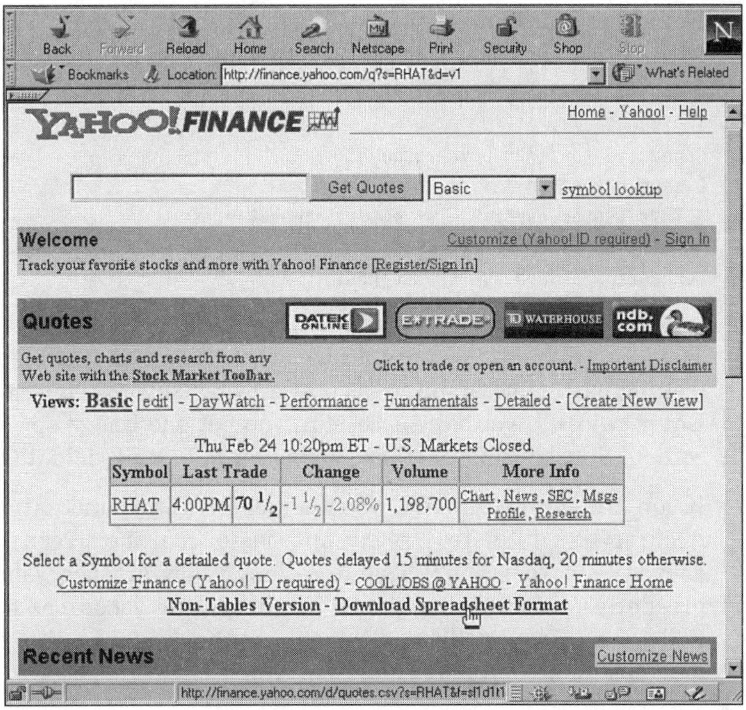

Figure 18.1: *A screen shot of Netscape after obtaining a stock quote for* RHAT *at* `http://finance.yahoo.com`.

From here, you have three choices:

- Move the mouse over the `Download Spreadsheet Format` link and note the URL that shows up on the status line (Netscape 4.7 shows the link URL there).

- Select from the menu item `View->Page Source`. Look through the HTML code for the link that looks something like `<a href="/d/ quotes.csv?s=RHAT &f=sl1d1t1c1ohgv&e=.csv">Download Spreadsheet Format</a>` (find it by looking for "Download Spreadsheet Format").

- The best way this information can be captured with Netscape is to right-click on the `Download Spreadsheet Format` link. From the pop-up menu, select the item `Copy Link Location`. This will copy the link reference to your Clipboard. Then, you can later paste this information into a file.

From this information, you will have all that you need. Test the facility with `telnet` as follows (remember to supply `80` after the hostname):

```
$ telnet finance.yahoo.com 80
Trying 204.71.201.75...
Connected to finance.yahoo.com.
Escape character is '^]'.
GET /d/quotes.csv?s=RHAT&f=sl1d1t1c1ohgv&e=.csv
"RHAT",168.9375,"11/24/1999","4:00PM",0,147.5625,175.5,145.6875,3061700
Connection closed by foreign host.
$
```

The `GET` command is issued after you are connected, along with the strange-looking pathname and a press of the Enter key (you might need to press Enter twice). If you are successful, you get one line of spreadsheet data in return! Substituting another symbol for `RHAT` will yield different data.

If you are not having any luck, then check your punctuation and spelling. Accuracy is vital here. Use cut and paste from the screen if possible. If this doesn't help, then you'll need to research how `finance.yahoo.com` is doing it presently (you might even need to start at the `yahoo.com` home page). Follow the steps outlined previously so that you'll be able to find out the new hostname and pathname required.

This is a summary of the quote fetch procedure:

1. Connect to `finance.yahoo.com` on port `80` (this hostname might change at a future date).

2. Issue the `GET` request with the magic pathname shown (the word `GET` should be uppercase).

3. A line of spreadsheet format data is returned on the same socket as a response.

4. The socket is closed.

That is all there is to it! Remember these steps when you examine the source code listings later.

The following sections will illustrate and describe the modules that make up the server and client programs. Unfortunately, space does not permit a full listing of the source code. The full source code and `make` files are available, however, at `http://www.quecorp.com/series/by_example/`.

Table 18.1 lists all the source files that you will need. Some of the more interesting ones will be listed and described within this chapter.

Table 18.1: Source Modules for the Quote Server and Client

Source File	Description
Makefile	The project make file.
bcast.c	Implements the function that performs the quote broadcasting to the local area network.
connect.c	Implements a function that connects to the remote Internet quote server.
csvparse.c	Parser for the quote data that is returned.
gettick.c	Fetches the quote information from the remote Internet quote server.
load.c	Loads the stock market ticker symbols from file tickers.rc.
misc.c	Small miscellaneous functions.
mkaddr.c	The Internet address convenience function.
mktwatch.c	The market watch client program. This program receives the local broadcast information and displays it.
msgf.c	A module that logs server messages to the syslog logging facility.
qserve.c	The module that implements the local quote server program.
quotes.h	The common header file for all source modules.
tickers.rc	The list of ticker symbols to inquire about. Modify this file to change the tickers to the ones that interest you.

Examining the Quote Server Program

The logical place to start examining code is the qserve.c source module. This module forms the main program for the quote server itself. It is responsible for obtaining stock market quotes and then broadcasting them to the local area network. Listing 18.1 shows the source listing for qserve.c.

EXAMPLE

Listing 18.1: qserve.c—The Quote Server Module

```
1:   /* qserve.c:
2:    *
3:    * Stock Quote Concentrator Program:
4:    */
5:   #include "quotes.h"
6:
7:   static char *command = NULL;
8:
9:   /* Remote Quote Server Address */
10:  static char *cmdopt_a = DFLT_SERVER;
11:
12:  /* Quote Re-Broadcast Address */
13:  static char *cmdopt_b = DFLT_BCAST;
14:
```

continues

Listing 18.1: continued

```
15:  /*
16:   * Ticker Table:
17:   */
18:  static TickReq tickers[MAX_TICKERS];
19:  static int ntick = 0;
20:
21:  /*
22:   * Return server usage information:
23:   */
24:  static void
25:  usage(void) {
26:      printf("Usage: %s [-h] [-a address:port]\n"
27:          "where:\n"
28:          "\t-h\t\tRequests usage info.\n"
29:          "\t-a address:port\tSpecify "
30:          "the server\n"
31:          "\t\t\taddress and port number.\n"
32:          "\t-b bcast:port\tSpecify "
33:          "the broadcast\n"
34:          "\t\t\taddress and port number.\n",
35:          command);
36:  }
37:
38:  /*
39:   * Server Main Program:
40:   */
41:  int
42:  main(int argc,char **argv) {
43:      int rc = 0;              /* Return Code */
44:      int optch;               /* Option Char. */
45:      int z;                   /* Status Code */
46:      int x;                       /* Index */
47:      int s;                 /* Broadcast socket */
48:      time_t tn = 0;             /* Time Next */
49:      time_t zzz;                /* Sleep Time */
50:      time_t tm = 20;              /* Seconds */
51:      time_t td;              /* Time & Date */
52:      struct sockaddr_in bc_addr; /* bc addr */
53:      socklen_t bc_len;       /* bc addr len. */
54:      const int True = TRUE;  /* Const. TRUE */
55:      static char cmdopts[] = "ha:b:";
56:
57:      /*
58:       * Process command line options:
59:       */
60:      command = Basename(argv[0]);
```

```
61:
62:        while ( (optch = getopt(argc,argv,cmdopts)) != -1 )
63:            switch ( optch ) {
64:
65:            case 'h' :              /* -h for help */
66:                usage();
67:                return rc;
68:
69:            case 'a' :        /* -a quote_server */
70:                cmdopt_a = optarg;
71:                break;
72:
73:            case 'b' :      /* -b broadcast_addr */
74:                cmdopt_b = optarg;
75:                break;
76:
77:            default :
78:                /* Option error */
79:                rc = 1;
80:        }
81:
82:        /*
83:         * Check for option errors:
84:         */
85:        if ( rc ) {
86:            usage();
87:            return rc;
88:        }
89:
90:        /*
91:         * Form the broadcast server
92:         * address:
93:         */
94:        bc_len = sizeof bc_addr;    /* Max len */
95:        z = mkaddr(
96:            &bc_addr,           /* Returned addr. */
97:            &bc_len,            /* Returned len. */
98:            cmdopt_b,           /* Input address */
99:            "udp");             /* UDP protocol */
100:
101:        if ( z == -1 ) {
102:            msgf('e',"%s: -b %s",
103:                strerror(errno),
104:                cmdopt_b);
105:            return 1;
106:        }
```

continues

Listing 18.1: continued

```
107:
108:     /*
109:      * Create a UDP socket to use:
110:      */
111:     s = socket(PF_INET,SOCK_DGRAM,0);
112:
113:     if ( s == -1 ) {
114:         msgf('e',"%s: socket(PF_INET,"
115:             "SOCK_DGRAM,0)",
116:             strerror(errno));
117:         return 1;
118:     }
119:
120:     /*
121:      * Allow broadcasts on socket s:
122:      */
123:     z = setsockopt(s,
124:         SOL_SOCKET,
125:         SO_BROADCAST,
126:         &True,
127:         sizeof True);
128:
129:     if ( z == -1 ) {
130:         msgf('e',"%s: setsockopt(SO_BROADCAST)",
131:             strerror(errno));
132:         return 1;
133:     }
134:
135:     /*
136:      * Load tickers from tickers.rc:
137:      */
138:     if ( load(&tickers[0],&ntick,MAX_TICKERS) )
139:         goto errxit;
140:
141:     /*
142:      * Now monitor the remote quote server:
143:      */
144:     for (;;) {
145:         tn = 0;                 /* Refresh tn */
146:         time(&td);              /* Current time */
147:
148:         /*
149:          * Loop for all tickers:
150:          */
151:         for ( x=0; x<ntick; ++x ) {
152:             /*
```

```
153:                    * Skip tickers that are either
154:                    * unknown, or are producing parse
155:                    * errors in the returned data:
156:                    */
157:                   if ( tickers[x].flags & FLG_UNKNOWN
158:                      || tickers[x].flags & FLG_ERROR )
159:                       continue;    /* Ignore this */
160:
161:                   /*
162:                    * Pick up the earliest "next" time:
163:                    */
164:                   if ( !tn
165:                      || tickers[x].next_samp < tn )
166:                       tn = tickers[x].next_samp;
167:
168:                   /*
169:                    * If the current time is > than
170:                    * the "next" time, it is time to
171:                    * fetch an update for this ticker:
172:                    */
173:                   if ( td >= tickers[x].next_samp ) {
174:                       /*
175:                        * Get Quote Update:
176:                        */
177:                       z = get_tickinfo(
178:                           &tickers[x],cmdopt_a);
179:
180:                       /*
181:                        * Compute time for the next
182:                        * update for this ticker:
183:                        */
184:                       time(&tickers[x].next_samp);
185:                       tickers[x].next_samp += tm;
186:
187:                       /*
188:                        * If the quote fetch was OK,
189:                        * then broadcast its info:
190:                        */
191:                       if ( !z )
192:                           broadcast(s,&tickers[x],
193:                               (struct sockaddr *)&bc_addr,
194:                               bc_len);
195:                   }
196:               }
197:
198:           /*
```

continues

Listing 18.1: continued

```
199:             * Here the interval between updates is
200:             * progressively increased to 5 minutes
201:             * max. This provides a lot of initial
202:             * action for demonstration purposes,
203:             * without taxing the friendly quote
204:             * providers if this program is run all
205:             * day. Abuse will only force the kind
206:             * providers to change things to break
207:             * the operation of this program!
208:             */
209:          if ( tm < (time_t) 5 * 60 )
210:              tm += 5;     /* Progressively increase */
211:
212:          /*
213:           * Compute how long we need to snooze.
214:           * The time to the next event is
215:           * computed- sleep(3) is called if
216:           * necessary:
217:           */
218:          if ( !tn )
219:              tn = td + tm;
220:          if ( tn >= td )
221:              if ( (zzz = tn - td) )
222:                  sleep(zzz);
223:      }
224:
225:      return rc;
226:
227:      /*
228:       * Error Exit:
229:       */
230: errxit:
231:      return rc = 2;
232: }
```

Note the following highlights about the program organization:

- This program accepts the -a or -b options, which are stored in variables cmdopt_a and cmdopt_b, respectively (lines 9 to 13).

- The stock market tickers to be monitored are maintained in the table tickers[] (line 18). The variable ntick indicates how many active entries are in the table (line 19).

- Function usage() provides usage information upon request when option -h is provided (lines 24 to 36).

- The remainder of the program is the main program for the server (lines 41 to the end).

Now, examine the flow of control in the server main program:

1. Options are parsed in a getopt(3) loop (lines 62 to 88).

2. The broadcast address is formed in bc_addr by calling upon the mkaddr() function (lines 94 to 106).

3. A UDP socket is created by calling socket(2) (lines 111 to 118).

4. Enable the broadcast feature of the socket from step 3 (lines 123 to 133).

5. Call upon the load() function to load the tickers[] table from the initialization file tickers.rc (lines 138 and 139).

6. The server then executes an infinite server loop until the program is terminated (lines 144 to 233).

Now, examine the server loop steps that are used:

1. The "next time" value tn is cleared to zero (line 145). The current time is also placed into td (line 146).

2. A for loop in line 151 iterates through all ticker table entries (lines 151 to 196). This loop will later be described separately.

3. The value of tm represents the time to pause between ticker updates. It was initialized to a value of 20 (seconds) in line 50. In line 209, it is tested to see whether the value is greater than five minutes. If not, tm has five more seconds added to it (line 210). This is done so that the time interval will increase gradually (to a maximum of five minutes), in case the server is left running all day. This will prevent abuse of the Yahoo! quotation servers, which are kindly providing a free service to you.

4. If an event time is found in tn, the amount of time to sleep is computed and placed into variable zzz and sleep(3) is called. Otherwise, the loop immediately begins another iteration.

Now examine the more interesting for loop beginning in line 151:

1. The ticker table entries contain a flags member. If the flag bit FLG_UNKNOWN is set (line 157), this indicates that the ticker has been discovered to be unknown. After this bit is set, the ticker is never looked up again (continue in line 159 causes it to be ignored). Likewise, if flag FLG_ERROR is set (line 158), the ticker is not looked up again. This flag indicates that a data format error was encountered while trying to decode the quotation.

2. The current time and date in td are compared with the next event time for the ticker entry ticker[x] (line 173). The next event time is

stored in member `next_samp`, which indicates when the next sample should be taken. If the current time is greater than or equal to the next sample event time, then it is time to fetch a new quote for this ticker.

3. The function `get_tickinfo()` is called to obtain ticker information for this ticker symbol (lines 177 to 178).

4. A next event time is computed from taking the current time and adding the time period `tm` to it (which increases to a maximum of five minutes). This is done in lines 184 to 185.

5. A test is made to see whether the ticker quote fetch was successful (line 191). If it was, the function `broadcast()` is called in lines 192 to 194 to send the information out to all interested local area network client programs.

6. Repeat step 1, increasing x, until all ticker symbols have been processed in `tickers[]`.

That covers the operation of the main segment of the server code. The next sections will cover the operation of the quotation fetch and then the broadcast function.

Fetching Quotations via `get_tickinfo()`

This section will examine the source module `gettick.c` so that you can see how the quotation was retrieved by the C code. Before that module can be shown, however, you need to examine some of the structure references that are being used. Listing 18.2 shows the `quotes.h` header file used by the source modules in this project.

EXAMPLE

Listing 18.2: `quotes.h`—The `quotes.h` Header File

```
 1:   /* quotes.h:
 2:    *
 3:    * Project header file:
 4:    */
 5:   #include <stdio.h>
 6:   #include <unistd.h>
 7:   #include <stdlib.h>
 8:   #include <errno.h>
 9:   #include <ctype.h>
10:   #include <string.h>
11:   #include <getopt.h>
12:   #include <memory.h>
13:   #include <stdarg.h>
14:   #include <math.h>
15:   #include <syslog.h>
```

```
16:  #include <signal.h>
17:  #include <sys/types.h>
18:  #include <sys/time.h>
19:  #include <sys/socket.h>
20:  #include <netinet/in.h>
21:
22:  /*
23:   * Default Quote Server:
24:   */
25:  #define DFLT_SERVER "finance.yahoo.com:80"
26:
27:  /*
28:   * Default Broadcast Address:
29:   */
30:  #define DFLT_BCAST   "127.255.255.255:9777"
31:
32:  /*
33:   * *.CSV Parsing Parameter:
34:   */
35:  typedef struct {
36:      char    type;        /* 'S' or 'D' */
37:      void   *parm;        /* Ptr to parameter */
38:  } Parm;
39:
40:  /*
41:   * Timeout on Quote Fetch:
42:   */
43:  #define TIMEOUT_SECS    10
44:
45:  /*
46:   * Ticker load file:
47:   */
48:  #define TICKPATH        "tickers.rc"
49:
50:  /*
51:   * Maximum number of tickers:
52:   */
53:  #define MAX_TICKERS     256
54:
55:  /*
56:   * Ticker length:
57:   */
58:  #define TICKLEN         8
59:
60:  /*
61:   * Date Length:
```

continues

Listing 18.2: continued

```
 62:    */
 63:  #define DTLEN          10
 64:
 65:  /*
 66:   * Time field length:
 67:   */
 68:  #define TMLEN          7
 69:
 70:  /*
 71:   * Define TRUE & FALSE if not defined:
 72:   */
 73:  #ifndef TRUE
 74:  #define TRUE    1
 75:  #define FALSE   0
 76:  #endif
 77:
 78:  /*
 79:   * Ticker Request Structure:
 80:   */
 81:  typedef struct {
 82:      char    ticker[TICKLEN+1];    /* Symbol */
 83:      double  last_trade;       /* Last Price */
 84:      char    *date;                  /* Date */
 85:      char    *time;    /* Time of Last Trade */
 86:      double  change;              /* +/- Change */
 87:      double  open_price;   /* Opening Price */
 88:      double  high;               /* High Price */
 89:      double  low;                 /* Low Price */
 90:      double  volume;    /* Volume of Trades */
 91:      int     flags;           /* Server flags */
 92:      time_t  next_samp; /* Time of next evt */
 93:  } TickReq;
 94:
 95:  /*
 96:   * Ticker Flags:
 97:   */
 98:          /* Ticker unknown */
 99:  #define FLG_UNKNOWN     1
100:          /* Data format error */
101:  #define FLG_ERROR       2
102:
103:  /*
104:   * External Function References:
105:   */
106:  extern int load(
107:      TickReq *tick,int *pntick,int nmax);
```

```
108: extern int extract_parms(
109:      Parm *plist,short n,char *src);
110: extern void msgf(
111:      char type,const char *format,...);
112: extern int Connect(const char *addr);
113: extern int mkaddr(
114:      void *addr,
115:      int *addrlen,
116:      char *str_addr,
117:      char *protocol);
118: extern char *Basename(char *cmd);
119: extern char *strtick(char *str);
120: extern int get_tickinfo(TickReq *req,char *addr);
121: extern void broadcast(
122:      int s,TickReq *quote,struct sockaddr *bc_addr,
123:      socklen_t bc_len);
124:
125: /* End */
```

The items that are of primary interest to you are

- Macro `DFLT_SERVER` (line 25) defines the default hostname and port to contact for quotes (note that non-Yahoo! servers will likely use different spreadsheet data formats).

- Macro `DFLT_BCAST` (line 30) defines the default broadcast address. The default is to broadcast to the loopback network so that it will work for those readers that do not have a network card installed.

- Structure `Parm` (lines 35 to 38) defines a type that controls parsing of information into a C data type.

- Macro `TIMEOUT_SECS` is set to 10 seconds, and defines the maximum amount of time to wait for a stock quotation before giving up on a response (line 48).

- Macro `MAX_TICKERS` defines the table size of `tickers[]` in the module `qserve.c` (line 53).

- Structure `TickReq` (lines 81 to 93) defines one ticker symbol entry for the server. This structure is also used in the client program, but structure members `flags` and `next_samp` are ignored by the client program.

- Flags `FLG_UNKNOWN` and `FLG_ERROR` are defined in lines 99 and 101.

With the header file out of the way, examine Listing 18.3, which illustrates the `gettick.c` source module.

Listing 18.3: `gettick.c`—The `get_tickinfo()` Function Source Code

```
1:   /* gettick.c
2:    *
3:    * Get ticker info from inet:
4:    */
5:   #include "quotes.h"
6:
7:   /*
8:    * f is set TRUE when a request
9:    * for a stock quote has timed
10:   * out.
11:   */
12:  static int f = FALSE;
13:
14:  /*
15:   * Catch SIGALRM and Timeout:
16:   */
17:  static void
18:  sig_ALRM(int signo) {
19:      f = TRUE;    /* Mark timeout */
20:  }
21:
22:  /*
23:   * Get ticker info:
24:   *
25:   * RETURNS:
26:   *   0         Success
27:   *   -1        Failed:
28:   *
29:   * errno:
30:   *   ETIME     Timed Out
31:   *   EBADMSG   Field data format
32:   *   other     Network/system errors.
33:   */
34:  int
35:  get_tickinfo(TickReq *req,char *addr) {
36:      int z, er;            /* Status, errno */
37:      int s;                /* Socket */
38:      int n;                /* Byte count */
39:      char buf[256];        /* Receive buffer */
40:      char *tkr = NULL;     /* Extracted ticker */
41:      struct sigaction
42:          sa_new,           /* New signal action */
43:          sa_old;           /* Saved signal action */
44:      Parm parms[9];        /* Data parse table */
45:
46:      /*
```

```
47:         * Initialize parsing parameters. This
48:         * parameter list will need modification
49:         * if yahoo or your quote provider uses
50:         * a different format:
51:         */
52:        parms[0].type = 'S';     /* String */
53:        parms[0].parm = &tkr;    /* Ticker name */
54:        parms[1].type = 'D';     /* Double */
55:        parms[1].parm = &req->last_trade;
56:        parms[2].type = 'S';
57:        parms[2].parm = &req->date;
58:        parms[3].type = 'S';
59:        parms[3].parm = &req->time;
60:        parms[4].type = 'D';
61:        parms[4].parm = &req->change;
62:        parms[5].type = 'D';
63:        parms[5].parm = &req->open_price;
64:        parms[6].type = 'D';
65:        parms[6].parm = &req->high;
66:        parms[7].type = 'D';
67:        parms[7].parm = &req->low;
68:        parms[8].type = 'D';
69:        parms[8].parm = &req->volume;
70:
71:        /*
72:         * Initialize to catch SIGALRM:
73:         */
74:        sa_new.sa_handler = sig_ALRM;
75:        sigemptyset(&sa_new.sa_mask);
76:        sa_new.sa_flags = 0;
77:        sigaction(SIGALRM,&sa_new,&sa_old);
78:
79:        /*
80:         * Connect to finance.yahoo.com:
81:         */
82:        f = FALSE;
83:        alarm(TIMEOUT_SECS);
84:
85:        s = Connect(addr);
86:        if ( s == -1 )
87:            goto errxit;
88:
89:        /*
90:         * Send GET request:
91:         *
92:         * NOTE: This is subject to change-
```

continues

Listing 18.3: continued

```
 93:        * If finance.yahoo.com changes, you
 94:        * will need to adjust this formatting.
 95:        */
 96:       sprintf(buf,"GET /d/quotes.csv?"
 97:           "s=%s"
 98:           "&f=sl1d1t1c1ohgv"
 99:           "&e=.csv\r\n",
100:           req->ticker);
101:
102:       write(s,buf,strlen(buf));
103:       shutdown(s,1);
104:
105:       /*
106:        * Read response with a timeout:
107:        */
108:       do {
109:           z = read(s,buf,sizeof buf);
110:       } while ( !f && z == -1 && errno == EINTR );
111:
112:       er = errno;                /* Save error */
113:       alarm(0);              /* Disable timeout */
114:       close(s);                 /* Close socket */
115:
116:       /* Restore the signal action */
117:       sigaction(SIGALRM,&sa_old,NULL);
118:
119:       if ( !f && z > 0 )
120:           n = z;            /* Read n bytes OK */
121:       else {
122:           if ( f )                /* Timeout? */
123:               er = ETIME;    /* Yes- timeout */
124:           /*
125:            * Report error to log:
126:            */
127:           msgf('e',"%s: Get ticker '%s'",
128:               strerror(er),
129:               req->ticker);
130:
131:           errno = er;          /* For caller */
132:           return -1;       .        /* Failed */
133:       }
134:
135:       /* Remove CR, LF, or CRLF */
136:       buf[strcspn(buf,"\r\n")] = 0;
137:
138:       /*
```

```
139:         * Check for the unknown ticker case:
140:         */
141:        if ( strstr(buf,"N/A,N/A,N/A,N/A,N/A") ) {
142:            msgf('e',"Unknown Ticker: '%s'",
143:                req->ticker);
144:            req->flags |= FLG_UNKNOWN;
145:            errno = EBADMSG;        /* For caller */
146:            return -1;              /* Failed */
147:        }
148:
149:        /*
150:         * Parse quote results:
151:         */
152:        if ( (z = extract_parms(parms,9,buf)) < 0 ) {
153:            /* Report failed parse of data */
154:            msgf('e',"Field # %d: '%s'",z,buf);
155:            req->flags |= FLG_ERROR;
156:            errno = EBADMSG;        /* For caller */
157:            return -1;              /* Failed */
158:        }
159:
160:        /* Capture the exact case for this ticker */
161:        strncpy(req->ticker,tkr,TICKLEN)[TICKLEN] = 0;
162:
163:        /*
164:         * Update sample time in entry:
165:         */
166:        return 0;
167:
168:        /*
169:         * Error Exit:
170:         */
171: errxit:
172:        alarm(0);
173:        sigaction(SIGALRM,&sa_old,NULL);
174:        return -1;
175: }
```

This module defines the following major components:

- The timeout flag f in line 12. When this flag is set TRUE, it will indicate that the request has timed out.

- The signal catcher function sig_ALRM() that will catch the signal SIGALRM when the timer has expired. This function sets flag variable f to TRUE in line 19.

- The get_tickinfo() function occupies the remainder of the module, starting in line 34.

Now, examine the procedure used by get_tickinfo():

1. The data that this function hopes to receive is in spreadsheet format. To parse the data out of this formatted record, a parameter table is established in array parms[] (lines 52 to 69). Type 'S' indicates a string type of data, whereas the 'D' represents a C-type double value to be extracted.

2. The signal handler for SIGALRM is established (lines 74 to 77).

3. The flag f is initialized to FALSE and the timer is started (lines 82 and 83).

4. A connect request is issued by calling function Connect() with the address of our quotation server (lines 85 to 87). The source code for Connect() is provided in module connect.c.

5. A GET request is formatted (lines 96 to 100). This is one area of code you might need to change if the Yahoo! servers change.

6. The GET request is written out to the quotation server (lines 102 and 103). The call to shutdown(2) sends and end-file notification to the remote server without closing the socket. This is necessary so that the response can be received from the server.

7. Wait for and read the resulting spreadsheet record (lines 108 to 110).

8. Save the errno value in variable er in case an error has occurred (line 112).

9. Cancel the timer (line 113) and close the socket s (line 114).

10. Restore the signal handler for signal SIGALRM (line 117).

11. If flag f is still FALSE and z is greater than zero, then the program successfully received some quotation data (lines 119 and 120). The number of bytes received is recorded in variable n.

12. Otherwise, if f is TRUE, then set the saved error value in er to ETIME to indicate that a timeout occurred (line 123).

13. Lines 127 to 132 handle the timeout or error case when a quotation was not successfully received. The call to msgf() logs an error message to the syslog logging facility.

14. The carriage return or linefeed is removed from the received spreadsheet record (line 136).

15. A special sequence is tested for, which indicates that the ticker symbol is not known (lines 141 to 147). Yahoo! returns N/A for a number of fields if the ticker symbol is not known.

16. If the ticker symbol is known, then the spreadsheet record is parsed in lines 152 to 158. If a record parse or field data error occurs, the error exit is taken in line 157.

17. If the parse is successful, the ticker symbol itself is copied back into the entry `req->ticker` (line 161). This is done for some symbols that use a mixed case.

18. Finally, at long last, the `return` statement in line 166 indicates that the `req` member has been updated with new ticker information successfully.

The next section will examine the `broadcast()` function that was called upon by the server program.

Broadcasting Quotes via `broadcast()`

The server calls upon a function named `broadcast()` to share the information it has managed to obtain from Yahoo! with all interested local area network clients. The listing for this program is shown in Listing 18.4.

EXAMPLE

Listing 18.4: bcast.c—The `broadcast()` Function in bcast.c

```
1:   /* bcast.c:
2:    *
3:    * Broadcast Ticker Updates
4:    */
5:   #include "quotes.h"
6:
7:   void
8:   broadcast(
9:     int s,                    /* Socket */
10:    TickReq *quote,           /* Quote */
11:    struct sockaddr *bc_addr, /* addr */
12:    socklen_t bc_len) {  /* addr len. */
13:      int z;                  /* Status */
14:      char buf[2048];         /* Buffer */
15:      char *cp = buf;      /* Buf. ptr */
16:      int msglen;   /* Message length */
17:
18:      /*
19:       * Format a datagram for broadcast:
20:       */
21:      strcpy(buf,quote->ticker);
22:      cp = buf + strlen(buf) + 1;
23:      sprintf(cp,"%E",quote->last_trade);
```

continues

Listing 18.4: continued

```
24:        cp += strlen(cp) + 1;
25:        strcpy(cp,quote->date);
26:        cp += strlen(cp) + 1;
27:        strcpy(cp,quote->time);
28:        cp += strlen(cp) + 1;
29:        sprintf(cp,"%E",quote->change);
30:        cp += strlen(cp) + 1;
31:        sprintf(cp,"%E",quote->open_price);
32:        cp += strlen(cp) + 1;
33:        sprintf(cp,"%E",quote->high);
34:        cp += strlen(cp) + 1;
35:        sprintf(cp,"%E",quote->low);
36:        cp += strlen(cp) + 1;
37:        sprintf(cp,"%E",quote->volume);
38:        cp += strlen(cp) + 1;
39:
40:        msglen = cp - buf;
41:
42:        /*
43:         * Broadcast the datagram:
44:         */
45:        z = sendto(s,buf,msglen,0,bc_addr,bc_len);
46:        if ( z == -1 )
47:            msgf('e',"%s: sendto(2)",
48:                 strerror(errno));
49:  }
```

The broadcast() function uses the following basic steps:

1. The buffer buf[2048] is used to format the broadcast datagram (line 14). Pointer variable cp is used to build this datagram in stages (line 15).

2. Line 21 starts building the datagram by copying the null terminated ticker symbol into buf[]. A new pointer for cp is computed to point after the null byte that follows the ticker symbol in buf[] (line 22).

3. The last_trade value is formatted and placed after the null byte in the datagram (line 23). Again, cp is computed to point past the null byte that follows (line 24).

4. Lines 25 to 38 repeat this procedure for all other data components to be placed into the datagram. Note that each component is a null-terminated string unto itself, within this datagram.

5. The final length of the datagram is computed (line 40) and stored into msglen.

6. The sendto(2) function is called upon to broadcast the datagram out to the socket s, to the broadcast address provided in bc_addr. If an error occurs, it is logged to the syslog facility (lines 47 to 48).

That covers the interesting network code for the server program. Now, let's take a look at the client side of things.

Examining the Client Program

The client program mktwatch must bind itself to the broadcast address being used, so that it can receive the broadcast market quotations. Examine the mktwatch.c module shown in Listing 18.5.

Listing 18.5: mktwatch.c—The Market Watch Client Program

EXAMPLE

```
1:    /* mktwatch.c:
2:     *
3:     * Get datagram stock market
4:     * quotes from central quotes
5:     * server:
6:     */
7:    #include "quotes.h"
8:
9:    /*
10:    * -b option (broadcast) address:
11:    */
12:   static char *cmdopt_b = DFLT_BCAST;
13:
14:   /*
15:    * Display command usage:
16:    */
17:   static void
18:   usage(void) {
19:       puts("Usage:\tmktwatch [-b bcast]");
20:       puts("where:");
21:       puts("\t-b bcast\tBroadcast address");
22:   }
23:
24:   /*
25:    * Extract ticker information from
26:    * broadcast datagram packet:
27:    */
28:   static int
29:   extract(char *dgram,TickReq *tkr) {
30:       char *cp = dgram;
31:
```

continues

Listing 18.5: continued

```
32:        memset(tkr,0,sizeof *tkr);
33:        strncpy(tkr->ticker,dgram,TICKLEN)
34:            [TICKLEN] = 0;
35:        cp += strlen(cp) + 1;
36:        if ( sscanf(cp,"%lE",&tkr->last_trade) != 1 )
37:            return -1;
38:        cp += strlen(cp) + 1;
39:        tkr->date = cp;
40:        cp += strlen(cp) + 1;
41:        tkr->time = cp;
42:        cp += strlen(cp) + 1;
43:        if ( sscanf(cp,"%lE",&tkr->change) != 1 )
44:            return -1;
45:        cp += strlen(cp) + 1;
46:        if ( sscanf(cp,"%lE",&tkr->open_price) != 1 )
47:            return -1;
48:        cp += strlen(cp) + 1;
49:        if ( sscanf(cp,"%lE",&tkr->high) != 1 )
50:            return -1;
51:        cp += strlen(cp) + 1;
52:        if ( sscanf(cp,"%lE",&tkr->low) != 1 )
53:            return -1;
54:        cp += strlen(cp) + 1;
55:        if ( sscanf(cp,"%lE",&tkr->volume) != 1 )
56:            return -1;
57:        return 0;
58:    }
59:
60:    /*
61:     * Market Watch Main Program:
62:     */
63:    int
64:    main(int argc,char **argv) {
65:        int rc = 0;        /* Command return code */
66:        int optch;         /* Option character */
67:        int z;                  /* Status code */
68:        int s;                      /* Socket */
69:        socklen_t bc_len;          /* length  */
70:        struct sockaddr_in bc_addr; /* AF_INET */
71:        socklen_t a_len;       /* Address length */
72:        struct sockaddr_in adr;     /* AF_INET */
73:        char dgram[2048];        /* Recv buffer */
74:        const int True = TRUE;   /* True const. */
75:        TickReq tkr;              /* Ticker Data */
76:        const char cmdopts[] = "hb:";
77:
```

```
78:      /*
79:       * Parse command line options:
80:       */
81:      while ( (optch = getopt(argc,argv,cmdopts)) != -1 )
82:          switch ( optch ) {
83:
84:          case 'h' :              /* -h (help) */
85:              usage();
86:              return rc;
87:
88:          case 'b' :              /* -b bc_addr */
89:              cmdopt_b = optarg;
90:              break;
91:
92:          default :
93:              /* Option error */
94:              rc = 1;
95:          }
96:
97:      if ( rc ) {
98:          usage();            /* Option errors */
99:          return rc;
100:     }
101:
102:     /*
103:      * Form broadcast address:
104:      */
105:     bc_len = sizeof bc_addr;
106:     z = mkaddr(
107:         &bc_addr,    /* Returned addr. */
108:         &bc_len,     /* Returned len. */
109:         cmdopt_b,    /* Input address */
110:         "udp");      /* UDP protocol */
111:
112:     if ( z == -1 ) {
113:         fprintf(stderr,
114:             "%s: -b %s",
115:             strerror(errno),
116:             cmdopt_b);
117:         return 1;
118:     }
119:
120:     /*
121:      * Create a UDP socket to read from:
122:      */
123:     s = socket(PF_INET,SOCK_DGRAM,0);
```

continues

Listing 18.5: continued

```
124:     if ( s == -1 ) {
125:         fprintf(stderr,
126:             "%s: socket(2)\n",
127:             strerror(errno));
128:         return 1;
129:     }
130:
131:     /*
132:      * Allow multiple listeners on this
133:      * broadcast address:
134:      */
135:     z = setsockopt(s,
136:         SOL_SOCKET,
137:         SO_REUSEADDR,
138:         &True,
139:         sizeof True);
140:
141:     if ( z == -1 ) {
142:         fprintf(stderr,
143:             "%s: setsockopt(SO_REUSEADDR)\n",
144:             strerror(errno));
145:         return 1;
146:     }
147:
148:     /*
149:      * Bind to the broadcast address:
150:      */
151:     z = bind(s,
152:         (struct sockaddr *)&bc_addr,bc_len);
153:
154:     if ( z == -1 ) {
155:         fprintf(stderr,
156:             "%s: bind(%s)\n",
157:             strerror(errno),
158:             cmdopt_b);
159:         return 1;
160:     }
161:
162:     /*
163:      * Now listen for and process broadcasted
164:      * stock quotes:
165:      */
166:     for (;;) {
167:         /*
168:          * Wait for a broadcast message:
169:          */
```

```
170:          a_len = sizeof adr; /* Max addr len. */
171:          z = recvfrom(s,              /* Socket */
172:              dgram,        /* Receiving buffer */
173:              sizeof dgram,/* Max rcv buf size */
174:              0,            /* Flags: no options */
175:              (struct sockaddr *)&adr, /* Addr */
176:              &a_len);    /* Addr len, in & out */
177:
178:          if ( z < 0 ) {
179:              fprintf(stderr,
180:                  "%s: recvfrom(2)\n",
181:                  strerror(errno));
182:              break;
183:          }
184:
185:          /*
186:           * Extract and report quote:
187:           */
188:          if ( !extract(dgram,&tkr) ) {
189:              printf("%-*s %7.3f %s %7s %+7.3f %7.3f "
190:                  "%7.3f %7.3f %9.0f\n",
191:                  TICKLEN,
192:                  tkr.ticker,
193:                  tkr.last_trade,
194:                  tkr.date,
195:                  tkr.time,
196:                  tkr.change,
197:                  tkr.open_price,
198:                  tkr.high,
199:                  tkr.low,
200:                  tkr.volume);
201:              fflush(stdout);
202:          }
203:      }
204:
205:      return 0;
206: }
```

The interesting features of this program are as follows:

1. Command-line options are parsed (lines 81 to 100).

2. A broadcast address is formed (lines 105 to 118).

3. A datagram (UDP) socket is created (lines 123 to 129).

4. The SO_REUSEADDR option is enabled (lines 135 to 146). This is essential if more than one client program is to receive the same broadcasts on the same host machine.

5. The broadcast address is bound (lines 151 to 160).

6. A client listening for loop begins in line 166. This loop continues forever until the program is terminated (usually with the interrupt character such as Ctrl+C).

After the client begins listening for datagram broadcasts, the following steps are carried out in the for loop:

1. The program waits for a datagram to arrive (lines 170 to 183). The received datagrams will be the qserve server broadcast messages.

2. A function named extract() extracts all the string data contained within the datagram and places the converted data into a TickReq structure entry named tkr (line 188). The extract function is defined in lines 28 to 58.

3. If the datagram extraction is successful, the ticker data is reported to standard output (lines 189 to 201).

4. Step 1 is repeated until the program is terminated.

Now is the time to put all this code into action!

Compiling and Running the Demonstration

To compile the demonstration project, obtain the source code for Chapter 18 and type make shown as follows:

OUTPUT

```
$ make
gcc -c -g -Wall -Wreturn-type -D_GNU_SOURCE   qserve.c
gcc -c -g -Wall -Wreturn-type -D_GNU_SOURCE   csvparse.c
gcc -c -g -Wall -Wreturn-type -D_GNU_SOURCE   msgf.c
gcc -c -g -Wall -Wreturn-type -D_GNU_SOURCE   load.c
gcc -c -g -Wall -Wreturn-type -D_GNU_SOURCE   gettick.c
gcc -c -g -Wall -Wreturn-type -D_GNU_SOURCE   bcast.c
gcc -c -g -Wall -Wreturn-type -D_GNU_SOURCE   connect.c
gcc -c -g -Wall -Wreturn-type -D_GNU_SOURCE   misc.c
gcc -c -g -Wall -Wreturn-type -D_GNU_SOURCE   mkaddr.c
gcc -o qserve qserve.o csvparse.o msgf.o load.o gettick.o bcast.o connect.o
➥misc.o mkaddr.o
gcc -c -g -Wall -Wreturn-type -D_GNU_SOURCE   mktwatch.c
gcc -o mktwatch mktwatch.o mkaddr.o
$
```

This produces two executables:

- The qserve executable, which is the quotation server program

- The mktwatch executable, which is the broadcast listener client

The following sections describe how to run these programs.

Starting the `qserve` Quotation Server

If you have no network adapter card installed, simply use the default loop-back parameters (127.255.255.255:9777 is the default broadcast address and port number used). The defaults are used when the server is started as follows:

OUTPUT

```
$ ./qserve &
[1] 798
$
```

If you have a network adapter card, you can broadcast on one interface as follows (here, the interface broadcast address and port number used is 192.168.0.255:9777):

OUTPUT

```
$ ./qserve -b 192.168.0.255:9777 &
[2] 800
$
```

In both cases, the server is started, which should begin to contact the finance.yahoo.com Web site and start broadcasting. Before launching the client, you might want to start another window to watch for server errors in your /var/log/messages log file. You can do this by entering the following (as root if log file permissions require):

OUTPUT

```
# tail -f /var/log/messages
Nov 26 16:34:10 pepper qserve: 34 tickers loaded.
Nov 26 16:34:37 pepper qserve: Unknown Ticker: 'NEC'
```

In the log output, observe that 34 ticker symbols were loaded from the tickers.rc file, and that symbol NEC was not known by the finance.yahoo.com server. Any other server messages will be logged to the warning, error, and information logs.

> **NOTE**
>
> If you cannot find the log file as shown, examine your /etc/syslog.conf file to determine how your logs are configured on your system. If necessary, consult the syslog.conf(5) man page for details about the file format.

Starting the `mktwatch` Client

The client program can be started in any user's session. You simply must be certain that the broadcast address agrees with the way qserve was started. If you provided no command-line arguments to use the qserve defaults, then do the same for the client:

```
$ ./mktwatch
```

If you specified a broadcast address to qserve, then supply the same address to the client program with the -b option as follows (substituting your broadcast address and port):

```
$ ./mktwatch -b 192.168.0.255:9777
```

Be patient after starting the client program. The server program will pause 20 seconds or more between updates. After it wakes up, it will go through the list of tickers that it must update.

TIP

If you don't see any output within one or two minutes, then check to see that you have the server running. If it is, then you have probably not specified addresses correctly.

An easy error to make is to forget the port number that follows the IP number (:9777 in the examples shown). If this number is omitted, then zero is assumed by the mkaddr.c module, which allows the operating system to pick any free port number instead!

Whether you used the local loopback interface default or used your local area network, you should be able to obtain results that look something like this:

OUTPUT

```
$ ./mktwatch -b 192.168.0.255:9777
CHP.TO    20.000  11/26/1999   3:58PM   +0.550   19.750   20.500   19.600       7657
AMZN      93.125  11/26/1999   1:01PM   +5.875   91.062   95.125   90.500   11496000
AMD       27.688  11/24/1999   1:02PM   +0.438    0.000   28.125   26.750    1880400
CSCO      93.188  11/26/1999   1:01PM   +0.750   95.250   95.375   92.812   12171000
DELL      42.938  11/26/1999   1:01PM    -0.37   43.562   43.938   42.750   11280900
EMC       90.312  11/26/1999   1:00PM   +1.000   89.562   90.375   89.375    1739800
GTW       79.062  11/26/1999   1:01PM   -0.188   79.688   79.688   78.938     391700
MOT      119.031  11/26/1999   1:48PM   +2.094  118.562  120.688  117.750    1440400
NCR       32.938  11/26/1999   1:01PM   -0.062   32.750   32.938   32.500     134800
NN        24.312  11/26/1999   1:00PM   +1.875   23.375   24.625   23.062    1602000
NOK      146.750  11/26/1999   1:18PM   +7.500  144.938  147.125  144.500    1935000
NT        81.688  11/26/1999   1:00PM   +3.383   81.000   82.188   79.562    2226900
ORCL      73.625  11/26/1999   1:01PM   +1.812   71.000   73.875   70.812    4617500
XRX       28.188  11/26/1999   1:00PM   +0.000   28.312   28.750   28.000    2428600
YHOO     226.875  11/26/1999   1:01PM   -4.125  233.000  235.250  225.375    2008900
RHAT     213.500  11/26/1999   1:00PM  +44.562  184.000  219.938  181.000    2296600
COB        8.312  11/24/1999   1:00PM   +1.188    0.000    8.375    7.312     316300
ATYT      10.375  11/26/1999  12:59PM   +0.438   10.250   10.375   10.125      80800
```

This output should continue to scroll as the tickers become updated. The time between updates will increase to a maximum of five minutes if the server is allowed to run all day.

If the `finance.yahoo.com` Service Changes

If the `finance.yahoo.com` service should move or change in some way, you'll need to rediscover the service by checking out its Web pages. After you determine the new server address (if it changes), you can specify that on the `qserve` command line using the `-a` option, as follows (with or without the additional `-b` option):

```
$ ./qserve -a new.server.com:80 &
[1] 821
$
```

OUTPUT

Substitute the hostname for `new.server.com` and the port number (port `80` for the Web). The port number must be supplied—it is not optional. Check the `/var/log/messages` file for any errors.

If you see a number of data format errors being reported in the log file, then this suggests that the spreadsheet data format has changed. This will require some code change if this has happened. Module `gettick.c`—lines 52 to 69—is a good place to start making changes. The `sprintf(3)` statement starting in line 96 might also need to be adjusted.

C A U T I O N

The Internet remains a fun place to be if people don't abuse it. Please be considerate of `finance.yahoo.com` when running this example program. Please do not short-circuit the program to poll its server too frequently. This will spoil the fun for everyone.

What's Next

Now that you have reached the end of this book, it is my sincere hope that you have a certain feeling of satisfaction. Having covered a number of socket programming concepts in detail, you should now be well equipped to write any networking application you can think of.

However, there is much more that can be learned about networking in general. If this book has increased your appetite for networking topics, it is probably a good time to begin a study of the underlying network protocols. With an understanding of these, you then can advance to using raw sockets and other advanced techniques.

In conclusion, I want to thank you for reading this book. This book should continue to serve you as a useful reference for socket programming. Even though you've used Linux to learn socket programming here, you are actually well equipped to program sockets for any type of UNIX. Now might be a good time to join a GNU software development effort and contribute to GNU/Linux. Power to the networked penguins!

Appendixes

Appendix A

Socket Function Quick Reference

Socket-Specific Functions

socketpair(2)
```
#include <sys/types.h>
#include <sys/socket.h>

int socketpair(int domain, int type, int protocol, int sv[2]);
```

socket(2)
```
#include <sys/types.h>
#include <sys/socket.h>

int socket(int domain, int type, int protocol);
```

bind(2)
```
#include <sys/types.h>
#include <sys/socket.h>

int bind(int sockfd, struct sockaddr *my_addr, int addrlen);
```

connect(2)
```
#include <sys/types.h>
#include <sys/socket.h>

int connect(int sockfd, struct sockaddr *serv_addr, int addrlen);
```

listen(2)
```
#include <sys/socket.h>

int listen(int s, int backlog);
```

accept(2)

```
#include <sys/types.h>
#include <sys/socket.h>

int accept(int s, struct sockaddr *addr, int *addrlen);
```

Socket Addressing

getsockname(2)

```
#include <sys/socket.h>

int getsockname(int s, struct sockaddr *name, socklen_t *namelen)
```

getpeername(2)

```
#include <sys/socket.h>

int getpeername(int s, struct sockaddr *name, socklen_t *namelen)
```

Reading of Sockets

read(2)

```
#include <unistd.h>

ssize_t read(int fd, void *buf, size_t count);
```

readv(2)

```
#include <sys/uio.h>

int readv(int fd, const struct iovec *vector, int count);

struct iovec {
    ptr_t  iov_base; /* Starting address */
    size_t iov_len;  /* Length in bytes */
};
```

recv(2)

```
#include <sys/types.h>
#include <sys/socket.h>

int recv(int s, void *buf, int len, unsigned int flags);
```

recvfrom(2)

```
#include <sys/types.h>
#include <sys/socket.h>
```

```
int recvfrom(int s,
    void *buf,
    int len,
    unsigned flags,
    struct sockaddr *from,
    int *fromlen);
```

flags:

MSG_OOB	Process out-of-band data.
MSG_PEEK	Peek at a datagram.
MSG_WAITALL	Requests that the operation block until the full request has been satisfied (with some exceptions).
MSG_ERRQUEUE	Receive from the error queue.
MSG_NOSIGNAL	Turn off the raising of SIGPIPE.

recvmsg(2)

```
#include <sys/types.h>
#include <sys/socket.h>
```

```
int recvmsg(int s, struct msghdr *msg, unsigned int flags);
```

```
struct msghdr {
    void          *msg_name;
    socklen_t      msg_namelen;
    struct iovec *msg_iov;
    size_t         msg_iovlen;
    void          *msg_control;
    size_t         msg_controllen;
    int            msg_flags;
};
```

```
struct cmsghdr {
    socklen_t cmsg_len;
    int       cmsg_level;
    int       cmsg_type;
/*  u_char    cmsg_data[]; */
};
```

flags:

MSG_EOR	End of a record received.
MSG_TRUNC	Datagram was truncated.
MSG_CTRUNC	Control data was truncated.
MSG_OOB	Out-of-band data was received.
MSG_ERRQUEUE	Extended error info was returned.

Writing to Sockets

write(2)
```
#include <unistd.h>

ssize_t write(int fd, const void *buf, size_t count);
```

writev(2)
```
#include <sys/uio.h>

int writev(int fd, const struct iovec *vector, int count);

struct iovec {
    ptr_t  iov_base; /* Starting address */
    size_t iov_len;  /* Length in bytes */
};
```

send(2)
```
#include <sys/types.h>
#include <sys/socket.h>

int send(int s, const void *msg, int len, unsigned int flags);
```

sendto(2)
```
#include <sys/types.h>
#include <sys/socket.h>

int sendto(int s,
    const void *msg,
    int len,
    unsigned flags,
    const struct sockaddr *to,
    int tolen);
```

flags:
```
 MSG_OOB        Process out-of-band data.
 MSG_DONTROUTE  Bypass routing.
 MSG_DONTWAIT   Do not block waiting to write.
 MSG_NOSIGNAL   Do not raise SIGPIPE.
```

sendmsg(2)
```
#include <sys/types.h>
#include <sys/socket.h>

int sendmsg(int s, const struct msghdr *msg, unsigned int flags);
```

```
struct msghdr {
    void        *msg_name;
    socklen_t    msg_namelen;
    struct iovec *msg_iov;
    size_t       msg_iovlen;
    void        *msg_control;
    size_t       msg_controllen;
    int          msg_flags;
};

struct cmsghdr {
    socklen_t cmsg_len;
    int       cmsg_level;
    int       cmsg_type;
/*  u_char    cmsg_data[]; */
};
```

Other Socket I/O

select(2)
```
#include <sys/time.h>
#include <sys/types.h>
#include <unistd.h>

int select(int n,
    fd_set *readfds,
    fd_set *writefds,
    fd_set *exceptfds,
    struct timeval *timeout);

struct timeval {
    long  tv_sec;    /* seconds */
    long  tv_usec;   /* microseconds */
};

FD_ZERO(fd_set *set);
FD_SET(int fd, fd_set *set);
FD_CLR(int fd, fd_set *set);
FD_ISSET(int fd, fd_set *set);
```

cmsg(3)
```
#include <sys/socket.h>

struct cmsghdr *CMSG_FIRSTHDR(struct msghdr *msgh);
struct cmsghdr *CMSG_NXTHDR(struct msghdr *msgh, struct cmsghdr *cmsg);
size_t CMSG_ALIGN(size_t length);
```

```
size_t CMSG_SPACE(size_t length);
size_t CMSG_LEN(size_t length);
void *CMSG_DATA(struct cmsghdr *cmsg);
```

Controlling Sockets

shutdown(2)

```
#include <sys/socket.h>

int shutdown(int s, int how);

SHUT_RD       0
SHUT_WR       1
SHUT_RDWR     2
```

getsockopt(2)

```
#include <sys/types.h>
#include <sys/socket.h>

int getsockopt(int s,
    int level,
    int optname,
    void *optval,
    socklen_t *optlen);
```

setsockopt(2)

```
#include <sys/types.h>
#include <sys/socket.h>

int setsockopt(int s,
    int level,
    int optname,
    const void *optval,
    socklen_t optlen);
```

dup(2) and dup2(2)

```
#include <unistd.h>

int dup(int oldfd);
int dup2(int oldfd, int newfd);
```

fcntl(2) Using F_SETOWN

```
#include <unistd.h>
#include <fcntl.h>

int fcntl(int fd, int cmd, long arg);
```

The cmd value F_SETOWN allows ownership of the socket to be established, for the process ID given in arg.

ioctl(2) to Test for Mark

```
#include <sys/ioctl.h>

...

int z;    /* Status */
int s;    /* Socket */
int flag; /* True when at mark */

z = ioctl(s,SIOCATMARK,&flag);
if ( z == -1 )
    abort();           /* Error */
if ( flag != 0 )
    puts("At Mark");
else
    puts("Not at mark.");
```

Network Support Functions

byteorder(3)

```
#include <netinet/in.h>

unsigned long htonl(unsigned long hostlong);
unsigned short htons(unsigned short hostshort);
unsigned long ntohl(unsigned long netlong);
unsigned short ntohs(unsigned short netshort);
```

inet_addr(3)

```
#include <sys/socket.h>
#include <netinet/in.h>
#include <arpa/inet.h>

unsigned long inet_addr(const char *string);
```

inet_aton(3)

```
#include <sys/socket.h>
#include <netinet/in.h>
#include <arpa/inet.h>

int inet_aton(const char *string, struct in_addr *addr);
```

inet_ntoa(3)
```
#include <sys/socket.h>
#include <netinet/in.h>
#include <arpa/inet.h>

char *inet_ntoa(struct in_addr addr);
```

inet_network(3)
```
#include <sys/socket.h>
#include <netinet/in.h>
#include <arpa/inet.h>

unsigned long inet_network(const char *addr);
```

inet_lnaof(3)
```
#include <sys/socket.h>
#include <netinet/in.h>
#include <arpa/inet.h>

unsigned long inet_lnaof(struct in_addr addr);
```

inet_netof(3)
```
#include <sys/socket.h>
#include <netinet/in.h>
#include <arpa/inet.h>

unsigned long inet_netof(struct in_addr addr);
```

inet_makeaddr(3)
```
#include <sys/socket.h>
#include <netinet/in.h>
#include <arpa/inet.h>

struct in_addr inet_makeaddr(int net,int host);
```

getservent(3)
```
#include <netdb.h>

struct servent *getservent(void);
void setservent(int stayopen);
void endservent(void);

struct servent *getservbyname(const char *name, const char *proto);

struct servent *getservbyport(int port, const char *proto);
```

getprotoent(3)

```
#include <netdb.h>

struct protoent *getprotoent(void);
void setprotoent(int stayopen);
void endprotoent(void);

struct protoent *getprotobyname(const char *name);

struct protoent *getprotobyname(const char *name);

struct protoent *getprotobynumber(int proto);
```

Standard I/O Support

```
#include <stdio.h>

FILE *fdopen(int fildes,const char *mode);

int fileno(FILE *stream);

int setbuf(FILE *stream,char *buf);

int setbuffer(FILE *stream, char *buf, size_t size);

int setlinebuf(FILE *stream);

int setvbuf(FILE *stream, char *buf, int mode, size_t size);

mode:
 _IOFBF   fully buffered.
 _IOLBF   line buffered.
 _IONBF   no buffering.
```

Hostname Support

uname(2)

```
#include <sys/utsname.h>

int uname(struct utsname *buf);
```

gethostname(2)

```
#include <unistd.h>

int gethostname(char *name, size_t len);
```

getdomainname(2)

```
#include <unistd.h>

int getdomainname(char *name, size_t len);
```

gethostbyname(3)

```
#include <netdb.h>

extern int h_errno;

void herror(const char *msg);

const char *hstrerror(int err);

struct hostent *gethostbyname(const char *name);
struct hostent *gethostbyaddr(const char *addr, int len, int type);
```

sethostent(3)

```
#include <netdb.h>

void sethostent(int stayopen);
void endhostent(void);
```

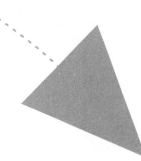

Appendix B

Socket-Related Structures Reference

Socket Address Structures

sockaddr
```
#include <sys/socket.h>

struct sockaddr {
    sa_family_t  sa_family;    /* Address Family */
    char         sa_data[14];  /* Address data.  */
};
```

sockaddr_un
```
#include <sys/un.h>

struct sockaddr_un {
    sa_family_t  sun_family;    /* Address Family */
    char         sun_path[108]; /* Pathname */
};
```

sockaddr_in **and** in_addr
```
#include <netinet/in.h>

struct sockaddr_in {
    sa_family_t     sin_family; /* Address Family */
    uint16_t        sin_port;   /* Port number */
    struct in_addr  sin_addr;   /* Internet address */
    unsigned char   sin_zero[8];/* Pad bytes */
};

struct in_addr {
    uint32_t        s_addr;      /* Internet address */
};
```

SPECIAL IPv4 ADDRESSES

```
adr.sin_addr.s_addr = ntohl(INADDR_ANY);

adr.sin_addr.s_addr = ntohl(INADDR_LOOPBACK);
```

sockaddr_x25 and x25_address

```
#include <linux/x25.h>

struct sockaddr_x25 {
    sa_family_t  sx25_family;  /* Must be AF_X25 */
    x25_address  sx25_addr;    /* X.121 Address */
};

typedef struct {
    char         x25_addr[16];
} x25_address;
```

sockaddr_in6 and in6_addr

```
struct sockaddr_in6 {
    sa_family_t     sin6_family;
    uint16_t        sin6_port;     /* port # */
    uint32_t        sin6_flowinfo; /* flow info */
    struct in6_addr sin6_addr;     /* IPv6 address */
};

struct in6_addr {
    union {
        uint8_t     u6_addr8[16];
        uint16_t    u6_addr16[8];
        uint32_t    u6_addr32[4];
    } in6_u;
};
```

sockaddr_atalk and at_addr

```
#include <netatalk/at.h>

struct sockaddr_atalk {
    sa_family_t   sat_family;
    u_char        sat_port;   /* port */
    struct at_addr sat_addr;  /* net/node */
};

struct at_addr {
    u_short       s_net;
    u_char        s_node;
};
```

`full_sockaddr_ax25`, `sockaddr_ax25`, and `ax25_address`

```
struct full_sockaddr_ax25 {
    struct sockaddr_ax25 fsa_ax25;
    ax25_address fsa_digipeater[AX25_MAX_DIGIS];
};

struct sockaddr_ax25 {
    sa_family_t    sax25_family;
    ax25_address   sax25_call;
    int            sax25_ndigis;
};

typedef struct {
    /* 6 call + SSID (shifted ascii!) */
    char           ax25_call[7];
} ax25_address;

#define sax25_uid        sax25_ndigis
```

Miscellaneous Structures

servent

```
struct servent {
    char    *s_name;          /* official service name */
    char    **s_aliases;      /* alias list */
    int     s_port;           /* port number */
    char    *s_proto;         /* protocol to use */
}
```

protoent

```
struct protoent {
    char    *p_name;          /* official protocol name */
    char    **p_aliases;      /* alias list */
    int     p_proto;          /* protocol number */
}
```

utsname

```
#include <sys/utsname.h>

struct utsname {
    char    sysname[SYS_NMLN];
    char    nodename[SYS_NMLN];
    char    release[SYS_NMLN];
    char    version[SYS_NMLN];
    char    machine[SYS_NMLN];
    char    domainname[SYS_NMLN];
};
```

hostent

```
struct hostent {
    char  *h_name;          /* official name of host */
    char  **h_aliases;      /* alias list */
    int   h_addrtype;       /* host address type */
    int   h_length;         /* length of address */
    char  **h_addr_list;    /* list of addresses */
};


/* for backward compatibility */
#define h_addr   h_addr_list[0]
```

timeval

```
struct timeval {
    long   tv_sec;          /* seconds */
    long   tv_usec;         /* microseconds */
};
```

linger

```
struct linger {
    int    l_onoff;
    int    l_linger;
};
```

I/O-Related Structures

iovec

```
#include <sys/uio.h>

struct iovec {
    ptr_t  iov_base;        /* Starting address */
    size_t iov_len;         /* Length in bytes */
};
```

msghdr

```
struct msghdr {
    void        *msg_name;
    socklen_t   msg_namelen;
    struct iovec *msg_iov;
    size_t      msg_iovlen;
    void        *msg_control;
    size_t      msg_controllen;
    int         msg_flags;
};
```

cmsghdr

```
struct cmsghdr {
    socklen_t cmsg_len;
    int       cmsg_level;
    int       cmsg_type;
/*  u_char    cmsg_data[]; */
};
```

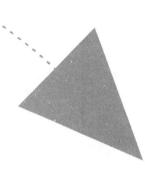

Appendix C

Useful Network Tables

Table C.1: Internet Address Classes

Class	Lowest	Highest	Network Bits	Host Bits
A	0.0.0.0	127.255.255.255	7	24
B	128.0.0.0	191.255.255.255	14	16
C	192.0.0.0	223.255.255.255	21	8
D	224.0.0.0	239.255.255.255	28	N/A
E	240.0.0.0⁻	247.255.255.255	27	N/A

Table C.2: Netmask Values by IP Class

Class	Lowest	Highest	Netmask
A	0.0.0.0	127.255.255.255	255.0.0.0
B	128.0.0.0	191.255.255.255	255.255.0.0
C	192.0.0.0	223.255.255.255	255.255.255.0

Table C.3: Private IP Number Allocations

Class	Lowest	Highest	Netmask
A	10.0.0.0	10.255.255.255	255.0.0.0
B	172.16.0.0	172.31.255.255	255.255.0.0
C	192.168.0.0	192.168.255.255	255.255.255.0

Table C.4: Amateur Radio Reserved IP Numbers

Class	Lowest	Highest	Netmask
A	44.0.0.0	44.255.255.255	255.0.0.0

Table C.5: The `/proc/sys/net/ipv4/tcp_stdurg` *Settings*

Value	Interpretation
0	BSD Interpretation (Linux default)
1	RFC793 interpretation

Table C.6: The `/etc/inetd.conf` *Configuration Record*

Field #	Description	Example
1	Internet service name	`telnet` (this may also be a port number)
2	Socket type	`stream` or `dgram`
3	Protocol	`tcp` or `udp`
4	Flags	`nowait` or `wait`
5	UserID to use	`root` or `nobody`
6	Pathname of executable	`/usr/sbin/in.telnetd`
7	Server arguments	`in.telnetd`

Glossary

address family   A set of acceptable address formats for use with a particular network protocol.

ancillary data   Control data that is sent or received with normal data in a packet. Ancillary data normally includes user credentials or file descriptors transmitted over a PF_LOCAL/PF_UNIX socket.

API   Application Programming Interface.

ARPA   Advanced Research Projects Agency.

auxiliary data   Another name for ancillary data.

AX.25   An amateur radio adaptation of the CCITT X.25 network protocol for digital radio transmission. See also *X.25*.

big-endian   The endian quality describes the byte ordering of a particular piece of digital hardware. Big-endian implies that the most significant byte occurs first in physical placement.

BPQ   In this book, BPQ refers to AX.25 support over Ethernet, developed by John Wiseman (radio callsign G8BPQ).

canonical hostname   A host machine on a network can be identified by several different names. However, each host must have one official hostname. All other hostnames are considered aliases of the canonical hostname.

CCITT   Abbreviation for International Telegraph and Telephone Consultative Committee, which is a standardization bureau. This has now been combined into the ITU-T (International Telecommunication Union) standards bureau.

connection-oriented protocol   A protocol that requires that a channel of communication be established. Only after establishing the connection can communication take place. This form of communication is like a telephone call, where the other party must be reached before the conversation can begin.

connectionless protocol   A protocol that requires no prior establishment of a connection. This form of protocol is like mailing letters[md]messages are sent, in the hope that they arrive at their designated destinations.

control data   When discussing PF_LOCAL/PF_UNIX sockets, this means ancillary data.

credential   A kernel testimonial that reliably identifies the userID and group of the requesting process.

daemon   A server process that runs without a controlling terminal. Usually a process that is started when the system boots and runs in the background until it is terminated or until the system is shut down. Other daemons are started by the inetd daemon, upon demand.

DARPA   Defense Advanced Research Projects Agency.

datagram   A finite unit of data that is sent and received as one unit. It is a network message that is delivered on a best-effort basis.

DHCP   Dynamic Host Configuration Protocol.

dichotomy   A division, or the process of dividing into two mutually exclusive or contradictory groups or entities.

domain   In the context of sockets, the domain represents one of a set of possible protocol families. For DNS name servers, a domain represents an area of influence or authority. A domain can also be applied to a set of machines cooperating with the use of NIS.

dotted-quad   An address notation that includes four decimal values separated by dots (periods). Also known as dotted-decimal notation; 127.0.0.1 is an example of a dotted-quad address.

endian   This quality describes the byte ordering of a particular piece of digital hardware. There are big- and little-endian CPUs, for example. Mixed-endians can also exist.

EOF   End of file.

Ethernet   A name chosen by inventor Bob Metcalfe of Xerox PARC in 1973 to describe a new local area network technology, which was based upon the University of Hawaii's ALOHA system. The word "Ether" was used by nineteenth-century physicists to explain how light passes through the vacuum of space.

FAQ   Frequently Asked Question.

firewall   A firewall is a metaphorical concept that separates harm (fire) on one side from valuable resources on the other side, by means of a wall. It can be implemented in software alone or as a piece of equipment with software, designed to screen out malicious access to the internal network.

flow control   A form of control exerted over the transfer of data within a stream. When too much data arrives at the receiving end, the sender is instructed to stop sending. When the receiver has caught up with the data it has already received, it then instructs the sender to begin transmitting again.

FTP   File Transfer Protocol.

`ftp`   A network client program that allows the user to perform file transfers over a network, using the FTP protocol.

GMP library   GNU Multi-precision Math library. This library permits the programmer to compute numbers that exceed the precision of the standard C data types.

in-band   The normal path for data on a stream socket can be considered as "in-band" data. Data within this stream must be delivered in precisely the same order it was sent. The opposite to in-band data is out-of-band data.

`inetd`   The Internet daemon. This process waits for a connect (or UDP request) and then starts the server that will handle the request. See Chapter 15, "Using the `inetd` Daemon."

inline   When applied to out-of-band data, the term inline means that the out-of-band data is received intermixed with the normal in-band data. See also *in-band* and *out-of-band*.

interface   In the networking context, an interface provides access to the network medium. It is normally a combination of a software driver and a piece of network hardware. See also *NIC*.

IPO   Initial Public Offering.

IPv4   Internet Protocol version 4, which is in use over the Internet today. The IP number used by this protocol is 32 bits in length.

IPv6   Internet Protocol version 6, which will be the next generation Internet protocol. The IP number used by this protocol is 128 bits in length.

IrDA   Infrared data communications.

ISP   Internet service provider.

little-endian   The endian quality describes the byte ordering of a particular piece of digital hardware. Little-endian implies that the least significant byte occurs first in physical placement.

localhost   The commonly accepted name of the local loopback interface that is normally assigned the IPv4 address 127.0.0.1.

loopback   This is a software network interface that permits processes on a local host to communicate to other processes on the same host. It is normally given the IPv4 address of 127.0.0.1.

man   A Linux/UNIX command for viewing online manual pages. Often simply called the man command for accessing man pages.

mirror site   An alternative site, which hosts the same services as the primary site. For example, a mirror FTP site will serve the same files that the primary FTP site provides. This is done to balance the load and provide a backup against service disruptions.

netmask   Network mask. When applied to a network address, it separates the network ID from the host ID.

NIC   Network Interface Card. This is one type of hardware that provides an interface to the physical network medium.

NIS   Network Information Service, formerly known as the Sun Yellow Pages (the name Yellow Pages is a registered trademark of British Telecom PLC in the United Kingdom). This is a service which provides centralized information services for a group of hosts within a network.

nslookup   Name Server lookup command. Permits the user to query name servers to turn hostnames into network addresses and vice versa.

NTP   Network Time Protocol. This is a protocol used to synchronize the time of different host computers. There are now several documents about NTP, but RFC 1129 is a good place to start.

out-of-band data   This is data that is sent outside of the normal data path to the receiving end. This permits out-of-band data to be received ahead of the data that has already been sent, and to be received separately from the normal data. Note that this is a more general concept than TCP's "urgent mode."

packet   A packet is a single unit of data that can be transmitted through a network. The term was originated by Donald Watts Davies in 1965 while performing research in London.

pad bytes   These are placeholder bytes, which carry no useful information in themselves. They are often zero bytes, placed into structures in order to fill out the structure to a particular size.

peek   A peek at received data implies that the data is read, without making it unavailable. Conversely, a normal read operation obtains data without the option of receiving the same data again.

peer   A peer is usually another host involved in communication with the local host. However, the local host can act as a peer when communicating with itself as one process communicates with another on the same host.

PID   The Process ID is used by the UNIX/Linux kernel to identify each task operating in the system.

pipe A pipe is a metaphorical concept representing a channel of data flow between one process and another on the same host. Most UNIX pipes are unidirectional.

port A port number, when combined with an IP address, allows a specific instance of a connection to be addressed. For example, one host can offer two services for the same IP number, differing only by the port numbers used.

resolve The process of converting a hostname into a network address. A hostname is converted into an IP number, for example.

RFC A "Request For Comments" Internet document. The first such document was written by Steve Crocker on April 7, 1969. It was labeled "Request For Comments" and subtitled "Host Software." The general tone of this document was warm and welcoming. It was so well accepted that it was subsequently followed by a series of further RFCs for Internet protocol and design documents. Many RFCs become defacto standards even though they continue to be referred to as RFCs.

rlogin A network client program that provides the current terminal user access to another remote host as a terminal session. See also *telnet*.

router A piece of network equipment that routes packets from one network to the correct destination network.

RPN Reverse Polish Notation.

run-level A systemwide mode that the overall system is in. For example, run-level 5 has the X Window server running on the console for many Linux distributions. Run-level 3 is usually for not having the X Window server running on the console.

setuid This is a UNIX feature where the execution of an executable can be performed under a different userID than the account that the user is logged on as. For example, the lpr command runs as userID root when a print request is made under Red Hat Linux 6.0.

socket A socket is an endpoint in network communications. A pair of sockets is required for connection-oriented communications (using TCP/IP, for example).

stderr Standard error output: This FILE control block is normally open for writing to file descriptor 2.

stdin Standard input: This FILE control block is normally open for reading from file descriptor 0.

stdout Standard output: This FILE control block is normally open for writing to file descriptor 1.

stream   In the socket context: A stream socket is a connection-oriented socket. This is different from a datagram socket, which is connectionless. In the standard I/O context: a stream represents a FILE control block that is open for reading or writing.

TCP   Transport Control Protocol layer, which is used on top of the IP protocol layer. This layer adds flow control and data integrity to the lower IP level.

telnet   A network client program that provides a terminal session for the user. See also *rlogin*.

thread   A sequential flow of control within a process. There can be several threads operating in parallel within one process, each representing an independent flow of control. All memory is shared between all threads within one process.

Trojan horse   A usually dangerous program designed to masquerade as some other program. By impersonating a normal program, it gets run by an unwitting user, which can then cause harm or capture information that should be kept secret.

UDP   User Datagram Protocol.

URG bit   A TCP protocol header bit that indicates urgent data is present.

urgent data   The special data that is sent in urgent mode. See also *urgent mode*.

urgent mode   The TCP protocol provides a facility where the sending end can indicate to the receiving end that "urgent data" has been placed into the normal stream of data. The receiving end then becomes notified that urgent data exists in its incoming data stream, but it remains up to the receiving end to determine how to process this data.

urgent pointer   This is a TCP protocol pointer that points to either the urgent data byte itself (RFC793) or the byte that follows the urgent data byte (BSD). This pointer is only computed and used at the receiving end when the TCP URG bit is set in the packet header.

wild socket address   This is a socket address that is left unspecified. This is often done when the choice of network interface is not known in advance, allowing the address to be dynamic.

X.25   A packet-switched network protocol recommended by CCITT in 1976, based upon the ISO networking model.

YP   Sun Microsystem's Yellow Pages is now known as NIS (the name Yellow Pages is a registered trademark of British Telecom PLC in the

United Kingdom). This is a service which provides centralized information services for a group of hosts within a network.

zombie   This is a UNIX process that has terminated or exited gracefully. Until the parent process inquires of the kernel about the child process's termination, a minimal process table entry is maintained by the kernel. This entry will display as a *zombie* process when all the processes are listed by the ps(1) command.

Index